The participants are: Senator Geo[rge Pearce, Minister for Defence in] the Fisher Labor Government, Aus[tralia; ...] General Sir William Nicholson, Chi[ef of the Imperial General Staff;] Sir Frederick Borden, Minister for [Militia and Defence, Canada.]

(without saying where they are going to) of mobilising an Expeditionary Force to be used, we do not specify where or for what purpose, so similarly as time goes on in Australia, for example, the General Staff should work out a scheme so that, if the Government of Australia so desires, they will have preparations made for mobilising a certain proportion of their force to proceed to certain ports for oversea action. In other words you would follow the same system that we have adopted here— Home defence as one thing and, if the Dominions so wish, a certain contingent or force for expeditionary action, without going into details of where it is to be used or when it is to be used, because it can only be used with the approval of the Government of the Dominion, and we cannot tell in the British Empire in what particular direction, though we have some idea where, it might be used. It is much better to hold our tongues about it and not say anything, according to the old Persian proverb "What two ears only hear, God himself does not know". Therefore in those matters we do not say anything and nobody else knows about it.'

Pearce: 'Then those schemes will be sent on by the local section of the Imperial General Staff to the Imperial General Staff here for the benefit of their advice.'

Nicholson: 'Exactly. The great use of your representative on the General Staff here is because he will be able to speak about these things. I think it much better we should do this thing quietly without any paper on the subject, because I am sure in some of the Dominions it might be better not to say anything about preparations.'

Borden: 'It gives mischievous people an opportunity to talk.'

Pearce: 'I quite recognise that, and I suppose we have as large a proportion of that kind of people in Australia as there are anywhere else . . .'

Nicholson: '. . . meanwhile there is no reason why in anticipation of its development certain steps should not be taken to formulate what would be done in the event of the Governments of your Dominions being willing to assist in a general war. If we take that as the conclusion, I would suggest that this paper might be withdrawn.'

Borden: 'Suppressed or withdrawn—I would hope so.'

Nicholson: 'We recommend its withdrawal provided it is understood that the resolution of the last Conference will be carried out.'

Borden: 'Yes.'

Pearce: 'On the understanding that it will be acted upon.'

The Source Document is 'Questions of Defence (Military)', WO 106/43, PRO.

AN ARMY FOR A NATION

AN ARMY FOR A NATION

A history of Australian military developments 1880–1914

John Mordike

ALLEN & UNWIN
in association with
The Directorate of Army Studies
DEPARTMENT OF DEFENCE

© The Commonwealth of Australia, 1992
All rights reserved. No reproduction without permission.

First published in 1992
Allen & Unwin Pty Ltd
8 Napier Street, North Sydney, NSW 2059 Australia

National Library of Australia
Cataloguing-in-Publication entry:

Mordike, John Leonard.
An army for a nation, a history of
Australian military developments, 1880–1914

Bibliography.
ISBN 1 86373 192 X.

1. Australia. Army—History. I. Title.
355.00994

Set in 10/12 Times by DOCUPRO, Sydney
Printed by Kim Hup Lee Printing, Singapore

Contents

Illlustrations		vii
Acknowledgments		ix
Abbreviations		xi
Introduction		xv
1	The origins of imperial and national priorities for an Australian military force	1
2	Major-General Edward Hutton: His command of the colonial force of New South Wales, 1893–1896	21
3	The Boer War and federation: Imperial aspirations and national realities, 1896–1901	44
4	The first Defence Bill: Its development and its failure, 1901	66
5	An imperial GOC and his hidden agenda, 1902	85
6	National reactions to imperial plans, 1902–1904	109
7	The GOC and the Australian military force: The implementation of Hutton's scheme, 1902–1903	131
8	The civil reaction: From GOC to military board, 1903–1905	148
9	The creation of a national defence agenda: Alfred Deakin's plans for a national guard, 1905–1907	165
10	Bridges, Hoad and the convergence of policy, 1908–1909	191
11	The achievement of the imperial objective, 1909–1914: An Australian imperial force	214
Appendix I: Commonwealth Ministries 1901–1914		248
Appendix II: Chiefs of the General Staff 1909–1914		250
Notes		251
Bibliography		294
Index		306

Illustrations

Members of the Volunteer Forces of Victoria in the 1860s	2
Colonel Sir William Jervois inspecting batteries, 1877	4
Departure of the NSW contingent for the Sudan, 1885	5
'Save us from our friends'	18
Major General Sir Edward Hutton	23
The Colonial Conference of 1897 in London	47
Sir John Forrest	67
'The Motherland's Misalliance'	95
Members of the 2nd South Australian (Mounted Rifles) Contingent who served in the Boer War	98
'Summed up'	106
'Alone'	114
Part-time militia forces in Goulburn, NSW, in the 1890s	140
Sir Edmund Barton with Alfred Deakin	167
Major General Sir William Throsby Bridges	171
Sir Thomas Ewing	192
Senator George Foster Pearce	199
Lord Kitchener visits Sydney, 1910	225
Melbourne welcomes Lord Kitchener, 1910	227
Horse-drawn Maxim machine gun on exercises	230
The Military Board outside Army Headquarters, Melbourne, 1910	237
The Imperial Conference of 1911 in London	240
Trainees march along Hunter Street, Sydney, 1913	245
Members of the 2nd Infantry Brigade and the 4th Light Horse Regiment parade in 1914	246

Acknowledgements

This book was commissioned for the Australian Army by the Army Historical Policy Committee. I am indebted to its members for the opportunity to undertake what has been an arduous but personally rewarding study. A number of senior Army officers have also assisted me in many ways, but primarily by simply taking an interest in my work. They probably never realised how much I valued their comments and assistance. I trust that this work will in some small measure confirm their judgement that the Army can benefit from an historical analysis of its own development.

I am especially grateful to the Australian War Memorial for the award of a research grant which enabled me to undertake vital research in the United Kingdom. I extend my sincere appreciation to the Memorial for its support. Without it this study could not have been completed.

Throughout the years this study has taken I have been most grateful for the assistance given by a number of people in their professional capacities. The staff at the Australian War Memorial and the Australian Archives Office, Melbourne and Canberra, deserve special thanks. In particular I wish to thank Mr Rod Stroud of the National Library of Australia for his dedicated assistance over a long period. I was always impressed by his competence. Dr Robert Hall of the Australian Defence Studies Centre, University College, University of New South Wales, Australian Defence Force Academy, was also an untiring source of encouragement. I wish to thank him for many hours of valuable discussion. Lastly, I extend my thanks to Lieutenant Colonel Robert Deane, whose professional competence was vital in bringing this book to publication.

Author's Acknowledgement

Students of Australian defence and foreign policy of the early Commonwealth period are indebted to Professor N. K. Meaney of Sydney University for his prodigious scholarship. His work has broken much of the ground for this study.

The work of Dr C. D. Coulthard-Clark on the military careers of William Throsby Bridges and James Gordon Legge is also acknowledged.

Abbreviations

AA	Australian Archives
AA & QMG	Assistant Adjutant Quartermaster General
ADB	Australian Dictionary of Biography
ADFAL	Australian Defence Force Academy Library, Canberra
ANL	National Library of Australia, Canberra
AWM	Australian War Memorial, Canberra
BPD	British Parliamentary Debates
BPP	British Parliamentary Papers
BL	British Library, London
BML	Bridges Memorial Library, Duntroon
BU	University of Birmingham
CA	Commonwealth Acts
Cab	British Cabinet Papers
CDC	Colonial Defence Committee
CID	Committee of Imperial Defence
CIGS	Chief of the Imperial General Staff
CG	Commonwealth Gazette
CGS	Chief of the General Staff
CO	Colonial Office

CPD	Commonwealth Parliamentary Debates
CPP	Commonwealth of Australia Parliamentary Papers
CSO	Chief Staff Officer
DAAG	Deputy Assistant Adjutant General
DAG	Deputy Adjutant General
DMO	Director of Military Operations
GOC	General Officer Commanding
HQ	Headquarters
IG	Inspector-General
IGS	Imperial General Staff
LAGD	Library of the Attorney General's Department, Canberra
MBPHI	Military Board Papers of Historical Interest
MF	Military Forces
PL	Library of the Parliament of Australia, Canberra
PRO	Public Records Office, London
RAA	Royal Australian Artillery
S of S	Secretary of State
WO	War Office

'Speaking for myself, I am content to trust the Australian people. I believe they are not only fitted to serve, but to command, and to rival in the arts of war, so far as they can be practised in times of peace, any of like experience against whom they may be pitted.'

Alfred Deakin, Prime Minister of Australia, 13 December 1907

Introduction

The Australian Army of the 1990s is facing one of the greatest peacetime challenges of its 90-year history. Already the implementation of a national strategy of defence is testing its leaders and its rank and file as they plan, organise and train to meet a new and complex range of demands. The permanent basing of key fighting units in Northern Australia, exercising in harsh terrain in the seasonal excesses of the wet and the dry, and the effective utilisation of the civil infrastructure are only a few of the issues now being addressed. But perhaps one of the biggest demands facing the Army is relinquishing its past, for it is a past dominated by expeditionary operations in co-operation with the forces of other, larger nations. It is in this environment that Australia's proud fighting traditions have been forged. In view of this, the organisation of the Army to meet credible contingencies in the defence of our homeland with our own resources is a novel challenge for which few are prepared. This study is therefore timely, because it reveals that many of the issues that are now being confronted are not new. It reveals that Australians in the first decade of the Commonwealth perceived the need for a national defence strategy and began to organise the Army for that very purpose as their primary defence objective. How did they change their minds?

In the introductory chapters of the first volume of the official history of Australia in World War I, Dr Charles Bean gave a brief account of Australian military and defence developments in the years before the outbreak of hostilities. According to Bean, they were inspired by perceptions of the need for self-defence and, as a result, Australia had 'provided only for the chance of an enemy raiding or invading her shores'. He believed (or he wanted us to believe) that there had been no specific preparations before August 1914 for Australia to provide an expeditionary force in the event of hostilities in Europe. There was, he wrote, 'no set scheme for common action with Great Britain in case of war' because, as an enlightened imperial power, Britain had realised that 'the unity of the Empire in war depended ultimately on the free will of each of its several parts . . .'. This policy, he emphasised, was in clear contrast with 'the rigid and calculating organisation upon which the German Empire was built'. Britain's policy, Bean announced triumphantly, was 'the essence of liberalism: it avoided all imposed control and placed its trust in the good sense and feeling inherent in men left free'.[1]

Continuing in this vein, Bean explained that, unlike Australia, New Zealand had 'agreed to a definite scheme for an expeditionary force' in 1913. Similar action was not taken in Australia and the other dominions because their 'ministers were nervous of the opposition which the mere suggestion might create among their respective people'. Indeed, when a young staff officer at Army headquarters, Major Cyril Brudenell White, had requested approval to draw up a provisional plan for an Australian expeditionary force, 'the permission was withheld'. However, Bean proceeded to point out that one Australian Minister for Defence, Senator George Foster Pearce, had at least considered joint military action with New Zealand. This work commenced in 1912 when New Zealand's Chief of the General Staff, Major General Alexander Godley, 'had chanced' to visit Australia. According to Bean, Godley's Australian counterpart, Brigadier Joseph Gordon, had suggested to Pearce that the visit presented an opportunity to make joint plans *in case either were invaded*'. Pearce agreed and, as a result, Brudenell White developed plans to raise and organise a force of 12 000 men, but Bean noted that it was for 'co-operation between Australia and New Zealand only'.[2]

When war broke out in 1914—Bean said it came with 'extreme suddenness', falling 'upon the British people out of a clear sky'—it was this 'one piece of forethought' which provided the plans for raising the expeditionary force for Europe. 'Major White could guarantee', Bean reported, 'that it was possible to raise and organise for service abroad a volunteer force of 12 000 men of all arms, and to have them ready for sailing within six weeks'. And not only were mobilisation plans ready but there was more than enough equipment and clothing for the force. But this, too, was more the result of good fortune than careful preparation, according to the official historian. 'During the previous three years,' Bean wrote, 'the Government had laid in large quantities of army stores *against the chance* of a sudden mobilization.' As a result, he could record with pride that it was claimed by many that 'no troops ever went to the front more generously equipped than this first Australian contingent'.[3]

Bean's account of Australia's entry into World War I is the authorised version which has endured for some 70 years since its first publication in 1921. It tells us that, at the first hint of danger to Britain, a united Australia reacted in a spontaneous outburst of imperial sentiment, rushing to the

Introduction

colours to provide unsolicited support to 'the last man and the last shilling'. The very speed of their response was a measure of their enthusiasm to fight, to suffer and to die far from their homes and their families. It is a noble story of readiness for service and sacrifice that is imbedded deeply in the Australian consciousness. It is a story which has been revered by successive generations of Australians and, indeed, emulated by many. But it is a story in need of revision.

During the course of research for this book, a document was discovered in War Office records which revealed that Australia commenced its preparations for World War I not in August 1914 but in June 1911, when Prime Minister Andrew Fisher, Minister for External Affairs Egerton Batchelor and Senator George Foster Pearce were in London for an Imperial Conference. During this conference, Pearce gave senior War Office officials an assurance that he would have staff officers at Army headquarters in Melbourne develop plans for an Australian expeditionary force to fight with Britain in a European war which was expected in 1915. Yet it was an undertaking which the British officials and Pearce shrouded in secrecy because they feared the opposition it might arouse in Australia. On their return from the conference, the Fisher Labor government proceeded with haste to establish a defence industry to equip the force while Pearce declared publicly that these preparations were necessary to defend Australia from attack. Japan, not Europe, posed the major threat to Australian security, Pearce claimed disingenuously. By playing on Australian concern about Japan, senior government members fabricated a cover for the substantial increase in expenditure on armaments and equipment. The Australian Imperial Force, as the expeditionary force was eventually named, was therefore the result of some three years of planning and preparation, not six weeks as Bean has led us to believe. But the preliminary steps did not end there. In 1912, Major General Godley was invited to Australia so that New Zealand's contribution to the European war could be organised concurrently.

None of the participants ever revealed the undertaking or the real purpose of the early preparations to the public and, although it might never be proved conclusively, it seems likely that Bean, too, was a party to the cover-up. It now remains for us to understand why. Why, if Australians were so willing to serve the empire, could they not be told the truth before—or perhaps more importantly after—this significant event in Australian history?

This study is concerned with the development of the Australian military forces from the colonial period to the outbreak of World War I. It reveals that, although Australians had both a constitutional and emotional attachment to the British empire, they also shared a common experience as Australians, an experience which, for many, defined their national interests as distinct from those of Britain. This was the basis of Australian nationalism, a nationalism which was at times muted and diffident but nonetheless influential and persistent in shaping Australia's response to its perceived strategic requirements. Yet, from our contemporary vantage point, it is also a nationalism we have not expected to encounter to any significant extent—at least not so far as its influence on defence developments is concerned. It seems that our expectations have been influenced by the effusive display of imperial fervour at the outbreak of World War I. This frame of mind has been encouraged by historians of imperial persuasion—historians like Bean—who have certainly acknowledged the existence of an independent element in early Australian defence thinking but who have portrayed Australia's commitment to World War I as a coalescence of imperialism and nationalism, as an act of unified resolve.

Taking a different line, the rationale for this study is that Australia's defence history was a contest between the two ideologies, a contest which resulted in victory for imperialists after a long and tenacious campaign when Australia entered the war. But, by believing accounts like Bean's authorised version, we have failed to recognise this and have tended to emphasise the imperial aspects of our early defence history while the independent, national aspects remain largely unrecognised and unreported. It has meant that a few isolated imperial episodes have acquired an exaggerated importance: the Sudan campaign and the Boer War both exemplified the outbreak of the imperial sentiment of the Great War—albeit on a smaller scale—and both enjoy prominent positions in Australian military and political history. However, the more mundane (but much more persistent) efforts before federation to raise military forces and build fortifications for defence against the threat of raids by Russia, France or Germany have received less attention. Indeed, taking a national view of defence, Australians of the late nineteenth century were alert to threats within their region, threats with direct implications for Australia's livelihood rather than the empire's. Yet we have tended to overlook the strength of this local defence consciousness in the colonies. Similarly, the steps taken in the early Commonwealth period to maintain and develop the Army as a national body for the defence of Australia, while rejecting overtures from Britain to participate in an imperial military force, now appear incongruous. And, remarkably, Prime Minister Alfred Deakin's national defence strategy of 1907, a strategy which was as comprehensive as the Hawke Labor government's strategy of 1987,[4] has been ignored, even though with some prescience it identified Japan as the prime threat to Australian security. It is as though Deakin's strategy never existed. Yet these important national developments were as much an extension of colonial defence policies as the more spectacular inclination to rush to the call of empire in time of crisis.

Australian ambivalence on the defence question—the tension between national and imperial priorities—is perhaps best illustrated by the first *Defence Act*, which was proclaimed on 1 March 1904. Developed immediately after Australia's involvement in the Boer War, it contained a provision which denied an Australian government the power to send any soldier, and

Introduction

hence any military unit, outside Australian territory. The restriction was included because a sufficient number of parliamentarians were wary of future involvement in imperial operations. Effectively, it meant that the Army could not be sent overseas, the force being maintained for the defence of Australia. Yet, in the same Act, the imperial connection was also acknowledged by the inclusion of a provision which enabled Australians to volunteer as individuals for service overseas in the defence of empire. This is the reason why the Australian Imperial Force was a special force raised from volunteers specifically for the war. But it was this *Defence Act*, with its provision for voluntary imperial service, which worried British strategists. Would men volunteer in sufficient numbers? Would they be experienced and adequately trained? Would they have sufficient equipment? Would they be organised and equipped in a way that was compatible with the Imperial Army? And how could a suitable force be mobilised in time to meet the need?

The same questions also worried people like Pearce. They feared the problems which might be created by nationalists if they mobilised against the war preparations. Although the imperial attachment had begun to assume greater prominence with the Dreadnought crisis of 1909 when it was feared that Germany's naval strength might eclipse that of Britain within a few years, national priorities for defence could still become a rallying point for an alternative path for Australia's future development. Referring to the apparent strength of nationalism, Bean commented that: 'For at least a generation before the war . . . [Australians] . . . had tended to act as a nation of themselves'. Indeed, the Australian character displayed a 'marked independence' which, misleadingly, Bean claimed had been 'fostered in him by Great Britain'. It had sometimes led 'outsiders' to believe that Australia 'was aiming at complete separation from the parent country'. But Bean's inference is clear: 'outsiders' did not understand that beneath the Australian's tough, independent exterior was not a nationalist, but an imperialist. The outbreak of war therefore provided the means of proving the real feelings of Australians for Britain. 'Was this critical hour the time when the Australian would dream of deserting her?' Bean challenged. Happily, 'no' was the answer and he could record that 'the attitude of Australia was from the first *perfectly definite* and *united*'.[5]

Certainly, Britain was assured of substantial support from Australians, but total commitment and early preparation for the war were considered vital. The cover-up was therefore critical in achieving unity by denying the public an issue around which an alternative view could rally during the period from June 1911 to August 1914. There were obvious benefits for the Fisher Labor government in this approach: there is little political risk in telling a nation that you are preparing to defend it, but, of enduring significance, it also assisted in the emasculation of Australian nationalism, thus ensuring the triumph of the imperial ideology. In this sense, the day

An Army for a Nation

the men of the Australian Imperial Force stormed the beach at Gallipoli was not the day Australia became a nation. Quite the opposite. It was the day when Australia was committed unreservedly to imperial defence strategies, a commitment which would last for at least another generation. When Australia again turned to the question of national defence in response to Japan's southward thrust in 1941–42 it would be almost too late.

For their part, the British authorities could be encouraged by Pearce's commitment to the undertaking. Despite Bean's claim to the contrary, they had spent some 30 years planning how to implicate the colonies in imperial defence strategies, but this was the first time they had received such a positive response from Australia's political leadership. The British authorities well knew that Britain had the authority to declare war for the empire but were always unsure whether the self-governing colonies would come to their assistance in sufficient strength and appropriately prepared. They had also learnt through long, bitter experience that open intervention in colonial defence matters ran the very real risk of driving the colonies into independence. Therefore, while some doubts would remain about the extent of support when the crisis broke, they too were more confident that the questions of training, equipping and planning were finally being addressed in a timely fashion. They only had to await the outbreak of war when, hopefully, a surge in imperial sentiment would produce unified, spontaneous support.

This study commences in the colonial period. It was then that Britain began to develop an imperial defence strategy in the hope that the empire would be able to count on appropriately structured and trained elements from the colonial military forces. Likewise, this was the period when the Australian colonies began preparations for their own defence and began to consider a force structure based on a national defence strategy. It is through the denouement of these two influences—the imperial and national priorities for defence—that we are able to achieve a more balanced understanding of Australia's early defence history, which provides important insights into Australian defence developments during the remainder of this century.

1
The origins of imperial and national priorities for an Australian military force

In the mid-nineteenth century, Australians enjoyed a life free from war and the threat of war. Those unhappy trials had been left behind at the other side of the globe. Surrounded by sea and distant from the troubles and tensions of Europe, security seemed assured. There was no menace. Defence received scant attention. Only occasionally was there some fear of hostile enemy action. One such scare arose over concern about the possibility of a raid by a Russian force at the outbreak of the Crimean War in 1854. New South Wales raised one troop of cavalry, one battery of artillery and six companies of infantry, called the 1st Regiment of New South Wales Rifles.[1] In Victoria, the Volunteer Rifle Corps was raised at Geelong and, in the capital city of the colony, the Melbourne Volunteer Rifle Regiment was established. A year later, a mounted unit, the Victorian Yeomanry Corps, was raised and a mounted company was added to the Melbourne Volunteer Rifle Regiment. In both colonies the recruits were volunteers serving on a part-time basis without pay, but it was an unsatisfactory method of service because few men could devote time to military training at the cost of losing income from their normal occupations. Consequently, at the end of the Crimean War in 1856, interest in the volunteer forces in Victoria declined, enlistments dropped and units became less efficient.[2] In New South Wales, the volunteer units virtually ceased to exist.[3]

The threat of war between Britain and France in 1859 caused a revival of interest in colonial military forces. During the 1860s, each of the six Australian colonies raised units of part-time volunteers, but the problem of maintaining enthusiasm and attracting sufficient enlistments remained. Incentive was provided in New South Wales and Queensland with land grants in return for the completion of five years' service. Pay was also introduced for part-time soldiers in South Australia.[4] One lesson had thus

Members of the Volunteer Forces of Victoria in the 1860s. Each unit had distinctive uniforms of its own design. Members of the Volunteer Forces received no pay.
(NATIONAL LIBRARY OF AUSTRALIA, PHOTO: CHARLES NETTLETON)

been learned: there could be no sustained development of colonial forces until recruits were offered some form of remuneration for their service.

A mercenary approach was also used to raise a regular force of colonists for the Waikato Campaign in 1863. Francis Dillon Bell, the Minister of Native Affairs in New Zealand, visited Australia, offering generous conditions of service for recruits. James Bodell, unemployed and formerly a British soldier, was immediately interested when he saw one of the Waikato recruiting posters in Melbourne. 'My old soldiering propensities revived and my Friend and myself put our names down for New Zealand,' Bodell wrote, seeing an end to his plight. 'I would have gone to any Part of the World to get out of Victoria.' In addition to grants of a 50 acre (20 hectare) farm lot, a town lot and twelve months' free rations after completion of service, there was pay, which started at the daily rate of two shillings and sixpence for privates, and free rations and quarters for all recruits. In Bodell's opinion, these were 'not bad terms'—especially so, it seems, because Melbourne was experiencing economic hardship at the time and a labourer could get only five shillings for an occasional day's work.[5] Responding to New Zealand's recruiting campaign, more than 2000 men were enlisted in Victoria, New South Wales, Tasmania and Queensland.[6]

The participation of Australian colonists in New Zealand, unrelated to any threat to Australian security, exemplified the possibility of using colonists in an expeditionary role to serve imperial ends. Yet the primary impulse in colonial defence consciousness remained local and colonial rather than imperial. The withdrawal of the last British regular regiment from Australia in 1870—a decision inspired by Cobdenite economic doctrine, which considered the colonies to be millstones around Britain's neck in a period of increasing free trade—reinforced this impulse. As a result, the first permanent soldiers were enlisted in New South Wales and Victoria. But—quite suddenly it seems—Australians were beginning to lose their sense of isolation and security. A significant turning point was the linking of Australia to Britain by telegraph in 1872. As never before, news of tensions and skirmishes, common to this age of imperial expansion, reached the streets of Sydney and Melbourne on the day it was published in London. There were also rapid advances in the development of fast, reliable steamships, putting Australia within closer reach of possible belligerents. Indeed, the growing imperial ambitions of France, Germany and the United States in the Pacific region were becoming a cause for concern. Attention therefore turned to more elaborate schemes and plans for colonial defence.

At the request of the governments of New South Wales, Victoria, Queensland and South Australia, two imperial officers, Colonel Sir William Jervois and Lieutenant-Colonel Peter Scratchley, inspected and advised on colonial defence in 1877 and 1878. Their recommendations were based on the principle that the colonies should rely, for their first line of defence, on armed vessels at sea. The immediate protection of major ports and cities would then be provided by powerful forts operating in conjunction with mobile forces consisting of paid, part-time soldiers and a small number of colonial regulars.[7] The recommendations of the two imperial officers were given urgency by another Russian war scare in 1878, producing the incentive to proceed with the fortifying and arming of key points of strategic interest.

In the early 1880s the Australian colonies reached a watershed in defence organisation and development. Encroachments by Germany and France to the near north and northeast of Australia were treated as potential threats to security. Early in 1883, Queensland annexed Papua in the name of the British empire, hoping to exert control over the area and curtail German expansion. It was a move which gained the general support of all Australian premiers, although some had reservations. While enthusiasm for Queensland's action varied, all could agree that if such action were not taken in the name of the British empire then a foreign power would feel free to act first. Similar fears arose over the French annexation of the New Hebrides, producing a note of concern at an Intercolonial Convention in the same year. Included in the convention's final resolutions was a condemnation of any future incursion by foreign powers into the South Pacific.[8] Combined with this threat of European expansion into the region, the possibility of war between Britain and Russia over Afghanistan in 1885

Colonel Sir William Jervois inspecting the Inner South Head batteries, Sydney Harbour, in May 1877. The colonial governments of New South Wales, Victoria, Queensland and South Australia had invited Jervois and Lieutenant Colonel Peter Scratchley, both Imperial officers, to advise on local defence. (NATIONAL LIBRARY OF AUSTRALIA)

revived fears of a Russian raid. The result was dramatic. In 1883 the combined strength of permanent and part-time soldiers in the colonial forces was less than 8000 men; by 1885, the forces had increased to a combined strength of nearly 22 000 men.[9]

The expanded colonial forces were comprised predominantly of citizen soldiers, with barely 1000 of the members serving full-time. These permanent men were the administrative staff on headquarters, the instructors and, in the more technically demanding areas of the military forces, the artillerymen, the submarine miners and the artificers. The prominent regiments which were raised at this time, such as the Victorian Mounted Rifles and the New South Wales Lancers, owed their existence to the interest and energy of part-time soldiers.[10] Primarily these units were maintained for local defence, but it is apparent that some members looked further afield. Another unit to be raised in the colony of New South Wales was the Upper Clarence Light Horse. Charles Chauvel, a grazier of Tabulam and father of General Sir Harry Chauvel, initially offered to raise this unit to fight the Russians on the northwest frontier of India. 'His offer was declined but he was authorised to raise two troops of Volunteer Cavalry,' Sir Harry recalled. 'Some 120 were sworn in early in January 1886, most if not all of whom

Priorities for an Australian Military Force

agreed to serve abroad.'[11] Such complexities of motivation and function were to lie at the heart of Australian military history—and planning—for several generations.

The impulse to serve on imperial operations was dramatically illustrated by the Sudan episode. In February 1885, the Australian colonies were shocked to learn that General Charles Gordon, revered hero of the empire, had been killed in Khartoum by the forces of an insurgent known as the Mahdi. Gordon, whose exploits were well known to the men, women and children of the colonies, was the embodiment of Victorian virtues; a devoted Christian, philanthropist and soldier, he served selflessly as an inspired missionary of the empire. His death at the hands of an Islamic rebel demanded retribution. The Acting Premier of New South Wales, William Bede Dalley, cabled Britain with an offer to send 'two batteries of our Permanent Field Artillery, with ten sixteen-pound guns, properly horsed; also an effective and disciplined battalion of infantry, five hundred strong'. This force, Dalley informed the British government, could arrive in Sudan thirty days after embarkation.[12] The conception and execution of this offer depended entirely on the recent advances in communication and transportation.

There was an immediate response to Dalley's call for recruits. Two

The departure of the New South Wales contingent for the Sudan on 3 March 1885. Some 200 000 people of a total Sydney population of 300 000 turned out to farewell the men. Fast, reliable steamships and the telegraph had put Australia in touch with the rest of the world. (NATIONAL LIBRARY OF AUSTRALIA)

weeks after the force was offered, its 770 men and 218 horses were ready to go. The departure on 3 March was watched with intense public interest and support, with some 200 000 of the 300 000 residents of Sydney turning out to farewell the contingent. Yet in the midst of apparent unanimity there was dissent. Sir Henry Parkes, a former Premier of New South Wales on the verge of re-entering the colonial parliament, denounced the undertaking. His complaints were trenchant. He believed the contingent from New South Wales could make no difference to the outcome of the campaign; it was economic folly to encourage able-bodied men to migrate to the colony as labour while sending others overseas to war; furthermore, it was improper to commit money to such an undertaking, as Dalley had done, without the sanction of parliament. Significantly, Parkes was also upset because Dalley's action overturned the tradition that the local military forces were raised exclusively for service at home.[13] Underlying the outcry by Parkes was the concern that Australians were powerless to influence the determination of imperial policy and should therefore be more circumspect about their involvement in imperial operations. Australia's impotence had been demonstrated a few years earlier when Britain had failed to support the annexation of Papua by Queensland. Although southern New Guinea was subsequently proclaimed a British protectorate, there had been angry charges that Britain had neglected Australian interests when it was learned in December 1884 that Germany had annexed territory of its own in New Guinea.[14] Graham Berry, a noted Victorian politician, recalled that it was at this time that the idea of colonial federation first enjoyed widespread currency because it would add weight to Australian representations in Downing Street.[15] Likewise, Parkes claimed that he had no doubts that 'if there had been a central government in Australia—if Australia could have spoken with one voice in the year 1883, New Guinea would have belonged to Australia'.[16]

Australian anger over the New Guinea issue did not go unnoticed in Britain, and evoked some concerns that it might lead to Australian independence. Dalley's offer to send troops to the Sudan was therefore greeted with relief because it confirmed colonial loyalty to the empire, probably explaining why the offer was accepted so readily.[17] The long-term worry for British imperialists was that, as reassuring as the spontaneous Sudan offer was, it did not constitute a reliable commitment by the Australian colonies to imperial defence. In particular, there was no colonial defence *structure* on which the empire could rely. Britain sought the comfort of something more predictable and permanent than the Sudan model. This problem had concerned Benjamin Disraeli when he had contemplated the liberal *laissez-faire* policies which had granted self-government to the colonies. Preoccupied with imperial consolidation and repudiating Cobdenism, Disraeli had asserted in 1872 that colonial self-government should have entailed binding economic arrangements and 'a military code, which should have precisely defined the means and responsibilities by which the Colonies should be defended, and by which, if necessary, this country should call for aid from the Colonies themselves'.[18] Indeed, as European imperialism gained momentum during the last quarter of the nineteenth century, so the idea of sharing the burden of imperial defence gained support. The imperial defence agenda developed during this period by new and powerful Whitehall committees contained measures designed to entwine colonial defence resources of money and men into a centrally controlled defence strategy.

As a consequence of the threat of war with Russia in 1878, Britain had instituted an inter-departmental committee of the Admiralty, War Office and Colonial Office to inquire into the defences of the colonies and seaborne trade. It was dissolved in 1879 when a royal commission was appointed under Lord Carnarvon to examine the same questions in greater detail. The commission's attention was directed to the imperial possessions of strategic or commercial importance with the object of determining whether an organised system of imperial defence was required under the umbrella of protection provided by the Royal Navy. Recommendations were sought on the composition of defence forces which might be required—imperial troops, colonial troops or a combination of both—and on arrangements for cost-sharing between Britain and the colonies.[19]

In reviewing the defence of the Australian colonies, the Carnarvon commission examined the detailed reports compiled by Sir William Jervois in 1877 and 1878. At that time, Jervois, who had since been appointed Governor of South Australia, had determined that the Royal Navy would protect the seaways while the Australian colonies would provide local forces at their own expense for the defence of the principal Australian ports. In keeping with these earlier reports, Governor Jervois therefore advised the Carnarvon commission from Adelaide that the colonial forces of Australia were intended only for local protection. The possibility that two or more colonies might combine their forces to provide a military contingent for 'the general service of the Empire' was, as Jervois informed the commissioners, 'a project which can only be contemplated as looming in the far distant future, when the population has greatly increased and federation has been accomplished'.[20]

The commissioners rejected the advice offered by Jervois because they believed the time had arrived when the Australian colonies should become directly involved in imperial defence. To begin with, the colonies could make a financial contribution to naval defence, but the commissioners warned that central control of naval units should not be relinquished by Britain in return for any financial contributions the colonies might make. Furthermore, they anticipated assistance from the colonial military forces. The commissioners were hopeful that, in time of war, the Australian colonial governments would 'readily come forward' and approve participation in combined operations with the forces of the other colonies or with Britain. To facilitate this goal, they recommended that the standard of training and efficiency of colonial forces should be improved. Australian soldiers were 'of good physique, with zeal and every disposition to perfect themselves in drill' but the officers were 'less satisfactory' because they lacked sufficient training. Accordingly, the establishment of a military college like the one in Canada was suggested as the best long-term solution for training military leaders. Until then the commissioners believed that the colonial forces would benefit from the guidance of imperial officers, either on a temporary basis or a long-term attachment, because they would 'tend to raise the tone of discipline and bring about uniformity in organization and equipment'. Such attachments were to be encouraged, the commissioners recommended. Therefore, requests from the Australian colonies for the services of officers from Britain 'should receive prompt compliance'.[21] It would give imperial officers the opportunity to encourage the colonial governments 'with tact and judgement' to combine their various forces from time to time for joint training. 'The growth of the Colonies in wealth and population will, in all human probability, be relatively more rapid than that of Great Britain,' Carnarvon concluded, 'and their power to take a fair share of the defence of the Empire will be constantly on the increase.'[22]

Following the commission's report, the British government established the first permanent body to take an interest in colonial defence. Known as the Colonial Defence Committee, its role was to review the state of colonial defences, to establish basic defence principles and to advise colonial governments accordingly.[23] The Committee became an important agent for encouraging uniform standards and practices throughout the colonial forces of the empire, working gradually towards the distant, idealistic goal of an integrated imperial force. It was an end some perceived with clarity. In 1886, the defence question suggested immediately to Henry Thring, a British parliamentary counsellor, 'the expediency of forming an Imperial force as distinguished from a mere British force'. It also raised the possibility of political consolidation of the empire. 'I believe that in a well-considered scheme for creating an Imperial military and naval force would be found the true solution of the problem of Imperial federation,' Thring concluded.[24] These views were shared by the first secretary of the Colonial Defence Committee, Sir George Clarke.[25] However, while Imperial federation was a sensitive and difficult issue to address, as Thring acknowledged, there were alternative, less intractable, methods of working towards a consolidated imperial defence scheme. The Admiralty, for example, was at that time finalising arrangements to control naval developments in Australia which would effectively lock the Australian colonies into dependence on the Royal Navy.

In 1884, a senior officer of the Royal Navy, Admiral George Tryon, was posted as Commander-in-Chief of the Australia Station with instructions from the First Sea Lord, Admiral Sir Cooper Key, aimed at eliminating the nascent naval forces of the colonies and delivering Australian naval defence into the hands of the Admiralty. The plan had evolved from Key's wish to impose uniform standards on the colonial naval forces. It called on the colonies to forgo the development of their own seagoing navies in return for protection from an additional number of warships from the Royal Navy for the Australia station. Crews for the ships were to be provided by Britain and the colonies were to meet capital and running expenses. However, when put to the colonies, there was disagreement over their respective financial contributions. Despite this initial setback, the resolute Tryon eventually negotiated an agreement with the colonial governments which fulfilled Admiralty aims but involved some expense for the British taxpayer. The colonial governments were also insistent on retaining their own port defence capability. To be known as the auxiliary naval squadron, the additional ships were essentially a branch of the Royal Navy, manned entirely by personnel of the Royal Navy and financed, to some extent, by colonial contributions. Significantly, the colonial governments had no control over the movements of the squadron, except for the power of veto on its removal from the Australian station.[26] A formal agreement was drawn up for ratification by the premiers of the Australian colonies at the first Colonial Conference which was convened in London in 1887.

The inaugural meeting of colonial leaders was held to coincide with Queen Victoria's golden jubilee, which provided a ceremonial outlet for the growing imperialistic fervour of the late 1880s; the convenors were hopeful that the celebrations would encourage a deeper sense of imperial unity among the colonies. But the pomp and circumstance, the ceremony and the excitement were only the veneer. Beneath this elaborate display of imperial pride lay the disconcerting knowledge that colonial trade with Britain had been in decline since 1883 in favour of foreign nations. At the same time, Britain's imports had risen sharply, sounding an ominous note for a country which depended heavily on international trade.[27] There was also a distinct possibility that commercial competition with the other European nations, driven by a desire for territory, wealth and power, might eventually lead to armed conflict. Such matters were viewed with increasing concern in Britain, providing the incentive to consolidate the empire.

Defence was a vital subject for consideration at the Conference. British concerns about French designs on Egypt and conflict with Russia in Afghanistan combined with Australian worries about the South Pacific to set the tone for the agreement between the governments of Britain, Australia and New Zealand to establish the auxiliary naval squadron in Australian waters. Under its terms, Australia would contribute £106 000 each year and New Zealand would provide £20 000. Effectively, this agreement eliminated any seagoing naval capability in the colonies of Australia and New Zealand. The British authorities then turned their attention to the colonial military forces. The Secretary of State for the Colonies, Sir Henry Holland, put a proposal to participants that, should colonial governments consent to combining their military forces for active service outside their colonies, then an obligatory condition would be that the forces were subject to British control.[28] Holland's proposition illustrated Britain's role as an imperial power, attempting to dictate terms and conditions to its colonies, but the difficulty was that the colonies, who had enjoyed self-government for some 30 years, were free to make no contribution to imperial defence if they so desired. Indeed, it would become increasingly clear that the first interest of the colonies was self-defence. Therefore, it is not surprising that no commitments were given in this instance.

The colonial attitude to defence was illustrated when Sir Samuel Griffith, the Premier of Queensland, informed the conference that he did not believe that the Australian colonies were free from the threat of invasion. According to the Queensland Premier, some powerful nation might suddenly turn on Australia because such little use was being made of its available resources. 'Here is a large part of the world you are not using . . . ,' Griffith thought an imperial power might soon say to Australians, 'make way for somebody who will.'[29] Griffith therefore suggested that a periodic inspection of the colonial military forces by an Imperial officer was warranted. Primarily, he was concerned that each Australian colony possessed different military organisations operating under different defence legislation, but he also thought there might be other shortcomings.

Griffith's suggestion was welcomed by Edward Stanhope, the Secretary of State for War, who took a note of it, while Sir Henry Holland informed participants that it accorded with certain recommendations of the Carnarvon commission. Holland, of course, was referring to Carnarvon's suggestion that Britain should take full advantage of any opportunity to advise the colonies on defence matters. Therefore, the British authorities were quick to respond to Griffith's suggestion. The next day Holland informed the conference that Stanhope had already discussed the matter with the Duke of Cambridge, Commander-in-Chief of the Imperial Army, and that agreement had been given to an occasional inspection of the Australian forces by an imperial general.[30] The first inspection would be undertaken as soon as arrangements could be made.

Agreeing with Griffith, the British authorities perceived the lack of uniformity in the colonial forces to be the primary problem. Accordingly, in January 1888, the new Secretary of State for the Colonies, Lord Knutsford, proposed that the inspecting officer would, as a first priority, provide advice to enable the colonial forces to organise on a uniform basis so that they might 'co-operate effectively in the event of joint action becoming necessary'. However, despite the manifest benefit of co-operative defence for the Australian colonies, the arrangements for the inspection stalled for some months because the colonial governments could not reach agreement over sharing the costs. It was not the first time this problem had arisen over questions of defence; the proposal to establish the auxiliary naval squadron had foundered on the same issue. Stanhope, however, was determined to avoid further delay and rescued the military inspection from colonial bickering by defraying the cost from War Office funds.[31] Yet the difficulty in organising the colonies for defensive purposes would remain a source of irritation, bringing Sir George Clarke to the conclusion that, as a first priority, the British government should encourage unity of action by the Australian colonies.[32] For this reason alone, federation of the Australian colonies was suggested in Britain as a desirable goal. It was an obvious means of encouraging the military uniformity and combined operational capacity that the British authorities wanted Australians to establish.

Major General Sir James Bevan Edwards, the newly appointed commander of the British forces in the treaty ports of China, arrived in Australia late in June 1889. Ageing yet decisive and energetic, Edwards commanded the immediate respect of Australians. His gracious, confident manner was founded on the experience of 38 years' service in the Imperial Army. Early in his career he had served with distinction in the Crimea and the Indian mutiny, but more recently, as a Colonel on the headquarters staff, he had commanded the Engineer elements of the British force in the Sudan campaign. Promoted to the rank of Major General in 1887 in recognition of his long and distinguished service, Edwards was assured of an attentive audience in the colonies, both official and public.[33] For three months he toured Australia, inspecting all colonial forces in turn, paying special attention, as Lord Knutsford had proposed, to the possibility of their undertaking joint operations. Everywhere, the imperial officer was greeted with warmth and enthusiasm by the public, who took great interest in the inspection.

In Brisbane, Edwards inspected the fort at Lytton, where the garrison artillery engaged a target at Luggage Point and the engineers detonated several submarine mines. He also inspected the naval stores, concluding his visit with a review in the Domain of 1100 members of the metropolitan division of the military force.[34] Sydney was next, where Edwards inspected the forts at South Head, Middle Head, George's Head and Botany. Travelling north and south of Sydney, he also visited the defence establishments at Newcastle and Wollongong. As a finale to his inspection in New South Wales, he reviewed a parade of military units at Moore Park. It was the largest review yet held in the colony and possibly the largest in Australia, with 3500 part-time and permanent soldiers coming from the metropolitan area and the country districts.[35] In Melbourne, he reviewed manoeuvres by 2400 members of the force at Albert Park, visited Western Port to examine likely sea approaches to the city and travelled overland from Dromana to Cape Schank to study the local topography. A searching inspection of the artillery batteries at the Heads and Swann Island followed.[36] His tour then took him to Adelaide, where he reviewed manoeuvres at Montefiore Hill, then inspected the Glanville Fort, the police barracks and the gunboat *Protector*.[37] His Australian inspection tour concluded with a visit to the distant and smaller forces in Western Australia and Tasmania. Before his departure from Australia, Edwards submitted a separate report to each colonial government on the state of their defences.

Edwards considered that New South Wales alone possessed a force organised in such a way that it was suitable to meet the requirements of Australian defence, 'as distinguished from purely local defence'. Victoria had an efficient force, but its organisation had no 'power of expansion' and was suitable only for the local defence of Melbourne. The South Australian force compared unfavourably with those of New South Wales and Victoria. Its standard of training was low and its members were paid too little, thus failing to attract recruits from the 'better classes'. Of more concern, the standard of the Tasmanian and Western Australian forces was so low that Edwards considered they were of little value as defence forces. Encouragingly, the General thought the force in Queensland was in a 'fairly satisfactory condition' but there would have to be some improvements before it could be considered efficient. The northern colony also presented a unique defence problem because of the extent of its coastline and the lack of internal communications. Edwards therefore proposed that the colony be divided into two defence districts. One district, from Mackay northwards, would depend primarily on naval defence while military forces provided local static defence. In the other district, from Rockhampton southwards to the border with New South Wales, the military forces would be organised to operate with the forces of New South Wales, Victoria and South Australia.[38]

Overall, the state of development of the colonial forces could not have been too encouraging for the visiting officer. He believed that many improvements were needed before the various forces could hope to operate efficiently on a combined basis and, to this end, he provided an additional report. In it, he recommended that combined defensive operations would be 'more economical, and more effective, than the present system of purely local defence'. Yet, as desirable as this goal was, it would not be easily achieved. Not only was there a lack of uniformity in colonial military organisations, but there were also important legal impediments—the legislative power of colonial governments did not extend beyond their own borders, thus raising difficulties with the employment of troops outside their colony of origin. However, Edwards suggested that these problems could be solved by adopting both uniform organisations and identical defence legislation in each of the colonies. The introduction of a standard railway gauge to facilitate troop mobility and the establishment of a military college to train officers were additional recommendations.[39]

Edwards advised that a total number of some 30 000 to 40 000 men were required for Australian defence, about the size of a corps in a European army. To build a force of this strength, Edwards recommended that the colonies adopt a brigade organisation for their forces. Infantry would be the major arm in each brigade with mounted riflemen, artillery, engineers, supply and medical staff adding flexibility, fire-power and organic support to the force. The peace establishment for each brigade would be 1910 men. He believed Queensland and South Australia could provide one brigade each while New South Wales and Victoria could provide three brigades each, producing a total of eight brigades. By combining two brigades into a division, the Australian colonies would then have four divisions. It was also an effective means of achieving a measure of integration of the colonial forces because the single brigades of South Australia and Queensland could be paired with the odd brigade in Victoria and New South Wales, respectively.[40] The recommendations by Edwards therefore went beyond the elementary stage of uniformity of organisation for the separate colonial forces, and approached a unified corporate structure for an Australian force.

As helpful as the Edwards report might have been to the colonial governments as a basis for planning the development of their military forces, it did have some shortcomings and inconsistencies. For example, it recommended that the combined colonial forces be commanded by an officer of the rank of Lieutenant General in wartime, while in peace this officer would be inspector to the forces. The question of who would direct the General, particularly in war, was not addressed by Edwards, possibly because the obvious imperial answer—British military control—would not please colonial public or political opinion. Similarly, an assessment of the likely threat to Australia's security was also ignored. There was also no hint given by Edwards that he envisaged an expeditionary role for the forces. Instead, he referred only to local defence and briefly cited an example where an enemy might attack and capture Newcastle in New South Wales. If this happened, the colonies could 'at once supply a powerful force to retake it', he said. 'The fact that 30 000 or 40 000 men could be rapidly concentrated to oppose an attack, upon any of the chief cities,' Edwards claimed, 'would deter an enemy from attempting such an enterprise.'[41]

But there was a flaw in Edwards' reasoning. While the proposed structure might form the basis of a sizeable, integrated colonial force, the recommendations made by Edwards could not achieve the rapid concentration of 30 000 to 40 000 men required for the type of action he had cited as his only example. His proposal was that each of the eight brigades would have a strength of 1910 men, thus producing a total strength of 15 280 men who were trained and equipped for immediate operations. In the event of war, Edwards had continued, each brigade could be 'quickly expanded' to 3000 men and, after 'a reasonable time' had expired, to a full strength of 5000 men of all arms. The final result, Edwards had claimed, was that a force of 30 000 to 40 000 men could be assembled anywhere along the Australian coastline from Spencer's Gulf in South Australia to Moreton Bay in Queensland.[42] Clearly this could be achieved only after the elapse of some months.

The major inconsistency with the Edwards report, therefore, was that he had laid the groundwork for the mobilisation of a force of some 30 000 to 40 000 men on the basis of rapid concentration to oppose an attack on an Australian city but had overlooked the reaction time required to expand, equip and train a force to that level from a core force of 15 280 men. This problem is resolved, however, if the primary function of the integrated force is seen in a wider context of imperial need rather than local defence. This became more obvious after Edwards returned to London and explained his reasoning in the light of comments on his report by the Colonial Defence Committee.

In London, the Colonial Defence Committee was impressed by the ability and care shown by Edwards, but it was unable to agree with all that the officer had written because he had failed to present and justify his recommendations within the context of imperial strategy. To start with, the committee believed, the requirements of Australian defence should be based 'solely upon the probable nature and strength of the attack'. But, in its opinion, no part of the British empire was less likely to be attacked because of its location and size of population. Indeed, the landing of a small body of troops on Australian soil 'would be to court disaster'. Therefore, an enemy incursion would need a large, fully equipped expeditionary force capable of holding an important strategic point or a considerable portion of territory 'under the certain condition of losing its communication by sea'. And the committee advised that such an expeditionary force could not be assembled in Europe or at an advanced base without the knowledge of the British authorities, thus allowing time for the Royal Navy to be deployed in a defensive role. It was a factor which Edwards had overlooked. Therefore, the committee overturned his conclusion that Australia should prepare for an attack. It held resolutely to its belief that British naval supremacy and the other difficulties and risks associated with an invasion of Australia meant that it was 'almost inconceivable that the attempt would be made'. All that the Australian colonies need worry about, the committee advised, was the possibility of chance raids by enemy cruisers. Consequently, the Colonial Defence Committee concluded that Edwards was wrong in stating that the colonies needed to concentrate a force of 30 000 to 40 000 men to defend Australian territory. 'This appears to be a contingency so excessively improbable,' the Committee informed the colonial governments, 'that it need not be taken into account as one of the requirements of Australian defence.'[43] Yet, significantly, while the logic of this argument might seem to point to a conclusion that no integrated colonial force was necessary, the Colonial Defence Committee proceeded with a very different line.

The committee supported Edwards' call for Australian governments to organise the various colonial forces on a uniform basis. The ability to move troops from one colony to another for combined operations was highly desirable as defence against the type of raids contemplated by the committee, but it was also desirable as a precaution in the event of a great war in which the military resources of the empire would be taxed heavily. If war should break out, the committee claimed, a large number of trained, part-time soldiers would be required so that disruption to industry could be minimised. This extensive reservoir of men could then provide relief forces, because the role which the Australian colonies would probably play in the event of war was 'not likely to be limited to the passive defence of ports little liable to attack'. There was a strategic advantage of the first importance to be gained by undertaking 'a vigorous offensive at the outset of war against points which might subsequently prove menacing'. It was not spelt out in its comments, but the inference was clear : the Colonial Defence Committee anticipated the participation of the Australian forces on imperial operations. For all these reasons, the committee, while acknowledging its disagreement with aspects of Major General Edwards' report, concurred with the strength of the military force which he had recommended to the Australian colonial governments. [44]

While addressing the Royal Colonial Institute on the subject of Australasian defence after he had returned to London, Edwards, now aware of the criticism of his work by the Colonial Defence Committee, firmly embraced its policy. 'The idea that local defence will suffice for the needs of a commercial country and that the interests of Australasia end with her territorial waters, is utterly false,' the General informed the audience. 'The real defence of the Australasian Colonies and their trade will be secured by fleets thousands of miles from her shores.' By acknowledging a role for the Royal Navy, Edwards was now in harmony with imperial policy. 'I am sure there is nothing which would be objected to by those who found some fault originally with his . . . plans,' commented Sir Charles Dilke, a member of parliament and prominent student of imperial defence, after hearing the address by Edwards. Significantly, it was not that the Navy's pride had been injured by Edwards' original omission. Far more important issues were at stake. The notion that Australian security depended ultimately upon Britain bound Australia into the imperial family and discouraged Australian independence. Another member of the Royal Colonial Institute to hear Edwards' address, Sir William Jervois, now back in London after his vice-regal appointment, mentioned fears 'as stated in some quarters', that federation of the Australian colonies 'means probable separation from the Mother Country'. To Jervois this was an improbable outcome and, agreeing with Edwards, he pointed to the unifying effect of an imperial defence strategy by commenting that 'if the British navy were withdrawn . . . you would have the grass growing in the streets of Sydney and Melbourne'.[45]

But ascribing pre-eminence to the Royal Navy for Australian security also placed Australia in a position of dependence, putting the colonies under an obligation. 'As the main burden of defence of Australasian commerce will fall upon the Mother Country, and as other Colonies are sharing this burden by contributing to the defence of the coaling stations,' Edwards told his London audience, 'may we not in return receive from Australia assistance in the shape of military forces to co-operate with the national navy in the capture of the enemy's bases and coaling stations?' Nowhere in his recommendations to the Australian governments was such a proposal mentioned. The omission, it seems, had been quite deliberate, because to raise the possibility of Australian military involvement in imperial defence ran the very real risk of arousing colonial opposition to the military reforms he had suggested. Yet to his London audience Edwards explained that adequate imperial defence demanded the ability 'to assume the offensive against our enemies' in order to 'capture his naval bases'. To this end, his recommendations to the Australian colonies provided 'an organisation which, without increasing the number of men now under arms, would not only lay the foundation of a sound military system but form a rallying-point around which a force might be formed . . .'. This idea had occurred to him when he had witnessed the arrival of the military contingent from New South Wales during his service in the Sudan, he said. 'If a desire to join in defending [Britain's] interests has been manifested in such small wars, in which assistance was not actually required,' Edwards reasoned, 'what may we not expect when [Britain] is engaged in a struggle for existence, and when the Colonies can only protect their own interests by joining heartily with the Mother Country in presenting a united front to the enemy?' At such times, it was his confident belief that the Australian colonies would 'place the whole of their forces at the disposal of the Mother Country'.[46]

Once Edwards had made his thinking clear, the major inconsistency in his original report was resolved. He had begun preparing the way for Australia to provide a balanced federal force capable of expansion to a strength of 30 000 to 40 000 men for imperial operations. During a major war when the Imperial Army was involved in Europe and the Indian Army was committed to the land frontiers of India, Edwards explained in his address to the Royal Colonial Institute, the 'land forces best suited for the attack of the enemy's bases in the Pacific and Indian oceans would be found in the Australasian Colonies'. Jervois summed it all up rather neatly when he observed that Edwards' presentation to the Royal Colonial Institute was now 'more properly a paper on Australian Federation, Australian defence, and Imperial defence combined'.[47]

The report by Edwards produced an immediate reaction in Australia. During his visit to Sydney, the Imperial General had had several discussions with Sir Henry Parkes, the Premier of New South Wales,[48] and it is obvious that the two men had realised that mutual benefit could be derived from the report on military defence.[49] Later, recalling his visit to Australia, Edwards especially mentioned meeting with Parkes. 'I gathered that there was a consensus of opinion favourable to Federation,' Edwards recounted, 'but that the realisation of some common need was required to bring it about.'[50]

Within a week of the Edwards report being published, Parkes broached the subject of federation with other colonial premiers and before the end of the month he made his famous Tenterfield address.[51]

'The Imperial General who inspected the troops of the colony,' Parkes told his audience, 'had recommended that the whole of the force of Australia should be united into one army.' If this recommendation was accepted, Parkes said, then some central executive authority was required to control the army. Suggestions had been made by some colonial statesmen that the Federal Council was the appropriate authority, he continued. This body had been established by the colonies in 1883, but New South Wales had never been a participant. There were, however, more fundamental reasons why Parkes rejected the suggestion that the Federal Council could become the authority to control the federal army. The Federal Council 'had no power to do anything of the sort, as it had no executive function; and, moreover, was not an elective body, but merely a body appointed by the Governments of the various colonies . . .'. It did not, therefore, 'carry with it the support of the people', Parkes argued. Another suggestion, according to the Premier, was that the Imperial parliament should be requested to pass legislation authorising the colonial forces to unite as a federal army. But this, too, was unacceptable because it did not provide an appropriate solution to the problem of control. 'The colonies would object to the army being under the control of the Imperial Government, and no one of the colonies could direct it,' Parkes told the audience. As he believed it was essential to preserve the security and integrity of the colonies by establishing a federal army, the New South Wales Premier then asked 'whether the time had not now come for the creation on this Australian continent of an Australian Government'?[52]

The proposal by Parkes answered some of the questions posed by major Australian newspapers when they had commented on the recommendations by Edwards. The *Age* had referred to them simply as 'political difficulties'.[53] The *Sydney Morning Herald* had been more specific, discussing Edwards' recommendation to appoint a commander-in-chief for the combined colonial force. It posed 'certain questions of a delicate nature' concerning the basic issue of control and co-ordination of an Australian force, the newspaper had observed. The newspaper report had referred to the recent arrangements for the auxiliary naval squadron where control rested with the British Admiral in command of the Australia station. This senior officer was 'only hampered by the condition that he cannot take the ships . . . out of Australian waters without the consent of the Australian Governments'. 'Are the colonies prepared to entrust corresponding powers to the military Commander-in-Chief?' the *Sydney Morning Herald* had asked.[54] The same question also troubled the *Brisbane Courier* because the Queensland newspaper had presumed that the military commander would be appointed from the Imperial Army. '[B]ut will he take his orders from the Horse Guards [in London]?' it had wondered. 'This arrangement would be most strenuously resisted by

Save Us from Our Friends

VULTURE: *'Come under my wing and I'll defend you.'*
LAMB: *'What will it cost?'*
VULTURE: *'Oh, Not much—a pound or two of your wool to feather my nest with, so to speak!'*
LAMB: *'Thanks. You're much too fond of mutton to be trusted.'*
This cartoon appeared on the title page of *The Bulletin* in 1889 during Major General Sir James Bevan Edwards' inspection of the colonial military forces of Australia. The vulture depicts England. Note the words 'British Army' emblazoned on its left wing. The lamb depicts Australia. (NATIONAL LIBRARY OF AUSTRALIA)

the colonies.'⁵⁵ The underlying nationalist sentiment had been given more radical expression in the pages of the *Bulletin* while Edwards was still in Australia. The journal had published one correspondent's letter which called for the formation of an Australian republican force to serve as a national guard. 'The imperialists would not dare put it down,' the writer had claimed. 'The men would only be banded together for national defence.'⁵⁶ The next edition of the weekly journal had featured a cartoon on its title page which depicted an English vulture with British Army emblazoned on its wing. The bird stood, wings spread, menacing an Australian lamb. The vulture would provide protection, the lamb was informed, in return for 'a pound or two of [its] wool'. 'Thanks,' responded the lamb, declining the offer. 'You're much too fond of mutton to be trusted.'⁵⁷ In the conservative and radical press of Australia, therefore, there was agreement that defence and military development were questions related directly to Australian interests. Wisely, Parkes had selected an uncontroversial subject to initiate the difficult process of federation.

In response to the issues raised by the Premier of New South Wales, a meeting of colonial politicians was convened in Melbourne in February 1890. Here, it was acknowledged that there were benefits to be derived from political federation and a formal conference, the National Australasian Convention, was subsequently convened in Sydney in March 1891. Taking a leading role, Parkes proposed four principles on which the federal government should be founded. Together with the preservation of colonial rights, intercolonial trade and the power to impose customs duties, the New South Wales Premier moved: 'That the military and naval defence of Australia shall be entrusted to Federal Forces under one command.' This was duly resolved by the convention.⁵⁸ However, while defence shared prominence in initiating the move to federation, it attracted little debate during later conventions in Adelaide, Sydney and Melbourne, but not because it was unimportant. Federal control of Australian defence forces and the attendant benefits were considered to be beyond question.⁵⁹

The prominent place of defence in promoting the federation movement illustrated a significant change in Australia's outlook since the 1850s. The major influence was the growing European imperial interest in the southwest Pacific. Advances in communication and transport also made the colonies more aware of the proximity of likely threats to their security. Their sense of isolation eroded, Australians began to develop a defence consciousness which promoted a significant growth in defence forces in the early 1880s. In practical terms, this development was a much more important, if much less remembered, feature of colonial military history than the episode of the Sudan contingent. However, as the Sudan episode illustrated, there was an impulse to serve on imperial operations. But, despite this brief imperial episode and its minor military involvement, the primary and sustained influence was the growing perception that defence was a national issue. The next evolutionary step was the development of a national army. While its achievement was motivated by the wish to enhance the defence of Australia, it is also apparent that British strategists had more ambitious imperial purposes in mind. The danger for Britain was that colonial nationalism was easily offended by imperial intervention in local affairs, especially where colonial resources of finance and manpower were concerned. For this apparent reason Edwards omitted any reference to possible military involvement by Australian troops on imperial operations. However, this was not the case when he returned to London where he was more frank about such a role for an Australian force. For similar reasons, it seems, Edwards failed to make any reference to a method of controlling a federal force. It is almost certain that the question of control would have been raised during his discussions with Henry Parkes and Edwards would have realised that it was a sensitive issue with important implications for Australians. Indeed, when Parkes used the report submitted by Edwards to promote Australian federation he left no doubt on this issue. Imperial intervention in the control of the proposed federal military force was rejected unequivocally. According to Parkes, any future Australian army would be controlled totally by an Australian federal government.

2
Major-General Edward Hutton: His command of the colonial force of New South Wales, 1893–1896

Despite a promising start, the movement towards federation of the Australian colonies had lost some momentum by 1892. Its achievement demanded hard, prolonged negotiation to surmount colonial and regional jealousies and to gain a national market free of intercolonial barriers. While such domestic issues were not resolved easily, there was no dispute in Australia over the obvious benefits of federal defence. The British authorities, too, perceived the desirable goal of enhanced Australian security but they also realised that a combined Australian military force could satisfy certain, broader requirements of imperial strategy. Growing impatient with the tardiness of the colonies, they came to believe that a federation of colonial military forces could be achieved before political federation. Gentle pressure was therefore applied to the Australian colonies to adopt uniform military developments within an imperial framework.

In 1892, Major-General Alexander Tulloch, an imperial officer who commanded the Victorian force, was appointed by the colonial government of New South Wales to lead a royal commission in a review of its military force. Tulloch, a staunch imperialist, had earlier used his position as Victorian commandant to plead publicly the imperial defence case. He had argued that Australia should not entertain separation from Britain, claiming that the colonies were not strong enough to defend themselves from invasion. '[W]ithout a British fleet to protect Australian commerce from even a maritime enemy, the prosperity of the colony would be at an end,' he said. As it relied on the Royal Navy for security, Australia should 'remain a portion of the British Empire, and . . . take its share in defending itself against the common enemy'. Giving an indication of what he thought this entailed, he added that '[t]he defence of Australia commences in India'.[1] To participate effectively, the Australian colonies should combine their forces for imperial operations, Tulloch asserted. Not surprisingly, these imperial considerations also influenced his findings in the royal commission.

Tulloch, while reporting that he believed there were serious deficiencies in the New South Wales force, again recommended the federation of the colonial military forces. Furthermore, he urged that the commandant and the principal staff officer of the New South Wales force should be specially selected imperial officers. As the Carnarvon commission had concluded earlier, it was desirable for Britain to have imperial officers appointed to the colonial forces, especially as commanders and senior staff. Remarkably, Tulloch also recommended that the power and military authority of the colonial governors should be significantly increased by empowering them to act as commanders-in-chief, unfettered by the requirement to conform with ministerial advice.[2] He thus brought the imperial defence objective out into the open, at least temporarily. The combination of a British governor and an imperial officer exercising autonomous command over the colonial military force was the pinnacle of imperial audacity. It revealed Tulloch's naive, if not contemptuous, understanding of the practice of constitutional democracy in New South Wales.

On receiving Tulloch's report in London, Sir George Clarke, the first secretary of the Colonial Defence Committee and a leading imperial strategist, wrote to Robert Meade, permanent undersecretary for the colonies at the Colonial Office, advising him that 'the time is ripe for a manner of military federation [in Australia]—with encouragement from you it might become an accomplished fact—great results would follow'. Referring to Tulloch's recommendation for the colony to appoint a commandant from Britain, he added cryptically: 'the Imperial government ought to be represented by a sailor and soldier who know'.[3] Meade was soon presented with the opportunity to follow this advice. In 1893, the government of New South Wales implemented one of Tulloch's recommendations by appointing an imperial officer, Colonel Edward Hutton, as commandant of its force.[4]

Colonel Hutton was born in 1848 at Torquay, Devon, the son of Edward Hutton, a banker, and step-son of General Sir Arthur Lawrence, Colonel-Commandant of the Rifle Brigade. After receiving his education at Eton, his military career commenced in 1867 with his appointment as an ensign in the 60th Rifles, a decision influenced by his step-father. His first experience of active service was with the 3rd Battalion, 60th Rifles, in the Zulu war of 1879, and, two years later, he commanded a squadron of mounted infantry in the first South African war. In 1882, he participated in the occupation of Egypt, including the battle of Tel-el-Kebir, and from 1884 to 1885 commanded the mounted infantry force in the Nile Expedition. It was an arm of the service which attracted his deep interest for the remainder of his career. On his return to Aldershot, his experience in Africa was put to good use in organising twelve companies of mounted infantry for home service. To complement his extensive field service, Hutton attended the staff

Major-General Edward Hutton

Major General Sir Edward Hutton. Hutton commanded the Colonial Force of New South Wales from May 1893 to March 1896. He returned in January 1902 to become the first GOC of the Australian Army. When this appointment came to an end in December 1904, the Australian government abolished the position of GOC and established the Military Board in an attempt to increase parliamentary control over the Army. (NATIONAL LIBRARY OF AUSTRALIA)

college, Camberley, in 1881 and subsequently held various staff appointments. He was deeply interested in his chosen profession and applied himself to its various aspects with diligence, taking a leading role in organising the military society at Aldershot as a forum for professional discussion. He became a recognised member of the 'Wolseley Ring' of reformers and also played a prominent part in achieving improvements in the standard of food served to British soldiers. In June 1889, Edward Hutton married Eleanor, daughter of Lord Charles Paulet and granddaughter of the 13th marquis of Winchester, at St Paul's Anglican Church, Knightsbridge. His subsequent promotion to Colonel and appointment as *aide-de-camp* to Queen Victoria in 1892 were indications that his prospects for promotion to senior rank were good. As commander of a colonial force, Hutton would have been keen to impress his superiors in London.[5]

Before leaving London for his Australian appointment, Hutton was given a thorough briefing by Robert Meade, as Sir George Clarke had suggested. He was told that his primary role in New South Wales was to organise the military force for the defence of the colony but he was also expected to fulfil other important imperial requirements. In this regard, Meade informed Hutton that the federation of the Australian colonies was 'within the sphere of practical politics'. Therefore, as a preliminary step, it was considered possible 'to shortly bring about a Federation . . . for Defence purposes'. Because Meade believed this development could be achieved before political federation, he told Hutton that the federated military force would 'act under the direction of a Council of Federal Defence, or under the command of a chief nominated by such a Council'. Hutton was therefore expected not only to reform the forces of New South Wales but to influence

Australian military development on a federal basis. To begin with, he was told that, as far as possible, there should be uniformity in the administration, arms and equipment of the various colonial forces. In a very important additional charter, Meade also advised Hutton to encourage imperial loyalty because, although imperial federation for defensive purposes was considered unlikely in the foreseeable future, he believed it was 'very possible that should a serious emergency arise in which the safety of the Empire is jeopardized the Colonies may be invited to assist by a contingent of troops or otherwise'. Specifically, Meade stated that, in the event of war with France, 'the Australasian Colonies might be called upon to take the offensive in the Pacific and to provide an Expeditionary Force for the occupation of New Caledonia or other such possessions in those seas'. Yet the need to keep this imperial objective at least partially hidden was recognised candidly. The permanent undersecretary for the colonies took care to warn Hutton that, although there was strong imperial sentiment in Australia, it was also apparent that there was an increasing 'party of opposition' towards the imperial attachment in each colony; this was especially so in the 'rising' generation. The imperial officer was therefore advised 'to omit as a question of practical imperial policy, any reference to the possibility of Colonial Forces being necessarily expected to take part in Imperial military operations'.[6] Hutton was requested to fulfil his imperial instructions without disclosing the aim to Australians.

Meade's immediate concern about the possibility of conflict with France was sparked by a threatened clash of British and French imperial interests in Southeast Asia. A year earlier, in 1892, France had made a desperate bid to persuade Britain to accept the Mekong River as the line of demarcation between their respective spheres of influence in Indochina and Burma. France had feared that Britain would pursue the territorial claims of their recently conquered Kingdom of Ava on the east bank of the upper Mekong. This British conquest threatened French plans to control the entire east bank of the Mekong so that they could use the river as a great waterway to the southern Chinese provinces of Yunnan and Szechuan. Wishing to frustrate French designs and to create a buffer zone between British and French possessions, the British Foreign Secretary, Lord Rosebery, had given his approval to a suggestion to cede Britain's territorial claims on the east bank of the upper Mekong to the stable Asian powers of China or Siam. There was immediate uproar in Paris when Britain's intentions became known at the beginning of 1893 and France began to assert itself in the region. French attention turned immediately to Siamese territory on the east bank of the middle Mekong which also blocked achievement of its ultimate objective. In March, the month when Meade briefed Hutton, France despatched gunboats up the Mekong to take possession of islands belonging to Siam. Alarmed at the speed of this development and wishing to avoid war with France, Rosebery decided not to intervene in the hope that the French would be satisfied once they had taken the east bank of the middle Mekong. Yet the situation remained tense and the extent of French ambitions uncertain. It could easily escalate. Contemplating the likely outcome, the permanent undersecretary at the British Foreign Office, Sir Philip Currie, feared that the French were 'working themselves up into a state of excitement against Siam with a view to plundering her'.[7] In that event, the threat to British possessions and strategic interests in Asia was clear; war was possible. Such a disturbing outcome was obviously in Meade's mind when he briefed Hutton, prompting him to suggest the contingency of an Australian expeditionary force to attack the French possession of New Caledonia.

In addition to his briefing from the senior Colonial Office official, Hutton was briefed by the intelligence departments of the War Office and the Admiralty as well as the Colonial Defence Committee.[8] Captain Peacocke, secretary of the Defence Committee and a friend from staff college days, also gave Hutton 'the papers upon imperial defence and its probable developments which [Sir George] Clarke had prepared as the basis for the expansion and solidification of the great self-governing Dependencies of the Empire'. Hutton therefore came to New South Wales in May 1893 fully primed with an understanding of imperial defence requirements and strategy. His prime object, he recalled later, was to establish 'a system of co-operative defence between the six [colonies] of Australia, and ultimately . . . a complete federation of the Island Continent'. To achieve this, he planned to reform the force of New South Wales in such a manner 'as to prove a model to the other remaining [colonies]', hoping that they would follow suit 'so as to make immediate co-operation simple and effective, and to facilitate . . . further development later into complete federation'. Successful achievement of this goal, he thought, would provide an example to be emulated throughout the empire. Hutton was convinced that it would strengthen the empire's military capability and might lead ultimately to imperial federation, as men like Clarke were proposing.[9]

Fortuitously, Hutton (who was to hold the local rank of Major-General for the duration of his colonial command) and his wife Eleanor travelled to Australia on the RMS *Parramatta*, a ship of the Peninsular and Oriental line which also carried the new Governor of New South Wales, Sir Robert Duff, his wife, Lady Duff and their five children. The voyage brought the two families together and, on their arrival, one Sydney newspaper reported that the new military commandant was 'evidently quite a member of the Governor's party, and on the best of terms with them all'.[10] To Hutton and his wife, such an association was natural and they continued to mix frequently with Sir Robert Duff and his family, but it is apparent that some colonists began to suspect that the commandant's attachment to the viceregal office suggested something more than a social relationship. It would soon be asked whether Hutton considered himself to be an imperial officer taking his orders from the Governor rather than a colonial officer under the sole authority of the colonial government. These questions were not confined to the radical elements of colonial society. The Premier of the colony, Sir George Dibbs, harboured similar concerns, it seems, from the moment Hutton arrived in Australia at the end of May.

Hutton disembarked from the *Parramatta* in Melbourne and completed his journey to Sydney by express train, so enabling him to greet the new Governor as the military commandant when the ship arrived in Sydney one day later.[11] Quite by chance, Hutton travelled north on the same train as Sir George Dibbs, who had been in Melbourne on official business. Apparently the two men took the opportunity to converse during the journey but, according to later accounts by supporters of Dibbs, after arriving in Sydney Hutton failed to report formally to the Premier or to any representative of the government. It was claimed that over a week passed before Hutton responded to a curt reminder from the principal undersecretary of the colony and paid an official visit to Dibbs, who also held the portfolio of defence.[12] As improbable and exaggerated as this account might seem, Hutton noted that there was 'something of truth in it' in his private papers.[13] It was certainly true that Hutton's first visit to the Premier's office occurred one week after his arrival in Sydney.[14] Whether Dibbs had taken offence over this incident, as his supporters subsequently suggested, is not certain but, without doubt, the working relationship between the Premier and the commandant was fragile; the two men managed to co-operate effectively only for the first few weeks. Eventually, differences arising from their perceptions of the authority and status of their respective offices were to erupt in an unseemly public exchange.

Apart from his apparent indiscretion with the Premier, Hutton and his wife Eleanor made a favourable impression on their arrival in Sydney. He was dark, not tall, but of solid build with a frank, open countenance.[15] She was 'fair and slight, and very bright and pleasant in manner'.[16] Together, they were a confident couple; their enthusiasm for their new roles was obvious. 'My wife and I were fortunate in securing a beautiful house and grounds upon Darling Point,' Hutton recorded. 'The house stood in a lovely garden with views of the celebrated Sydney harbour, and this delightful setting was a great asset to us in entertaining Sydney society.'[17] *Greenoakes*, as their residence was named, provided the ideal venue for garden parties, dinners and dances, and the Huttons established a reputation as gracious and frequent entertainers. Eleanor was preoccupied chiefly in planning their busy social life while her husband applied himself to his new command— there were never any children from the marriage. She also became the inaugural president of the Soldiers' Wives League which aimed to encourage camaraderie and mutual support among the wives of servicemen.[18] Eleanor was dedicated to her role as wife of the commandant, providing assistance and support to her husband in the demanding task that confronted him.

Hutton had arrived at a difficult time for the colony. An economic depression placed severe constraints on the amount of money available for public expenditure, especially for defence. Yet, to his credit, Hutton was unperturbed, taking up command of the force of 600 permanent and 4700 citizen soldiers with energy and enthusiasm. At 44 years of age he possessed the drive and knowledge to undertake the reforms required to mould the military units of New South Wales into an efficient, cohesive force. It was an 'herculean task' which confronted him, he told officers at a social function three weeks after his arrival, but he reminded them that it was their duty to support his endeavours to improve the force.[19] One week later, the first important step was taken by introducing a reform at the most senior level of military administration.

Under previous arrangements, the command and control of the force had been vested in the commandant while administrative functions concerning finance, soldiers' pay, stores and equipment had been the responsibility of a senior civilian officer called the military secretary. Both these senior officers were responsible directly to the Minister for Defence for their separate functions. Understandably, it was an arrangement which Hutton found unsatisfactory, especially since the military secretary also advised the minister on general military subjects. One month after his arrival, the new commandant gained the approval of Dibbs to assume control of the military secretary, thereby becoming the pre-eminent military authority and sole defence adviser to the minister.[20] This was an important achievement for Hutton. Control of all military assets and functions gave him far greater freedom to introduce comprehensive reforms. Dibbs undoubtedly agreed to this arrangement because of the commandant's persuasive claim that increased efficiency and reduced expenditure would be achieved, both highly desirable goals in the depressed economic conditions.[21]

In the commandant's opinion, there were no serious problems with most of the individual units in the force; it was more a question of rationalising the force structure and introducing efficient procedures. Indeed, he thought that the units of the citizen forces were of a 'fair' standard. Writing to the Duke of Cambridge, Commander-in-Chief of the Imperial Army, Hutton informed him that the New South Wales Lancers and the Mounted Rifles had 'the element of being quite first rate'; the engineers were 'quite excellent' and the engineer field companies would 'even run some of our Royal Engineer Companies close for knowledge'; the four regiments of infantry were comprised of 'really magnificent men' and their officers, although wanting in theoretical knowledge and training, were 'very zealous' with the result that, overall, '[f]or steadiness, physique, shooting and turnout these four Regiments would bear comparison with most imperial Regiments'. Similar compliments, however, could not be extended to the artillery units because Hutton thought they alone were in 'a very discreditable state, due to ignorance, want of technical knowledge, and scientific training'.[22] It was this arm which received the most attention from the new commandant, resulting in the introduction of comprehensive reforms.

The artillery consisted of a number of garrison and field batteries mixed together in various combinations as units without corporate identity. Hutton organised this arm into distinct field and garrison units with standard establishments, calling it the New South Wales Artillery Regiment. Furthermore, he established a school of artillery to overcome the shortcomings in training and made improvements to the arming of forts. The Corps of Engineers needed less attention but he reorganised it to achieve greater efficiency. And so Hutton proceeded, leaving no quarter untouched. Cooking and transport units were rationalised to form the Army Service Corps and a mounted brigade was formed from the various mounted units throughout the colony. The barrack and ordnance departments were also reorganised. Other important reforms were introduced for the employment and training of officers. To prevent stagnation in key positions, the tenure of command and staff appointments was limited to four and three years respectively. Schools of instruction for officers and non-commissioned officers were also established, while officers of promising ability were sent to India and England for further training with the Imperial Army. The sensitive issue of payment for citizen soldiers also received attention, with the introduction of monthly, instead of quarterly, payments. A zealous reformer, Hutton was also enterprising. When parliament imposed financial reductions by not providing funds for annual camp training, he conducted a number of smaller camps in various localities throughout the colony without exceeding the reduced budget allocation.[23]

In addition to his efforts to impose organisation and efficiency on the force, Hutton also promoted its image in the public arena. A few months after his arrival he held a military display at Minto where the New South Wales Regiment of Cavalry, two companies of the Mounted Rifles, and 'A' Battery of the field artillery entertained the public with a review and, to the special delight of spectators, a mock battle.[24] On the following Saturday, he organised a highly successful open day at Victoria Barracks. As the artillery band performed and refreshments were served, visitors were treated to impressive displays of gun drill, horsemanship and military equipment. 'A Brilliant Success' was the judgement of the *Daily Telegraph*, describing the function as 'one of the most successful military social festivities of late years'.[25] Hutton's energy and enthusiasm raised the morale of the force and drew the admiration of colonists.

Despite these initial successes, there was some scepticism when it was announced a few weeks later that a military tournament would be held in the grounds of the Royal Agricultural Society at Moore Park. Spectators would be charged an entry fee but, because of the depressed economy, there were fears that costs would not be covered. Doubts also arose about the propriety of such an enterprise. 'But is it quite dignified of the military department to run a show of this kind,' asked one Sydney newspaper, 'and enter into competition with the many entrepreneurs who are engaged in catering for the public amusement in so many ways? And if Major-General Hutton's great tournament happens to prove a monetary failure, how will the deficit be met?'[26] But such questions were quickly dismissed when large numbers of spectators flocked to Moore Park over the three days of the tournament to watch soldiers from all over the colony compete at tent-pegging, lemon-cutting, sword and lance duelling and wrestling on horseback. Costs were more than covered and the profits were donated to the hospitals of the colony. Impressed by this benevolent gesture, one evening newspaper observed also that the tournament had 'afforded valuable indications that the military instruction for which the country pays pretty dearly has by no means been wasted'.[27] Not only did the military force enjoy new heights of public approval, but Hutton's reputation as a competent organiser was established.

A remarkable feature of the military tournament was the accomplished performance of horsemen from the country districts. To the surprise and delight of Sydneysiders, mounted detachments from the country centres of Camden, Inverell, Tenterfield and the Hunter Valley outclassed representatives from the city-based Lancers.[28] The results were especially significant because a team from the Lancers had recently performed well at similar tournaments in London and Dublin. Remarking that there was obviously 'plenty of untravelled talent' able to beat the highly regarded Lancers, the *Evening News* concluded that the colony possessed 'within its own borders the makings of a cavalry force equal to any that could be raised anywhere'.[29] Significantly, it was a conclusion which Hutton had already reached. He had expressed this opinion a few months earlier, when he had inspected the 4th Infantry Regiment at the rural town of Singleton. 'During the manoeuvres on the town common,' it had been reported in the *Daily Telegraph*, 'the General called a number of young men spectators on horseback to him and addressing them said they wanted no teaching to ride. Australians never did, and were the finest material for cavalry he had ever seen'.[30] Yet, as much as he wished to do so, the commandant was unable to raise additional mounted units because of the restricted military budget.[31] Nevertheless, the skilful horsemanship of men from the country districts left a lasting impression on Hutton, priming his plans and aspirations for the future.

Despite the limits imposed by the depression, Hutton's military achievements during the three-year period of his command were remarkable. Without question, he had achieved one of his major objectives in making the force of New South Wales a model of military organisation and efficiency to be emulated by the other colonies. Importantly, he had also enhanced the credibility of the force in the eyes of the public. However, in attempting to fulfil all of his confidential imperial instructions, he encountered grave difficulties, as Robert Meade had expected.

An Army for a Nation

Soon after his arrival, a vice-regal review of the force was held in Centennial Park for Sir Robert Duff.[32] Speaking to the troops after the manoeuvres, Hutton complained that they had not performed well. He urged them to strive to reach higher standards. The mounted troops and the infantry, in particular, would have to apply themselves to their training. 'Suppose the Imperial authorities wanted troops to help England in her hour of need,' the *Bulletin* claimed he told the Mounted Rifles. 'It is men of your stamp that would be required.' Not surprisingly, the nationalist journal objected to such statements. 'All through his peppery talk the Commandant seemed under the ghastly delusion that he was here to train Australian men for the Imperial service,' the *Bulletin* concluded. 'But Australians will never again play the Soudan [sic] goat.'[33] It was the first of a series of allegations which soon appeared in other publications claiming that Hutton was motivated primarily by imperial interests.

One week later, a letter was published in the *Daily Telegraph* under the *nom de plume* of Verite. It referred to Hutton's suggestion that the Mounted Rifles might be required for imperial service. 'Well, I venture to say the Mounted Infantry will never be required for anything else,' Verite wrote, 'and I hardly fancy the taxpayer will contribute for the upkeep of a body of men who can never be useful in time of war in Australia.'[34] In a matter of days, this and related issues attracted more intense interest when it was revealed publicly that recent developments in Siam were serious enough to suggest the possibility of war between Britain and France. Already, Britain had taken the precaution of despatching two naval vessels to Siamese waters before Rosebery learned, in July, that the French had also laid claim to the east bank of the Mekong right up to the upper reaches. This claim, the French *chargé d'affaires* in London informed Rosebery, would be dropped in return for British acquiescence to the French annexation of the Siamese provinces of Siamreap and Battambang. It placed Rosebery under extreme pressure. If the two provinces fell into French hands, the Siamese capital of Bangkok and Siamese independence would be threatened, placing British commercial and strategic interests at risk.[35]

Alerted by the developments in Siam, a reporter from a Sydney newspaper, the *Evening News*, called on Hutton at Victoria Barracks and asked him directly whether he thought there was a possibility of war. 'Certainly not,' the commandant replied. But the reporter persisted and asked him if, as an imperial officer, he would be recalled in the event of hostilities. 'No,' was his response. 'I am bound to a three-years service in Australia, and my post is here unless . . .'

'Unless our soldiers are ordered to the front?' the reporter prompted. 'You think that in the event of trouble in [Indo]China, the contingency of calling upon colonial troops for foreign service is possible?'

'I can scarcely answer that question,' Hutton replied cautiously. 'The policy in that event would rest not with me but with the Colonial Office. But I think such a contingency is possible.'

Clearly, the commandant was in no position to confirm that, four months earlier, a senior member of the Colonial Office staff had briefed him on the possibility of Australia being 'called upon' to supply an expeditionary force to take the offensive against the French in New Caledonia. At the same briefing, he had also been instructed to remain silent about the possibility that colonial forces would be expected to participate in imperial military operations. Therefore, regardless of the truth of the matter, it is not surprising that the interview with the reporter at Victoria Barracks ended with a denial by Hutton that he had received any official intimation about the possibility of serious complications in Siam.[36] But that same day, the assiduous reporter from the *Evening News* discovered more compelling evidence to support his suspicions when he learned that the Victorian commandant, Major-General Alexander Tulloch, was staying overnight at Sydney's Hotel Australia, after a rushed trip to New Caledonia.

In an interview with the reporter, Tulloch claimed that his trip had been simply for pleasure and relaxation. 'It was not with any official purpose that I went,' said Tulloch. 'The labors [sic] and worry attendant upon the presidency of the Military Commission in this colony, the cares connected with my own position as chief of the Victorian forces and other matters, acted adversely on my nerves, and being an old sailor I took a sea trip as a tonic and very well I feel after it.'

It is unlikely that Tulloch was telling the truth; his trip was almost certainly taken with the prime object of gathering intelligence for a military operation against the French, as Robert Meade had suggested to Hutton as a contingency in March. But, in response to further questions from the reporter, Tulloch claimed that there was no possibility of a war with France and, attempting to create a diversion and avoid further questions about New Caledonia, Tulloch nominated Russia as the greatest threat to Australian security. 'Russia's desire to possess itself of British territory in Asia will sooner or later but inevitably provoke war,' he warned. In that event, he was asked by the reporter whether he would be recalled to serve with the Imperial Army.

'No; I, like other Imperial officers, have made an engagement for a certain time. I am bound to fulfil that engagement and could not leave without the sanction of the colony, whose servant I am. But the colonies will be expected by England to do their duty.'

'They would be expected, you mean, to contribute a contingent of troops for service abroad?' he was asked.

'Decidedly,' replied Tulloch forcibly. 'A war with Russia would mean a war of the Empire against Russia. The colonies in such an event would be expected if necessary to offer their last dollar [sic] and their last man.'

The interview concluded with a statement by Tulloch that nothing would please him more 'than to lead a force of Australians in the field against an enemy of England, and I hope, as a soldier that the opportunity may yet be afforded me'.[37]

Despite the public assurances by Hutton and Tulloch, the developments in Asia were ominous; within days of the two interviews the situation appeared critical when France announced a naval blockade of Siam. But it came to nothing. In the end, war would be avoided and, in 1896, tensions would be resolved diplomatically. At the time, however, publication of the comments by Hutton and Tulloch in the *Evening News* sparked immediate expressions of concern in the Australian press.

'The Australian nationalist who pays heavy to maintain a "defence force",' the *Bulletin* observed, referring specifically to Tulloch's comments, 'will now understand what the Australian military and naval establishments are really meant for.'[38] The *Sydney Morning Herald,* too, was worried about the suggestions that the local force might be used for more extensive purposes than local defence. It reported that '[a] considerable degree of uneasiness prevails in military circles' which had led to the resignation, in 'one or two instances', of 'popular, experienced and efficient officers'. The cause of the problem, according to the newspaper, was 'an Imperialising tendency which is unpalatable to not a few'. Hutton was not named, but the comments were clearly about him. There had recently been several military conferences, 'necessarily conducted behind closed doors', the report continued, at which it had been suggested that the mounted troops, at least, would be assimilated to the Imperial Army, 'so that the two could fight side by side'. Bombay or Calcutta had been suggested as likely destinations for Australians 'so that they might co-operate with Imperial troops in maintaining British supremacy in that part of the world'. As a result, it was claimed by some Australian military officers, co-operation with the Imperial Army had become the primary influence dictating the choice of equipment and structure for the colonial force. This was a disturbing development. The Sydney newspaper reported the belief that proposals to copy British military practice were welcome if they meant 'improvements in regard to organisation, training, and equipment'; however, this was as far as assimilation should go. Any suggestion, the *Sydney Morning Herald* concluded, that 'one or the whole of the colonies might send a contingent to India or some other place where Great Britain might require assistance, was scouted by many as being of a character that would not be tolerated in the colony'.[39]

The *Sydney Morning Herald* also reported that there was concern in the force at a suggestion that pay rates would be reduced. It became clear two days later, when Hutton responded publicly to these allegations, that the adjustment to pay was simply another step in the assimilation program. The new pay rates proposed by the commandant would be the imperial rates. Rates of pay for Australian soldiers were significantly higher than those for their British counterparts, so creating a virulent source of discontentment should soldiers from both countries serve side-by-side in the same imperial force. Of course, Hutton was careful not to elaborate on this point. Being a time of economic hardship, the commandant diverted attention by stating that he intended simply to introduce 'economy in all military matters, [as well as] careful organization, and the highest state of efficiency possible'. This was the reason why he was following the example of the Imperial Army, he claimed. Nothing was done by the military authorities in England 'except on absolutely the most stringent lines of economy'. Continuing his calculated distraction, he explained that his aim was to make the defence of New South Wales 'as complete and perfect as possible' because in the event of war the imperial authorities 'did not contemplate having to send troops to Australian shores'.[40] Hutton therefore exercised caution on this occasion, albeit belatedly, by publicly avoiding any suggestion of a wider role than local defence for the military forces.

Despite his careful statement to the *Sydney Morning Herald,* widespread conjecture about Hutton's motives continued. The *Newcastle Morning Herald* reported one rumour that the British authorities had directed the colonial governors to introduce measures which would make the colonial forces 'available in other parts of the British Empire'. If this were true, the newspaper continued, then it was 'a very grave and serious innovation on the relations which have hitherto subsisted between the mother country and these colonies'.[41] Similarly, the *Daily Telegraph* charged that Hutton had confidential plans to have amendments introduced to colonial defence legislation 'of a decidedly Imperialistic nature'. If he was successful, the newspaper had been informed, it would mean the 'alteration of our military constitution to such an extent that the Australian soldier was in future to take his orders from the Imperial head, and was to hold himself in readiness for *foreign* service when called upon'. When pressed for a response to these allegations by the newspaper, the commandant was evasive and failed to confirm or deny them.[42] His behaviour in this and other instances, the *Newcastle Morning Herald* observed, gave weight to the belief that he considered the colonial force to be 'an outlying picket, or one which ought to be so, of the Imperial Army'. However, the newspaper continued, if his many reforms were aimed simply at achieving a high state of efficiency for the force, 'then the commandant is rightly discharging the duties which he is being paid to perform'. But if he was acting on instructions from the British authorities for imperial purposes, the *Newcastle Morning Herald* concluded, then it was 'a mischievous and dangerous policy'.[43]

One week later, on 30 August 1893, the commandant was a little more forthcoming than he had been with the press when he spoke in the more exclusive forum of the United Service Institution of New South Wales. He informed members that the existing defence legislation of the colony prevented employment of the troops beyond the borders. 'It will be for the constituencies of this colony,' Hutton advised suggestively, 'to decide as to whether they wish the clauses of the Army Act enlarged so as to admit of their Military Forces serving in a larger area—we will say Australia.' The commandant then hinted that the colony was obliged to consider more than local interests in relation to defence. 'Complete security for life and property must be assured, not only to the population here, but that security must be further assured in the eyes of the commercial world beyond its immediate shores,' Hutton continued. Neglect in this area would result in the loss of confidence by 'those capitalists who have so largely promoted the commercial enterprise of this colony'. It was therefore vitally important 'that the security of capital invested in this country should be assured in the event of any possible warlike complication in which Great Britain might be involved'. The implications of the commandant's address were clear: Australia should not adopt an independent stance on the defence issue. Indeed, the colonies were responsible to Britain for making appropriate defence arrangements. Hutton therefore proposed that the military force of the colony should be organised to defend Sydney, Newcastle, Wollongong and Bulli as well as 'provide an adequate, well-organised and thoroughly equipped force, which shall be capable of being moved, in whole or part, into any part of the colony at the shortest notice'.[44] Clearly, effective defence of the colony demanded the establishment of mobile units to operate in conjunction with the fixed defences, but Hutton was not motivated primarily by this objective in developing his mobile force. He had another object in mind. Surreptitiously, the commandant prepared the groundwork to fulfil Meade's prescription for an expeditionary force. Imperial requirements had become a force structure determinant for the local military force.

As reports and rumours about Hutton's hidden imperial objective reverberated throughout the colony, so his relationship with Sir George Dibbs deteriorated. Persistent allegations that Hutton looked to Whitehall rather than Macquarie Street for guidance disturbed the Premier's peace of mind. Doubt surrounded one of the fundamental requirements of democratic government that the military commander was subject totally to the constitutional authority of parliament. Furthermore, as Premier and Minister for Defence, Dibbs was totally reliant on Hutton for proper advice on defending the colony. Their relationship was more than a constitutional form: mutual trust was essential.

To fulfil his role as the military adviser to the government, Hutton had arranged at the beginning of his appointment to meet with Dibbs at 3.00 p.m. each Monday and Friday.[45] To Hutton's anger, he soon found that his arranged meetings with Dibbs lapsed. As a result, he protested that the Premier was misunderstanding documents and correspondence sent to him on military subjects. 'It is quite beyond my power,' Hutton complained to Dibbs, 'to act up to the spirit of your wishes and the interets [sic] of the Colony unless I have personal access to you as the Minister to whom I am responsible.'⁴⁶ It was an indication of the strain between the Premier and the commandant. An additional reason for increasing tension was a difference of opinion over Hutton's plans to fulfil one of Meade's instructions by introducing new military developments aimed at producing a federal military force. 'My proposals for the reform of the Military Forces of New South Wales, upon which hinged the scheme, already formed in my mind, of a system of Federal Defence based upon co-operative lines between the six [colonies] of Australia did not commend themselves to Sir George Dibbs,' Hutton noted in his private papers. Dibbs, perhaps suspicious of Hutton's motives, therefore prevented the commandant from implementing one of his imperial instructions. In response to his determination to introduce these reforms, the commandant claimed that Dibbs 'endeavoured by every means in his power to make my position untenable, and to this end subjected me to numerous acts of official discourtesy and incivility'.⁴⁷

The antagonism between the two men became public on 4 November 1893. A reduction in the defence estimates by Sir George Dibbs contrary to the advice of Hutton prompted the commandant to speak to a newspaper in Sydney before departing for Melbourne to watch the running of the Melbourne Cup. The subsequent article, which recorded the commandant's displeasure over the Premier's action, upset Dibbs. Publicly asserting his authority, the Premier gave an interview to the *Daily Telegraph* explaining that Hutton's action was a challenge to the authority of parliament. 'If he had his own way,' Dibbs told the newspaper, 'I should merely become his recording clerk.' In addition, the Premier echoed the numerous charges already published in the newspapers of the colony by complaining that Major-General Hutton 'has come here with a lot of strong Imperial opinions, and he has to learn that things in the colony have to be done in a far different style'.⁴⁸ In response to an earlier complaint from Hutton over their working relationship, Dibbs then called the commandant to his office for a meeting after his return from Melbourne.⁴⁹

'I was summoned to the office of the [Premier] at 9 pm on 13th November 1893,' Hutton recorded in his notes, 'and so apprehensive was I of what might occur from Sir George Dibbs's [sic] well-known hasty temper that, being in uniform at the time, I arrived on the scene with my revolver concealed in my great-coat pocket.' Hutton had decided that he was 'quite determined' to make his position clear and reassured himself that he 'had the great mass of public opinion . . . behind [him] and the Militia force to a man'.⁵⁰

On one level Hutton's action provides an insight into the aggressive nature of his personality. There were no apparent grounds for Hutton to believe he was under some bodily threat from the Premier. It is astonishing, therefore, that Hutton believed physical violence, or the threat of violence, could assist him in asserting his position with the Premier. There could be only dire consequences from such action. And beyond the immediacy of their personal relationship there was the important question of the relationship of the military arm of the state to the institution of parliament. As the Premier had informed the *Daily Telegraph,* he was under no illusion on this question and had every legal right to demand the subservience of Hutton as commandant, particularly after Hutton's recent public indiscretion over the estimates. Yet it is implicit in Hutton's actions and his recorded thoughts that he was prepared to challenge this authority, even to the extent of involving the militia.

It is clear that Dibbs did not guess the lengths to which Hutton might go, but he did, at least, perceive the commandant as a troublesome personal challenge to his authority as Premier. '[H]e writes and talks too much,' Dibbs stated publicly, '[and] has much to learn in regard to his official duties.'[51] The Premier obviously realised that he needed to keep a tight control on the commandant. It is therefore not surprising that Dibbs resisted Hutton's proposal to constitute a federal force. Such a proposition would only pose further difficulties for the authority and autonomy of the colonial government.

Despite Hutton's sinister preparations, his meeting with the Premier was conducted on an amicable basis, at least superficially. Perhaps the presence of Mr Critchett Walker, the principal undersecretary, discouraged any animosity between Hutton and Dibbs. Hutton simply renewed his complaint to the Premier about his failure to meet with him on a regular basis, but, significantly, Dibbs rebuked Hutton for treating the Governor, Sir Robert Duff, as his principal rather than himself, the Premier.[52] Clearly, Dibbs was deeply concerned about where Hutton's loyalty lay.

The meeting between the Premier and the commandant undoubtedly relieved some of the tension between the two men, but neither of them retreated from his original position. Despite urging by Hutton, Dibbs still refused to entertain the commandant's proposal for a federal military force.[53] In October 1893, the Colonial Defence Committee, too, had added its support but with no immediate success. Noting Tulloch's recommendation for the federation of colonial military forces in his royal commission of 1892, the Defence Committee urged that the 'time is now ripe for some legislative action in this much-desired direction'.[54] But still Dibbs resisted. Frustrated by the failure of the colonial Premier to respond to prompting, Hutton then tried to mobilise public support for the proposal.

Speaking at Bathurst in January 1894, the commandant advocated the development of a military federation for Australia.[55] For this statement he was quickly admonished by Sir Henry Parkes, who was now 78 years old and reaching the end of his political career. 'I have read the report of your speech at Bathurst with some concern,' Parkes wrote to Hutton on the day the speech was published. 'The ground you take is all old ground with us, which has been examined time and time and virtually abandoned.' There could never be a federal army unless it was under the direct control of a federal government, the elder statesman informed the commandant. It was quite impossible, Parkes wrote, to achieve a common defence act, the union of colonial forces and control by a council, as Hutton had suggested, without first establishing a federal legislative body.[56]

'My chief hope in making the speech I did at Bathurst,' Hutton responded to Parkes, 'was to indicate the direction which our military changes should take, so that such changes might make Federal Defence easy of accomplishment as soon as statesmen like yourself considered the moment had arrived.'[57] But the military commandant still failed to acknowledge the democratic necessities which Parkes had explained to him. The politician again wrote to the commandant. 'It is curious how you insist upon misunderstanding me,' Sir Henry despaired. He then proceeded to point out, 'as I have pointed out a hundred times', that the Australian military forces could only be brought under one federal law and one federal command 'by the Australian colonies uniting under one federal government'.[58] Given the suspicion which surrounded Hutton's imperial motives and the apprehension Parkes had expressed earlier to Duncan Gillies, the Premier of Victoria, about the need to insulate local forces from imperial control,[59] Sir Henry Parkes was insistent in placing national claims on any future Australian force.

Confronted with resistance from Dibbs, there was little that Hutton could do. But, ignoring the advice from Sir Henry Parkes, he continued to believe that the government of New South Wales could take action to encourage the adoption of a federal defence scheme. Indeed, the intransigence of the colonial government on this point annoyed him intensely. 'The troops are easy enough to manage, the real difficulties lie with the Government with which political wirepulling and consequent influence make it occasionally very trying to deal,' he informed the Duke of Cambridge in February.[60] Yet the commandant had little choice but to wait, and in August he was rewarded. The Dibbs ministry moved on to the opposition benches to be replaced by a government under the leadership of George Reid. ' "Federation" is one of the leading party cries of the new Government,' Hutton wrote to the Duke of Cambridge optimistically, 'and I am in hopes that the Schemes for Australian Federation for Defence, prepared for, but pigeon-holed by the late Government may now see the light.'[61]

It appeared that Hutton's optimism was fulfilled. Reid quickly accepted his recommendation to attempt to establish a federal defence scheme. The new Premier was satisfied with the action which had been taken already to plan and organise for the defence of New South Wales.[62] However, in addition, he thought it would 'be well to endeavour to work out a general scheme of defence applicable to the Colonies as a whole'. Significantly, Reid approved Hutton's proposal because he believed it would enhance Australian defence.[63] With the support of Victoria, South Australia, Tasmania

An Army for a Nation

and Queensland, a conference of military commandants was convened in Sydney in October 1894, with Tulloch as president.

The draft federal defence scheme, which Hutton submitted to the conference, was based on principles laid down by the Colonial Defence Committee.[64] The threat to Australian security and the defence requirements of the Australian colonies described in Hutton's draft scheme agreed with the appreciation originally developed by the committee in 1890 in its comments on the report on Australian defence by Major-General Sir James Bevan Edwards. The Australian colonies were under little threat of invasion and, even if this proved to be wrong, the Royal Navy would provide an effective barrier to the large expeditionary force which would be required to undertake such an operation. Therefore, the defence of the Australian mainland would have to contend only with relatively minor raids by enemy cruisers 'which might or might not be accompanied by ships carrying troops'. In addition to defence from raids, however, Hutton's draft submission drew attention to the need to maintain a secure environment for capital investment and seaborne trade. It should not be overlooked that the economic welfare of the Australian colonies depended on the supremacy of the Royal Navy, Hutton concluded. Accordingly, he asserted that Australia 'must . . . be prepared, out of its own resources, to protect the Naval bases, to secure the important strategical positions, and to guard all that the Navy needs for its free action at sea'. [65] From the outset, therefore, it was clear that the federal defence scheme was cast within the wider framework of imperial strategy.

The scheme proposed that each colonial force should be comprised of two elements to fulfil the dual roles of 'passive defence' and 'active defence'. 'Passive defence' was the protection of commercial centres and varied according to local requirements, while 'active defence' concerned the general defence of Australian soil and would be undertaken by the federal force comprised of elements from each colony.[66] It was necessary, Hutton continued, to have the men for the federal force 'ready to hand and trained' but, for 'passive' or local defence, 'men who had been hastily raised and armed would meet the case'.[67] The 'active defence' force, or field force as it was soon called,[68] was therefore designed to fulfil the role of the federal force originally proposed by Edwards but, instead of being organised as four divisions, Hutton proposed that it be organised as one infantry division and one mounted brigade.[69] Perhaps Hutton thought that it was an appropriate force for operations in New Caledonia.

Nowhere in the draft scheme did Hutton mention the possibility that the force would serve with the Imperial Army. Yet, as he explained in a private letter to the Governor of Queensland, General Sir Henry Norman of the Imperial Army, his proposals for the federal force were on 'the lines indicated to me by the Intelligence Departments of the War Office—Admiralty and the Imperial Defence Committee [sic] as being those which would most conduce to the efficiency of the Military Forces of Australia and enable these Forces hereafter to be rendered available for joint operations with Imperial troops should the Colonial policy allow it'.[70] In the draft scheme, he therefore included measures which would facilitate this end by proposing that the officers of the field force should have rank and authority identical with the Imperial Army and that, when mobilised, the force was to be subject to the British *Army Act* of 1881.[71]

Like the report submitted by Edwards, Hutton's draft scheme raised difficult questions about self-government and the practice of parliamentary democracy in the colonies. When mobilised for active service, the proposed field force was to be controlled by a federal defence council,[72] as Meade had suggested to him. The military commander of the federal force and the senior officer of the Royal Navy in Australia were to be members of the council together with two representatives each from New South Wales and Victoria and one representative each from the other colonies. No explanation of how this council was to relate to the government of each colony was made. 'What would be the Government responsible for the direction of the Federal Army?' the *Sydney Morning Herald* asked. 'If it had a commander-in-chief, to what Government would he be subordinate and from whom would he take his orders?'[73] As difficult as his proposal was to reconcile with parliamentary democracy and self-government, Hutton, like Tulloch, also wished to bestow prerogative powers on colonial governors, even though the British monarch had long since lost them in relation to control of military forces.

Presumably Hutton wished to overcome the situation where a colonial government could choose to withhold its portion of the federal force from active service because he proposed that a colonial governor could order the government to mobilise its contribution to the field force.[74] As Hutton was well aware, concerted federal action by the colonial forces was fraught with difficulty because six colonial governments were involved. Indeed, he had become quite frustrated by colonial politics and complained to Peacocke about the difficulties which he had encountered with '[t]he local Governments blowing hot and cold to suit the Labor Parties here and in Victoria . . . and the difficulty of meeting everyone's views and opinions'.[75] To the Duke of Cambridge, he confessed that he looked 'forward in the near future to a system of Australian Federal Defence which will remove the control of the Military Forces of the various colonies from the hands of the Local Parliaments and place them directly under the Federal controlling authority, whether a Federal Council of Defence, a Federal Parliament, or a Federal Military Head, it matters not which'.[76] Hutton was determined to remove as many barriers as possible which could prevent or impede the employment of the federal force.

Despite the careful preparation included in the draft defence scheme, Hutton could not ignore the limits colonial attitudes placed on the service of the military forces of New South Wales. A few weeks before the conference of commandants sat to consider Hutton's draft scheme, Arthur Griffith, a member of the New South Wales legislative assembly, railed against Hutton's 'imperialistic tendencies'. 'We know perfectly well that every Australian considered that the destiny of Australia is to be worked out within the boundaries of the island continent, not on the frontier of India,' expounded Griffith. 'We do not want any more Sudan contingents . . . [and] . . . We do not want our forces educated in the hope that there will be any.' [77] By now Hutton realised that such views were not to be dismissed lightly. Three days before the conference sat, he wrote to Peacocke informing him that the federal scheme 'must be based upon Defence alone', otherwise his draft scheme would not be accepted by the colonies. Nevertheless, Hutton explained that he had gone as far as he could to fulfil his imperial instructions and asked the secretary of the Colonial Defence Committee to 'note the "Federal Force" proposed by me would be available for service wherever the policy of the Australian Colonies might indicate'.[78]

Hutton's mood of resignation was reflected in the proceedings of the commandants' conference. During discussions, Colonel Drury, the Queensland commandant, proposed an amendment to Hutton's scheme which would have effectively allowed the field force to operate anywhere outside Australia. Reluctantly, Hutton could not support the amendment on the grounds that 'we have also to deal with practical politics'. Any proposal to employ Australian forces beyond Australian shores 'opens up a great political question', Hutton advised the other commandants, 'which I am quite sure the Government [of New South Wales] is not prepared to take up at present'.[79] Drury was probably unaware that it was also a sensitive issue in his own colony. Just three years earlier, James Drake, the member for Enoggera in the legislative assembly of Queensland, had moved an amendment to the *Defence Act* of the colony to restrict deployment of its military force to Australian territory. He had explained that the measure was needed to guard against 'Imperialism and the movements of those known as "Imperialists", whose headquarters were in London'. Sympathising with Drake's view, the legislative assembly of Queensland had taken the more extreme precaution of amending the *Defence Act* to restrict the movement of the force to the area within the boundaries of Queensland.[80] Among the commandants at the conference in 1894, at least Hutton and Tulloch had become aware of the underlying strength of such sentiments. Because of likely opposition from colonial governments, another clause in Hutton's draft scheme allowing the field force to be moved by sea to defend or seize any strategic position considered to be in Australian interests also had to be deleted. Tulloch thought it was 'very far reaching in its meaning and might provoke much hostile criticism'.[81] *Realpolitik* prevailed. The proposed federal agreement drawn up by the commandants as a result of their discussions on Hutton's submission restricted military service to Australia and adjacent waters.[82] The area was prescribed as that bounded by longitudes 110°E to 170°E and latitudes 5°S to 44°S.[83]

As much as Hutton might have wished to ignore the vagaries of democratic government, it was this very fact which prevented the federal defence agreement ever becoming more than a paper proposal. The military commandants were in a difficult position. Keen to achieve a federal defence force, their proposed scheme pre-empted political federation. 'This question of Federation has been going on for the last five years and is no nearer accomplished now than then,' complained Tulloch, 'if something is not done at once . . . our scheme falls to the ground.'[84] However, there was to be no relief for Tulloch's frustration. Reid took the commandants' proposed federal agreement to a meeting of colonial premiers in Hobart in January 1895, but to no avail. Although the premiers acknowledged the obvious benefits of federal defence, they were not inclined to create a federal force before a federal government had been established because of the problem of imposing executive control on a federal military commander.[85] The issue was so fundamental that there was no formal discussion by the premiers on the commandants' proposal.[86]

Taking a different view from that of the premiers, the Colonial Defence Committee was initially satisfied with the proposed agreement drawn up by the conference of military commandants because it represented a move towards military federation. It hoped that 'after this great step in advance has been taken the matters may not be let go asleep again'.[87] However, after further consideration the committee found a problem because it failed to grasp the need for compromise which even Hutton, after some time in Australia, had reluctantly recognised. While the federal defence scheme was based on the Defence Committee's strategic assessment for Australia and laid the groundwork for an Australian federal force to be deployed on imperial operations, 'this special point has been rather obliterated by the references to the action of the Federal Forces being confined to Australia or Tasmania,' the new secretary, Captain Nathan, complained to Hutton. This prevented the Australian forces undertaking an offensive role on imperial operations, as British strategists intended. 'To me personally,' Nathan informed Hutton, 'this seems the chief *raison d'être* of the whole scheme.' However, coming to the realisation that it was a delicate subject, the committee deliberately avoided a specific reference to this shortcoming in its official comments on the scheme.[88] Hutton, of course, was in no doubt about the wishes of the British defence planners and needed no reminding. Overseas service for the Australian forces, Hutton hastened to assure Nathan, was an object which he had kept in mind continually but at which he had 'never dared to hint publicly'. There was 'a strong, and very blatant party, who denounce the Soudan [sic] Contingent and any idea of helping the old country', Hutton reiterated. 'It would do more harm than good just now to court this opposition considering the condition of party politics,' he warned.[89] But there was one consolation for the committee. In its official comments it had urged the convening of a conference of representatives of the colonial government to discuss implementation of the federal military scheme.[90] Fortuitously, Hutton informed Nathan, a further meeting of military commandants would be held in the near future. The conference would review the federal defence scheme and Hutton promised that he would include the points raised by the Colonial Defence Committee for discussion.[91] Two weeks later, Hutton also advised Nathan that George Reid had decided to place the results of the imminent military conference on the agenda of a meeting of colonial premiers to be held in February 1896.[92]

No matter how much prompting Hutton might receive from London the imperial officer had to face colonial realities. At the subsequent meeting of colonial commandants, held in January 1896, the clause in the proposed agreement which prevented Australian soldiers being sent overseas remained intact.[93] The senior military officers realised that an amendment to this important provision would attract considerable opposition, perhaps placing the whole scheme in jeopardy. In a desperate move, however, the commandants attempted to circumvent this restriction covertly by amending the area described as 'Australia and Tasmania' in the interpretation clauses of their proposed federal defence agreement. The area was now defined by longitudes 110°E to 180°E and latitudes 0° to 50°S.[94] It included not only Australia, but also New Zealand, New Caledonia, the New Hebrides and New Guinea, as well as parts of Borneo and Java. It was a futile amendment designed to permit imperial operations of the type indicated by Meade when he briefed Hutton before his departure from England, but it would not have survived close public scrutiny. Perhaps recognising this, the commandants made one further concession to imperial wishes by including a clause which empowered the proposed federal defence council to despatch members of the field force on overseas service if they volunteered to do so.[95]

But it was all to no avail. Referred to a conference of colonial premiers in February, ratification of the defence agreement was again rejected. Instead, the premiers resolved that political federation of the colonies was essential before a federal defence scheme could be completed for Australia. In the interim, however, it was considered desirable that colonial legislation should be amended to permit combined operations by the separate forces in any part of Australia specifically to oppose foreign aggression. Uniformity in control, discipline, arms, equipment and pay were also to be secured as soon as possible.[96] The decisions by the premiers, therefore, were concerned with national control and local defence. They fell far short of the imperial designs behind the federal defence agreement drawn up by the commandants.

Hutton departed from Sydney in March 1896, returning to London at the cessation of his military command in New South Wales. At a subsequent interview with Meade, Hutton was praised for his work on the forces of New South Wales and for his efforts to bring about federal defence. Undoubtedly, his achievements had been considerable, but in introducing his various organisations and reforms and in developing his proposals for federal defence, he had kept imperial requirements firmly in mind. The issue of local defence and its unique requirements had not been addressed seriously. Hutton had been more interested in establishing an Australian force for an expeditionary role. However, while he assured Meade that he had tried to follow his imperial instructions to the letter, he pointed out that it was 'impossible' to arrange for a federal force to serve outside Australian waters because of 'public and political opinion'. An attempt had been made to overcome this problem, Hutton informed Meade, by greatly expanding the geographical definition of Australia in the amended scheme of 1896. Failing to appreciate that the draft defence agreement was now a defunct document in Australia, Meade believed that this amendment would at least permit the capture of New Caledonia in the event of war with France. This was 'the important factor', Meade told Hutton. Hutton then advised Meade, as he had already advised the Duke of Cambridge and his successor as Commander-in-Chief, Lord Wolseley, that pressure should still be applied to the Australian colonies to adopt federal defence before political federation was achieved. Otherwise valuable time would be lost. Concluding the interview, Meade requested Hutton to pass the same information to the Colonial Defence Committee.[97] The Colonial Office official obviously failed to appreciate the reality of the Australian situation or perhaps, like Hutton, he simply tried to ignore it.

The European imperial expansion of the late nineteenth century promoted the development of an imperial and an Australian defence agenda. The ideal solution for both requirements was the development of a federal military force from the separate military forces of each colony. Yet imperialists found that it was a step which the Australian colonies were not prepared to take until a federal government had been established in Australia. Australians were determined to maintain control of the development and deployment of an Australian force. Nationalism and the realities of colonial self-government conspired to frustrate British attempts to guide and influence colonial military developments. Despite the efforts of men like Hutton, there was little that Britain could do to rush the Australian colonies towards the desirable objective of federal military action. The real risk for Britain was that excessive imperial meddling in colonial affairs could drive the colonies to greater independence. Yet, rather than leave the Australian colonies to work out their own solution, the British authorities would continue to search for ways to achieve their imperial objective.

3
The Boer War and federation: Imperial aspirations and national realities, 1896–1901

From 1896, the prospect of integrating the human and other resources of the colonies into a global policy of imperial defence began to receive practical consideration at the highest levels in Britain. Field-Marshal Lord Wolseley, intent on military reforms, had assumed in the previous year the position of Commander-in-Chief of the Imperial Army, and found that his suggestions for an expeditionary force structure enjoyed support from outside the War Office. In 1896, members of the Royal United Service Institution were told by Vice-Admiral Phillip Colomb, a leading defence exponent, that the empire was 'not safe' because Britain could despatch only a small military force at short notice for service overseas. A larger expeditionary force was required, but resources were limited. The problem facing the policymakers, then, was to rationalise the use of resources available for defence. Colomb suggested that, because the Royal Navy was such a dominant force in controlling the seas, the threat of invasion was diminished and therefore money spent on static defences throughout the colonies was largely wasted. So he advocated 'a larger and mobile Army, to be obtained by suppressing all over the Empire . . . those exaggerated ideas of localised and immobile defences which are now so strongly advocated and which absorb funds that could and should go to the mobile Army'. In the discussions which followed, members of Colomb's audience agreed that economic realities dictated such a solution to the imperial defence problem. The chairman, Earl Cowper, stressing the latter point, concluded: 'we can never hope more money will be spent on the two Services than is spent now.'[1]

The increasing financial demand of defence was an immense burden for late nineteenth-century Britain. In 1850, defence had consumed 27.2 per cent of the annual budget, but by 1896 the allocation had increased to 38.0 per cent, and showed no sign of diminishing.[2] A major drain on funds was the maintenance of the two-power standard for the Royal Navy, especially with the increasing complexity of ship construction. Hand in hand with the financial problem was a shortage of suitable recruits for the Army. British soldiers were not well paid and the Army faced a perennial recruitment problem. Not only did military service fail to attract men in sufficient numbers but those who did apply for enlistment were generally in poor physical condition. A survey of British recruiting reports from 1896 to 1902 brought Major-General Sir John Maurice to the conclusion that 'out of every five men who are willing to enlist only two are fit to become effective soldiers'. The causes, Maurice believed, were years of poor diet and the unhealthy conditions in the vast industrial slums where large sections of the population lived. He concluded that the shortage of suitable human resources placed Britain in a perilous situation.[3]

Resource problems also weighed heavily on Wolseley. Since assuming the duties of Commander-in-Chief he had been examining the ability of the Imperial Army to execute its duties. He saw the Army's roles as home defence, the maintenance of colonial garrisons and the mounting of foreign expeditions, and concluded that the Army needed more men. 'But how does it find these men?' Wolseley asked the Permanent Undersecretary of State for War in February 1896. 'It finds them,' he explained sadly, 'by a perpetual series of makeshifts, by transfers, by enlarged depots, by bounties, by robbing Peter to pay Paul, by the denudation of the home cadres, by a succession of struggles and expedients which combine to keep it in a weak and exhausted condition, and leave it unfit to fulfil other requirements, such as the garrisons for home ports, and the Army-Corps for home defence or for abroad, which are also an important part of its functions. We live from hand-to-mouth, like the insolvent debtor who meets his daily liabilities by shifts invented upon the spur of the moment, and with any money he can lay his hands on regardless of the ultimate loss he is incurring.'[4] Granted such deep concerns on the availability of resources, it is little wonder that defence planners turned their minds to the human and financial potential of the colonies.

The combination of strategic requirements and limited resources dictated new approaches to imperial defence. In May 1896 the Colonial Defence Committee considered that its policy of encouraging improvements in the defence of each colony while promoting co-operation between adjacent colonies in time of war—an object of the federal defence scheme proposed earlier for Australia—was only the beginning. The committee looked forward to a time when the increasing strength and resources of the self-governing colonies would enable them to assist Britain 'by placing at her disposal for operations in any quarter of the globe bodies of troops formed from the excellent material of strong self-reliant Colonists'. Until this goal could be achieved, the committee believed that the best contribution the colonies could make to imperial defence was the development of their resources and their local defences. However, if England suddenly became embroiled in a conflict which posed no direct threat to the colonies, then it considered that an immediate offer of colonial assistance 'would be prized not only for its real value, but also as evidence of that solidarity on which the greatness of the British Empire must ultimately rest'.[5] There was a distinct advantage, the committee believed, in demonstrating that, militarily, the members of the empire acted as one.

Such long- and short-term goals represented a new stage in the development of imperial defence. In particular, they went beyond the expedient of requesting an Australian federal force to capture regional objectives, such as New Caledonia or German New Guinea. It was now envisaged that colonial troops might be employed on general imperial service under British control. There were therefore pressing reasons why the colonial forces should evolve along imperial lines. The Colonial Defence Committee set out to formulate a comprehensive statement of imperial standards for the colonial forces.

The committee believed that small numbers of permanent soldiers were required in each colonial force to care for armaments, defence installations and stores. The permanent members should also assist in training a larger force which would be comprised of part-time citizen soldiers. The citizen soldiers should be either militia who were paid for their service, or volunteers who were unpaid. However, better results would be achieved, the committee thought, if the majority of the force was militia. This type of service was more suited to rural areas where pay for military training would compensate men for time lost to the consistent demands of primary production. Volunteer service was more suitable for towns and well-populated districts where military training could be arranged more easily to avoid interference with normal working hours. While militia and volunteers should be organised into discrete units, they should all belong to higher formations which comprised a field force, the committee advised. It also stressed the importance of supply, transport and medical services as organic support for the field force.[6]

All these recommendations were suitable for colonial circumstances, it was considered, where a force of citizen soldiers could be maintained during peace for a relatively small cost. In war, the citizen force could be mobilised into its formations, ready for either home defence in the unlikely exigency of invasion or, more likely, for an expeditionary role abroad. This was a departure from the widely held concept of a citizen defending hearth and home—a concept which essentially tied a citizen force to discrete localities. The development of a mobile field force with organic support permitted greater flexibility in choosing the area of operations. Therefore, to permit combined operations on an intercolonial or imperial basis, the committee recommended standardisation of small arms, the adoption of a common disciplinary code for active service—the British *Army Act* of 1881—and the introduction of rank structures and insignia as used in the Imperial Army.[7]

The Colonial Conference of 1897 in London. The Colonial Secretary, Joseph Chamberlain, is seated at the front. A keen grower of orchids, Chamberlain is following his usual practice of wearing a bloom in his buttonhole. Sir George Reid, the Premier of New South Wales, is the large gentleman with the umbrella standing immediately to the right of Chamberlain. (NATIONAL LIBRARY OF AUSTRALIA)

These recommendations were sent to all the colonies in July 1896 by the colonial secretary, Joseph Chamberlain.[8]

Chamberlain was deeply imbued with a centralist view of empire and a desire to develop imperial defence in a more substantial fashion. 'I and those who agree with me believe in the expansion of the Empire and we are not ashamed to confess that we have that feeling, and we are not at all troubled by accusations of Jingoism,' Chamberlain had stated in the Commons in March 1893.[9] Originally a radical Liberal, he had returned from the political wilderness in 1895 to join Lord Salisbury's Conservative cabinet. His choice of portfolio, the Colonial Office—until then a political backwater—was unexpected, for Chamberlain was a man of considerable energy, talent, popularity and ambition. But he saw the Colonial Office not as a sinecure but as an exciting administrative challenge which provided the means of fulfilling his grand vision of empire.[10] Chamberlain was committed to the goal of integrating the colonies within an imperial defence scheme. His strategy was to wait for 1897 when the imperial fervour of the sixtieth anniversary of Queen Victoria's accession to the throne offered promising opportunities.

An Army for a Nation

A Colonial Conference—the second—was to be held in London to coincide with the celebrations for Queen Victoria's long reign. Defence, Chamberlain decided, would be one of the topics for discussion. In setting the agenda, he received a recommendation from the Colonial Defence Committee to institute a program of interchange of military units between Britain and the colonies because, as the committee explained, it would be 'a practical step in the direction of Imperial Unity'.[11] Chamberlain was in full agreement and decided to put the proposal to the conference.

Queen Victoria's Diamond Jubilee on 22 June 1897 was a spectacular celebration of the imperial family under the leadership of the British crown. The premiers of the empire's eleven self-governing colonies all participated in the ceremonies which emphasised imperial pride, achievement and, above all, unity. Two days later the premiers of Canada, the Cape Colony, New Zealand, Newfoundland, Natal and the six Australian colonies assembled for the Colonial Conference chaired by Joseph Chamberlain.

Chamberlain presented the conference with his vision of a united, strong British empire. He suggested the establishment of an imperial federation governed by a federal council comprised of representatives from Britain and the colonies. Economic incentives would be a feature of such an organisation, with free trade uniting the empire. Common defence would also be an issue of primary importance. And while on that subject, Chamberlain explained that Britain already faced a heavy financial commitment in maintaining her naval and military forces. 'If we had no Empire,' he said, 'there is no doubt whatever that our military and our naval resources would not require to be maintained at anything like their present level.'[12] But he emphasised that imperial security was not Britain's responsibility alone. According to Chamberlain, each of the colonies faced some threat from a potential enemy. Unlike the approach previously taken by the Colonial Defence Committee, the colonial secretary moved to disturb the sense of security shared by the Australian colonies. Australian interests, Chamberlain asserted, 'have already, on more than one occasion threatened to come into conflict with those of two of the greatest military nations of the Continent . . . who also possess each of them a very large, one of them an enormous fleet'. In a move calculated to unnerve the Australian premiers, the colonial secretary referred to the possibility of conflict 'with Japan or even with China'. The point Chamberlain wished to stress to those present was that they shared a common interest with Britain for their security and were therefore obliged to contribute to imperial defence.[13]

Chamberlain was pleased that the Australian colonies made an annual financial contribution to the Admiralty for naval defence as well as taking steps to provide for their own military defence, but he wanted the other members of the empire to consider contributions they might make. Turning to the colonial military forces, Chamberlain pointed to the benefit to be gained from early preparation, the use of common arms and equipment, and

The Boer War and Federation

standardised training. Then, following the proposal made to him by the Colonial Defence Committee, the colonial secretary suggested that the colonies might exchange units of their military forces with British units for joint training exercises. If the colonies sent military units to the United Kingdom for the purpose of training and 'if it were their wish to share in the dangers and glories of the British Army and take their part in expeditions in which the British army may be engaged, [Chamberlain saw] . . . no reason why these Colonial troops should not, from time to time, fight side by side with their British colleagues'.[14] It was an invitation to the colonies to do more than simply organise for their own defence—that is, to participate in imperial military operations beyond their own borders.

If Chamberlain was expecting an immediate, positive response to his proposals, appropriate to the buoyant mood of imperial pride and unity engendered by the Diamond Jubilee, he was to be disappointed. His opening proposal for imperial federation was quickly despatched. While Australians were at that time finalising arrangements for national federation, imperial federation was not a popular issue. The mood of the Australian representatives was admirably illustrated by an exchange between the Premier of South Australia, Charles Kingston, and Joseph Chamberlain. When asked by Kingston whether the proposed imperial federal council would be comprised of two houses with one of them giving equal representation to the colonies regardless of the size of their population, Chamberlain immediately replied: 'I should say certainly *not*.' The exchange was then abruptly terminated by Kingston with a terse comment that arrangements should therefore remain as they were.[15] The colonies would not surrender their political autonomy under such conditions. Similarly, Chamberlain received little support for his defence proposition. The premiers gave no commitment but promised to consider the proposal when they returned to their colleagues and parliaments in the colonies.[16] Having avoided a direct answer, the colonial leaders were, however, quick to assure Chamberlain that, in the event of war, Britain could rely on support from the Australian colonies. 'You would find they would cast all . . . narrow ideas [on defence of the Empire] to the winds,' George Reid, the Premier of New South Wales, advised. They would, he said, be ready to 'do anything, go anywhere'. But in time of peace Australians were reluctant to make any contributions.[17] Like other parts of the empire, Australia would respond to a major threat to Britain because of its loyalty, but until then, local defence enjoyed precedence.

Before leaving Australia for the Diamond Jubilee, the Australian colonial leaders had participated in a four-week session of the National Australian Convention in Adelaide. The result, which they brought with them to London, was the first draft of the constitution for the proposed Commonwealth of Australia. As the constitution was to be enacted ultimately by the British parliament, comments were sought on the preliminary document.

However, the British authorities, while determined to encourage Australian federation, were quite worried by what they read in the draft. [18]

On 19 June, three days before the Diamond Jubilee celebrations, a worried Sir John Anderson, head of the Australian section at the Colonial Office, noted that it was 'impossible to view [the draft constitution] as entirely satisfactory, especially in regard to the unity of the Empire'. One of Anderson's major concerns was that Section 70 of the draft implied that in all cases the Governor-General was to act only on the advice of his Executive Council, so preventing the Governor from fulfilling his role as an imperial officer by receiving instructions from Britain and representing imperial interests in the business of parliament. The fear was that the unity of the empire was threatened unless the British government retained ultimate control over colonial legislation.[19] John Bramston, Assistant Under Secretary of Australasian Affairs, shared Anderson's trepidation that Australia might become 'at once an independent state'. Indeed, he feared that this was the underlying intention. The drafters of the constitution of course had no such aim, but it must have caused Chamberlain some concern for his plans for imperial federation and combined military operations as he read John Anderson's concluding comments: 'while everyone is talking of "unity" and praying and hoping for it, it is discouraging to find united Australia putting forward as the product of its united statemanship a distinctly disruptive measure'.[20] Chamberlain shared the concern of his advisers and decided to take action 'against the objectionable provisions pointing out their separatist character but making no threats'.[21]

The colonial secretary instructed his staff to prepare memoranda which expressed the views held by Her Majesty's government on the draft constitution together with suggested amendments. Aware of the potentially explosive nature of direct and open intervention in colonial affairs, Chamberlain took action to attempt to have the imperial amendments incorporated surreptitiously in the draft constitution. The colonial secretary approached George Reid, the Premier of New South Wales, confidentially, and asked him to introduce the amendments at the next National Australian Convention to be held in Sydney later that year.[22] Undoubtedly, Chamberlain reasoned that the amendments would be accepted more readily by Australians if it was believed that they came from Reid rather than himself. Reid, perhaps motivated by a mixture of unprincipled opportunism and loyalty,[23] agreed to co-operate and was sent copies of the Colonial Office memoranda by Chamberlain for his 'private and independent' consideration. Some of the amendments, the colonial secretary advised Reid, were 'very desirable to meet objections which might otherwise be taken' when the constitution was presented to the British parliament. Chamberlain urged Reid to give the matter his personal attention as he was 'anxious to avoid the possibility of friction hereafter'.

Among the suggested amendments were several aimed at preserving the discretionary powers of the Governor-General so that he could protect imperial interests. As the Colonial Office missive put it, 'he may have constitutionally to act without the advice of his ministers'.[25] But one suggested amendment, which had not been raised previously in the lengthy record of observations by the Colonial Office staff (it was probably introduced by Chamberlain) concerned the command of Australia's military forces. It proposed to amend Section 68 of the draft constitution which provided that the Commander-in-Chief of the Australian military and naval forces would be 'the Governor-General as the Queen's Representative'.[26] The British authorities wanted the reference to the Governor-General deleted and the Queen instead to be designated as the Commander-in-Chief.[27] The motive of the British authorities is clear. This amendment would have given the British parliament a constitutional basis to command Australia's forces; the Queen was compelled to act on the advice of her ministers and in this instance they would have been British ministers. As the noted constitutional authority, Alpheus Todd, commented in 1894 in relation to the prerogatives of the Crown, 'it is now obvious that any attempts on the part of the Sovereign to retain in his [sic] own hands power, in respect to military administration or diplomacy, would be as inconsistent with constitutional usage as would be the personal and direct interference by the Sovereign in domestic affairs'.[28]

It is inconceivable that Chamberlain could have contemplated exercising control over Australian forces without the consent of an Australian government, but the proposed amendment is a clear indication of the British determination to prepare the way for combined operations by an imperial force. Certainly, in terms of international law, the British parliament was recognised as the authority for declaring war for the empire, but the colonial secretary undoubtedly had more practical considerations in mind. Once Britain had made a war declaration, the degree of colonial commitment to its prosecution rested with the respective colonial parliaments. It was after the colonial contribution had been made—assuming that it was a positive response—that the proposed amendment was to take effect. Its successful introduction into the Australian constitution could have been an important step in removing legal problems associated with the command of an imperial force by placing its ultimate control, at least as far as Australians were concerned, in the hands of one central authority, the British parliament. It was, in short, the latest in a series of possible answers to the question of ultimate control of Australian federal forces, a question posed originally by the report on Australian defence by Major-General Sir James Bevan Edwards and echoed, to the concern of the Colonial Defence Committee, in the proposed federal defence scheme.

The command and control of colonial troops on imperial operations raised difficult legal issues for which some effective solution had to be found. Problems first occurred, in relation to the Australian colonies, when

An Army for a Nation

New South Wales sent the contingent to the Sudan in 1885. The military forces of the self-governing colonies were raised and controlled under the terms of colonial legislation—at least while they remained within their respective colonies. But complications arose when the troops left the colony because the legislative power of colonial governments did not extend beyond their own borders. One attempt to overcome this problem resulted in the inclusion of Section 177 in the British *Army Act* of 1881, which attempted to make colonial military law binding on forces when serving inside and outside the colony. It also gave precedence to the *Army Act* when colonial troops were serving with British troops and the colonial legislation was thought to be inadequate. Nevertheless, there were substantial doubts about the legality of Section 177, doubts which were shared by the Judge Advocate General of the Imperial Army, Sir Francis Jeune. It was his belief that an imperial Act could not in itself be binding on troops raised in and belonging to the colonies.[29] The issue was clouded with uncertainty. 'I do not think it would be possible to construct any effective system,' General Sir Henry Norman, a senior and influential officer of the Imperial Army, complained in 1898, 'by which a [British minister] should be able to give positive instructions to forces that belong to self-governing Colonies.'[30] But the proposed amendment to the Australian constitution was clearly such an attempt, giving a clear indication of the scope of Chamberlain's thoughts on imperial consolidation. If nothing else, it prepared a legislative basis for implementing his proposal to interchange military units.

The reason given confidentially to Reid for the proposed constitutional amendment was that the command of the military forces was usually vested in the General Officer Commanding, not the Governor-General. Therefore it was 'undesirable to use any language which would require any alteration of their relative positions'.[31] On this pretext, Chamberlain recommended deletion of the reference to the Governor-General in favour of the Queen. In the context of the constitution, however, his explanation was nonsense, as Chamberlain would have been well aware. He was ignoring the fundamental necessity of Australian parliamentary control. But the men who drafted the constitution were well informed on the realities of constitutional law. Chamberlain's spurious reasoning therefore would not have confused them and there can be no doubt about their reaction had the amendment been proposed by Reid. Participants in the final Constitutional Convention of 1898 were in complete agreement in their view that, as Commander-in-Chief, the Governor-General should act solely on ministerial advice—the advice of Australian, not British, ministers. It is therefore not surprising that Reid apparently made no attempt to introduce the amendment proposed by the British authorities.[32] The command of Australian troops was an issue on which there was no second opinion. One prominent participant in the final Convention, Alfred Deakin, succinctly captured the sense of the debate when he concluded that: 'In no case is [the Governor-General] to be endowed

The Boer War and Federation

with the personal power to act over the heads of Parliament and the Ministry, by whom these [Australian naval and military] forces are called into existence and by whose contributions they are maintained.'[33] Australians were clearly determined to exercise ultimate control over their forces in accordance with the accepted practice of constitutional democracy.[34] The two versions of the clause for the constitution—Chamberlain's and the National Australian Convention's—therefore illustrate a point of friction for a nation emerging within an imperial framework. Notwithstanding Australia's formal position as a member of the empire, the self-esteem associated with perceptions of national status and the autonomy inherent in constitutional democratic government placed important limits on the ways in which Australian soldiers could be integrated into centralist defence plans for the empire. Such difficulties would continue to emerge in the search for an imperial defence scheme.

In August 1897, immediately after the Colonial Conference, Lord Brassey, the Governor of Victoria, wrote to Joseph Chamberlain with a suggestion to raise a military force in Australia for general service under the control of the British government in time of war. However, it seems that Brassey did not first discuss the proposal with the government of Victoria. 'There is nothing to show that Ld. [sic] Brassey's suggestion was not a purely private one or that he ever consulted his Ministers' it was noted by one of Chamberlain's officers when the letter was received at the Colonial Office.[35] In his submission, the Victorian Governor recommended that advantage be taken of the strong military spirit and the abundance of very cheap horses by retaining a force of 5000 mounted troops in Australia at a cost to the Imperial Exchequer of £20 for each man. This force could then be mobilised when required by the British government for imperial operations.[36] An interested Chamberlain referred the suggestion to the Colonial Defence Committee for its consideration.

While the committee applauded the intent of Brassey's suggestion, it had reservations about its form. In addition to doubts about the financial cost of the proposal, it was concerned about the probable efficiency of the force because it believed that it would lack sufficient experienced officers. Moreover, the Defence Committee anticipated political problems in using the force if the colonial governments were opposed to a particular operation. 'However desirable Imperial Federation may be and is,' the committee observed, 'it would be impossible at the present time for the Imperial Government to accept the dictation of local popular feeling in Australia on a point such as a campaign on the frontiers of India, or a war with the Transvaal.' In the worst case, the British government might find itself without the troops in wartime that it had paid for in peace. [37] Nevertheless, the committee considered 'the creation of an Imperial army as a great step towards Imperial unity'. It therefore concluded, with War Office approval, that discussions should continue with Brassey to determine 'how Australian troops can be brought into the Imperial system of defence in such a way as to minimize the difficulties [it had] pointed out'.[38] This suggestion was followed up in mid-1898 when Brassey returned to London for a visit.

Attending a meeting of the Colonial Defence Committee on 17 June 1898,[39] Brassey portrayed Australia as an ideal source of mounted infantrymen. Horses were plentiful and 'the hard life of the up-country farmer' produced men with a 'special aptitude for the work which would fall on mounted infantry in a campaign in rough country and a hot climate'. Yet, despite Brassey's enthusiasm, the committee still held to its original reservations and did not support the suggestion. As an alternative, it raised a proposal of its own, suggesting the establishment of a regular Australian Regiment as a unit of the Imperial Army. 'If a battalion (and eventually two or more battalions) of Australian infantry could be raised for general service,' the committee observed, 'it would tend to relieve the present strain on the infantry at home caused by the large requirements of India and the Colonies.' The unit would serve under the same conditions and pay as the Imperial Army and be maintained from a base depot in Australia. The committee believed it was a better suggestion than Brassey's because Australian soldiers would be serving constantly by the side of those from the United Kingdom and 'the idea of Imperial unity would be much more advanced'. Furthermore, the unit would be a part of the Imperial Army and would therefore be firmly under British control. The training and experience received by the soldiers would also enhance Australian defence in the future, the committee concluded.[40]

This suggestion promised imperial benefits similar to those arising from the proposal to exchange units which the colonial secretary had put to the premiers at the Colonial Conference. Chamberlain therefore gave the committee his support.[41] Wolseley, too, was enthusiastic about the suggestion. 'I think the close union of the Colonies with the Mother Country to be of such great importance to our Empire, that I would willingly see a small Battn. raised in Australia,' the Commander-in-Chief observed. It would be 'a great result' if the other colonies took similar action, he added.[42] One major shortcoming of the suggestion, however, was the problem of attracting recruits from Australia, where wages were relatively high, in return for the low wages paid to imperial soldiers. 'In view of the high rate of wages for unskilled labour in Australia do you consider it worthwhile at the present time to pursue this subject any further?' Wolseley was asked by his Adjutant-General, Evelyn Wood. The senior staff officer realised that this question worried the commander and also the Secretary of State for War, Lord Lansdowne. However, despite their reservations, both Wolseley and Lansdowne agreed that an attempt should still be made to implement the suggestion. 'I am not sanguine as to the result but I would on no account throw cold water on the proposal,' Lansdowne concluded.[43] Although pessimistic about the outcome, the possibility of integrating an Australian unit

The Boer War and Federation

into the Imperial Army promised to overcome a major problem for imperial defence by settling the difficult question of control. For on this issue the War Office was emphatic. 'It must . . . be clearly understood that an Australian regiment, if raised, will be required to serve out of Australia, in peace as well as in war, and that it will be under the *Army Act*, and subject to exactly the same conditions of service as regards pay, quarters, rations, &c., as the rest of Her Majesty's Army,' the War Office informed the Colonial Office.[44]

The British authorities had now developed two similar proposals for involving colonial forces in their military plans: Chamberlain's suggestion to exchange military units and the Colonial Defence Committee's suggestion to raise an Australian Regiment as part of the Imperial Army. They were both modest in their scope, increasing the probability that either proposal might win the approval of the cautious colonial governments and, as a result, establish precedents for more ambitious imperial schemes. Yet they hardly seemed adequate foundations for future developments. The dream of the War Office and the Colonial Defence Committee for an imperial army was far from being realised, and the urgency of the matter was becoming more pressing as the international situation began to appear unstable. The strengthening of the alliance between France and Russia, the crisis with the United States over Venezuela in 1896, the Jameson raid against the Boers in the Transvaal with the subsequent liaison between President Kruger and the German Emperor, and tension with France over the Fashoda incident of 1898 all served to presage a major international conflict. 'These are the dangers,' the British Prime Minister, Lord Salisbury, observed in 1898, 'which threaten us in the period which is coming on.'[45]

Against this background of mounting urgency, Edward Hutton, already blooded in the difficult arena of colonial defence planning, was prompted to draw up more ambitious plans for an imperial military force. 'The advent of the Salisbury Government to power in 1895, with the Rt. Hon. Joseph Chamberlain as Colonial Minister,' Colonel Hutton recorded, 'gave an opportunity for the adoption of some definite scheme upon which the unity and solidification of the Empire could be based.'[46] On the night of 19 April 1898 Hutton presented a paper to the Royal Colonial Institute in the Hotel Metropole, London, on the subject of 'A Co-operative System for the Defence of the Empire'. According to Hutton, his paper was an attempt to show how a pronouncement by Chamberlain of January 1898, that 'the Sons of Britain throughout the world shall stand shoulder to shoulder to defend our mutual interests and our common rights' could be put into practice.[47] Since that time, Hutton had been working on his paper, taking care to discuss his ideas with Major-General Sir John Ardagh, Director of Military Intelligence at the War Office. 'I saw at once that I had [Ardagh's] full concurrence, although he was careful to avoid committing himself to any official approval,' Hutton noted.[48]

An Army for a Nation

Hutton introduced his paper by informing the audience that no scheme of organised military defence 'in which all portions of Her Majesty's dominions shall take their share' had ever been developed for the empire. A British expeditionary force of two army corps numbering 60 000 men, or even three army corps, would be totally inadequate to fulfil the requirements of imperial defence, Hutton claimed. What was needed was a large imperial field force of 173 000 men, or six army corps, incorporating infantry, artillery, cavalry and administrative elements. Its organisation and composition would make the force capable 'of taking part in active offensive operations in the field'. Contingents would be drawn from the militia forces of the colonies in proportion to their overall population, Australia's contribution being 12 000 men.[49]

The idea for this scheme had grown out of Hutton's experience as commandant of the force in New South Wales. 'It seemed clear, even at this early period, while studying the methods for effecting a co-operation for defence among the six [colonies],' Hutton subsequently recalled, 'that this system, if successfully launched in Australia, might easily become the prototype of a similar system which could be adopted by Canada, by New Zealand, by South Africa, and ultimately by the Mother Country.' [50] The model for the imperial defence scheme, Hutton therefore told his audience at the Hotel Metropole, was the federal defence scheme drawn up for Australia. The underlying principles would be mutual defence between colonies, reliance on the supremacy of the Royal Navy at sea and acceptance of the notion espoused by the Wolseley school[51] that 'the true defence of the Empire may be best served by a vigorous offensive—that hostilities should be forced upon the enemies of the British Empire, and fought out upon other than British soil'. According to Hutton, the members of the empire would be bound by 'some system of offensive–defensive alliance, or Federal Agreement, which shall include the creation of a central controlling council, having, in peace, the limited administrative powers necessary for the organisation and maintenance of the federal force agreed upon, and, in war, its control and distribution'.[52] Hutton's proposal for imperial defence therefore repeated the major shortcoming of the federal defence scheme for Australian defence: it failed to consider the political ramifications of the controlling body. Indeed, in military terms, it had much to commend it as a solution to the problem of imperial defence; in reality, however, the proposal had virtually no hope of accommodating the autonomous aspirations of the colonies. Hutton failed to understand the nature of democratic society and the strength of sub-imperial nationalism.

Hutton's address was heard by a number of influential British defence experts, parliamentarians and service officers. Prominent among them were Sir Charles Dilke, Liberal member of parliament and co-author with Spencer Wilkinson of *Imperial Defence*; Sir John Colomb, member of parliament, and his brother, the recently promoted Admiral Phillip Colomb, who both

The Boer War and Federation

enjoyed substantial reputations in the defence field as leading proponents of the 'Blue Water' theory of naval concentration; Lieutenant-General Sir James Bevan Edwards, erstwhile adviser to the Australian Colonies; General Sir Henry Norman; and Mr Arnold-Forster, member of parliament and future Secretary of State for War. Major-General Sir John Ardagh was also present. Each of these men contributed to the discussion following Hutton's address and established a consensus of support for the general principles which were fundamental to his proposals.[53]

Dilke, who spoke first, believed that the possibility of war made the subject of common defence of the empire 'a pressing one indeed'. It was impossible to exaggerate the importance of the subject, he told the audience. The piecemeal defence of each colony was inadequate. 'What we may be called upon for at any moment,' Dilke believed, 'is the most strenuous effort that can be put forth to wage an offensive war for the purpose of destroying those who have attacked us.' Similarly, Sir John Colomb thought passive defence was without value, adding that Britain required an 'offensive means or striking power through the military arm'. Britain had been pursuing the wrong military policy by 'locking up too many men for purely local defence'. To meet the demands of a war, he continued, the combined resources of the empire had to be organised to produce a military force 'free to be applied in offensive operations whenever necessary to bring the war to a finish'. Admiral Phillip Colomb was inclined to the same views. The 'speed and certainty of transport', he told the audience, meant that military forces could now be moved quickly to 'deter the enemy from stirring in the most effective way'.[54]

The statements of a number of the speakers were motivated by an underlying sense of urgency. Equally obvious, however, was the frustration caused by the intransigence of the colonies. While it was acknowledged by some that colonial support would be received at the outbreak of a major war, by then it would be too late. Undoubtedly, the empire needed a scheme which entailed early preparation by all its members. With the reticence demanded by his senior position at the War Office, Sir John Ardagh therefore agreed that the colonies had to undertake 'co-operation in the great work of Imperial defence'. 'But I think we are yet a long way from coming to [this],' he concluded. This realisation was a source of considerable irritation to participants in the discussions at the Hotel Metropole. 'We had Mr Reid here last year,' said Dilke, referring to the attendance of the Premier of New South Wales at the Colonial Conference, 'but, to judge by his speeches before he came and after he went back, he really came home for the purpose of preventing our doing that which we believe, in the interests of the Empire, ought to be done.' 'I believe the time has come for plain speaking on this question,' Sir John Colomb agreed, 'and that real practical combination and self-sacrifice in the Colonies and Mother Country alike are necessary to achieve British security.'[55]

From the perspective of London, the problem was seen clearly but its solution was beyond reach. Dealing with the colonies was a problem, General Sir Henry Norman stated, because it was 'impossible to dictate to them that they shall expend certain sums in raising a force, or in organising means of defence or offence'. It was all very annoying. The colonies did not share Britain's sense of urgency and so did not consider military preparations to be a high priority. Arnold-Forster fumed that 'there is no country, large or small, no War Office, enlightened or uninformed, which ever thought it had provided for the elementary necessities of defence by taking the measures which commend themselves to the Government of the Australian Colonies'. The problem would be solved more easily, Dilke thought, if there were one parliament in Australia instead of six. It was still possible that all the Australian colonies might not federate so 'we have to do the best we can by raising our voices constantly and strenuously, and trying to bring the Colonies to feel with us on this question [of defence]'. Although driven to exasperation by colonial politicians, Dilke was consoled by the attitude of the men serving in the various colonial military forces. 'They understand and have thought on this question,' Dilke informed the meeting, 'and I believe they are an admirable element in approaching to proper views of the question.'[56]

The general aim of Hutton's proposed scheme thus received the support of members of the Royal Colonial Institute. Yet, however attractive Hutton's plans were, as a solution to the defence problems perceived by the British authorities, they were of little practical use. Their implementation was virtually impossible without some form of imperial federation and this proposal had been rejected by the colonial premiers at the Colonial Conference in 1897. It is not surprising, therefore, that Hutton's scheme was not considered by the Colonial Office or the War Office. The first step towards involving the colonies in imperial defence had to be less ambitious and more cautious. Therefore, Chamberlain's unit exchange proposal, which enjoyed War Office support on the condition that colonial troops serving in the United Kingdom were subject to the *Army Act*,[57] was put to the colonies in August 1898.

Since initially raising the proposal a year earlier at the Colonial Conference, Chamberlain had developed a definite plan. He was also keen to open negotiations because he was worried that his original suggestion would languish if the colonies were not prompted. 'Unless we enter into more detail,' Chamberlain believed, 'I am afraid there will be delay and misunderstanding.'[58] However, because only permanent soldiers could participate in long-term exchange programs, the scope of Chamberlain's proposal was restricted to certain types of units. For a start, the Colonial Secretary suggested that Canada exchange a field artillery battery with Britain while New South Wales and Victoria, perhaps with participation by Queensland, should each exchange a garrison artillery battery. But it is evident that

The Boer War and Federation

Chamberlain had further developments in mind as a result of this first step. 'It seems most desirable,' he told the colonial governments in seeking their comments, 'that the mother country should have the option of employing Colonial units (other than garrison artillery) on Field Service abroad.'[59]

As unambitious as this initial proposal was, the response was not encouraging. The Victorian government envisaged legal problems. According to the Victorian Attorney-General, Isaac Isaacs, there was no adequate legislative basis to permit Victorian troops to serve in Britain. It was therefore considered appropriate to wait until the Australian colonies had federated before proceeding with such a proposal.[60] The government of Western Australia, which had only one permanent artillery garrison, stationed in Albany, also suggested that the proposal should be considered after federation.[61] The Tasmanian government supported the idea but said it was unable to participate because the colony had very few permanent soldiers.[62] South Australia, too, was unable to participate, but made the point that it was also unwilling.[63] 'We expected this,' John Anderson noted on the Colonial Office file, 'Mr Kingston [the Premier] is a provincialist not an imperialist.'[64] Some encouraging comments came from Queensland, but for various reasons, particularly the small size of its permanent artillery force, the Queensland government proposed that the exchange be limited initially to two lieutenants.[65] The New South Wales government alone was prepared to undertake the exchange on the basis Chamberlain had proposed.[66]

This reply took the Colonial Office by surprise. The Victorian response had already been received, and Colonial Office officials expected that New South Wales, too, would want to defer participation in the exchange until after federation.[67] Indeed, an initial examination of the legal questions raised by the Victorian government had convinced the Colonial Office officials that an exchange of a battery of garrison artillery with New South Wales could not proceed at that time. '[T]he question must now wait for Federation,' John Anderson concluded, 'when we may be able to get something done if we get an energetic patriotic War Minister for Australia.'[68] But three weeks later, Anderson changed his mind on the legal question. It now appeared that the *Defence Act* of New South Wales *was* compatible with the British Act because, on 26 July 1899, John Anderson observed that it was 'most desirable that the [exchange] should be pushed through'. Anticipating further developments, he added: 'it will be an excellent beginning'.[69]

Despite Anderson's optimism, the War Office suddenly became too busy to proceed with the exchange of a battery of garrison artillery with New South Wales.[70] In August and September of 1899, war in South Africa was imminent. Chamberlain's interest in gaining colonial involvement in imperial operations was now more urgent, although not for the reason that he believed a war in the Transvaal would unduly tax British military resources. The Colonial Secretary wanted a spontaneous offer of military assistance from the colonies to serve as a display of imperial unity and strength. The proposal to exchange units was therefore put to one side. It was now also unimportant that the Victorian government and the New South Wales government were not enthusiastic about the Colonial Defence Committee's suggestion to recruit an Australian regiment. Responding to an approach from the Colonial Office on establishing such a unit, both colonial governments believed the low imperial rate of pay would prevent the scheme from working. In each case, it was recommended that further consideration of the suggestion should be deferred until after federation.[71] As a matter of some urgency, Chamberlain now concentrated his efforts on gaining a spontaneous offer from the colonies for the war in South Africa.

The war promised to be a useful catalyst for hastening long-term plans. The difficulty of involving the colonies in imperial defence had long worried the British authorities. They dreamed of an imperial army, yet the reality was that the Colonial Secretary could get immediate agreement from only one Australian colony to exchange a single artillery battery. The war now provided a significant opportunity to introduce military co-operation on a wave of imperial patriotism. But, moderating Chamberlain's optimism, the early responses were not encouraging. Queensland alone responded in July 1899 with an offer of 250 volunteers for operations in South Africa. The other colonial governments, despite expressions of enthusiasm for active service from a number of Australians, displayed some reluctance to become involved. Joseph Chamberlain was not pleased. Like Sir Charles Dilke, however, Chamberlain was well aware of the attraction active service on imperial operations would hold for some Australian citizen force units, at least in the major colonies of New South Wales and Victoria. These units could possibly provide Chamberlain with assistance in gaining a more substantial and unified colonial commitment to the war.

At the time Chamberlain was busy reviewing the possibility of colonial military operations in South Africa, a detachment from the New South Wales Lancers was in England undergoing training. The trip had been organised by the commanding officer of the unit, Lieutenant Colonel James Burns, and was financed by the War Office and private contributions; the government of New South Wales provided no assistance. 'I entirely refused to grant any money towards the trip of the Lancers to the mother country,' Premier Reid informed the parliament. 'In fact, my own opinion was that if we did send any men to the mother country at the public expense, the other branches of the service were entitled to at least equal consideration, if not more.'[72] Public expenditure on trips to England by citizen force units was a sensitive issue, demanding great care from Reid, because, since the elections of July 1898, he had depended on Labor Party support for a majority of four seats. Yet it seems that finance might not have been the sole consideration. Reid had also turned down an earlier application from Burns, a principal of Burns, Philp and Company, for a squadron of the Lancers to serve in the Afridi campaign in India because he 'did not want

The Boer War and Federation

to see a spirit of unrest and military adventure' fostered in the colony.[73] Yet, despite the lack of support from Reid, during a business trip to London, Burns had little difficulty gaining War Office approval for 100 men with horses to be rationed, quartered and trained at Aldershot for a period of six months free of charge.[74] This offer was presented to the government in Sydney as a *fait accompli* by the Colonial Office in December 1898, leaving it no reasonable grounds for opposition. However, in giving its approval, the government informed the British authorities, rather pointedly, that it considered the trip to be 'more or less of a private nature'.[75]

It was an encouraging development for Chamberlain. The enthusiasm of the Lancers to train in England had provided the colonial secretary with a degree of military co-operation he had been unable to achieve by dealing directly with the colonial government of New South Wales. Chamberlain quickly realised how he might be able to use the visit by the Lancers to achieve united colonial contributions for South Africa. In July, when his plans to exchange units with the colonies finally stalled, the colonial secretary telegraphed a request for co-operation to the governments of New South Wales and Victoria. He asked whether the contingent of Lancers at Aldershot and also a contingent from the Victorian Mounted Rifles would offer to serve with British troops 'in the event of necessity arising for a military demonstration against the Transvaal'.[76] But the responses were disappointing. Ignoring Chamberlain's reference to the Lancers, the New South Wales government promised to assist the enlistment of volunteers in the colony if Britain requested them, but made it clear that it did not want to commit any funds to such an undertaking.[77] A similar reaction came from the Victorian government, which informed the Colonial Office that some men would volunteer, but asked whether the British government would pay for their preliminary training.[78]

Chamberlain and his staff were particularly annoyed by the reply from New South Wales because it was the senior Australian colony and, like Victoria, also influenced the smaller colonies by its actions and decisions. Furthermore, he had not intended to call publicly for volunteers, hoping for a spontaneous offer of co-operation by the colonies which he might then welcome as a display of imperial unity. He therefore decided to send another telegram to the colonial government.[79] On receiving it, Beauchamp, the Governor of New South Wales, undertook to approach Reid again, but he advised Chamberlain that there was little reason to be optimistic if the offer which he sought involved any expense for the government.[80]

As Beauchamp had suspected, Reid's government still refused to make the spontaneous offer of troops that Chamberlain wanted so earnestly. The Colonial Secretary was advised that the cabinet of New South Wales did not believe that the situation in the Transvaal warranted such an offer. Because of its tenuous claim to power, the government also believed that 'it would not be advisable to submit such a proposal for Parliamentary sanction'.[81] Therefore, it stated that it was not prepared to bear the expenditure involved in raising and offering troops on its own initiative.[82] Nevertheless, Reid advised that there would be large numbers of volunteers from New South Wales if Britain required them and, by inference, was prepared to pay for them.[83]

Testily, Chamberlain rejected Reid's offer of assistance to recruit volunteers, as Britain 'of course' possessed 'ample resources for any emergency'. However, the colonial secretary added suggestively that he was still prepared 'to welcome any offer of assistance from Governments of any Colony *if made spontaneously* . . . as proof of sympathy with Mother Country and identity of feeling and interest in all that concerns the Empire'.[84] Yet, despite such prompting, Reid's government remained obdurate. The assistance Chamberlain wanted from New South Wales, however, eventually came from the Lancers.

The imperial officer who commanded the New South Wales forces, Major-General French, joined James Burns in a plot to force the hand of the New South Wales government by having the detachment of Lancers, who were then nearing the completion of their training in Aldershot, diverted to South Africa. It appears that Burns instructed the officer commanding the Lancer contingent in England, Captain Charles Cox, to offer the service of his men to the War Office. Cox was then instructed to ask Lord Carrington, the Lancers' Honorary Colonel and a former Governor of New South Wales, to cable news of the offer to Sydney with a request for reinforcements. The cable, duly received by Burns, contained the specified information as well as an expression of hope that the government would sanction the Lancers' offer to serve in South Africa.[85]

The new colonial government of William Lyne, replacing the government of George Reid, assumed power in New South Wales in September 1899. The Premier and most of his ministers were dismayed at the prospect of a military commitment in South Africa, but by October were under some pressure to change their attitude. New Zealand, South Australia, Queensland, and Victoria had already made offers of troops, thus isolating Lyne's government on the issue. The new cabinet quickly came to a decision when Carrington's cable arrived in Sydney.[86] Chamberlain was advised that the cabinet of New South Wales had on 3 October approved the Lancers' application to serve in South Africa.[87] The offer had the outward appearance of 'spontaneity' required by Chamberlain, putting further pressure on the remaining Australian colonies of Western Australia and Tasmania. Within a few days, they too made offers.

The Boer War was an important event in the development of British plans for imperial defence, at least as far as the Australian colonies were concerned. Unlike the Sudan campaign of 1885, it involved all the Australian colonies and over 16 000 Australian men and some 60 nurses ultimately

The Boer War and Federation

served in the war.[88] It represented a far greater test of resolve and commitment than the earlier limited operation. The South African campaign therefore stood as an important precedent, fulfilling Australian promises of the past and priming British expectations for the future that Australians would stand by Britain in time of war. As expected, a mood of heightened military enthusiasm also emerged in Australia. After the declaration of war in October 1899, membership of the colonial military forces in Australia increased from 22 000 men to 29 000 within a year,[89] making Major-General French optimistic about future military developments. It was proof, he informed the Premier of New South Wales in May 1900, that 'the English-speaking people throughout the Empire are willing to take their share in its defence, and provide the men, and possibly the money, therefore'. As a result, French proposed that war reserves, comprised largely of mounted men, be established in Australia for imperial service in future operations.[90] 'This well deserves serious consideration,' Wolseley observed when he read the suggestion which French had also sent to Lord Lansdowne in London.[91] 'There can be no doubt that it would strengthen our Military position very much and tend to bind the Colonies still more to the Mother Country if in each we had some thousands of men always held to serve in our Army in the event of war.'[92]

The Colonial Defence Committee could now look to the future with optimism. As Captain Nathan, secretary of the committee, observed in January 1900, there were two important matters 'bearing on the question of troops from Australia for Imperial Service in war'. Firstly, the federation of the Australian colonies which would 'remove many of the difficulties in the way of a scheme involving the cooperation of all the colonies of Australia has advanced considerably nearer consummation'. Secondly, Nathan observed, the Australian colonies had already 'furnished, without previous agreement, over 2500 men, largely mounted infantry, for active operations in South Africa and are preparing to considerably add to their contingent'. He therefore gained the concurrence of each member of the committee to defer further consideration of French's suggestion until after the federation of the Australian colonies.[93] Joseph Chamberlain endorsed this decision by the committee,[94] believing that the experience gained in South Africa would suggest 'the best method of organising and utilizing Col. troops for Imperial service' in future.[95]

In the interim, Nathan was confident enough to start work on plans to establish an imperial expeditionary force having a total strength of 160 000 men. The United Kingdom would provide 120 000 men and the remaining 40 000 men would come from the self-governing colonies. Nathan believed that, with such a force, offensive operations could be undertaken in any part of the world within two months of the outbreak of war. The fact that the security of Australia was 'guaranteed by the Imperial Navy will without doubt make its inhabitants desire to largely assist the Empire in land operations', Nathan reasoned. The Australian contribution to the expeditionary force would be 14 000 men—Nathan appears to have rejected the scheme proposed by French because of its limited scope. He knew the participation by Australia and the other colonies in his proposals would require amicable agreement to co-operate in an imperial military organisation in advance of a specific requirement. Britain should be able to rely on colonial support with 'reasonable certainty', he emphasised. Therefore, according to the secretary of the Colonial Defence Committee, there was a need to start early planning for future wars.[96] The areas in which it was envisaged that Australians might fight were the Pacific coast of the United States, New Caledonia, French Indochina, the northwest frontier of India, New Guinea and China.[97] That Australian military forces might fight on Australian soil was clearly considered to be an unlikely contingency. Nathan proposed that his plans be discussed at the next Colonial Conference.[98]

On 1 January 1901, Sydneysiders made their way to the centre of the city to witness the inauguration of the Commonwealth of Australia. Contingents from each Australian colonial military force, the New South Wales Lancers, the Royal Australian Artillery band and guard of honour, and school cadets all marched in the celebratory procession, adding a military dimension to the sense of pride in national achievement. A reminder of Australia's imperial attachment was provided by two contingents of Australians who had participated in the Sudan campaign and the Boer War, and, even more vividly, by the participation of a large Indian military contingent and representatives from 39 famous British regiments. Indeed, the *Sydney Morning Herald* thought these military visitors gave 'the utmost pleasure and satisfaction' to spectators. It was 'valuable and inspiring' that Australian soldiers were regarded 'as brothers in arms by such splendid fellows'. 'Their helmets, their bearskins, their busbees, their keen bright swords, and cuirasses,' observed the newspaper, 'drew the admiration of the crowd, as readily as they caught the sunlight.' The presence of the Indian and British troops, concluded the *Herald*, 'seemed . . . as they were intended to do, to embody our unity with the mother country and identification with its Indian and colonial empire'.[99]

That night, when a state banquet was held in the Sydney Town Hall, the imperial officer commanding the large British contingent, Colonel Wyndham, used the occasion to express the hopes which Britain had long held, often privately, for Australian federation. He told guests that Australia's soldiers were Britain's 'blood relations, [their] brothers in arms, brothers in suffering and brothers in death'. Accordingly, Wyndham hoped that detachments from Australia's military forces would be sent to Britain to attend camps and manoeuvres in order to learn of the latest developments in drill, tactics and staff duties. The imperial officer was encouraged that soldiering was so popular in the new nation and he expected that Australians would claim it as their right to fight with their British comrades in the next campaign. Perhaps Australia might even contribute an army corps and with such a force Britain would 'be able to checkmate any enemy that may cross or block the road of freedom and prosperity'. 'That is the message we have come half across the world to deliver,' Wyndham concluded.[100]

4
The first Defence Bill: Its development and its failure, 1901

With the federation of the Australian colonies came the foundation of the Australian Army. On 1 March 1901, the Commonwealth assumed control of the former colonial military forces by proclamation under Section 69 of the Constitution.[1] The forces had a total membership of 28 500 men and were comprised of three types of soldier: firstly, permanent soldiers numbering some 1500 men; secondly, 18 000 members of the militia; and thirdly, 9000 members of the volunteer forces. The Army was and would remain predominantly a citizen force. In addition to its active members, 29 000 men were enrolled as members of rifle clubs, another 2600 were in the military reserves and there were 9000 school cadets.[2] Fortunately for Prime Minister Edmund Barton's Commonwealth government, there was no lack of public interest in military training; it was engendered by Australian participation in the Boer War which continued until May 1902. Yet the development of an Australian military force posed certain difficulties. The major problem confronting the government was that the Army was national in name only. There was little uniformity in organisation and no rational force structure. Furthermore, until federal legislation was enacted, the troops in each state would be administered according to six different sets of colonial legislation. The task of moulding the separate colonial forces into a cohesive national body was a major task of reorganisation and administration. There were many years of hard work ahead of the Commonwealth authorities, and the task was made more difficult by a lack of military knowledge and experience in establishing a national force.

The First Defence Bill

Sir John Forrest. Forrest was Minister for Defence in the first Commonwealth government. He held this portfolio from 17 January 1901 to 7 August 1903. (NATIONAL LIBRARY OF AUSTRALIA)

The major administrative responsibility fell on the shoulders of Sir John Forrest, the second Minister for Defence. The first, Sir James Dickson, died on 10 January, never having left his sick bed since assuming office. The sudden and unexpected ministerial vacancy produced an immediate review of portfolios. Initially Forrest's appointment had been as Postmaster General, but he had not contemplated this role with enthusiasm. The Department of Defence would be more to his liking, he believed, because it would be less complex.[3] With disarming honesty, he confessed publicly six months later that he had looked forward to 'a haven of rest in taking charge of . . . an easy department—the management of the defences of Australia'. He had not anticipated 'a great deal of work or trouble'.[4] Clearly, Forrest did not perceive his department's immediate responsibility of raising and equipping Commonwealth units for active service in South Africa as a major commitment; nor was the security of Australia under threat. Defence was not a high priority for the Barton government.

Forrest was born in 1847 at Preston Point, near Bunbury, Western Australia. A man of humble origins, he trained as a surveyor and, in 1865, was appointed to the staff of the Surveyor-General's office. There he quickly gained widespread public recognition for his skill and courage in leading several challenging survey expeditions across the vast, forbidding wilderness of Western Australia. Professionally competent, by 1883 he had risen to the position of Surveyor-General and Commissioner of Crown Lands with a seat in the executive and legislative councils of the crown colony government. With the advent of a local parliamentary system in 1890, he was elected unopposed as member for Bunbury in the legislative assembly. Popular, politically experienced and forceful, he became the first and only Premier of the colony, dominating public affairs for a period of ten years until federation. The considerable weight of his public influence was matched only by his imposing physical stature—on entering the federal arena, he stood 183 centimetres tall and, with a girth of 137 centimetres, weighed 127 kilograms.[5]

Understandably, Forrest was reluctant to leave his commanding, influential position in his home state to become a member of the first federal government in Melbourne. He regretted deeply the 'great inconvenience and sacrifice' of relinquishing the premiership of a colony to become one of nine federal ministers on the other side of the continent. His greatest achievements were behind him and before him lay the daunting prospect of hard work and little recognition. Already he had acquired wealth; there was little to attract him. 'It is . . . a great wrench, leaving Western Australia and my Home,' he wrote to Joseph Chamberlain, informing him of his misgivings, 'but I have decided to do it for a short time at any rate.'[6] To make his new parliamentary and ministerial life more tolerable while in Melbourne, Forrest rented a large suite of rooms in the Grand Hotel where he entertained on a lavish scale.[7] Yet his tenure of the defence portfolio was to be anything but a pleasant experience. Lacking military knowledge and motivation, Forrest was not a good choice as Minister for Defence.

As a first step towards developing a national force operating under federal defence legislation, Forrest appointed a federal military committee comprised of the six state military commandants. The task of this committee was to give advice on military force structure and integration. Its first recommendation was the appointment of a formal inquiry into the state of the forces, their organisation and equipment. A comprehensive inspection of defence installations was also recommended.

The inquiry and inspection, which were completed in 1901, revealed several problems. Low stocks of small arms ammunition in the various military stores were of particular concern. Victoria, being the worst case, possessed only seventeen rounds for each rifle in its force. It was revealed also that the coast defence artillery employed different fire control systems from state to state; indeed, New South Wales had two different systems in operation. Guns and equipment were also in a bad condition. Ignorance and neglect prevailed because, with the exception of New South Wales, there were no periodic inspections of military equipment and ammunition. The serious consequences were obsolete ammunition, unserviceable field guns, guns without mountings and mountings without guns—it was even claimed that some of this artillery equipment had originally been 'bought by mistake'. Defence depots also held obsolete submarine mining stores and equipment. Over many years there had been haphazard procurement of stores and equipment and poor management of defence assets. Expensive equipment had been bought without first determining its role within an overall defence plan and, in many instances, no supporting equipment, accessories or replacement parts had been procured for future operation and maintenance.[8]

In relation to the organisation of the forces, the inquiry reported that there were no service corps elements in Queensland, South Australia and Western Australia and no veterinary departments in any of the states. Only one state, New South Wales, had both a medical department and an ordnance store department which were organised as military units.[9] These had been introduced by Hutton during his command from 1894 to 1896. For future military operations, the inquiry believed, it would be necessary to establish similar functions on a national basis. On the vital question of force structure, however, the military inquiry had been pre-empted to some degree by the federal military committee itself.

In their original recommendation to the government, the commandants had stated that the inquiry should make no attempt to suggest a detailed organisation for the forces. Instead, the commandants urged, it 'should be instructed that the Commonwealth Forces will be organized' according to the recommendation made by Hutton in 1894 for his proposed federal force. Accordingly, the Australian military forces should be divided into two separate forces. One would be a field force for active operations and the other would be a local force for passive defence. The commandants also stipulated that the field force should be 'capable of being moved to any part of the Commonwealth that may be threatened'.[10] Such operational functions required a balanced combat component of infantry, mounted troops, artillery and engineers as well as organic logistics elements to move, supply and maintain the force. However, because state forces were organised only on the basis of local defence, the commandants concluded, a major reorganisation would be required.[11]

The defence of Australia presented unique problems because of the size of the country, the sparse population and the limited development of transport facilities. The areas where the population was most dense—Brisbane, Sydney, Melbourne and Adelaide—were linked by rail. Otherwise, water craft, horses and horse-drawn vehicles provided the only substantial means of transport. Yet, beyond the capital cities, port facilities were few and roads were poorly developed. The concentration and deployment of a large field force within Australia, especially in locations outside the south-eastern quarter of the continent, would be extremely difficult and its subsequent maintenance virtually impossible. But these same problems would also face an invading force—assuming there was a country with this intention and capability. Invasion of the remote areas of Australia was not a credible contingency.

Why, then, did the federal military committee suggest to the government that there was a requirement to develop a discrete field force for operations in any part of Australia? Undoubtedly the defence of Australian cities and inhabited localities demanded the ability to field mobile forces to operate in conjunction with the somewhat restricted capacity of static defences. However, such citizen force units should have been designed primarily to operate within the region in which the soldiers lived and trained. More flexibility and combat power could be achieved by organising units in the more densely populated regions into formations, say brigades, for independent operations within a locality. Such a force structure would also be suitable for responding to simultaneous attacks in various places. But the formation of a large national field force clearly was not an appropriate solution to the problems of Australian defence. The insistence by the committee to establish such a force suggests that the military officers who headed the various colonial forces were thinking in terms of the imperial agenda long cherished in Whitehall. In particular, their suggestion that a field force could be transported by sea to Thursday Island, or even Albany, to provide defence in case of attack was unconvincing. The commandants presumably had more realistic contingencies in mind. Clearly, the development of a large field force did not address the special problems of Australian defence, but it did provide a structure suited ideally to expeditionary operations outside Australia.

The real intentions of the federal military committee became more obvious when, at the request of the government, it drafted a federal Defence Bill. Meeting in Melbourne, the committee was comprised of Major-General George French, representing New South Wales, who presided, Major-General Francis Downes from Victoria, Colonel George Chippindall of Western Australia, Colonel Harry Finn of Queensland, Colonel Joseph Gordon of South Australia and Colonel William Legge of Tasmania. French, Finn and Chippindall were imperial officers on loan to the Australian forces, while Downes, Gordon and Legge originally had served with the Imperial Army. These men were therefore predisposed by their training, experience and loyalty to imperial service. French, in particular, had clearly displayed his imperial inclination when, in May 1900, he had written to the Premier of New South Wales, Joseph Lyne, with the suggestion that: '[T]he real way . . . to help Old England to keep the flag flying all over the Empire is to form war reserves in the colonies.' Australia could have 10 000 men, most of them mounted, ready to fight for the Empire, he had enthused. 'I have now been asked to prepare [a defence] Act,' French had informed Lyne, 'and it can readily be imagined what an immense advantage it would be if in the Federal Defence Act for all Australia . . . the necessary powers could be taken for the formation of a war reserve of the nature . . . indicated.'[12]

A week earlier, French had also written privately to Lord Lansdowne, the Secretary of State for War, making the same suggestion and seeking his

The First Defence Bill

advice on drafting an Australian defence act and military regulations which would be suitable for the maintenance of an Australian force for imperial service. 'Any information that you may be pleased to give will be considered strictly confidential,' French informed Lansdowne.[13] The British authorities responded cautiously to this conspiratorial suggestion, however. French was informed that, while Britain desired military co-operation with the colonies, he should not proceed with his proposal without consulting the colonial government.[14] With federation pending, the political climate certainly was against the assertion of imperial over national aspirations, and Lansdowne knew it. Nevertheless, the federal military committee, with French as president, proceeded to follow imperial objectives while being less than forthright with the Australian government.

The committee's draft Defence Bill proposed that the Australian military forces be comprised of active forces, reserves and rifle clubs. The active forces, in turn, were to be constituted of permanent troops, militia and volunteers as developed in the colonial period. In peace, enlistment was to be voluntary for periods of three years' duration for the active forces, with those soldiers who had served efficiently in the active ranks being drafted into the reserve on completion of their engagement. The proposal that rifle clubs would become an arm of the military forces was an acknowledgement of the skills possessed by those men who participated in this popular pastime. The committee also proposed the establishment of a military nursery in the form of a senior cadet corps for boys aged 14 to 16 years.[15] Having determined the basic constitution of the forces, the commandants then proceeded to draft the legislative framework for Australian involvement in imperial operations. Undoubtedly, it was the future employment of their proposed field force which was kept firmly in mind during this exercise.

The commandants planned that the Governor-General, acting on the advice of the executive council, was to play the key role in mobilising the Australian forces. It could hardly be otherwise. But, once mobilised, they proposed that the forces could be sent on active service anywhere in the world in response to the somewhat indefinite circumstances of 'war, invasion, national emergency, or the imminency of any of them'.[16] Clearly, the scope was sufficiently wide to admit contingencies unrelated to the maintenance of Australian security; the commandants were taking a liberal view of what actions might be undertaken in the name of national defence. While the constitutional obligation for the federal parliament to protect Australia from invasion and domestic violence[17] was clear and uncontroversial, the provisions of the draft Bill were potentially provocative where they defined procedures for sending Australian forces to support imperial operations. Indeed, the commandants included a provision that any members of the Australian military forces could be placed under command of the senior British commander wherever it was felt desirable. This provision applied not only to the regular forces, the militia, the volunteers, the reserves and

An Army for a Nation

rifle clubs, but also, through powers of conscription, to ordinary male members of the population between the ages of 18 and 60. Similarly, it was proposed that additional war reserves could be created and maintained in Australia in consultation with the British government.[18] The commandants intended that Australia would become a recruiting ground for compulsory service on imperial operations.

To ensure compatibility with Britain's forces, the commandants also proposed that the rank and relative authority of officers of the Australian forces were to be identical with officers of the Imperial Army. The disciplinary code was to be determined by the provisions of the British *Army Act* and the King's Regulations and Orders; the only exception was that the volunteers and reserves were not to be subject to corporal punishment. Command structures were also designed to facilitate imperial interoperability. The draft Bill proposed that the position of senior professional military officer, designated General Officer Commanding-in-Chief, was to be reserved for a regular officer from the Imperial Army, unless the Australian parliament specifically chose otherwise. Imperial officers were also to be given special access to all positions in the forces, including the influential positions of district, or state, commandants.[19]

On enlistment, members of the active forces and the rifle clubs were to take an oath or affirmation having 'the effect at law of a written agreement with His Majesty'. This measure recognised the titular status of the British monarch as a supreme military commander, but it seems the commandants were also motivated by more practical considerations. Their intentions became more obvious in view of the special role which they envisaged for the Governor-General. In accordance with constitutional convention, the commandants referred to the Governor-General in two ways. As Commander-in-Chief, they described him as 'His Majesty's representative'. This role was distinguished clearly from the more routine powers and administrative functions with respect to which the Governor-General was to follow the more familiar constitutional practice of acting on the advice of his Australian ministers. In this role 'His Majesty's representative' became the 'Governor-General-in-Council'. Effectively, the Governor-General could have no special powers in either capacity but it seems that the commandants thought differently. Like Chamberlain in his suggested amendment to the draft Australian Constitution, the commandants were apparently preparing the legislative basis for the British parliament to command Australian troops when deployed on imperial service. It is in this context that their reference to the Governor-General as 'His Majesty's representative' was to be understood. Having described the Governor-General in this special way as Commander-in-Chief, they then included the extraordinary provision that the senior military officer, as commander, was to be directly responsible to the vice-regal office. His relationship with the minister was that of military adviser.[20]

The First Defence Bill

The commandants submitted their draft Defence Bill for the approval of Sir John Forrest. But Forrest was not happy with all its provisions and amended it accordingly. Significantly, he moved to curb the powers of the Governor-General, insisting that the vice-regal office should be constrained by the advice of his Australian ministers on all matters.[21] Furthermore, Forrest proposed to make the senior professional military commander directly responsible to the minister, not the Governor-General, as the commandants wished. Administration of the forces was also to be exercised by the minister.[22] Forrest, in short, sought a more prominent and central role for the minister at the expense of the Governor-General. When, on 12 June 1901, they met to discuss these ministerial amendments, the commandants disagreed with Forrest and directly challenged him on this issue. They correctly drew his attention to the Australian Constitution, which had enacted during Queen Victoria's reign. Here the Governor-General as the Commander-in-Chief was referred to uniquely as 'the Queen's representative', while elsewhere the Constitution constrained the Governor-General to act with the advice of the federal executive council.[23] In view of this apparent difference, the commandants suggested that legal opinion be sought on the Governor-General's role as Commander-in-Chief of the forces. In the meantime, they were 'strongly of the opinion' that their original clause should remain unaltered.[24]

There was no doubt about the position of the Governor-General in the minds of the contemporary constitutional authorities, John Quick and Robert Garran. The distinction between the two ways of referring to the Governor-General in the Australian Constitution, they explained, was 'historical and technical, rather than practical or substantial'. One recognised the traditional prerogative powers of the crown and the other, those powers and functions controlled by statute law. In practice, however, there was no real difference. 'The Governor-General could not wield more authority in the naval and military business of the country,' observed Quick and Garran, 'than he could in the routine work of any other local department.'[25] The royal prerogative of command of the military forces could be exercised only in a constitutional manner.

Such limitations to the vice-regal powers were, of course, well understood and appreciated by the Attorney-General in the first Australian government, Alfred Deakin.[26] The commandants therefore had no hope of enshrining a special role for the Governor-General in defence legislation; they could do no more than preserve the niceties of constitutional terminology. However, failing to appreciate this, the commandants still attempted to defend the inclusion of special powers for the Governor-General by arguing that such a measure protected the operational command of the forces from ministerial intervention. Accordingly, they advised Forrest that they believed his amendments would result in the situation where the minister, and not the senior professional military officer, would command the forces. The danger, they warned, was 'that in the case of invasion or war the Officer Commanding-in-Chief could not freely and independently exercise his command'. They also stressed that it should be the commander, not the minister, who should exercise responsibility for maintaining discipline in the forces. Furthermore, they informed Forrest that the authority for convening courts martial, according to the British *Army Act*, was derived from the monarch and therefore, in Australia, 'the authority must come from . . . the Governor-General as His Majesty's representative'.[27] These were hopeless arguments, however. The commandants were ignoring the legal realities of a constitutional democracy where, while it was not the practice for the minister to intervene in the internal command function of the forces, ultimate authority did rest with parliament. The Barton government harboured no doubts on this fundamental issue and was not about to relinquish control of the military forces. Indeed, Forrest had already received prime ministerial censure and advice on the scope of his responsibility as Minister for Defence.

In late February, Forrest had instructed the military commandants in the states to continue to administer the forces under the terms of their respective colonial *Defence Acts* from 1 March, the date when the Commonwealth assumed control, until a federal Defence Bill was enacted. There was little choice in this matter. But Forrest also instructed the commandants to consult their former colonial defence ministers should they require an urgent decision with ministerial authority.[28] Barton was not pleased when he learned of this instruction and drew the minister's attention to his transgression. After 30 April, state authorities no longer had any power in defence matters, Barton informed his Minister for Defence. All authority was vested in the Commonwealth. 'I should think it a very wise step,' the Prime Minister advised Forrest tactfully, 'if you were to consult Deakin privately on the subject.'[29] Barton's rebuke and Deakin's advice undoubtedly stiffened Forrest's resolve in his subsequent dealings with the commandants.

To the further disappointment of the commandants, Forrest, although he retained the principle of conscription during war, amended their draft Bill to restrict deployment of the military forces to Australian territory. Such an amendment clearly upset the private hopes of those wishing to facilitate a possible expeditionary involvement in imperial operations. The committee therefore unanimously reasserted its recommendation that the government should have the power to order compulsory overseas service. Forrest's decision should be overturned, the commandants argued, because there could be reasons why 'it may be desirable not to await attack till the enemy is fully prepared'. The senior military officers wanted the power to undertake offensive operations beyond Australian shores. A field force—or, more precisely, an expeditionary force—could not be properly organised and prepared if the government had to wait on men to volunteer for service when war broke out, they pleaded.[30]

The First Defence Bill

To support their case for offensive operations outside Australia, the commandants told Forrest that the intercolonial military conference of 1896 had proposed that the field force should not be restricted to service in Australia.[31] But this advice was misleading. In deference to political and public opinion, the intercolonial military conference of 1896 had no choice but to include a clause in the proposed federal defence agreement which prevented Australian soldiers being compulsorily sent overseas. Service abroad could be undertaken only on a voluntary basis.[32] Certainly, the commandants of 1896 felt the same way about this issue as the commandants of 1901, and had attempted to circumvent the restrictions imposed by local opinion by surreptitiously defining an extended geographic area as Australia. But it was a futile move. The bogus definition was never examined, nor was the proposed federal defence agreement ever ratified. For the military commandants to quote the proposals of the 1896 conference in support of powers for compulsory overseas service was therefore tendentious.

Five of the six committee members—the dissenter remained anonymous—also registered their disapproval with Forrest's deletion of their special provision for the senior commander to be an imperial officer. Furthermore, they were upset by Forrest's removal of similar provisions concerning the positions of district commandant, thus opening these posts to officers from the militia or volunteers. On this, too, the commandants remained adamant, asserting that 'the important position of District Commandant should only be filled by an officer from His Majesty's Imperial Regular Service, or from the Commonwealth Permanent Service'.[33] They voiced additional reservations about the minister's terminology, the control of school cadets and the retirement ages of servicemen, but such concerns were minor. The crux of their dissatisfaction focused on the role of the Governor-General and the elimination of provisions for overseas service, for these were amendments hampering the operation of an expeditionary force.

On 15 June, the commandants presented Forrest with their objections to his amendments, and five days later they had Forrest's reaction to this submission in the form of Forrest's latest draft of the Defence Bill. However, they remained far from happy because their advice had not been followed. 'As the principles embodied in the Bill drafted by [us] have been repeatedly altered, and as [our] recommendations upon the alterations previously submitted to [us] . . . have not been adopted,' observed the commandants, 'we consider it unnecessary to repeat [our] former objections which in [our] opinion still hold good.' Provocatively, the military commandants challenged Forrest, should he present the Bill to cabinet or to parliament, to make it plain on behalf of the committee 'that it is not recommended by [us] and does not meet with [our] approval'.[34] The commandants were abandoning the minister's Defence Bill.

An Army for a Nation

Forrest was concerned about the stand taken by the military commandants. He moved quickly to place the stamp of federal parliamentary control on the military forces when he introduced his Defence Bill to the House of Representatives for its second reading on 9 July 1901. It was a very different Bill from the one prepared by the commandants. The minister informed the House of this fact, thus emphasising the authority of his office. Diffident about his portfolio and unwell when he introduced the Bill, Forrest was nevertheless obliged to deliver a major speech and he gathered himself to refute the challenge mounted by the military leaders. The Governor-General, acting on ministerial advice, would be the 'sole power in regard to the army', he explained to members. By way of reassurance, he stressed that he knew of no example where the executive government had been 'interfered with or restricted in its control of the military and naval forces'. Australia's forces would be commanded by a general officer, he explained, but it was not the government's intention to be too intrusive, or to ignore the advice of the senior military commander. At most times the commander's opinions would be accepted. But Forrest warned that such opinions would 'not be followed without demur in all cases, and instead of the Government being under the thumb or under the foot of the military authorities, they will be responsible to Parliament, and in time of difficulty will be able to say "No" '.[35]

Forrest went on to explain that the next tier in the command structure of the forces would be executed by commandants, one in each state, or military district. 'The idea in calling the different places districts,' Forrest explained, 'is that we wish to break down as far as we can . . . the notion that the permanent forces belong to any particular part of Australia.' For the same reason, permanent soldiers would not remain in one place for long periods but would be moved around Australia in various postings. Officers above the rank of major and adjutants, in particular, were to have a limit of five years' duration on their tenure of each posting.[36] The government was determined to prevent the development of parochial loyalties in the forces, ensuring that they would be responsive to federal control.

Equally, the federal government was determined to entrench as law the subordinate role of the military in a civilian democracy. So the Bill included measures aimed specifically at restricting the power and authority of military officers. One proposed restraint on military officers seemed quite practical. Finance, Forrest explained, 'should be as far removed as possible from the control of the military authorities'.[37] Another was quite absurd: 'the tendency to have too many high sounding titles in the army should not be encouraged,' he observed naively. Therefore, except for the commander, the highest rank would be colonel.[38] It seems that an unwitting Forrest had been influenced by the commandants on this issue. They had included a similar provision in their original Defence Bill but there can be little doubt that their aim was different. They were probably motivated by a wish to limit the experience gained by Australian officers, thereby encouraging a dependence on senior, experienced officers from Britain.[39]

Forrest's Bill also made a determined effort to prevent the ascendancy of permanent officers over part-time officers. Accordingly, the positions of district commandant were to be open to part-time as well as permanent officers, although the minister did not explain how a part-time officer could effectively fulfil the demands of such a position. His intention was clear, however. There would be one seniority list for all officers because the government thought there should be no 'difference whatever between those in the permanent forces and those who are only partially paid'.[40] Forrest wanted to avoid the creation of a professional military *élite*.

The principle of conscription survived. The Bill provided for the government to call out all Australian males between the ages of 18 and 60 years for compulsory military service.[41] However, the minister's ambitious claim that this would provide a force of 974 000 men was instantly deflated by John Watson of the Labor Party, who asked where the government would find sufficient weapons to arm the men.[42] Declining to answer, Forrest proceeded to address the sensitive question on where the Australian forces might serve.

Here at least the strength of the persistent imperial argument had influenced the legislation. Forrest evidently had modified his original intentions to accommodate the representations of the commandants. It was now proposed that the small number of soldiers who had voluntarily enlisted on a permanent basis could be ordered overseas on active service to any location. Acknowledging the unlimited scope of this provision, Forrest responded to an interjection from Henry Bournes Higgins by confirming that, in an emergency, such a destination might be India.[43] But citizen soldiers and those men who had been conscripted in an emergency were not to be subjected to such unlimited powers. They could only be ordered outside Australia for service which related directly to Australian defence—or at least, that was what the minister intended. It seems that Forrest had accepted the commandants' persuasive advice to the extent that local security might depend on striking an offensive blow outside national boundaries. Imperialists could take some heart, however, because such a provision was open to liberal interpretation, especially since the Bill retained the word 'emergency' as originally used by the commandants. Therefore, a glimmer of hope for the expeditionary option remained, despite Forrest's attempt to emphasise the regional limits to his intention by nominating Fiji as a possible destination.[44]

Forrest's Bill, like the personal loyalties he shared with most of his countrymen, was ambivalent on issues of national versus imperial priorities. While the Bill did fall short of the imperial aspirations of the state commandants, it recognised the contemporary reality that Australians were serving in the Boer War by including provisions for Australians to volunteer for imperial service under the command of British officers.[45] On a personal level, Forrest was quite keen to assist Australians to go to the war as volunteers, and he was certainly a supporter of the imperial cause. He saw himself as a member of an imperial fraternity, paying the dues and enjoying the privileges. When seeking the colonial secretary's agreement to award an imperial honour to John Winthrop Hackett, one of Forrest's staunch supporters and editor of the *West Australian*,[46] Forrest had reminded Joseph Chamberlain in January 1901 that, as a colonial premier, he had 'readily joined in sending two more units [of] about 250 men to South Africa—[and furthermore] about 2500 men [were] about ready and . . . waiting transports'. 'During the 10 years I have been Premier [of Western Australia],' Forrest had told Chamberlain, 'I have only asked for one *C.M.G.* and one *K.C.M.G.* which is not I think a long list.'[47] In August, he drew Chamberlain's attention to the statistic that Western Australia had sent more men to the war in proportion to its population than any other colony. 'I am with you heart and soul in regard to your policy in South Africa,' he had assured Chamberlain, 'and I am pleased that I have been able to assist in ever so small a degree as in sending some troops to help.'[48] As the Minister for Defence, however, Forrest remained adamant about the need for national political control of Commonwealth forces and the undesirability of compelling Australian conscripts to serve on imperial operations.

Forrest's introduction of his Defence Bill was followed by a lengthy parliamentary debate in which 41 of the 75 members of the House of Representatives chose to speak. Three parties were represented in the House. The Protection Party held a narrow majority over the next largest representation from Free Trade and formed the government by gaining the general support of the Labor Party in return for concessions. But there was little solidarity in party organisation at this early stage, with many members feeling relatively free to express personal views. Furthermore, many of the speakers evidently found Forrest's Bill difficult to interpret on some key issues and felt compelled to participate in the debate. The Bill had been poorly drafted, but the ambivalence of defence planning, especially over the crucial matter of imperial interoperability, had also clouded several key provisions. Henry Bournes Higgins, a Protectionist, described it as a 'scissors and paste bill, [with] its provisions having been cut from the existing Acts of the states, with a certain dash of the commandants' wishes thrown in'. For William Morris Hughes of the Labor Party it was 'a jumble of clauses . . . without any regard to symmetry, or to the important nature of the question'.[49] Doubts about Forrest's own interest and competence in his portfolio prompted searching criticism from a few members and encouraged others to hope that the Bill might be defeated or amended. Their opposition was invigorated because the minister was absent during the whole debate following his introductory speech. He had gone home to Perth following the death of his brother Alexander, a family bereavement of particular poignancy because of the recent death of Alexander's 16-year-old son in the Boer War.[50] Therefore, without ministerial direction, the debate was protracted, piecemeal and repetitious. The *Age* reported that the speeches of two members sent George Reid to sleep 'and drove other members to the lobbies or somewhere else where things were more to their taste'.[51] Some members, however, offered comprehensive, lucid comments, and despite the diverse quality of presentation, a remarkable degree of consensus emerged on certain fundamental issues.

Twenty-eight members made statements opposing what they called the excesses of militarism, especially conscription or the maintenance of a large permanent force. Such speeches also typically supported the principle of voluntary service.[52] Only two of them justified their statements on the grounds of thrift;[53] most believed that militarism and compulsory service were inimical to the values and ideals of Australian society. 'There will be no need for conscription,' said James Wilkinson, an Independent Labor member, 'and no need for pressing men into the defence forces to defend Australia when her needs arise.' Richard Edwards of the Protectionist Party thought compulsion or conscription 'would prove very distasteful to Australians'. Likewise, John Kirwan of the Free Trade Party believed conscription was 'almost an insult to Australians'. Underlying such expressions was the belief, articulated by some speakers, that Australians were patriotic and would voluntarily defend their country in time of need. Others found that the idea of coercion offended their liberal philosophical outlook. 'I put aside the whole idea of compulsory service,' Sir William McMillan of the Free Trade Party said tersely. Some members of the same persuasion broadened their attack and denounced militarism in general. Henry Bournes Higgins, a Protectionist, referred to the 'ghastly bane of militarism' and the desire of Australia's founding fathers to get rid of 'the burdens and dangers of war which have oppressed the people of Europe for so many years'. William Sawers of the Protectionist Party supported Higgins, while another member of the same party, James Hume Cook, railed against the 'octopus of militarism' whose spreading tentacles threatened to spread in all directions 'and grasp with a power which may eventually crush us'. Similarly, Sir Edward Braddon, a Free Trader, described militarism as a 'thing monstrous and inconceivable to us of modern times and of advanced liberal opinions'.[54]

Adherents of other political persuasions came to similar conclusions for more pragmatic reasons. Labor members could remember troops being used to coerce workers during the strikes of the 1890s. William Morris Hughes even rejected the proposal for a small permanent force of troops because 'while it is wretchedly inadequate to repel a foreign invader [it] . . . is sufficiently strong to overawe on some occasions—perhaps on many—the citizen in his pursuit of constitutional reform or in the maintenance of civil liberty and right'.[55] Hughes therefore argued the case for a military force comprised only of part-time soldiers. A force recruited from wage-earning citizens, he believed, was likely to be more egalitarian in outlook and less amenable to sectional interests. This was a popular view. At least 21 other members also argued that the forces should be predominantly based on part-time soldiers.[56] 'It required very little perception,' the *Age* newspaper reported on the debate, 'to ascertain that the feeling of the House is strongly in favor [sic] of a true citizen soldiery.'[57]

The debate thus displayed the powerful liberal values pervading the parliament, placing a further, perhaps unforeseen, obstacle in the path of imperialist ambition and confirming the nationalist inclination to define the limits of military activity. Liberalism continuously attempts to refashion the institutions of war to suppress their military characteristics. The civil state aims to contain and control military impulses. Its most obvious manifestation has been the idea of the small standing army—and, obversely, the perception that a large permanent military force is a threat to a free society. Primary reliance is therefore placed on a citizen force with defence becoming the responsibility of every citizen. Democratic practices are also encouraged in the forces, even to the extent of electing officers. The ultimate objective is to restrict the appropriation of power and authority by a select group of professional military officers and to subject the forces to civil control. [58]

In the case of Australia, however, there was a further motive for curtailing the authority of military leaders. The civil authority had to contend with the impulse for imperial service. During the debate on the Defence Bill, national interests were therefore emphasised in an attempt to define the military forces as a discrete national body subject to national control. Awareness of this need was sharpened by the contemporary involvement in the Boer War, and members were worried about encouraging British and Australian enthusiasm for future imperial commitments. 'I am inclined to think that we have just overstepped the mark in our anxiety to be loyal and serve the old country,' Samuel Mauger, a Protectionist, informed the House during the debate. Explaining this view, he added: 'we have engendered here a spirit of militarism that is likely to be detrimental at some distant date.' Joseph Cook, a Free Trader, was adamant that he did not want the Executive Council to be empowered 'to commit the Commonwealth behind the back of the people in connexion [sic] with any secret negotiations as to the defence of the Empire at any point'. Cook wanted parliament 'to control our military operations, no matter where they may be undertaken'. George Reid, also a Free Trader, denounced 'dreams of military adventure in other lands' and warned that they should 'not let the statesmen of England think, because we are ready to send our men to Africa, that Australians are infected with any lust of military enterprise'. Similarly, Charles McDonald of the Labor Party hoped that 'the day will never dawn when Australia shall become a recruiting ground for the British Army'. 'There is no justification for sending men abroad to assist in looting other people's country,' he emphasised. Two more members of the same party expressed similar, but more restrained, views. John Watson referred to 'the foolishness of our seeking to engage in every trivial contest that England has on hand', while William Spence thought it was 'rather unfortunate that recently we have had an experience which has somewhat drawn us into the Empire's troubles'. It was a view shared by members from all political parties. Indeed, George Edwards, a Free Trader, thought it was 'a fatal mistake that Australia ever interfered in the South African war'. However, he felt proud because the debate had shown that members from both sides of the House held the view 'that we should not go outside Australia to fight battles in the interest of we do not know what'. Of particular concern to Edwards was the possibility that Australians would be placed under the command of British officers.[59] Service on imperial operations therefore prompted many concerns about national control and Australian autonomy.

The debate on imperial service went beyond the House of Representatives. The Reverend Professor John Rentoul and the Reverend Lambley, representing the Peace, Humanity and Arbitration Society, not only objected to the provisions in Forrest's Bill for compulsory overseas service on liberal grounds, but also objected to reports in the London *Times* which regarded Forrest's Defence Bill as an attempt to make the Australian force an 'integral part of the British Empire'. In reply, Barton, who kept close watch on the parliamentary and public debate on the Bill during Forrest's lengthy absence in Western Australia, affirmed that it was not the government's intention to 'join in the schemes of European militarism', but he believed that Australians should be able to volunteer for overseas service if they wished.[60] There were, of course, many Australians who wanted this option but there was also apprehension, as Rentoul's and Lambley's protest illustrates, that the Bill's provision for compulsory overseas service in the name of Australian security might, in practice, be interpreted to include imperial operations. The journal of radical nationalist opinion, the *Bulletin*, expressed such concerns. The provisions in Forrest's Defence Bill for soldiers to operate beyond national limits solely for the defence of Australia were desirable, the *Bulletin* observed, but, regrettably, such provisions also made 'the way easier for an unlimited amount of expensive and idiotic contingenting which may lead to any amount of trouble hereafter'. Nevertheless, the journal concluded that no law could be devised which would prevent Australians serving on imperial operations if they wished to do so.[61] The Labor Party, however, decided to attempt legal remedies. By amending the Bill they hoped to close loopholes and place certain limitations on overseas service by Australians.

The Labor Party caucus discussed Forrest's Defence Bill on 24 and 25 July 1901, and decided to deny the government the power to order the Australian military forces to deploy outside the national boundaries. Such was the party's sensitivity on the issue that caucus even rejected Forrest's provision that members of the citizen forces could be sent beyond the national boundaries for the express purpose of defending the Commonwealth. Significantly, the conscription provision raised no comment. The issue of voluntary overseas service by individuals was not discussed either; it was obviously an acceptable proposition. Of course, it was in this way that volunteers were being enlisted and organised into units expressly for service in South Africa while the existing Australian force remained intact. But another aspect of the Bill which concerned caucus was the provision that the existing forces could be mobilised in response to a 'sudden emergency'. Labor members believed that such a term could be interpreted too liberally and agreed that more precise terminology was required. '[S]udden emergency,' caucus decided, was to be deleted in favour of 'actual or apprehended invasion', and only then could the forces be mobilised 'to repel such invasion'.[62] The Labor caucus was determined that the Australian forces were to be maintained exclusively for local defence. While the other parties did not share the same degree of discipline and cohesion, there were many non-Labor members who agreed on this issue.

During the debate on the Bill, at least ten speakers—five were Labor Party members—stated their belief that the military forces were to be maintained solely for national defence.[63] Effectively, the same ground was taken by at least another eleven speakers—one was a Labor member—when they stated their opposition to compulsory overseas service for the Australian forces. '[W]e are forming an army for the defence of the Commonwealth,' George Cruickshank, a Protectionist, claimed, 'the danger to English interests outside the Commonwealth is a matter for consideration when the time arises.'[64] It was clearly the dominant view of the House that, when war broke out, imperial service would be a voluntary option. Indeed, only two speakers acknowledged their support for compulsory imperial service and even they had reservations. Winter Cooke, a Free Trader, believed that the government should have the power to send men 'to assist Britain against her enemies', but he was adamant that Australians should not participate in 'any aggressive war' which Britain might enter. Sir William McMillan, another Free Trader, believed that the powers of compulsion for imperial service should be restricted to the small number of permanent soldiers.[65]

The strongest argument for the principle of voluntary service, and, indeed, one of the most detailed criticisms of John Forrest's Bill, was delivered by Henry Bournes Higgins. A member of the legal profession and a man of liberal persuasion, Higgins referred to the constitutional provisions which empowered the Australian government to raise military forces to protect Australia from invasion. 'What does the word "invasion" mean?' he asked, assured that '[i]t does not mean the invasion of some other country'. Yet, he continued, the Bill made provision for the forces to be employed outside Australia while under the command of British officers. 'Is that consistent with the idea that our forces are to be called out only to meet an invasion of the Commonwealth?' he queried. Like the Labor caucus, he

The First Defence Bill

was also critical of the lack of precision in the word 'emergency' and claimed that some of the clauses had no meaning unless it applied to virtually any war outside Australia. It could, for example, mean 'any emergency which the British Government think to be a national emergency'. Evidently suspecting a sinister intention behind the Bill, he was gratified that the Constitution restrained the power of military authorities. 'I do not accuse the Prime Minister in this matter,' he stated, probably believing that Forrest had been unduly influenced by the military commandants, and went on to tell the House that 'the Bill has been very discreetly drawn with a view to the wedging in of powers which do not appear to be given at first sight'.[66] Much of the ambiguity, in fact, could have been attributed to clumsy drafting, but not all. So detailed was Higgins' elaboration of the full implications of key clauses and terms in the bill that Barton began to realise that several amendments, or even a total revision of the Bill, would be necessary. As it stood, there was too much conjecture about the aims of the Bill, especially on the contentious issue of compulsory overseas service. 'On the flimsiest pretext,' Higgins had pointed out, 'there might be a legal obligation put on the citizen soldiers of Australia to go and serve in India against the Afghans or Sikhs. I think that that is not what we mean.' Attempting to clarify government policy, Barton interjected immediately: 'It is not what the Bill means either.'[67]

The Prime Minister's stated intention and the debate in the House illustrate just how hopeless the military commandants' cause was. In short, their original plan to maintain a field force for unrestricted, compulsory service on imperial operations was quite unacceptable to federal members. The politicians were intent on organising a military force comprised predominantly of citizen soldiers with the primary object of national defence and security. While there was a significant body of opinion which approved of imperial service, overwhelmingly, it was on the basis of voluntary service. This alone precluded the formation and training during peace of a force for imperial operations. Units would be organised from volunteers when the crisis came, as they had been for the Boer War. Until then the primary motivation for maintaining a military organisation was the defence of Australia.

The day after the federal military committee had withdrawn its support for Forrest's Defence Bill the federal government had sought the advice of the Colonial Defence Committee on the organisation of the Department of Defence and the constitution of Army headquarters.[68] Even before the advice had been received, however, the government had decided—on Forrest's recommendation[69]—that a general officer would be requested from the Imperial Army to become the first commander of the Australian military forces. Forrest believed that a local officer might not have sufficient experience and knowledge for the position. 'We want one of the best men in the Empire to start this machine, whatever we may do afterwards,' he said in justifying this decision. 'We want a really good man to initiate our system of defence.'[70] This slight to the various state military commandants probably was intentional for, in the period before this officer arrived in Australia, Barton, on behalf of Forrest, chose not to appoint one of the military commandants as military adviser.[71]

In its response to the Australian government's request, the Colonial Defence Committee was strong in insisting that the new Commonwealth defence forces should be commanded by a general officer, not a military board—advice made easier by the knowledge that the Australian government intended to appoint an Imperial Officer to the position. Encouraging other appointments of this type, the Committee advised that this would be an important step 'to securing uniformity of training with the Imperial army'.[72] Therefore, while a powerful political lobby in Australia suspected Forrest's Bill of being overly imperial, there was pressure on the government to go further in this direction. Faced with this dilemma, the government decided to withdraw Forrest's Defence Bill and await the appointment of a commander from Britain able to advise the Minister on the drafting of new legislation.[73] Given the strength of nationalist sentiment however, hopes that the appointment would resolve the tensions which Forrest's Bill had revealed were bound to prove excessively optimistic.

5
An imperial GOC and his hidden agenda, 1902

The Boer War strained Britain's resources. What the Secretary of State for the Colonies, Joseph Chamberlain, at first thought would be a short war lasted for a period of three years, consuming men and money. In 1901, 65.5 per cent of the annual public expenditure of Britain was devoted to the defence forces.[1] This was nearly double the allocation in 1897 when Chamberlain had complained to the colonial premiers about the rising cost of imperial defence. Total expenditure on the war in South Africa alone exceeded £200 million and there were more than 100 000 casualties among the 365 000 British and 82 000 colonial soldiers who participated.[2] As a result of this experience, the prospect of war with a major European nation was alarming. On the other hand, as Chamberlain had anticipated, the Boer War provided reassuring experience in organising and utilising colonial volunteers on combined operations, creating a model and an expectation of future military co-operation. 'The evidence establishes that the Over-sea Colonial Forces were great value and did good and useful service throughout the War and that such forces, if provided, could be an important adjunct to the Army as mounted rifles in any future war', the Elgin commission on the conflict in South Africa reported to the British parliament.[3]

More specifically, as far as the development of military organisation in Australia was concerned, the war also brought the erstwhile commandant of the New South Wales colonial force, Colonel Edward Hutton, back to the centre of defence planning in Australia. While serving in the war, Hutton wrote to the Chief of Staff of the British forces, Lord Kitchener, bringing to his attention the benefits to be gained by forming a composite brigade of mounted infantry from colonial troops. 'There is no question,' Hutton informed Kitchener, 'but the association together of the various representative units from each of our self governing Colonies will contribute more than anything else to the consolidation of the Military Forces of the Empire.'[4] Hutton, of course, saw the Boer War as a practical step towards the implementation of his proposals for co-operative military defence. It was one of several opportunities the enterprising officer had taken to promote his scheme since he first described it to the Royal Colonial Institute in 1898.

Shortly before going to South Africa in 1900, Hutton met Joseph Chamberlain in the Colonial Secretary's private rooms at the House of Commons. It was on the occasion of Hutton's return from Canada where he had commanded the militia since 1898. Hutton used this meeting to promote his proposals for co-operative defence. He told Chamberlain that he had reformed the Canadian militia on a national basis as a complete army 'above all party political intrigue and interference' and ready to become 'part of a Militia System of Cooperative Defence for the whole Empire'.[5] These claims undoubtedly surprised Chamberlain. Before Hutton had departed for his Canadian posting, the Colonial Secretary had told him that he was expected to use his influence as militia commander to encourage and support any proposals to exchange Canadian military units with Britain. But Chamberlain had believed there were strict limits to what might be achieved. He had advised the military officer that it was only possible to *'press'* and not *'force'* colonial governments to follow imperial policy.[6] Now, enthused by Hutton's sanguine account of his achievements, the colonial secretary arranged an immediate meeting with the deputy Prime Minister, Lord Balfour, during which the Colonel repeated his ambitious plans for co-operative defence.

Hutton told Balfour and Chamberlain that Britain should organise an imperial force which included its own militia and the militia forces of each of the colonies. To achieve this, he explained, the reforms which he had started to introduce in the Australian colonies from 1893 to 1896 and repeated in Canada had to be extended to the militia forces of the United Kingdom.[7] Major changes were therefore required because Britain's militia forces had evolved primarily as a local defence force which the British government was not empowered to deploy beyond British shores; overseas service by members of the militia could be undertaken only on a voluntary basis. This hampered Britain's ability to plan with any certainty for the despatch of a large expeditionary force. Certainly, some units had volunteered for service in the Peninsular War, the Crimea and South Africa, but the militia had never been regarded as a cohesive force in its own right.[8] Hutton thought that this was a shortcoming and believed that the military power of Britain would be greatly expanded if the full potential of its militia were realised. He believed the force had to be organised properly with supporting services to achieve mobility, enabling it to take its place with the colonial militia forces in an imperial expeditionary force. The co-operative scheme described by Hutton was therefore an answer to the problem of imperial defence which concerned Chamberlain. Encouraged by Hutton's views, the Colonial Secretary was optimistic about future developments and terminated his discussions with Hutton by agreeing that the whole military question would be 'taken in hand' on an imperial basis at the end of the Boer War.[9] Hutton was convinced that his grand plan was close to achievement.

In Hutton's mind, his co-operative defence scheme was more than a practical solution to a military problem; it became his obsession. He promoted the scheme with a passion and energy which gratified his ego but distorted his judgement. During the Boer War he wrote that the colonial troops were 'the very foundation stones upon which a great and Imperial nation must be raised and maintained', and he looked forward to the 'consolidation of the Empire, which so many of us are striving to achieve, and which in some crisis not far distant perhaps will prove the salvation of the mother country and her children'.[10] And, if co-operative defence was to contribute to the salvation of the empire, then Hutton's eminence, as its architect, was assured. Early in October 1900 he wrote to the Secretary of State for War, Lord Lansdowne, about rumours that he was to be appointed commander of the Australian Army when it was formed after federation. He told Lansdowne that no formal approach had been made to him, 'but if the opportunity presented itself of being called upon to put in practice the principles of the Federal Defence Scheme which [he] had drafted for the six Australian Colonies in 1894–96 [he] should certainly, feel it [his] duty to accept'.[11] Hutton's special interest in Australia was sparked by his conviction that it was the best recruiting ground for his favoured arm of the service, the mounted infantry. This, he thought, would be Australia's contribution to the imperial force, and he wanted to organise it.

In late 1900, no one in Australia was looking for a commander for the military forces to be formed after federation. Furthermore, Lansdowne was almost immediately shifted from the War Office to the Foreign Office in a cabinet reorganisation. Yet Hutton's letter to the Secretary for War was not entirely without result. Lansdowne's replacement in the defence portfolio, Mr St John Brodrick, contacted Hutton in December requesting his views on a proposal to establish a force of mounted troops in Australia and Canada for imperial operations.[12] Hutton's well-publicised interest in future military developments in the colonies and his experience made him an appropriate source for such advice.

Brodrick's request arose from the suggestion by Major-General George French, commandant of the New South Wales force, to maintain an imperial reserve in Australia. But it was not as ambitious and comprehensive as Hutton's proposal and, in his reply, Hutton repudiated French's suggestion.

An Army for a Nation

Instead, he took the opportunity to promote his own grand imperial plan for co-operative defence. 'I have taken the liberty,' he informed Brodrick in his written response, 'to add a Preface dealing in brief with the whole question of the Defence of the Empire upon the principle of Co-operation between Great Britain and her Colonies.' Then, in a succinct but comprehensive submission, which the Secretary for War must have found persuasive, Hutton laid down the elements of his scheme.

The time was propitious for the introduction of the scheme, Brodrick was reminded. Australia was on the verge of federation, a development, according to Hutton, 'very largely' influenced by the awareness of the defence principles which he had enunciated during his command in New South Wales from 1893 to 1896, and by the rise of Japan as a military and naval power. Furthermore, Canada had recently adopted military reforms according to his design. He also believed that the voluntary offer of troops for the Boer War from all parts of the empire, especially Australia and Canada, was an unsurpassed display 'of patriotism and of mutual sympathy' for the empire. Hutton therefore pressed Brodrick to organise a conference where representatives from the self-governing colonies could discuss his proposals for co-operative defence.[13]

Under the scheme he envisaged, mounted troops from Australia would become part of an imperial force operating under the terms of a defence agreement similar to that proposed for the Australian colonies by the military commandants in 1896. This agreement, Hutton advised the secretary for war, had been accepted by the Australian premiers in March 1896.[14] But this was a deliberate mistruth.[15] In his zeal for an integrated system of imperial defence, Hutton clearly was willing to mislead not only Australian politicians but also his civilian superiors in Whitehall. The military commandants' proposal had in fact been rejected by premiers unwilling to surrender control of their forces to a defence council. Yet a similar defence council was the cornerstone of Hutton's imperial scheme. Indeed, apart from the size of the proposed force, this was the essential difference between French's suggestion and Hutton's co-operative defence scheme. To inform the Secretary for War that the Australian premiers had rejected this aspect of the federal defence proposal would have been to admit a serious flaw in Hutton's plans. So in promoting his own scheme, Hutton's enthusiasm led him into error and extravagance. 'I am strongly of opinion,' he asserted enthusiastically, 'that a movement on the part of the Imperial Government such as that above suggested will be warmly welcomed by the very great majority of Australians and Canadians.'[16] It seems that colonial participation in South Africa encouraged Hutton to be optimistic about the success of his scheme.

Hutton's proposal fell on sympathetic ears in London. On 8 March 1901, while introducing financial estimates for the Imperial Army, Brodrick informed the Commons that he hoped 'the day is not far distant when some of our colonial brethren who have given us mounted assistance during [the

Boer War] will be willing . . . to keep up mounted contingents . . . who . . . will be available to join our own yeomanry should they ever Volunteer to go abroad'.[17] Invigorated, Hutton took his crusade into the public arena. In May he advocated colonial participation in imperial operations in an article he published in *Empire Review*. Before the Boer War, he wrote, the latent military strength of the self-governing colonies had never been realised. He especially believed that 'the mounted troops which Australia and . . . Canada could provide would some day prove of incalculable advantage to the Empire'. 'Even now,' he continued, 'the Empire has not learnt the full fighting strength which is available in Australia and Canada.'[18] The Colonial Defence Committee had also reached the same conclusion. In the same month that Brodrick made his statement in the Commons, the Colonial Defence Committee considered that imperial requirements should influence the future development of the Australian military forces. In a memorandum to the Australian government, Captain John Clauson, secretary of the committee, praised the performance of Australian mounted infantry in South Africa and suggested that Australia might concentrate on the development of forces of this type so that they could be 'regarded as a possible source of supply of troops for over-seas service in time of war'.[19] It is not known with certainty whether the committee had been influenced by Hutton's energetic promotion but it seems likely. The committee appears to have taken its lead from Brodrick, whom Hutton had primed in January on the principles of his co-operative defence proposal.

The overture by the Colonial Defence Committee evoked no immediate reaction from the Australian government. Such a direct approach would have been a source of discomfort for colonial sensibilities, confirming nationalist fears about the need to protect Australian men from the demands of imperial militarism. But Australians did not wish to reject all associations with the Imperial Army, and in 1901 Hutton's hopes of a new and larger Australian command were strengthened when Britain was requested to nominate a military officer to command the Australian Commonwealth forces.

In seeking an officer from Britain, the Australian government requested an enthusiastic soldier of varied experience which included active service in the Boer War. An understanding, sympathetic interest in citizen soldiers was also a requirement. Yet, simple as this prescription seemed, its fulfilment proved difficult. A number of senior officers were approached but all declined the Australian command. The annual salary of £2500 was too low to entice a British general to Australia, and the Australian cabinet resisted British suggestions to increase it by £500.[20] Eventually, Colonel Hutton's name was suggested to Joseph Chamberlain by Lord Roberts, Commander-in-Chief of the Imperial Army, as an officer 'of considerable ability, energy and administrative power'.[21] Needless to say, the relatively junior officer was a willing candidate. Some seven months after the original request was made, the Prime Minister, Edmund Barton, announced that Sir Edward

Hutton—he had been knighted for his service in South Africa—was to be appointed to the position of GOC of the Australian military forces.[22]

Some eminent British observers were worried about Hutton's appointment. Realising that it was essential to preserve imperial harmony as the basis of co-operation, they were concerned about Hutton's personality and recent performance. During his command of the Canadian militia he had engaged in a number of public confrontations with Canadian politicians. At the centre of these problems was Hutton's conviction that the Canadian force was an element of a larger imperial organisation. While these views had antagonised nationalist sensibilities, his propensity for speaking out publicly on sensitive political issues was a further source of irritation.[23] 'The remarks of General Hutton at the banquet at the Garrison Club last Saturday,' the Canadian Prime Minister, Sir Wilfrid Laurier, had written to Lord Minto, the Governor-General, in November, 1899, 'are I submit to Your Excellency, absolutely out of place.' 'It is not in the traditions of the British Army that outside of Parliament soldiers of high or low rank should ever venture on political ground. If there ever was a person who should have remembered this it was General Hutton.'[24] But Hutton had been unable to submit to the Canadian government and had proceeded to behave in an insubordinate manner. In February 1900, when the Canadian cabinet could no longer tolerate his challenge to its authority, Laurier had dismissed him.[25]

Now that Hutton was to be posted to Australia, Minto, an old school friend of the colonel, took the precaution of warning the Australian Governor-General, Lord Hopetoun, confidentially, that 'the danger with Hutton is his inclination to oratory'. With the public disputes between Hutton and the Canadian government fresh in his mind, Minto recalled that Hutton had spoken publicly on too many occasions while in Canada and repeatedly failed to take Minto's advice to refrain from doing so. '[T]he peace of his command [in Australia],' Minto informed Hopetoun, 'must largely depend on his keeping quiet.'[26] Major-General Sir Ian Hamilton held similar fears and counselled Hutton against public speaking and dealing directly with the Australian press. 'One thing you will have to look out for, my dear Hutton, is not to get into hot water with Ministers,' Hamilton warned him. 'For heaven's sake, be deferential and agreeable to them, and to their wives, and fill them up with Champagne, whenever you get a fair opening.'[27] Chamberlain also was uneasy. 'I hope that Hutton's appointment will be satisfactory,' he wrote to Hopetoun. 'It is not in my opinion the best that could have been made.'[28] Despite these reservations about the appointment, however, the British authorities knew they could rely on Hutton to use his influence in Australia to further imperial interests. His ends were precisely those required; his patrons had to worry only about the means he might employ to achieve them.

On the afternoon of 19 December 1901, immediately before his departure for Australia, Joseph Chamberlain interviewed Hutton at the Colonial

Office. During this discussion the Colonial Secretary, trying to avoid a repitition of the Canadian episode, revealed his concern about the danger of provoking nationalist sympathies in Australia. He advised Hutton carefully that he was to be the servant of the Australian government, and that 'it must never appear that he was acting as the Agent of the Imperial Government'. So much for appearances and formal relationships. In reality, as both men knew very well, Hutton certainly would be 'acting as the Agent of the Imperial Government'. Indeed, Hutton explained to Chamberlain that he would proceed to organise the Australian forces along the lines he had introduced in Canada. Chamberlain would have understood precisely what this meant, because of the briefing Hutton had given him and Lord Balfour in March 1900 on his efforts to implicate Canadian force development into a wider imperial military scheme. Explaining that he would shape the Australian forces 'in accordance generally with Mr Chamberlain's views', Hutton went on to state explicitly what this meant: an Australian militia force designed not only for local defence but also for 'offensive operations outside of the local area'. To do this, Hutton told Chamberlain, he intended to use his influence to ensure that Australian defence legislation empowered the federal government to deploy the military forces on overseas service.[29]

For Hutton to succeed in these plans would have delighted Chamberlain. But any hint of imperial meddling in Australian military affairs would be inflammatory. So Chamberlain repeated his warning that Hutton must ensure that there was to be no appearance of collusion between the two of them.[30] Having established a clear understanding of this clandestine relationship, the Secretary of State for the Colonies left Hutton to work towards the introduction of his co-operative defence scheme, satisfied that there would be no further correspondence between the two men.

Immediately after his interview with Chamberlain, Hutton repeated the points which he had discussed with the Colonial Secretary for the benefit of Sir Montagu Ommanney, permanent undersecretary for the colonies, and Sir John Anderson, head of the Australian section at the Colonial Office.[31] Yet, while Hutton received no specific instructions from Chamberlain and his senior Colonial Office staff on military organisation, two days later, when he met with King Edward, Brodrick and Lord Roberts, it was a different matter. Hutton gave these men an undertaking that he would organise a force of 20 000 Australian mounted troops for imperial operations.[32]

Hutton was filled with enthusiasm for his Australian appointment. He had been given another opportunity to implement an important part of his imperial scheme and he approached the task with concurrence from the most senior levels in Britain. Yet, while it bolstered his confidence for the difficult work which lay ahead, it also made him less able to countenance failure; coming to Australia for his second, most important, command, he was under extreme pressure to produce the results which he had promised his patrons.

Therefore, despite the counsel of men like Chamberlain and Hamilton, he was in a less conciliatory, more ruthless, frame of mind than he had been in in 1893 when he went to New South Wales. Indeed, he later recalled that he had gone to Australia on the second occasion determined that, in the absence of support for his proposals from the federal government or the Minister for Defence, 'I would initiate a Defence Policy of my own and carry it into effect at any cost to myself.'[33]

On his arrival in Australia Hutton was promoted to the local rank of Major-General and assumed command of the military forces on 29 January 1902. Avoiding direct contact with Chamberlain as they had agreed, Hutton kept the Colonial Secretary informed by using his permanent undersecretary as an intermediary.[34] 'It is truly a *tabula rasa*,' he wrote to Ommanney, 'and arriving with my portmanteau and a general's sword only, I have to create everything.'[35] Wasting no time, the new GOC had several long discussions with Prime Minister Edmund Barton and Defence Minister Sir John Forrest on the subject of their first ill-fated attempt at a Defence Bill. The major concern for Hutton was the provision in the Bill which had been designed to restrict the deployment of the citizen soldiers to the area of mainland Australia and the immediate region for the sole purpose of defence. This was far too restrictive for Hutton, who planned that the Australian forces would be available for general imperial service wherever required. He therefore tried to convince Barton and Forrest that no restrictions should be placed on the deployment of the military forces. 'I pointed out to them,' Hutton informed Ommanney after the talks, 'the unsoundness of the principles in the bill which restricted the services of Australian Troops to operations within Australian waters.' The GOC advised Barton and Forrest that the defence of Australia was best served by having the ability to undertake vigorous offensive operations in any location rather than the purely defensive operations envisaged by the government.[36] Whether Barton was aware of the motives behind Hutton's argument for forward defence is not clear, but the military commander soon had reason to be encouraged by the results of this first briefing.

Speaking at a dinner on 15 February to mark the arrival of Major-General Hutton, the Prime Minister informed the guests that Australia would not necessarily be involved in every imperial war, but he believed that the Commonwealth must be prepared to fight for the integrity of the empire. Furthermore, Barton told the audience, military forces might be sent overseas to defend Australia.[37] Flushed by Barton's reference to the defence of the empire and overseas service, Hutton was quick to exploit what he believed was an early, unexpected success. The GOC responded to the Prime Minister's address by telling the audience that Australia should have the ability to field a force of 'say, 20 000 mounted men' for the 'protection of Australian soil or for the defence of Australian interests elsewhere.' Another force would be required for purely local defence, he said. Although feigning spontaneity in suggesting the strength of the mounted force, it was the precise number of men which he had promised earlier to the King, Brodrick and Lord Roberts for imperial operations. However, the GOC was careful to make no specific reference to imperial service in his speech.[38]

Hutton had every reason to believe that his mission was off to an encouraging start, but he was more delighted than he should have been about the manner in which newspapers published reports of the speeches. He was especially surprised by a leader article in the *Age* which echoed his own words when it reported without dissent his suggestion that Australia should maintain a force of 20 000 mounted men, 'whether for the protection of Australian soil or for the defence of Australian interests elsewhere'.[39] But Hutton misunderstood the way the *Age* was using the notion of 'Australian interests'. For him it was easy to identify such interests with those of the empire, but for Australians the two were not necessarily synonymous. However, jumping to this comforting conclusion, Hutton assured Ommanney, when he sent him a copy of the article, that the *Age* was 'by far the most powerful newspaper in Victoria and indeed in Australia'. Another cause for optimism, Hutton assured the senior Colonial Office official, was that Barton had told him privately after his welcoming dinner that the principles espoused in his speech would become his government's policy. Concluding that it was all very promising, he informed Ommanney that he believed the new Defence Bill would include his own recommendations which would permit imperial service. 'It is curious to return to Australia,' he continued euphorically, 'and to find what a marvellous change has come over the whole continent as regards the public feeling towards the Empire and the Imperial connection!' Hutton suggested to Ommanney that this information should be passed to Chamberlain.[40]

Brodrick, unlike Chamberlain, received the good news directly from Hutton. Referring to their discussions prior to his departure from London, Hutton informed Brodrick that his proposals 'for a force of 20 000 mounted men, equipped and organised for service *wherever Australian interests are threatened* was received with a most satisfactory acquiescence'. Barton had declared 'a broad policy as regards defence', Hutton explained, which made him hopeful of securing imperial interests in the new Defence Bill shortly to be drawn up. 'The objectionable clauses restricting military service to Australian waters, will be withdrawn and many of the other clauses either omitted or modified,' Brodrick was told.[41]

As a result of Hutton's advice, the earlier optimism of the British authorities about Australian participation in imperial defence seemed to be justified. In reality, however, the matter was far from settled. In his speech, Barton had mentioned fighting for the empire, but he apparently envisaged that forces for such service would be raised on a voluntary basis as exemplified by Australian involvement in South Africa. The prospect of the government taking action to deploy a force overseas was mentioned by the

Prime Minister only in connection with the defence of Australia. Yet the one source of encouragement for British imperialists was the acceptance by Australians of the idea that their security depended on overseas service by the military forces. Even if potential disagreements remained about where to deploy such a force, this was at least a basis on which to erect the legislative and organisational framework for an Australian expeditionary force. It was in the imperial interest to encourage this development. The Governor-General, Lord Hopetoun, therefore added his support. '[T]hat possibly Australians might be called upon to fight elsewhere than on this continent in order to protect the soil of Australia,' Hopetoun wrote to Barton about his speech, 'was a very wise and very statesmanlike utterance.'[42]

If Hutton and the British authorities interpreted Barton's dinner speech to be the first step in a general commitment by his government to participation in imperial defence, they were wrong. Henceforth, the Prime Minister's pronouncements on the role of the military forces changed. As Hutton complained to Brodrick some eighteen months after Barton's speech, the Prime Minister never again spoke publicly on the subject of defending Australia beyond the national boundaries.[43] It was quite a sudden change. Undoubtedly, the fundamental issue underlying this new mood on defence was the perception that imperial and national interests might not always coincide. Indeed, at this very time, there was an important development in imperial affairs which emphasised this potential point of divergence.

Two days before the dinner welcoming Hutton, a surprise announcement by the Foreign Office in London gave serious cause for Australians to begin to question aspects of imperial policy in the southwest Pacific. On 13 February, a cable reached Australia confirming the ratification of a treaty of alliance between Great Britain and Japan.[44] Although caught unawares, Barton gave the appearance that he was unconcerned by telling the press the next day that, '[a]s to the effect which the new treaty will have on the naval and military position of the Commonwealth, I think that it will be rather beneficial than otherwise'. In relation to the *Alien Immigration Act*, which the Barton government had quickly erected to exclude Asians and other coloured races, the Prime Minister said that he did not believe that 'the treaty itself will make any difference'.[45] Despite these public comments, Barton privately sought reassurance for his optimistic outlook from Lord Hopetoun, 'for you understand these things so much better'.[46] Hopetoun was no better informed than his Prime Minister but, nevertheless, enthusiastically supported the initiative while noting that 'there has always been a feeling that the electors would look upon a "yellow alliance" as something unnatural and distasteful'. Yet, to his surprise, Hopetoun confessed, judging by initial newspaper reports on the treaty, that 'they have now swallowed it without a murmur'.[47] It was a rash judgement by the Governor-General.

One week after ratification of the treaty, the *Bulletin* announced that 'Australia wants to remain the same color [sic], outwardly anyhow as is JOE

The Motherland's Misalliance

'London, 12th February—The Foreign Office has announced the conclusion of a treaty of alliance between Great Britain and Japan.'
BRITANNIA: *'Now, my good little son, I've got married again; this is your new father. You must be very fond of him.'*
Australians were surprised by the announcement that Britain had ratified a treaty with Japan, a country which they viewed with apprehension. Their fear of Japan drew heavily on racist attitudes. Note the words 'White Australia' on the door which protects the young Australia from the outside world. (NATIONAL LIBRARY OF AUSTRALIA)

CHAMBERLAIN and KIPLING and the Duke of York'. Furthermore, the *Bulletin* pointed out, the Australian people 'had no voice, directly or indirectly, in the making of the Japanese treaty', and they were therefore not morally bound by its terms. 'Amid all these circumstances, it is too early yet to sit down with the restful assurance that because the Aliens Restriction Act [sic] is passed White Australia is safe,' the report concluded. 'It is no easy matter to remain white, and yet to remain part of an Empire that grows blacker every day.'[48] While the *Bulletin* exaggerated such issues, there were good grounds for Australians to question imperial policy in relation to what they perceived as their national interest. There can be little doubt that this issue acted as a catalyst for the change in Barton's future statements on defence.

In determining its defence policy, the government had to consider some important issues. Uppermost in its mind was the question of its own survival—the Barton administration did not enjoy an absolute majority in the House of Representatives. The Labor Party held the balance of power and its policy had already been determined when the Labor caucus had decided to amend Forrest's Defence Bill by removing the power to commit troops to overseas service. By restricting compulsory service to Australia, a purely defensive role for the military forces was assured and excessive involvement in imperial operations was avoided. Similar views were held by several members of other political persuasions as the debate on the first Defence Bill had revealed.

Understandably, Hutton was upset by what he considered to be the Labor Party's undue influence on the government's defence policy,[49] but the underlying issues also divided Barton's own cabinet. To Hutton's great disappointment, he learned that, while Barton and Forrest were 'anxious to compass some system of Military Co-operation with the Imperial Government', two other members of his seven-man cabinet, Sir George Turner and Charles Kingston, were 'violently opposed to such measures'.[50] Therefore, it seems probable that, with the exception of Forrest, Barton had consulted no other member of cabinet before making his speech at the dinner. But even if this were not the case, the unexpected announcement that Japan was an ally of Britain was probably sufficient to tip the balance towards the nationalists, giving them grounds to argue against overseas deployment for Australian troops as a possible first step towards involvement in imperial defence strategies. Not only did the Prime Minister never again advocate the forward defence of Australia, but, within four weeks of the dinner, he began carefully to spell out limitations to Australian involvement in imperial operations.

A disillusioned Hutton interpreted the Barton government's modified approach to defence as weakness.[51] Suggesting that it had bowed to the pressure of its political opponents, the GOC informed Sir Arthur Bigge, secretary to King Edward, that its members were 'reeds shaken by the wind'.[52] This was not a fair assessment of the government's position on the matter, however. Its policy was not simply influenced by the views of its political opponents, threatening as they were. It also reflected genuine bipartisan concern about the dangers of organising the Australian defence forces for imperial ends, concern which was given a special national emphasis with the unexpected ratification of the Anglo-Japanese alliance.

The government's wariness was immediately obvious in the position it took on a proposal to establish an imperial military reserve. In October 1901, Barton had received correspondence from Joseph Chamberlain informing him that the government of New Zealand intended to establish a military force as a reserve for imperial operations. Chamberlain specifically drew Barton's attention to comments on the proposal by the Colonial Defence Committee and requested the Australian government to consider following New Zealand's example.[53] In March 1902, reports on the New Zealand initiative were published in Australian newspapers, suggesting that the subject would be discussed at the Colonial Conference in June. When pressed publicly for a response, Barton did not commit himself. Instead, he signalled a lack of enthusiasm for the suggestion with the arresting comment that 'as matters are at present [such proposals] sound very much like taxation without representation'.[54] It is scarcely possible that in choosing these words Barton was unaware of their historic significance as the revolutionary slogan on which eighteenth-century Americans had asserted their independence from imperial Britain, but, strong as they were, they probably did not reflect Barton's personal views; it seems they were designed primarily for domestic consumption. However, Barton was beginning to realise that, despite his personal convictions, there was a need to be circumspect in dealing with Britain on questions of defence.

Clearly an informal commitment by Australia to assist Britain in facing a major threat was one thing, but the routine employment of an Australian force on general imperial service raised difficult and sensitive questions for the Australian government. First and foremost, as Barton's statement implied, the Australian government was unable to have a direct role in the political process which might lead to military action. On a more elemental level, the government feared the derogation of its authority, the loss of control over Australian manpower and resources and increasing demands for the commitment of men and equipment. Barton had experienced all these problems in the previous twelve months over Australian involvement in the Boer War, but late in March there was an important development, causing him to take a special interest in the welfare of Australian soldiers in South Africa. It came to a head immediately after his public statement on the imperial reserve, confirming his cautious approach to the issue.

The problem had originated in June 1901 when the 5th Victorian Mounted Rifles had fared badly in a surprise attack by a Boer force at Wilmansrust.[55] Subsequently accused of cowardice in colourful, but intemperate, language by an imperial general—the Australians were not only a 'fat-arsed, pot-bellied, lazy lot of wasters' but also 'white-livered curs' according to General Beatson[56]—three members of the humiliated unit had been sufficiently stung to utter statements considered to be mutinous. For this the three soldiers had been court-martialled, found guilty and sentenced to death. The sentences, however, had been commuted to a term of imprisonment when the Judge Advocate General ruled that the proceedings were legally flawed.[57] A disturbing aspect of the affair was that news of the trial and convictions had not reached Australia until the men had been imprisoned in England, some months after the court-martial had concluded. Then, after requesting an explanation from Chamberlain, the Australian government had received only a terse, official statement on the proceedings.[58] As a result, Barton had been hard put to provide satisfactory answers to questions from an enquiring electorate; it had been an embarrassing, demeaning experience for the Prime Minister.

There was an obvious need for the Australian authorities to be kept fully informed in future. Barton therefore had taken action to have Kitchener, the British commander-in-chief, advise the Australian government periodically of punishments and terms of imprisonment awarded to Australian soldiers under his command as a result of court-martial proceedings in South Africa.[59] Yet, in doing so, it seems that it had not occurred to the Prime Minister that a capital sentence might actually be carried out before

Eight men of the Second South Australian (Mounted Rifles) Contingent who served in the Boer War, 1899–1902. The mounted rifleman third from the left on the light coloured horse is 'Breaker' Morant. Experienced, self-reliant horsemen of this type proved to be excellent soldiers in South Africa. (AUSTRALIAN WAR MEMORIAL, AWM NEG. NO: P220/03/01)

the Australian government had been advised. Undoubtedly, Barton felt he had taken appropriate action in requesting periodic advice, thereby ensuring that he was adequately informed of the fate of Australian soldiers in future. He could only have been reassured when Kitchener promised to report to him on such matters at the end of each quarter after 1 January 1902.[60]

One can imagine how the Prime Minister felt when, towards the end of March 1902, Major Robert Lenehan, late of the Bushveldt Carbineers, landed in Melbourne after a trip from South Africa with the information that two of his Australian officers, Lieutenants Harry Morant and Peter Handcock, had been executed in Pretoria on 27 February, following court-martial proceedings.[61] The upsetting feature was that the Australian government had not been consulted on the matter; Lenehan's account was the first news it had of the executions. The authorities in Britain, however, were not ignorant of the proceedings. Brodrick had sought Chamberlain's advice before the sentences were carried out, undoubtedly for the reason that colonial officers were involved. 'Two executions ought to be sufficient,' Chamberlain had responded to Brodrick's inquiry on 21 February. The life of a third officer, Lieutenant George Witton, who was also involved with Morant and Handcock, could be spared, in the opinion of the colonial secretary.[62] Although this advice confirmed a similar recommendation by Kitchener, Brodrick still had been tempted to show no leniency. 'I should myself have been inclined to shoot all the three officers,' he had informed Kitchener, 'but you are in the best position to judge and I am agreeing with you.'[63]

Barton, of course, was not aware of this correspondence, but perhaps he suspected that Kitchener had consulted with the authorities in Britain before the executions. Regardless of this, he had good cause to be offended that, only three weeks after giving his undertaking to keep him informed, Kitchener had presided over the executions of Morant and Handcock without making any attempt to notify him. The British commander-in-chief had disregarded the Australian Prime Minister's obvious wish to know what was happening to Australian soldiers under his command. Barton must have been deeply disturbed at being treated in such a fashion.

The Prime Minister's position was made more difficult by the reluctance of the British authorities to provide information after the execution. Ignorance fuelled speculation in the minds of a number of Australians and gave greater prominence to the case. 'All Australia has lately been deeply moved at the Trial and execution of these two ex-Australians in Pretoria,' Hutton wrote to Brodrick, adding: 'It was a pity that the facts were not communicated here by the C. Chief [Kitchener], I think, as much adverse, and ill-advised comment would have been saved.' His failure to provide information, Hutton assumed naively, was probably due to the senior military commander's wish to spare Australians from the gruesome details of the crimes committed by their fellow countrymen.[64] The truth was that Kitchener simply believed that capital punishment could be inflicted on Australian officers under his command without providing any explanation to the Australian government.

Kitchener, Brodrick and Chamberlain displayed a callous disregard for the Australian authorities and the families and friends of the executed men. It was reported that Mrs Handcock, who lived in Bathurst with her children, first learned of her husband's demise from the pages of a newspaper. 'The reticence observed by the authorities in South Africa in this matter is, to say the least, singular,' the *Age* commented indignantly.[65] Edmund Barton was under extreme pressure to provide information. When Isaac Isaacs, the Member for Indi, asked the Prime Minister to explain the circumstances surrounding the case because of the 'very intense interest in Australia', Barton could say little more than had been published in newspapers, whose stories had been based on secondary sources. 'They were not in any sense employed by Australia, nor were they in a corps that was raised in Australia, or was distinctly Australian,' was Barton's lame response to Isaacs. He was trying to obtain more information, 'but it rests entirely with the military authorities in South Africa,' he explained.[66]

Despite his public air of detachment, Barton privately pressed the Governor-General for information. Hopetoun, in turn, despatched a strongly worded cable to Kitchener. 'If I fail to get proper satisfaction from him direct I shall turn all the screw through Mr Chamberlain and St John Brodrick,' the Governor-General assured Barton. 'These soldiers must not be allowed to have things all their own way.'[67] But the execution of Australian servicemen was not a subject on which Barton's government had ever intended that soldiers would have their own way. Forrest's Defence Bill of the previous year had included a similar provision to the colonial defence legislation of Queensland, Tasmania and New South Wales, by decreeing that no death sentence found by a court-martial could be carried out until it had been confirmed by the Governor-General, who, in accordance with constitutional practice, would seek the advice of his ministers.[68] The Morant–Handcock affair sounded a clear warning in March and April 1902 for the Barton government to protect the interests of Australian soldiers from imperial domination. The unfortunate incident also raised important questions about the authority of the government in relation to Australians serving with the Imperial Army.

Meanwhile, Hutton was pressing on tenaciously. Since his arrival in Australia, he had been hard at work preparing a report for the government on Australian defence. During its preparation, he frequently consulted the former secretary of the Colonial Defence Committee, Sir George Clarke, who had recently been appointed Governor of Victoria.[69] 'A really great work lies straight upon you,' Clarke had told Hutton when welcoming him to Melbourne. Offering his assistance, Clarke added: 'I know that you will add permanently to the strength of our Empire.'[70] It was this object which

An Imperial GOC

Hutton kept firmly in mind as he worked on his report. He presented the completed work to the government on 7 April 1902.

The report outlined the traditional British evaluation of Australian defence requirements. Australian security and the protection of Australian commerce, Hutton claimed, depended to a large measure on the supremacy of the Royal Navy. Indeed, according to Hutton, the strength of Britain's naval forces would in all probability limit hostile enemy action against Australia to raids by cruisers. But, in a departure from previous imperial advice, Hutton also considered that a large, well-equipped invasion could land although, in the GOC's opinion, this would be 'difficult in the extreme'. This obviously called for the ability to defend the major centres of population, but, appealing to the lessons of history, Hutton also stressed that the best means of defence was a vigorous offensive. Australia depended for its commercial success and future development on its seaborne trade and on 'the existence, maintenance and extension of fixed and certain markets for its produce outside Australian waters', Hutton explained. 'It therefore follows,' he claimed, 'that Australian interests cannot be assured by the defence alone of Australian soil.' It would be a dereliction of its national responsibilities if Australia did not undertake defence outside its national boundaries. The Australian government therefore had to address two defence requirements when organising its military forces: first, the defence of Australian soil; and, secondly, the defence of Australian interests wherever they might be threatened. Hutton did not specify what Australia's overseas interests were, but he felt compelled to warn that they were 'peculiarly open to foreign interference, and to possible destruction by an enemy in time of war'.[71] Well aware of the sensitivity of the subject, the imperial officer had been careful to couch his report in terms which discussed Australia's defence from a national perspective. It suited his imperial goals to use national requirements to fabricate the case for overseas service for the military forces.

The imperial officer knew precisely what he was doing. 'I have been careful to avoid any direct reference to assistance to the Empire in time of war except inferentially,' he confided to Brodrick when he sent him a copy of the report.[72] Similarly, he informed Ommanney that he had been 'careful to leave the deduction to be drawn as to what is really comprised under the head of "Australian interests" '. 'The keynote,' he explained, taking Ommanney into his confidence, 'is a *"Co-operative System of Defence"* in which all parts of the Empire shall combine with the Mother Country.'[73] But before Australian audiences, including his direct political masters, he made no such disclosures.

Hutton proposed that the Australian government divide the military forces into two separate organisations. One would be a garrison force of nearly 16 000 men for the defence of strategic centres and places of commercial importance. The other was to be a field force of 14 000 men in peace which could be expanded to a strength of 29 000 in war. Both forces were essential for the protection of Australian soil, Hutton claimed.[74]

Hutton did not envisage that all the garrison force would be tied to static defences. The word 'garrison' was a misnomer which has misled some historians in the very way it was intended to mislead Hutton's contemporaries.[75] He had originally called it the 'passive defence force' but changed it when Sir George Clarke suggested that the term 'garrison force' would be more acceptable.[76] There can be little doubt that the change in designation was meant to ward off difficult questions about the intended role of the garrison force in relation to the field force, especially since the latter had been described originally as the 'active defence force'. However, while Hutton did not describe the function of the garrison force in detail, careful reading of his report reveals that it would possess some mobility and organic support which would permit it to undertake operations in the field while simultaneously manning fixed installations. This deduction is confirmed by organisational details published in 1903. The garrison force was comprised not only of garrison artillery, but also of field artillery batteries, engineer field companies, infantry companies, light horse squadrons and supporting services. For example, of the 2775 men in the garrison force of Victoria, only 1446 were designated to man forts. The remaining men were organised as a mobile force, providing the capability of defending localities, cities and towns.[77]

Like the garrison force, the name of the field force had also been selected with some care. Hutton's somewhat euphemistic title of 'active defence force' was rejected for the less provocative one on the suggestion of Clarke.[78] According to Hutton, this force would operate in the extended remainder of Australia and therefore required greater mobility and a higher degree of self-sufficiency. The force was to be well trained and well equipped, and ready for active operations at short notice. As if it were an afterthought, the GOC added innocently that the defence of interests outside Australia could, 'if the necessity arose', be provided by the field force.[79] But the field force was not intended primarily for local defence. It was the Australian contribution to the imperial force. If Hutton could win acceptance for his scheme he would have laid the basis for an Australian expeditionary force for imperial operations.

When Hutton turned to the implementation of the scheme it became clear where his primary interest lay. 'I propose to deal later, when the Field Force has been created, with the Garrison Force,' he informed Major-General Sir William Nicholson, Director General of Mobilisation and Military Intelligence at the War Office. 'I conceive the latter to be of less importance than the former,' he explained.[80] His plan was that the field force would be comprised entirely of militia soldiers who received pay for their part-time service, whereas the garrison force would be formed entirely of unpaid volunteers. The difference was significant. The British authorities believed that experience in Australia revealed that militia were easier to recruit and retain, achieving a higher degree of efficiency than volunteers.[81] Hutton agreed, and was 'absolutely certain' that the men in the volunteer ranks would be of inferior efficiency in time of war.[82] However, the GOC was quick to advise the Australian government that unpaid volunteer forces were the pride of all Anglo-Saxon communities and that, in the unlikely event of Australia being attacked, it would be 'safe to accept the fact that . . . a sufficient number of citizens [would] always be found ready and willing to voluntarily undertake the duty of defence'.[83] As consoling as this reflection might have been, Hutton clearly wanted the more efficient troops for his field force because, as he had claimed in his earlier address to the Royal Colonial Institute, he believed that volunteer forces 'by their training, organisation or discipline' were not suitable matches for 'the trained soldiers of the Continent'.[84] Once again, however, he deliberately failed to inform the Australian government of the primary goals underlying his proposal.

In a letter to Forrest, Hutton explained the principle behind his proposed organisation without mentioning the possibility of imperial operations. The key was that the military force was to be capable of expansion when required. In peacetime the units and formations would have their full complement of officers and non-commissioned officers but the ranks would be left about half filled. In time of emergency the existing framework could then absorb the additional 15 000 men who would complete the war establishment. But while Hutton did not specifically alert the minister to the fact,[85] all the expansion in manpower was to be absorbed by the field force. However, Brodrick was not left to draw this conclusion for himself. Hutton informed the British minister that, in drawing up his proposal, he had 'carefully kept in view' the future expansion of field force units.[86] With equal deliberation, Hutton also planned that all expenditure on new equipment was to be for the field force.[87] Existing stores might suffice for the garrison force, Hutton believed, but as equipment for the field force such stores would leave 'much to be desired'.[88] In effect, the scheme being proposed would divert most of the Australian defence resources to the maintenance of a force intended for imperial operations. Inferior equipment and inefficient men were to be committed to local defence.

The suggested organisation of the field force amounted to a radical restructuring of Australia's citizen forces. Hutton proposed that the force be comprised of six brigades of light horse and three brigades of infantry, supported by field artillery and logistic services. Each brigade was designed to operate as an independent unit.[89] He never planned to combine the brigades into a higher formation. His reason was simple, but it was not stated publicly. 'I have advisedly restricted the proposed organisation to that of Brigades,' Hutton informed Nicholson confidentially. 'There are at present no Australian Officers who are fit for high command, or even high positions on the administrative Staff of so large a unit as a Division.'[90] He might have added that such a structure was ideally suited to situations where Australian brigades would be expected to join larger formations under the command of British generals. Indeed, this and not the defence of Australia was the determinant of force structure. Just how inappropriate the resulting field force organisation was for local defence requirements becomes clear when the detailed organisations—published more than one year after Hutton's original report—are examined. The 3rd Infantry Brigade was comprised of regiments located in Queensland, South Australia, Western Australia and Tasmania. Worse still, one half of its headquarters staff was in Adelaide and the other half was in Brisbane. Similarly, the 4th Light Horse Brigade had regiments in Tasmania and Victoria with its headquarters in Melbourne and the 6th Light Horse Brigade had regiments in South Australia and Western Australia with its headquarters in Adelaide.[91] Apart from the difficult problems surrounding the concentration and deployment of this organisation for local defence, such a wide dispersion of citizen force units made effective peacetime training at brigade level virtually impossible. But Hutton was not thinking in these terms when he chose such an organisation as the basis for the field force.

The internal organisation of each type of brigade would mean that a total eighteen light horse regiments and twelve infantry regiments would be raised throughout Australia. Operating on the proposed war establishment, a total of over 10 000 men would be mounted—twice the existing number—and this strength would be achieved by converting some of the existing infantry units to mounted units. 'This change,' explained Hutton to the Australian government, 'is not only consistent with the characteristics of the Australian people, but provides exactly that description of fighting man which has proved so valuable in South Africa, and which without doubt, would constitute a most powerful, if not a controlling, factor in any campaign in which Australian troops might be engaged.'[92]

While the eighteen light horse regiments would not provide the 20 000 mounted men he had promised before he left London, Hutton explained to Brodrick that the infantry regiments would also be trained as mounted infantry.[93] The same information was given to the Director General of Mobilisation and Military Intelligence at the War Office. 'I propose that the whole of the 12 Regiments of Australian Infantry . . . shall be convertable [sic] *en bloc* into Mounted Infantry when required,' he informed Nicholson.[94] Attempting to honour his undertaking to the British authorities, Hutton realised that he could not justify the establishment of a mounted force of 20 000 men to the Australian government. Therefore, while maintaining the guise of a national military organisation, the GOC planned to satisfy imperial requirements without stint.

It remained for Hutton and his imperial patrons to sell the scheme to the Australian government. Three weeks after Hutton submitted the report, the Governor-General, Lord Hopetoun, wrote to Barton at some length on the subject of defence to prepare him for his imminent trip to London to attend the 1902 Colonial Conference. The Governor-General's interest in defence perhaps reflected his education at the Royal Military College, Sandhurst, but it is clear that he also perceived such matters to be part of his vice-regal office.

Hopetoun's letter to Barton was replete with echoes of Hutton's report and encouraged Barton to consider defence from the imperial perspective. It may be taken for granted, Hopetoun counselled Barton, that 'success to the British Arms at sea means the safety of Australian soil'. '[S]o long as Australia is under the British Crown,' wrote the Governor-General, 'her safety and prosperity are so inseparably bound up with the Empire that it is not possible to view [naval defence] from a purely Australian standpoint.' Therefore Australians should not develop their own naval forces but rely on the Royal Navy, the Governor-General advised. To this end Hopetoun suggested that Barton should consider either increasing Australia's financial contribution to the upkeep of the naval squadron, or giving approval to an amendment of the naval agreement which would allow the vessels to be removed from Australian water in time of war. If the Australian Prime Minister adopted either course, Hopetoun believed that the British government would react favourably by sending better, safer ships to the Australian station.[95]

On the matter of force development, the Governor-General advised, Australia should concentrate on its military capabilities. 'You here in Australia,' he observed, 'can produce already three parts made, an article which it takes months of patient training to make in the Old Country—I mean the Mounted Infantrymen.' Thus the Governor-General delivered a tactful, persuasive argument for Australia to adopt imperial defence policy and to develop military forces in accordance with Hutton's recommendations. Australians needed to encompass defence objectives by using the natural attributes and inclinations of the people, Hopetoun continued. Then, in a less than subtle attempt to recruit the Prime Minister as an imperial ally, the Governor-General explained that he appreciated 'the strong objection which many have to any hint of taxation without representation.' [96] In this way, Hopetoun exerted his vice-regal influence to soften the Prime Minister's attitude on the eve of the Colonial Conference.

Barton was also being subjected to contrary pressures, however. On the day Hopetoun wrote to Barton, the Committee on Supply discussed the defence estimate of £937 000 for the financial year 1901–2. In reaching this amount, Forrest simply had aggregated the defence estimate of each state at federation and submitted them without any review or adjustment.[97] Hutton had added his support by advising the government that he thought the estimate was adequate for the time being, but he also claimed that the equipment for the field force would require an additional amount of approximately £500 000.[98] However, the estimate, in spite of Hutton's

An Army for a Nation

SUMMED UP.

Summed Up

A *Bulletin* comment on what it believed Prime Minister Edmund Barton would do in response to overtures by Britain for Australia to contribute to an imperial military reserve. Barton has cut the kangaroo's throat in return for an imperial honour from 'Joe' [Chamberlain], Britain's Colonial Secretary. It was published shortly before Barton left Australia to attend the Colonial Conference of 1902 in London. (NATIONAL LIBRARY OF AUSTRALIA) recommendation, was too high for the members of the House of Representatives and it met with widespread criticism.[99] One expectation of federation had been improved efficiency and economy in the administration of the defence forces. A defence estimate of £750 000 had been considered an appropriate amount at the Constitutional Convention of 1897.[100] Apparently a similar figure was now expected and Sir Edward Braddon, deputy leader of the opposition, received substantial support for his proposal to reduce Forrest's estimates by £200 000. Forrest, lacking confidence in his own submission, responded to the pressure by undertaking to reduce the next year's estimate by £131 000.[101] 'It was unmistakeably [sic] shown during the debate that a still larger reduction was desired,' Forrest informed Robert Collins, secretary for the Department of Defence, 'and it was only upon the assurance of the Government being given that the Estimates next year would be reduced by at least £131 000 and that every endeavour be made to still further reduce expenditure that the Estimates were allowed to pass without a direct instruction that the amount of the reduction should be £200 000.'[102]

The members of the House of Representatives were not simply seeking to save money. Despite Hutton's caution, some Australians were immediately suspicious about his report on Australian defence. 'If he can't get all that he wants directly, General Hutton is willing to get some of it indirectly,' announced the *Bulletin* when it reviewed the proposed field force. 'Hutton can no more be expected to frame an Australian military policy than could a French general.'[103] Similar thoughts occupied the minds of some members of the House of Representatives. They sensed 'that there must be something rotten in the state of Denmark', recalled Sydney Smith, a Free Trader.[104] Added to this suspicion was apprehension about the recent reports of British intentions to discuss the establishment of an imperial reserve at the Colonial Conference.

It was John Watson, leader of the Labor Party, who raised the subject of 'wild suggestions' by Britain for an imperial reserve during the debate on the defence estimate. He was also upset that the Prime Minister of New Zealand, Richard Seddon, supported the proposal. 'It shows how dangerous a man like Mr Seddon may become,' remarked Patrick Glynn of the Free Trade Party. Sir Edward Braddon, another Free Trader, was inclined to the same views. It was 'exceedingly remote', he said, that Australian forces would again serve overseas. James McCay, a member of the Protectionist Party and an infantry officer in the militia forces, believed that if Hutton's recommendations for a field force were adopted then the Minister for Defence 'should be designated the Minister for War'. 'It is time we put a stop to this sort of thing,' clamoured William Spence of the Labor Party, 'and the only way in which Parliament can do so is by the House of Commons cutting off supplies.' It was a pleasing turn in the debate for Henry Bournes Higgins, coming so close as it did to the departure of Barton and Forrest for the Colonial Conference. Higgins hoped that the Minister for Defence would not be swayed by 'the powerful influences which will surround him in London'. Forrest would now know how to respond to the British authorities when they called for support in organising an imperial force, Higgins taunted. 'I feel sure that he will know very well the view of this House that [it] is not prepared to go in for any extravagant scheme.'[105]

It soon became apparent that Barton had decided to adhere to a national approach to defence. The Prime Minister took the opportunity to signal his government's policy at a farewell dinner given by the mayor of Melbourne immediately before his departure for the Colonial Conference. In his address to the 700 guests, Hutton included, Barton said his government accepted responsibility for the defence of Australia and would continue financial contributions to the Royal Navy. In future, however, Australia might establish a navy of its own. As for participation in imperial defence, Barton added explicitly, it would mean levels of financial commitment which Australia was not in a position to make.[106] Hutton, whose unrealistic optimism had led him to inform the British authorities in late February that the Australian government appeared favourably disposed to adopting some form of imperial co-operation, must have been appalled by this statement, especially as Barton was about to carry it to the Colonial Conference in London.

In the space of four months in Australia Hutton's initial optimism had suffered a significant setback. Since his arrival in late January 1902, he had never broached the subject of his co-operative defence plans with the Australian government for fear of arousing an antagonistic reaction. By May it had become obvious that this caution had been justified. The Barton government had given a clear indication that it was not prepared to commit itself to imperial defence schemes. Yet Hutton had not passed this information to the British authorities, leaving them instead with his favourable opinion of late February that his efforts to change the direction of Australian defence planning were meeting with success. The likely explanation is that Hutton, with characteristic arrogance and tenacity, simply would not countenance failure or even compromise. He was making no attempt to revise his proposals for organising the Australian forces, even though they were designed primarily to provide a field force for the kind of imperial operations which Barton had now ruled out. As Hutton had determined at the outset, his risky course was simply to ignore the Australian government and pursue his own objectives.

6
National reactions to imperial plans, 1902–1904

The extent of Major-General Hutton's problems with Australian national sensibilities was not fully appreciated in Britain, partly for the obvious reason that Hutton had failed to brief his superiors there on precisely this point. He had, however, ensured that the men in Britain who had a special interest in imperial defence were aware of his plans for the Australian military forces. He sent them copies of his report on Australian defence which he had completed in April 1902. Among those who received his work were King Edward, the Duke of Connaught, the Duke of Cambridge, Sir Charles Dilke and Secretary of State for War, Mr St John Brodrick. Hutton did not send a copy directly to Colonial Secretary Joseph Chamberlain. As he explained to Sir Montagu Ommanney, permanent undersecretary for the colonies, Chamberlain 'seemed to think it better that I should not do so, and run the risk of it being supposed that I was in any way influenced by his instructions'. The GOC therefore sent two copies of his report to Ommanney, one being for himself and the other being for Chamberlain.[1]

Without sufficient knowledge of Hutton's political constraints, the report seemed strangely deficient. Lord Roberts, Commander-in-Chief of the Imperial Army, and Major-General Sir William Nicholson, Director General of Mobilisation and Military intelligence, were not entirely satisfied when they read a copy, possibly the one sent to Brodrick. After examining its proposals, the two senior imperial officers sent comments to Hutton in June 1902. Not the least of their concerns was that Hutton's scheme 'would leave it to the Australian Government to decide, when the emergency arises, whether the force proposed for expeditionary purposes will or will not be at the disposal of the central authority who is responsible for the defence of the Empire as a whole'. Clearly, Roberts and Nicholson were in no doubt about the intended imperial role of Hutton's field force, but they did not appreciate the limits imposed on their military plans by colonial sensibilities. They failed to realise that Hutton had been unable to mention the possibility of imperial involvement for the Australian forces because of the controversy it would arouse. 'Our view here,' Nicholson informed Hutton, 'is that it is desirable that that authority should be able to rely for certainty on Colonial contingents of definite strength being available for defensive or offensive operations in any part of the world as soon as the Navy has acquired such command of the sea as will permit of the transmarine movement of troops.' It was this issue that Roberts and Nicholson were anxious to discuss with the Australian Prime Minister, Edmund Barton, and his Minister for Defence, Sir John Forrest, at the imminent Colonial Conference.[2] The two senior military officers were obviously under the impression that the Australian participants, who had just arrived in London, would be willing to comply with their proposals.

What was not explained to Hutton was that staff at the War Office had recently drawn up a comprehensive plan to employ colonial troops on imperial service. It was this new scheme which Roberts and Nicholson wanted to place before the colonial representatives at the Colonial Conference for their concurrence, principally because it overcame the shortcomings in Hutton's scheme by making provision for imperial control. Furthermore, the War Office staff were coming to the belief that the field force which Hutton planned to establish in Australia was too large. Their latest plan for an imperial force had been developed primarily by the Assistant Quartermaster General, Lieutenant Colonel Edward Altham, and was based on experience gained in South Africa. Australia's contribution to the imperial force, Altham suggested, would be two mounted brigades and one infantry brigade totalling 9000 men which 'in time, Australia may fairly be expected to considerably increase'. This force would be called the 'Imperial Australian Force' and, in the event of war with a European power, it would be placed 'at the disposal of the Imperial Government for general service'. Under such circumstances it would be commanded by an imperial officer.[3]

Altham's work was submitted originally to Lord Roberts in December and he wasted no time approving it.[4] 'The expense likely to be involved is not heavy,' the commander-in-chief informed Brodrick, 'while the advantage to be gained is considerable.' The only worry in Roberts' mind was that the colonial governments might not give control of their forces to the British government 'without being given some voice in the general policy of the Empire'.[5] Brodrick, too, doubted whether the colonies would co-operate to the extent desired. The advantage to be gained by Britain in making a direct approach to the colonies, as the War Office was now suggesting, had to be weighed against the possibility of provoking a nationalist reaction in the colonies. In mid-February, Brodrick sought Chamberlain's advice on the possibility of holding discussions between the War Office and the Colonial Office on the subject of Altham's suggestion before the Colonial Conference was convened in June 1902.[6]

The Colonial Secretary was certainly interested in the scheme put forward by Altham. Its timing was auspicious because New Zealand had also submitted a proposal to the Colonial Office suggesting that the colonies should maintain military reserves for imperial operations. New Zealand wanted its suggestion discussed at the Colonial Conference which would coincide with Edward's coronation.[7] Brodrick therefore agreed with Chamberlain that the two proposals should be examined together by the Colonial Defence Committee.[8] By this stage, the War Office and the Colonial Office officials had also received letters from Hutton who claimed that Australians were coming around to the imperial outlook on defence.[9] The British authorities therefore had good reason to believe that they could enlist colonial co-operation; it remained for them only to formulate a satisfactory proposition for consideration by the colonies.

Meeting early in June, the Colonial Defence Committee welcomed both sets of proposals placed before it. The one by New Zealand, it was noted, provided the ability to 'despatch by sea a certain number of expeditionary forces' soon after the outbreak of war. This was an important step in establishing a comprehensive scheme of imperial defence, the committee enthused. It believed the colonial expeditionary forces could be used to reinforce local troops in any part of the empire or to take offensive action against the outlying possessions of an enemy. '[N]o European Power other than Great Britain,' the committee observed, 'is in a position to draw on large communities of white subjects outside Europe for military assistance, and the action of expeditionary forces based on Australasian and Canadian ports might be of great importance during the early stages of a war.' For New Zealand's proposal to be effective, the committee believed, it was essential that the co-operation of the colonies was assured in advance, and that colonial expeditionary forces were properly organised. These two essential requirements were addressed in Altham's scheme, the committee noted. Furthermore, it was satisfied that the assistant quartermaster general had assessed correctly the military resources likely to be available from each colony and had addressed the vital issue of the need for one central controlling authority. The committee was 'in entire accord' with the principles embraced in Altham's plan, and therefore recommended that assurances be sought from the colonies on the size of the contingents which 'they would be able to place at the disposal of His Majesty's Government for extra-Colonial service in a war with a European Power'.[10]

The British authorities had misjudged the mood in the colonies, taking too much for granted as a result of colonial involvement in the Boer War—and perhaps, in the case of Australia, being deluded by Hutton's optimistic advice. They had come to believe, incorrectly, that all of the colonies were ready to participate in imperial defence. Yet Altham alone realised the sensitivity of the issue and recommended, 'for military and political reasons', that reference to 'offensive expeditions across the seas' should be removed from both his paper and the Colonial Defence Committee's comments before publication. Chamberlain and Brodrick, however, rejected this advice, believing that the documents could be presented to the colonial representatives at the conference as they were.[11]

It seems that Chamberlain might have been the first to discover that the establishment of an imperial military reserve in Australia was not a foregone conclusion. Soon after his arrival in London, Barton, who was to be knighted before returning to Australia, wrote to the Colonial Secretary suggesting that confidential discussions be held before the conference commenced. 'In a conference the proceedings of which are to be reported and after time published,' the Australian Prime Minister informed Chamberlain, 'it will perhaps be found impossible for the representatives of self-governing colonies to address you with the absolute frankness which alone will enable you to quite know the reasons why we hold certain views.'[12] Perhaps Barton wanted to explain to the Colonial Secretary that, although the imperial proposals had his personal support, he was unable to embrace them publicly as Prime Minister because it would divide his own cabinet and mobilise damaging political opposition at home. However, while it is not clear whether the military reserve was discussed when they did meet,[13] Chamberlain certainly did not lose hope that he would eventually achieve colonial support for the proposal. The subject of colonial contributions to imperial military strength was an issue of the first importance. The resolute Colonial Secretary therefore tutored Brodrick on the approach he should take in order to stimulate colonial interest in New Zealand's proposal and so rally support.

Chamberlain advised the Secretary for War to encourage Prime Minister Seddon of New Zealand by telling him that he attached 'special importance to his proposal' because it would 'force the hands of the Commonwealth and the Dominions who cannot with decency remain behind after New Zealand has taken the initiative'.[14] Chamberlain was well aware of the colonial rivalry which arose as a result of the extent of New Zealand's support during the Boer War. Forrest, for one, had protested to the Colonial Secretary in August 1901 over reports that New Zealand had contributed more troops in proportion to population than any other colony. The Australian Minister for Defence sent figures to Chamberlain to show that Western Australia deserved the accolade.[15] It was therefore an astute move by the Colonial Secretary to attempt to encourage similar rivalry over the imperial reserve proposal, especially (as Chamberlain reasoned with Brodrick), if Seddon could see that his initiative was the centre of colonial attention. 'This will be true,' Chamberlain prompted Brodrick, *'and he will like it.'*[16]

National Reactions to Imperial Plans

At the conference table, the imperial authorities laid bare their intentions. Secretary of State for War Brodrick presented the paper drawn up by Lieutenant-Colonel Altham. The British authorities clearly had decided to press home their proposals and, in Barton's words, the representatives of the War Office 'absolutely pleaded' with the premiers for compliance with their military plans.[17] A similar, pressing case was also presented by Joseph Chamberlain. The Colonial Secretary argued that the idea of establishing an imperial force was not a momentary impulse arising from the Boer War, but rather the result of 'our whole progress in this country for the last twenty years'. The Boers had been a determined enemy, he continued, but they were not a well-organised military force. Britain now had to consider the possibility of a war against a European power. Diversity in the standard and organisation of the colonial military forces therefore had to be eradicated, Chamberlain explained, 'so that we may know exactly what we have to depend upon'. The colonies should maintain reserves, fully organised and equipped, trained on principles laid down in Britain and ready for active service as complete units, he insisted.[18]

Barton and Forrest, of course, knew that the realities of Australian politics prevented their agreeing to this proposal. Together with Sir Wilfred Laurier of Canada, they opposed it. Giving their agreement to uniformity in military organisation and equipment was as close as they dared come to accepting Chamberlain's proposition. Beyond that, they insisted, '[t]o establish a special force, set apart for general Imperial service, and practically under the absolute control of the Imperial government, was objectionable in principle as derogating from the power of self-government enjoyed by them'. The colonial governments would decide what military assistance would be given to Britain 'when the need arose'.[19]

Brodrick was upset by the failure of Australia and Canada to support Altham's plans. Writing to Chamberlain, the Secretary of State for War observed disconsolately that 'from a military point of view it is the wreckage of the scheme wh.[ich] would have saved us heavy expenditure'.[20] But Chamberlain, characteristically, was not yet beaten. He believed there had been some progress at the conference and, looking optimistically to the future, noted that Britain was 'reaching nearer with every successive Conference to Imperial Unity, as to which in spirit at least we are entirely agreed'.[21] Certainly, the Australian and Canadian representatives had made it very clear that the establishment of an imperial force would not be possible at that time, but the conference records noted that 'Imperial sentiment in the Colonies, was steadily growing, and their action in the late war left no room for doubt that such assistance would be given readily and effectively and to the utmost of their ability in any future emergency'.[22] The imperial authorities could be consoled also by the approval of Barton and Forrest to a renewal of the Naval Agreement of 1887. Under the terms of the new arrangement, the Australian representatives agreed to increase their annual

Vol. 23.—No. 1172. SATURDAY, AUGUST 2, 1902. Price 6d.

Alone!

'*London, Saturday afternoon*—At yesterday's sitting of the Colonial Conference, Mr St. John Brodrick (Secretary of State for War) proposed that the autonomous colonies should each maintain an imperial military (militia) reserve. He was disappointed that the co-operation of the Maoriland Premier, Mr R. [Dick] Seddon was alone available.

The Canadian and Australian Prime Ministers, Mr Wilfred Laurier and Mr Edmund Barton, emphatically indicated that they were not prepared to invite their respective Parliaments to sanction military expenditure except for purposes of local defence.'

BLOODTHIRSTY DICK: '*Pooh! It's not nearly so dangerous as it looks. Watch me!*'

(NATIONAL LIBRARY OF AUSTRALIA)

contribution from £106 000 to £200 000 and to relinquish any control they had over the deployment of the naval squadron.[23]

Chamberlain's faith in the growth of imperial loyalty in Australia was not ill-founded. He knew also that Forrest was a staunch imperialist who, although constrained in his official capacity, did give his unqualified personal support to the Colonial Secretary's imperial efforts. The Boer War had provided Forrest with the opportunity to impress Chamberlain with the strength of his convictions, especially when many people in Britain had become disillusioned over the wisdom and cost of the prolonged operations against guerrilla forces. 'I hope you stick to it and insist on absolute submission,' Forrest had encouraged Chamberlain in August 1901. '[W]e have conquered by the sword and we must be determined to hold as British territory what we have won.'[24]

The Colonial Conference therefore seems to have been a source of discomfort for Forrest because he could not officially embrace the imperial line on defence. Including a tour of Canada in his return trip to Australia, the Australian Minister for Defence continued to profess his imperial loyalty in letters to the Colonial Secretary. 'The contribution of £200 000 is far too small and it should at least have been £250 000,' he wrote apologetically to Chamberlain about the increased Australian payment under the terms of the Naval Agreement. Still, he observed hopefully, 'it is a new beginning and in the right direction'. Forrest also informed Chamberlain that, contrary to Laurier's assurances, the French Canadians and their newspapers did not support British action in the Boer War. 'From what I have heard,' Forrest wrote, 'I have not been pleased.' The Australian Minister for Defence therefore took the opportunity, while speaking at a dinner of the Board of Trade in Montreal, to tell Canadians that unless members of the empire were 'willing to pay the bill' they had no right to express an opinion in imperial affairs. Forrest cut the report on his speech from the pages of the *Montreal Daily Star* and sent it to Chamberlain.[25] 'I believe that you and I are absolutely in sympathy on this matter,' Chamberlain assured Forrest when he received the article. Encouraged by Forrest's support, the Colonial Secretary believed that the colonies were 'only just awakening to their responsibilities' which would make the empire 'safe against all its enemies'. 'Whatever the result,' he wrote to Forrest, 'you have done your part, and I cordially appreciate and respect your action.'[26] Responding to this praise, Forrest continued to foster Chamberlain's guarded optimism after his arrival in Australia. The Colonial Secretary was told that the Australian people seemed 'more British than the Australian Parliaments'. Therefore, Forrest informed Chamberlain, if it were ever put to the vote, then 'the little Englander and the selfish politician . . . will have a rude show, at any rate that is my hope and prayer'.[27] 'I appreciate your good opinion very much,' Chamberlain responded warmly, 'for I begin to think that you and I are the only true Imperialists in the British Empire.'[28]

There was a feeling of attachment and loyalty to Britain and the empire in Australia. But this did not mean, as Forrest seemed to be suggesting to Chamberlain, that Australians were about to acquiesce on all imperial issues. Unmistakably, Australians also had a keen sense of national pride and responsibility; support for the empire, although strong, was not unqualified. This was illustrated forcefully when reports of the British proposal for imperial reserves first reached Australia while the Colonial Conference was still in progress. The major Australian newspapers unanimously condemned the British proposal. The *Brisbane Courier* reported indignantly that 'to ask that any portion of the local forces . . . should be permanently handed over to the control of the War Office would be a surrender of the most vital principle of self-government'.[29] In Melbourne the *Argus* chided Mr Seddon 'whose Imperialism runs to impetuosity',[30] while the *Age* reported 'that the Prime Minister of the Commonwealth quite accurately interpreted public feeling here when he said that the Australian States would spend no money on military forces except for purposes of local defence'.[31] The *Advertiser* in Adelaide was surprised 'that in a country where "no taxation without representation" is a commonplace of politics any different decision could have been expected from colonial statesmen trained under the influence of the same idea'.[32] The *Sydney Morning Herald* believed the suggestion to establish imperial reserves displayed 'a vagueness of idea respecting the outlook and point of view of the dependencies which it may be hoped its rejection may remedy'.[33] Not surprisingly, the *Bulletin* also recorded its disapproval of Brodrick's proposal which, the journal noted caustically, entailed 'methods of fettering and plans of bleeding'. 'England must now recognise that Australia and Canada are only willing to give war-help, after judging the merits of the war, and then in purely voluntary fashion,' the *Bulletin* proclaimed emphatically. 'Not a soldier will be pledged beforehand.'[34]

Comment on the proposed imperial reserve was not confined to the newspapers in Australia. Cabinet publicly registered its support for Barton's and Laurier's rejection of the proposal.[35] More importantly, the controversy prompted Australian politicians to take a fresh and more careful look at Hutton's defence scheme which still awaited endorsement. Indeed, the increased interest in imperial defence plans came at a bad time for the GOC's recommendations. James Page, a member of the Free Trade Party, claimed that if parliament did not subject Hutton's proposals to scrutiny and place controls on him then he would 'land us in a queer mess' and 'put the collar and chain on the kangaroo'.[36]

The government, however, needed no such warning; appropriate action had already been taken. In Forrest's absence, the Acting Minister for Defence, Sir William Lyne, carefully examined Hutton's report on Australian defence and realised that it inferred that Australian troops should be sent overseas for offensive operations. 'I at once took an opportunity,' Lyne explained to the House of Representatives, 'to remove from the mind of the General Officer Commanding the impression that the Government or Parliament, would, for a moment, consent to such a proposal.'[37] Acting on Lyne's instructions, the secretary of the Department of Defence, Robert Collins, wrote to Hutton informing him that '[t]he Minister does not agree with any proposal to give control over Australian Troops to any but the Commonwealth Authority'. In addition, Collins pointed out, it might happen that, as in the case of the Boer War, a volunteer force could be sent abroad, but until that time arrived no expenditure could be incurred in maintaining any troops established 'on any consideration of undertaking such external operations'.[38]

Hutton decided to protest innocence. He challenged the minister to indicate anything in his report on the reorganisation of the forces which contained, or inferred, 'any proposal to give "the control, or implied control, over Australian Troops to any but the Commonwealth Authority" '. Hutton complained that he had made absolutely clear the principle that the Commonwealth government controlled the forces. And, up to a point, this was true. Yet the record of his earlier discussions with his superiors in London exposes his ultimate intention that control would rest with an imperial defence council. He was also being less than frank when he claimed that the organisations he proposed were considered necessary for the defence of Australian soil. The GOC also completely ignored the implications for his field force of the direction that no force would be maintained for external operations.[39]

Hutton was angered and embarrassed as a result of the proceedings at the Colonial Conference. Immediately after the newspaper reports were published in Australia, he wrote to Brodrick informing him that the proposal 'for the formation of a Militia Reserve in the Colonies has been followed by the strongest possible dissent from all quarters and all shades of public opinion'. Hutton had then condemned all previous suggestions which proposed to create an imperial reserve from colonial troops.[40] As he explained to Ommanney, Altham's scheme was simply based on the earlier suggestion by Major-General French to maintain military reserves in Australia. 'Major General French's scheme was that of an unthinking man,' Hutton wrote, 'anxious to meet War Office ideas without considering the feeling on the spot.'[41] The GOC also noted that Altham had completed his work on the scheme before his own departure from England to take up his Australian command. 'I need hardly say that if I had been made aware of the views therein expressed,' Hutton informed Ommanney, 'I would then have pointed out what from my previous knowledge of Australia I knew would have been impracticable to put into practice!' [42] The British authorities had to realise, Hutton exhorted, that Australians were 'peculiarly sensitive of any interference with what they consider to be their constitutional rights'. The only way to involve the colonies in imperial operations, Hutton therefore counselled Brodrick, was in the way he had originally proposed in his own co-operative defence scheme. He reiterated that the colonies should be induced to maintain forces in their own territory which they could then decide to commit to imperial operations under the control of an imperial council.[43]

Hutton was himself ignoring the reality of the situation, however. In his previous explanations of his co-operative defence scheme, he had provided information on military organisations and operational concepts but had never provided any substantial explanation of how he believed an imperial controlling council would be established or operate. Of course, it was essentially a problem to be solved by politicians, not military commanders, but Hutton's scheme would never work until a solution had been found. This was the fundamental flaw in his proposal. Hutton also failed to acknowledge that the colonial premiers of Australia had rejected his federal defence scheme in 1896 because its provision to vest control of the federal military force in an unelected council was not acceptable.

Considering the mood in Australia in 1902, there were no grounds to be optimistic about a different result in the future. Australians were not only reluctant to lose control of their forces on military operations but they also held fears of becoming embroiled in a series of imperial operations from which there was no easy release. For this basic reason, the Australian government opposed the creation of military organisations designed for an imperial role. As a result, Hutton could only continue to recommend his proposed military organisation by disguising the field force as a national defence force. The GOC therefore claimed that his scheme respected the constitutional rights of Australians, but, in practice, Hutton was attempting a grand deception of the Australian government and people.

Hutton had to be secretive in preparing the military organisations to fulfil his co-operative defence dream. But the controversy aroused as a result of the Colonial Conference now made his job more difficult. 'This will I fear,' Hutton informed the secretary for war when news of Altham's proposal reached Australia, 'be followed by outspoken criticism of even the indirect efforts which I have been making to induce the Australian Parliament and public opinion to accept the fact that the defence of Australian interests cannot be compassed by the defence of Australian soil.'[44] Indeed, as Hutton anticipated, more caution was demanded on his part. 'Ever since the publication of the War Office Scheme for an Australian Force to be maintained for Imperial purposes,' Hutton informed Ommanney, 'a section of the public, principally the Labour [sic] Party, have looked upon me as the War Office Apostle and my suggestions have therefore been viewed with more than suspicion.'[45]

Hutton was not deterred from his objective by increased suspicion about his motives. He told Ommanney in August 1902 that, having been requested to draft a new Defence Bill, he would still endeavour to include provisions which would enable the field force to serve outside Australia. The result, he hoped, would be considered by Chamberlain 'to be sound and to be the best possible under the circumstances'. As it was some months before the proposed legislation would be introduced to parliament, Hutton hoped the dissent arising as a result of the Colonial Conference would have subsided.[46] The GOC was still optimistic that the Australian government would eventually adopt the co-operative defence scheme. 'It is . . . , as I am sure you agree, the ideal to work for and in anticipation of!' he wrote to Ommanney. Accordingly, he still intended to prepare the way for the field force to operate as an expeditionary force.[47]

It seemed that his persistence would be rewarded. At the close of 1902 Hutton thought there were encouraging signs that the opposition and members of the Labor Party were beginning to accept his argument for military operations beyond Australian shores.[48] He therefore informed Ommanney that he should be left to work out the detail of military organisation in Australia by himself but he hoped that the Colonial Defence Committee would support any recommendations he made to the government. 'They will by doing so further the true interests of Australian defences as an integral part of the Defence of the Empire far more effectively than in recommending military ideals which are impracticable of adoption in the face of local political and personal considerations,' Hutton asserted.[49] But, early in 1903, Hutton was again plunged into a difficult situation by the actions of the British authorities.

In February, the new Governor-General in Australia, Lord Tennyson, received a despatch from the Colonial Office which included a copy of Altham's proposal with comments by the Colonial Defence Committee. Also enclosed in the same despatch were Colonial Defence Committee comments on Hutton's report to the Australian government of 7 April 1902. The Governor-General was obliged to pass the despatch to the government. This worried Tennyson and he conferred with Hutton, who had already seen a copy of Altham's plan a few months earlier. 'The paper . . . gave me a positive shudder,' he had informed Ommanney at that time, 'lest it should be pounced upon and published by the Press in Australia.'[50] The GOC and the Governor-General realised that considerable damage could be done to Hutton's cause if hostile members of cabinet chose to make the details of Altham's report generally known. Of far greater concern, however, were the Colonial Defence Committee comments on Hutton's report on the defence of Australia because they raised the very real threat that his proposed field force would be rejected if they were seen by the cabinet. Tennyson, in collusion with Hutton, therefore wrote to the Colonial Office requesting permission not to show the despatch to the Australian ministers.[51]

In its comments on Hutton's report, the Colonial Defence Committee stated its belief that the only real threat to Australian security was raids against centres of population and commerce. It therefore considered that

Hutton's proposed garrison force, which included mobile troops, was an adequate military force for the defence of Australia. Local defence requirements did not justify the establishment of the field force, the committee believed. Leaving no doubt on this issue, the committee went on to explain that employment of the field force 'in connection with the local defence of Australia is likely to be restricted'. Nevertheless, it believed strongly that the field force should be established and stated unequivocally that the main reason for this force was the desirability of having well-organised troops available at short notice for service outside Australia as an expeditionary force. Ideally, the committee thought that no restrictions should be placed on areas in which the force could be deployed, but that, at worst, the area of operations should be no less than that defined by the military commandants in 1896—broadly speaking, the southwestern Pacific region.[52]

The committee also believed Hutton's proposed organisation for the field force was too large. Specifically, it depended on an excessive expansion in war. '[A]bout half the war establishment of mounted troops and infantry and three-quarters of the field artillery personnel were left to be introduced into the ranks on mobilization,' it was noted. To avoid having too many untrained troops in the ranks for active service, the committee believed the gap between war establishment and peace establishment should be reduced. It suggested a reduction by one-third of the field force to four mounted brigades and two infantry brigades. One-half of those units could then be the expeditionary force while the remainder could be used as a reinforcement pool and form the nucleus for any subsequent expansion. The expeditionary force, which would be 'a real accession, to the military strength of the Empire', the committee concluded, could then be directed 'to any point which the Commonwealth Government might decide'.[53] With this later concession, the committee obviously hoped that Australia's self-governing status would be consistent with the maintenance of a force for imperial service.

The danger posed to Hutton's field force by the Colonial Defence Committee comments was obvious, but Tennyson's request to keep them from the Australian ministers was turned down by the Colonial Office officials, who evidently failed to understand the full extent of Australian feeling on the imperial defence issue.[54] There was good reason for this misunderstanding. Ommanney, for example, certainly realised why the colonies had rejected Altham's scheme and, furthermore, he sympathised with their attitude. 'I have always regarded the W.O. [War Office] schemes for using the Australian Colonies as a recruiting ground for a reserve as quite impracticable,' he explained to Hutton, 'and as being based on a complete ignorance of the constitutional position of our self governing Colonies and all a most extraordinary failure to appreciate the trend of public opinion in those Colonies.'[55] But Ommanney believed that the recommendations now made by the Colonial Defence Committee solved this problem. Indeed,

National Reactions to Imperial Plans

Ommanney informed Hutton that the committee had adopted 'a purely tentative attitude towards the question of co-operation in Imperial Defence in their recommendations' until the colonies had an effective voice in determining imperial policy.[56] The inference was that more substantial arrangements could be made when some form of imperial government was devised. Meanwhile the committee had explicitly placed the decision on committing the troops to imperial operations in the hands of the Australian government, just as Hutton had been recommending.

Hutton was in an embarrassing predicament. The Colonial Defence Committee had produced a proposal based on the co-operative principles which he espoused, but it was too candid. The GOC knew that it would be unacceptable to the Australian government. Hutton had been told that no military organisation was to be maintained for the purpose of service outside Australia. Apart from problems which would arise in Australia if the committee's comments were revealed, Hutton was now threatened with a serious loss of credibility in Britain. 'The difficulties of my position here have . . . been doubled as the criticism of the CDC [Colonial Defence Committee] upon my reconstruction will be difficult in the extreme to deal with and to answer in such a manner as will satisfy the conditions locally, and yet not get the opposition of the War Office at Home,' a worried Hutton explained to Tennyson.[57]

Faced with the almost certain failure of the field force proposal if the comments by the Colonial Defence Committee were to come into the hands of all members of cabinet, Tennyson and Hutton used their influence on Barton and Forrest to restrict their circulation. 'I have sent [the comments] to Barton and . . . to Forrest,' Tennyson informed the GOC, 'If they are wise they will lock them up in their drawers and not speak to you on the subject.'[58] But Forrest was concerned about what he read and on 6 March sent the Colonial Defence Committee comments and Altham's paper to Hutton requesting an explanation.[59] It put the GOC in a tight spot. Hutton's first reaction was to inform Forrest that '[w]ithout intending to do so the C.D.C. provided a weapon for argument on the part of those who would abolish our military forces altogether'. Exploiting this opening play, Hutton then entreated Forrest to consider 'very seriously . . . whether it would be wise to give the C.D.C. Minutes to the Cabinet'.[60] Remarkably, this argument, with assistance from Tennyson, was successful. 'I am glad to be able to tell you that Sir Edmund Barton, and Sir John Forrest, have decided to keep the contents of the two minutes of the Colonial Defence Committee confidential and not to promulgate them to the Cabinet,' a relieved Hutton wrote to Ommanney at the beginning of April. 'The Governor General has, I think, in this regard used all his influences, with the above happy result.'[61] Hutton, however, was still expected to provide advice for Forrest on the comments by the Colonial Defence Committee.

Initially worried about how he would respond to the comments by the Colonial Defence Committee, the GOC had decided that he would 'make as light of the criticism as [he could] both to the Minister and [his] own Staff'.[62] But now that Forrest had compromised himself by conspiring to withhold information from cabinet, the GOC was in a position of strength. Hutton therefore took his time in answering Forrest's request for an explanation. Only after being prompted did he provide his comments on 9 May, a delay of two months.

Hutton dismissed the Altham paper and the employment of Australian troops on imperial service as being none of his business. 'This appears to me to be a matter outside my province,' Hutton confessed to Forrest, assuming an air of innocence, 'and purely one of policy for yourself and the Commonwealth Government.' As for the Defence Committee's critical comments on his own proposals, Hutton noted that they commenced with the statement that the proposed organisation 'approaches the question of defence from the standpoint of United Australia, and has evidently been formulated with careful regard to Australian views and aspirations'. Hutton then calculated to confuse the minister by falsely claiming that the remainder of the committee's comments were based on Altham's proposals and, therefore, he would only offer further detailed comments 'if [he] was informed that the Commonwealth Government [would adopt] the principles on which the criticisms [were] based'. Hutton therefore neatly evaded the substance of the critical comments on the pretence that the organisation which he had proposed was different from Altham's organisation because it was based on national, not imperial, considerations. He then proceeded skilfully to cover his tracks by asserting that his original proposals had not been made without due consideration for Australia's vast expanse, therefore leading him to recommend an organisation which would spread comparatively small units over a large area. He had considered that this was better than confining larger units to the more populous centres. The GOC then delivered the *coup de grâce* of his masterful deception. He informed the Minister that his reorganisation had 'already to a large extent been carried into effect' and recommended that it not be interrupted 'unless the principles indicated in Lieut-Colonel Altham's paper are adopted by the Commonwealth Government'.[63] In a separate approach on 4 June, Hutton then applied pressure for final approval by the government of his proposed organisation and its publication in the *Commonwealth Gazette*.[64]

Forrest was not about to give in so easily to Hutton's bluff and bluster. On 23 June the minister directed further comments and questions to the GOC. He drew Hutton's attention to the fact that the reorganisation was only provisionally approved to the extent that it could be accommodated within the estimates for the oncoming financial year, and that these estimates had not yet been approved. Until then no new expenditure was to be incurred and no increase to any establishment or salary was to be approved unless it could be provided for from current financial allocations. Thus attempting to diminish the weight of Hutton's argument that his reorganisation had gone too far, Forrest turned to the major issues which Hutton had avoided so neatly. Understandably, the minister was concerned about the Colonial Defence Committee's comment that the prime object of the field force was service overseas, and that it would have only restricted scope for employment within Australia. Therefore, he wondered if there was a requirement for such a force, especially as the minister emphasised 'there is at present no intention on the part of the Commonwealth to maintain a force in Australia for other than local defence'. The minister was also particularly interested in the possibility of saving money if the government at least followed the committee's suggestion to reduce the size of the field force. Hutton was requested to comment on these observations in a more determined way than he had previously commented on them in May.[65]

If the minister expected the military commander to provide a positive response to his requests he was to be disappointed. On 1 July Hutton sent a minute back to the secretary for the Department of Defence which should have brought Forrest to the limits of his patience. Resorting to rather crude delaying tactics, Hutton pointed out that the minute containing the minister's last request contained information on the reorganisation scheme which had no formal security classification as well as information from the Colonial Defence Committee which was confidential. 'It will be advisable therefore,' wrote Hutton, 'for the Minute of the 23rd to be broken up into two portions, one open and the other "confidential" . . . I can then deal with [the Minister's request].'[66]

Hutton's play for time was successful to a point. It was July 1903, and, with the parliamentary session drawing to a close and an election due to be held before the end of the year, Forrest was anxious to produce some results for his two and one half years as Minister for Defence. His first Defence Bill, originally brought forward in 1901, had been withdrawn in the same year in the face of widespread criticism from the House of Representatives. As a result, the military forces were still being administered under six separate colonial Defence Acts and a national scheme of organisation for the forces had not been fully approved and implemented.[67] Forrest obviously felt he could delay no longer, and on 3 July advised Hutton that provisional ministerial approval had been given to his proposed reorganisation. However, he still pressed for a response to the Colonial Defence Committee comments.[68] Five days later Hutton despatched his answer but for some reason it was not seen by Forrest for nearly three weeks.[69] In the interim, Forrest, spurred on by the desire to achieve palpable results, implemented decisive action on the reorganisation.

On the night of 16 July, the Minister for Defence took the opportunity to introduce his newly drafted Defence Bill to the House of Representatives. While doing so, Forrest informed the House that he was proceeding with the formal approval of Hutton's reorganisation of the forces before his Bill had been enacted and before the imminent parliamentary recess. The minister explained that he would have felt 'absolutely ashamed' if the reorganisation had not been completed when parliament next sat.[70] As a result, Hutton's scheme, based primarily on the plan to provide a field force for imperial operations, was given formal approval on 25 July 1903.[71]

Two days later, Forrest saw Hutton's answer on the questions which had originally been put to him nearly five months previously. The military commander was once again evasive and in a lengthy, vigorous reply deliberately misled the minister with the assertion that his reorganisation was intended primarily to defend Australia. Hutton claimed that the Colonial Defence Committee had not been apprised of the details of the organisation of the garrison force and therefore had not realised that its mobile element was inadequate for effective defensive operations. It would have to be supplemented by the field force which Hutton now claimed had the dual role of 'the defence of the Commonwealth as a whole, and of a Mobile Force for the local defence of each State'. This was a plausible argument for enhancing the capability of the garrison force, but not for establishing a separate field force. Nevertheless, Hutton pressed on by observing that the garrison force would be comprised of volunteers and would therefore be an unreliable force. It followed, he argued, that the establishment of a militia field force was more urgent and took priority over the garrison element. But it was Hutton who had recommended that the garrison force be comprised of volunteers.[72] There was no reason why it could not have been a militia force.

The minister was now a little more critical of the advice he was receiving from Hutton. Contributing to this mood of discernment was Forrest's examination of a Defence Bill which Hutton had drafted and submitted in February.[73] In its various provisions Hutton had taken care to insert the necessary powers for the field force to be employed as an expeditionary force under the command of imperial officers, as Hutton's superiors at the War Office had long wanted. Firstly, he prepared the way for broad interpretations: 'active service' was defined as a military operation against an enemy in any place or country or the military occupation of any foreign country; 'emergency' was defined as war, invasion, national emergency or the threat of any of them. Secondly, he included a provision which empowered the government to despatch the permanent soldiers and the militia, who formed the field force, on 'active service anywhere' in response to an 'emergency'. Admittedly, in relation to the militia, he attempted to appease nationalist sensibilities by stating that such service was to be 'in defence of the Commonwealth', but in view of his terminology, the provision was open to liberal interpretation. Finally, he included a measure which empowered the government to place the Australian military forces 'under the orders of the Commander of the King's Regular Forces'. Complementing this last provision, another key clause was designed to subject Australian soldiers on active service to the provisions of the British *Army Act* 'save so far as they are consistent with this Act or the regulations'. This measure, he advised, was simply a convenient method of adopting an extensive disciplinary code which had been developed over a protracted period of British military experience. Otherwise, the GOC argued, the military authorities in Australia would have the arduous task of developing 'special Regulations for Australia which shall deal with all the technical and professional questions involved'. Furthermore, he claimed, the 'expense alone of our endeavour to frame and publish our own regulations is prohibitive at present'.[74] To some extent this was a truthful argument, especially since the clause claimed precedence for the Australian legislation, but Hutton had intended that this provision should endow the British military commander with sufficient legislative power to control the Australian field force on active service as an imperial force.

Needless to say, Forrest was aware immediately that much of what Hutton had included in his draft Bill was unacceptable. The minister might not have guessed the full extent of Hutton's scheming, but he understood enough to feel uneasy. In drafting his new Defence Bill, Forrest ignored some key aspects of Hutton's advice.

It was still difficult for Forrest to reconcile his imperial loyalty with his national responsibilities. In the preamble to his speech on the new Defence Bill, Forrest informed the House that he wished to defend himself from the charge that he was 'strongly Imperialistic'. 'I am proud to say that I am Imperialistic in the sense that I believe in Australia being as closely allied as is possible to the mother country,' Forrest professed, '[but] I am not prepared . . . to do anything that would in the slightest degree limit our freedom, or interfere with our constitutional rights.' [75] He did not explain the full significance of this statement, but it was clearly a signal for Hutton that the Defence Bill put the national interest first. Hutton would have realised that he had failed to achieve the results which he wanted so much. But the minister was obviously still troubled—perhaps apologetic—about the measures taken in the Bill to serve national interests at the expense of imperial wishes.

Forrest explained to members of the House of Representatives that, although he had been absent during the debate on his first Bill, he had since studied the numerous speeches which they had delivered. His new Bill, he believed, would dispel many of the worries which these same members had expressed previously. Attorney-General Alfred Deakin and his legal officers had also given their assistance to Forrest in drafting it. The ambiguity, lack of precision and poor structure which had caused so much confusion in his first attempt were therefore rectified. The new Defence Bill was clear and concise and was introduced by a more confident minister.[76]

'It is a machinery Bill providing for all the requisite powers of organization and control for our present forces and those which may be hereafter constituted,' Forrest said in his introduction. Other than a small number of permanent soldiers to man forts and provide technicians and instructors, the military forces would be 'almost entirely' comprised of citizen soldiers. But, allaying many of the concerns surrounding his first Bill, he emphasised that 'the primary duty of such forces is to defend Australia from invasion or attack'. The minister harboured no doubts on this issue. Indeed, Forrest informed members that the proposed legislation departed from certain recommendations made by the GOC, especially on this one important point. '[Hutton] does not approve of the provision that the citizen forces shall not be required to serve, in time of war, beyond the limits of the Commonwealth,' Forrest informed the House. 'The General Officer Commanding thinks that power should be taken to send them wherever they may be required. I do not take this view.'[77] Indeed, during final preparation of the Bill, Hutton had advised Forrest that he considered this decision 'with the gravest apprehension'.[78] Attempting to change Forrest's mind, Hutton had resorted to an argument based on military expediency and local interests. He had pointed ominously not only to the Dutch and German presence in New Guinea and French interests in the southwest Pacific but, further afield, to the growing military and naval strength of Japan and Russia. For good measure, Hutton also had tweaked the sensitive nerve of Australian racial attitudes by mentioning recent federal legislation designed to preserve Australia as a home for 'only certain defined Races'. 'It is strategically and politically unsound,' Hutton had argued, 'to restrict the operations of any Defence Force to passive defence within a given limit.'[79] But Forrest's only concession to the pleas of his military adviser was the inclusion of a provision which empowered the government to despatch the small number of permanent soldiers on overseas service.[80]

As bad as this was from Hutton's point of view, he was soon to suffer further disappointment, however. Other provisions within the Defence Bill had been framed to dispel objections of the type which had caused the original Bill to founder. The word 'emergency', for instance, was replaced throughout with 'war' or 'time of war', and these terms were defined explicitly to be an attack on the Commonwealth.[81] Likewise, although provisions for conscription were included, they were solely for the purpose of raising a force to protect Australia from invasion.[82] The new Defence Bill had therefore gone some way to closing the loopholes feared by nationalist politicians. As a result, it was generally well received and did not lead to a protracted debate of the kind which followed the introduction of the first Defence Bill. But, as the subsequent debate did illustrate, the new Bill still had not gone far enough.

Members remained apprehensive about excessive militarism and successfully amended the Bill to limit the growth of the permanent force by restricting permanent soldiers to administrative and instructional positions.[83] Significantly, members even rejected Forrest's provision for despatching the permanent soldiers to an overseas theatre. The Bill was amended accordingly, and as a result the Australian government was not empowered to despatch any troops outside Australia or its territories.[84] The subsequent Act provided only for voluntary overseas service in time of war. In these circumstances, members of the House did not object to Australian volunteers serving under the command of British officers.[85] However, the provision which sought to subject permanent soldiers and citizen soldiers to the provisions of the British *Army Act* aroused suspicion. Forrest had gone further than Hutton had originally suggested and proposed that the British legislation should apply in peace as well as in war, probably for the logical reason that it would mean that one disciplinary code prevailed at all times. When questioned on the reason for its inclusion, Forrest answered that he had been advised that to leave it out would mean 'we shall have to include another hundred clauses in the Bill'. This answer offended James McCay and, with the subsequent support of Henry Bournes Higgins, Richard Crouch and Charles McDonald, he stated emphatically that he would prefer to include another one thousand clauses rather than place 'our forces under an Act in regard to the provisions of which we have no control'. Yet the benefits of using the British disciplinary code, so long as certain provisions could be excluded, were appreciated by members. 'The Imperial *Army Act* is a code of penal law for the government of the Army,' Forrest reassured members. 'The Commonwealth forces are to be subject to it only so far as it is not inconsistent with this measure.' But McDonald, at least, was still sceptical and wondered whether the clause was 'another plank in the Imperial platform'. '[Forrest's] actions prove that he is amenable to any suggestions of an Imperialistic nature,' he told the House. Despite these suspicions, however, members accepted Forrest's advice that the clause adopted the *Army Act* as a disciplinary code only and left its application in Australian hands. It did not give total control of Australian forces to Britain, as some members initially feared. In addition, there were compelling pragmatic considerations for retaining the clause. Samuel Winter Cooke pointed out that if they decided to omit it along with all reference to the *Army Act*, then 'it will be necessary for us to go back on what we have already passed'. Members were clearly in no mood to start again. The only remaining problem was concern about the application of such a rigorous disciplinary code to citizen soldiers during peace. Therefore, on McCay's proposal and with Forrest's agreement, the clause was amended to apply to all members of the military forces, but only when on active service.[86] The minister's conciliatory mood was undoubtedly the result of his wish to ease the passage of the Bill through the House.

The Defence Bill was Forrest's swansong as Minister for Defence. On 7 August, it was announced that he was to become Minister for Home Affairs

An Army for a Nation

following a cabinet reshuffle precipitated by the resignation of Charles Kingston as Minister for Trade and Customs. 'I am glad that Sir John Forrest has gone out of the defence,' the GOC wrote to Ommanney. 'He was never in sympathy with the Troops, and had no real interest in the success of any military scheme.'[87] Another reason why the retiring minister was held in low esteem by Hutton was that, while professing loyalty to the empire, he did not publicly advocate a defence policy which encompassed imperial service for Australians.[88] Forrest 'silently avoided any personal responsibility as regards the policy of Defence', Hutton concluded contemptuously.[89] And as Forrest left the defence portfolio, so the Prime Minister terminated his own political career. On 23 September, Sir Edmund Barton made a permanent departure from politics for the High Court bench.

The *Defence Act*, which was proclaimed in March 1904, was a severe blow to Hutton's dream for his co-operative defence scheme for one important reason. The campaign for the vital objective of compulsory overseas service, an objective which he had promised Chamberlain before he left London, had been lost. The result, that Australians could only serve in an overseas operation on a voluntary basis, meant that much of his effort to organise an Australian expeditionary force, under the name of a field force, was to no avail. When arguing against the possibility of such a restriction, Hutton had cautioned Forrest that '[t]his would amount to the organization of Military Units for Active Service in the Field at the very moment when their services are required'. Peacetime organisations would be dislocated when war broke out, Hutton continued, and new organisations would have to be raised from volunteers.[90] But this argument was pushed to one side by a government determined to maintain the military forces for the primary reason of local defence. Hutton had failed totally to change the direction of Australian defence planning on this vital point. To his disgust, a field force had been established but the government was unable to deploy it outside Australia. The offending restriction in the *Defence Act*, Hutton told Ommanney, was 'much to be deplored'. 'I did my utmost, directly and indirectly, to educate politicians and the public generally to a broader view of the necessities and the strategical and political situation in Australia as it appears to those of us who consider the question from a broad Imperial standpoint,' Hutton continued, contemplating his failure. 'I should have had a better chance of success if it had not been for Mr Brodrick's unfortunate proposal for an Imperial Reserve suggested by Colonel Altham.'[91]

Yet, as easy as it was for Hutton to blame Altham, he tended to overlook the many pitfalls implementation of his scheme would face. Further limiting the utility of Australians as imperial troops were restrictions the government might place on Australian participation in certain imperial operations, even as volunteers. The treaty of alliance between Great Britain and Japan, for example, served as a potential point of divergence between imperial and Australian policy. In May 1903, Hutton, with the co-operation of Tennyson, had responded to a suggestion from the British ambassador in Tokyo, Colonel Sir Claude Macdonald, to exploit a visit to Australia by a Japanese naval squadron as an attempt to allay tension between the two countries. The Japanese had been offended deeply by their exclusion from Australia as a result of the *Alien Immigration Act* with its unashamedly racist aim of building a 'white Australia'. It struck a sour note, threatening the harmonious relations on which Britain was erecting its imperial strategy for the region. Understanding this, Hutton realised that the visit by the Japanese sailors 'had a peculiar and far-reaching significance, pregnant with important issues not so much to Australia as the Empire'. Yet the difficulty of convincing Australians that they should extend a warm welcome to the naval squadron was immediately obvious when the Barton government at first decided to ignore the visitors. Despite this setback, 'Lord Tennyson and I were equally determined that this visit by the Japanese should be treated with the consideration due to its great Imperial importance,' Hutton recorded. 'We therefore resolved that, come what might, a great public demonstration should be engineered which should allay the hostile feeling engendered in Japan by the recent Commonwealth legislation.' Lending his considerable influence to the achievement of this goal, Tennyson eventually convinced Barton and his cabinet that the naval squadron should be accorded a warm, public welcome. But, as Hutton observed, it was 'a task more difficult than he had anticipated'.[92]

Britain's alliance with Japan was motivated by a strategy aimed at containing Russian advances in the Far East, so protecting British interests in China and Korea. It was no secret that Russia had designs on Northern China, Manchuria and Korea as well as the ice-free Port Arthur on the Liaotung Peninsula.[93] Indeed, at the time of the visit by the naval squadron, there was a possibility of conflict between Japan and Russia over Manchuria. 'The shadow of the great struggle in the East between Russia and our Ally [Japan] for the supremacy, of the Northern Pacific loomed large,' Hutton noted, '[therefore] the value and importance to Japan and ourselves, with this war in sight, . . . of consolidating our alliance was never greater.'[94] It is evident that Hutton's particular interest in smoothing relations between Australia and Japan was promoted by the thought that Australia might be called on to give military assistance to Japan. But, even though a reluctant Barton government finally was persuaded to arrange reviews for the Japanese sailors in Melbourne and Sydney,[95] such trifling exercises had no hope of significantly changing Australian perceptions of Japan. It was simply inconceivable that Australia would become a military ally of the Japanese.

When the recently-promoted Lieutenant-General Sir Ian Hamilton, Quartermaster General at the War Office, asked Hutton confidentially in December 1903 whether 3000 to 4000 mounted troops were available in Australia to fight with the Japanese forces against the Russians he received a disappointing answer. Although Hutton could assure Hamilton that, despite some deficiencies of saddles and personal equipment, he was 'prepared with all detailed arrangements for placing in the Field from one to three Brigades composed of all three arms', there was little prospect that the force would be mobilised. This expeditionary force, Hutton explained, could be counted on only in the event of war which threatened the 'general interests of the Empire'. Such a war would enjoy popular support in Australia but a military undertaking in co-operation with Japan was a different matter. Therefore, while the GOC believed that sufficient men 'would be induced by high rates of pay to form an Australian Contingent fighting under a Japanese Government and Flag', he was convinced that the federal government 'would be bound to take steps to prevent such a Force being raised or dispatched from Australian soil'. [96]

The British authorities were not happy with the uncertainty of gaining military support from Australia. 'It is no use pressing it,' Brodrick noted disconsolately, 'but some day I cannot doubt that we shall get our Colonies to give us something which will be a dependable part of the regular army in case of emergency.'[97] Roberts held similar views. The Commander-in-Chief felt sure Australians would provide assistance in an emergency. 'Meanwhile we must leave Australian troops out of our general plans,' he concluded.[98] Reluctantly, the British authorities recognised that Australians were unwilling to commit themselves without reservation to imperial defence objectives. It had become clear that, under the terms of the 1903 *Defence Act*, the primary role of the Australian military forces was national defence.

7

The GOC and the Australian military force: The implementation of Hutton's scheme, 1902–1903

When Major-General Sir Edward Hutton took command of the Australian military forces on 29 January 1902 there was much to be done in organising a cohesive national force. As he had done in New South Wales in 1893, he proceeded to introduce sweeping reforms, demonstrating his characteristic energy and drive. On 1 March 1902, Hutton established his national headquarters in Melbourne with a staff of eight officers.[1]

Hutton's chief staff officer was the deputy adjutant general who, with the assistance of another officer, was responsible for discipline, training, enlistments, discharges, promotions and the issuing of orders and commands to the forces. The deputy quartermaster general, also assisted by another officer, was responsible for quartering, feeding and moving the forces and, in the event of war, for mobilisation. The artillery, the engineer services and the medical services each had a supervising officer on the headquarters. The remaining officer was responsible for the care, maintenance and repair of military stores and equipment. The position of chief paymaster was gazetted but not filled—the deputy quartermaster general performed the duties.[2]

In conjunction with Army headquarters there was a Civil Branch in the head office of the Department of Defence. Under the guidance of the secretary of the Department, Captain Robert Collins, it was responsible for administrative aspects of parliamentary work and ministerial decisions, financial accounting and the administration of defence contracts, stores and property. Neither the GOC nor the secretary enjoyed precedence; each was directly responsible to the Minister for Defence.[3] Yet, because of the functional responsibilities of the Civil Branch, the GOC found he did not enjoy complete independence from the secretary. Within seven months Hutton was complaining to the minister that his authority as a general was being reduced on a daily basis. He was concerned 'that such petty details as the discharge of a NCO and formation of a Committee upon technical military concerns form subjects of correspondence between myself and Captain Collins'. Whether or not it was necessary, Hutton observed, 'what is called in England "red tape" necessitates increased labour and additional Staff Officers'.[4] However, notwithstanding these tedious bureaucratic encumbrances, Hutton was still in a position to exercise considerable authority over the forces.

Beneath Army headquarters in the hierarchy of command were the state, or district, headquarters. These organisations had previously commanded the six separate colonial forces. Their retention was necessary not only because of the vast size of the country, but because, pending the proclamation of a Commonwealth *Defence Act*, the forces in each state were still to be administered under the terms of their original colonial defence legislation. This, however, did not impede Hutton in the exercise of his command. The GOC became involved personally in a wide range of issues concerning organisation, equipment and personnel, not only at Army headquarters, but down through the next level of command at district headquarters into the regions. Hutton's personality was seen to dominate the military forces, an impression enhanced by the GOC's frequent trips throughout the length and breadth of the country[5] and his predilection for public speaking. Sir George Clarke, former secretary of the Colonial Defence Committee and now Governor of Victoria, was annoyed by this behaviour, especially at the beginning of the GOC's appointment when he began publicly promoting his planned military organisation. Clarke dropped the moderate tones of his usually even-tempered judgement to note irritably that: 'Hutton is filled with gas which he blows off at short intervals.'[6] But it would be a mistake simply to dismiss Hutton's loquacity as an annoying idiosyncrasy. The GOC consistently tried to rally public support for his proposals in an attempt to place pressure on the government to adopt them. Indeed, it had been precisely this kind of exercise of power and authority which had caused so much friction with governments and politicians in his previous colonial postings. Clarke, no doubt, was worried that history might be repeating itself.

Initial inspections of the military forces by Hutton confirmed the results of the military enquiry which had been undertaken immediately after federation in 1901. The standard of military knowledge, organisation and efficiency varied widely, he discovered. There was a lack of uniformity and cohesion from state to state. New South Wales alone appeared to possess combat and logistic organisations fit for active operations in the field. This was largely the result of the military reforms introduced by Hutton in his previous colonial command. The forces of the smaller states, in comparison, were poorly organised and inefficient. Furthermore, the condition of military stores and equipment was everywhere unacceptable to Hutton. Except in isolated cases, training had not progressed beyond the elementary level of drill and ceremonial parades. Throughout Australia there had never been longer training periods than three to four days in a standing camp.[7]

The GOC and the Australian Military Force

While the GOC did not mention it, the low level of training was an inevitable result of maintaining a force comprised of citizen soldiers. Most working men had no annual holidays except for public holidays.[8] They worked for five and a half or six days a week. Some exceptions were self-employed men, public servants, school teachers and those employed in the pastoral or agricultural industries, where seasonal changes dictated working patterns which were less consistent, but at certain times more demanding. The longest break most men had from work was Easter, when a combination of public holidays and a Sunday provided a four-day period. This was the traditional time for citizen force camps, but the short duration placed a limit on the standard of training which could be achieved. Until this problem was overcome, Hutton believed, the troops of the Commonwealth could not be considered fit for active operations in war.[9]

Hutton acted quickly and energetically to rectify many of the shortcomings he had identified. Training programs were developed and plans were made to provide schools of instruction in each state for light horse, artillery, military engineering, infantry, medical services and supply and transport. A system of field training was introduced and camp training conducted. A service manual was published as the basis for the training and operation of mounted troops. Peace and war establishments were prepared for the forces and, to achieve an appearance and a sense of unity, a pattern of general service uniform was designed and approved. All this work was accomplished in the first eighteen months of Hutton's command.[10]

These reforms were important steps in laying the groundwork for a properly trained national force. They were largely the result of staff-work at Army and district headquarters which the GOC could direct and supervise without excessive interference from the Civil Branch. Nor were they related specifically to the imperial scheme which Hutton kept largely to himself. Rather, they were basic organisational improvements which any force, national or imperial, would require.

In July 1902, Hutton set out to form the Royal Australian Artillery Regiment out of artillery regiments and detachments in each state. He also organised the various submarine mining units and the field and electrical companies in each state into the Corps of Australian Engineers. Similar action was taken with the members of the various medical services and units by forming the Australian Army Medical Corps on a provisional basis; it was established permanently one year later.[11] These developments were relatively easy to accomplish because the elements of the new national organisations already existed in the colonial military forces before federation. Plans were also made to establish the Australian Army Service Corps, a Veterinary Department and a Chaplains' Department. Elements of these organisations already existed in some states, but the limited capacity of headquarters staff forestalled formation of national bodies at this stage.[12]

However, the establishment of an Ordnance Department and Ordnance Store Corps presented the GOC with difficulties of a different kind.[13]

The men who comprised the various organisations responsible for the custody and supply of military stores were predominantly civilian employees of the Department of Defence and, therefore, not subject to the GOC's military jurisdiction; only in New South Wales were a few storemen also members of the militia. The stores function was administered by the Civil Branch of the department. In an attempt to gain control of military stores, Hutton issued a general military order that the civilian members would be enlisted as militia and form the Ordnance Store Corps.[14] In this, however, the GOC was exceeding his authority and the order was ignored. Two years later no Ordnance Store Corps existed and Hutton was still fighting, without success, to gain control of the supply functions of the Department of Defence.[15] It would be nearly twenty years before an Ordnance Corps was finally established.[16]

As commendable as Hutton's argument for the military commander to control military stores was, he was unable to defeat determined opposition in the Civil Branch of the department. The issue at stake was not so much the enhancement of the defence capability but rather the preservation of power and prestige on a corporate and personal level. Similar resistance was to arise when the GOC tried to introduce structural changes and reforms to the established military units.

Hutton's plans to organise and reform the military forces and their practices called for significant, far-reaching changes. Disruption to the force was inevitable. Yet, in giving his approval to Hutton's proposals late in 1902, Forrest stipulated both that there was to be no overall reduction in the number of citizen soldiers, and that any redistribution of men was to be carried out with as little 'inconvenience or hardship to Corps as possible'.[17] Establishment of the field force and the garrison force commenced on 1 January 1903, with Forrest assuring the press that these new military organisations were intended for the 'internal defence of Australia'.[18] However, as subsequent events illustrate, the minister was as ignorant of the true purpose of the field force as he was of the radical changes its introduction entailed. Hutton had no intention of enlightening him, and at this stage Forrest had not seen the comments by the Colonial Defence Committee explaining that the justification for establishing the field force was imperial service. It seems that no one, least of all Forrest, was prepared for the upheaval which would result from the introduction of Hutton's scheme.

As various reports of inspections reveal, the standard and efficiency of citizen force units in 1902 varied greatly. Some were highly competent military organisations, but a few were little more than social clubs formed by men with little or no previous military experience. Most units had evolved as a result of the interest and motivation in several communities throughout the country. For this reason, and because of their strong regional association, they tended to consider themselves as individual units rather than integral components of a larger force. In varying degrees, many units therefore resented the loss of their identity as they were forced to conform with Hutton's national design: weapons, organisations, roles and, in the case of the Melbourne Cavalry Corps, independence were jealously guarded.

The Melbourne Cavalry Corps had been established late in the colonial period without any meaningful consideration of its role, its organisation and its relationship to the rest of the Victorian force. A Melbourne businessman, Alexander Rushall, had been the driving force behind the Corps, believing it would be 'an attractive one to Huntsmen and other Gentlemen around the city'.[19] But, in 1903, Rushall resisted the GOC's order that the Melbourne Cavalry Corps was to become a squadron of a light horse regiment in the nationally organised force. Writing to the chief staff officer at Army headquarters, Colonel John Hoad, Rushall asserted that his unit was 'to retain its own distinct command as a CAVALRY CORPS and not be connected with the Light Horse'. Therefore, 'to avoid complication and misunderstanding in the future', Lieutenant Rushall requested Army headquarters to approach the Minister for Defence for confirmation that his unit was to remain an independent cavalry force. Rushall also wanted ministerial approval for his unit to retain its unique establishment and its self-styled uniform, but he still expected stores and equipment to be provided at public expense.[20]

Understandably, Hutton was furious when he saw Rushall's letter. It was a direct challenge to his authority as GOC. 'I consider that the tenor of this young officer's minute is highly improper and should not have been submitted to me,' Hutton raged.[21] Now that the matter had been brought to the attention of the GOC, Alexander Rushall quickly recanted. The Melbourne Cavalry Corps became No. 6 Squadron, 10th Australian Light Horse Regiment.[22]

Hutton's reforms also upset the New South Wales Lancers who, as Labor Party leader John Watson observed sarcastically, 'are encouraged to prance round in fine uniforms with a pig-sticking instrument on their arm'.[23] Hutton agreed with Watson that the Boer War had demonstrated that the lance was no longer a suitable weapon for a military force. Writing to Lieutenant Colonel Burns in August 1902, Hutton had pointed out more tactfully than Watson, that to retain the lance as the primary weapon was 'to go back to the days of the Peninsular'. According to Hutton's plans, all Australian mounted troops would be converted to mounted infantry where horses provided mobility but the soldier fought dismounted with a rifle as his primary weapon. Hutton believed that the South African war had established the important tactical principle which supported his proposal. The increasing rapidity and range of gun and rifle fire combined with the improved concealment achieved with smokeless powder meant that troops of all descriptions had to operate in open formations.[24] The cavalry charge in close formation could no longer be considered a standard procedure for

An Army for a Nation

battlefield tactics. The GOC had therefore decided that mounted infantrymen would carry their rifles not in a bucket as cavalry, but across their backs with a sling. In deference to the traditions and *èsprit de corps* enjoyed by the Lancers, however, he recommended to the government that, although the unit would convert to the operational role of mounted infantry, they could retain the lance, but only as a secondary weapon. In practice this would mean that the lance would have little more than ceremonial value. In future, the GOC also decided, the unit would be called: 'Australian Light Horse (New South Wales Lancers)', thus signifying its new tactical role while acknowledging its cavalry origins.[25]

Despite the GOC's concessions, Burns was not happy and requested Hutton to reconsider the proposed changes. The change of name to Light Horse and the carriage of the rifle on the soldier's back, contrary to cavalry practice, were the 'most vital points' in the commanding officer's opinion.[26] Underlying the protest by Burns was an obvious desire for the unit to retain its tactical role as cavalry rather than convert to mounted infantry. But Hutton was adamant that it 'would be an anomaly for Australia to maintain a Lancer Regiment'. He insisted that 'the firearm must be made the first weapon'.[27]

The Lancers were not about to give in to the GOC's wishes. Hutton was soon made aware of strong opposition to his proposed changes from the officers and men of the unit.[28] The Premier of New South Wales, John See, also intervened with a request to the Prime Minister that the unit be designated as a lancer regiment and not light horse.[29] The resistance from the Lancers amounted to a direct challenge to the authority of the GOC as commander of the military forces. Hutton could not relent without a serious loss of credibility. He therefore insisted that the change in unit designation would occur as originally planned: the unit would retain the name New South Wales Lancers but it would also be allocated the Commonwealth designation of Australian Light Horse.[30] Hutton was obviously not about to concede the underlying argument on the operational role of the unit. Probably to allow Burns to save some face, however, it was decided that, instead of the rifle being carried on the soldier's back as Hutton had originally decreed, it would now be 'partly borne on men's shoulder and partly in [a] bucket on [the] near side of [the] horse'.[31] It was a pettifogging compromise, but obviously the GOC realised that some concessions were necessary if the co-operation of the unit was to be retained; the mounted regiments were the centre-piece of his imperial plan and therefore worthy of special attention. As Hutton informed Lord Roberts, the desire to retain the lance was so strong that had he abolished it altogether the Lancers would have disbanded.[32]

Parochialism could be an undesirable characteristic of citizen force units. The retention of the lance was an anachronism which was obvious to men of such diverse backgrounds and experience as Hutton and Watson. Yet

The GOC and the Australian Military Force

dedicated, sensible men in the Lancers reacted with emotion rather than reason to the direction that they adopt more appropriate weapons related to a modified tactical role. Burns and members of his unit challenged Hutton's reasonable plea that, as GOC, he must 'ask all ranks of the Military Forces of the Commonwealth to realise that each and all must be prepared to sink personal interests and individual wishes whether Regimental or otherwise for the general good of the whole Force'.[33] Like Alexander Rushall, Burns had to be persuaded to accept this principle. It would have been absurd for Hutton not to have had his way on the matter, but the Lancers did have more substantial grounds to object to another aspect of his reforms. In order to raise the large number of mounted regiments for the field force, the GOC decided to split the Lancers and another prominent mounted unit, the Australian Horse, into two separate units each, so establishing a recruiting basis for four complete regiments.[34] This decision was bitterly resented by the Lancers, but the GOC was unmoved and rejected their pleas to change his mind.

According to Hutton's plans for the two units to be formed from the Lancers, one regiment would have squadrons in Parramatta, Canterbury, Hawkesbury and Sydney and the other regiment would have squadrons located in the Hunter Valley. 'It seems hard after the big struggle we have had to get up to our present position,' Burns wrote to one of his officers, 'that we should be altered and chopped about as proposed.'[35] The Lancers were efficient and enjoyed a high level of *ésprit de corps* so their anger at the breakup of their unit can be understood. Furthermore, there were serious doubts that the Hunter Valley could provide sufficient recruits for a second regiment.[36] But Hutton would not relent, prompting a bitter outburst from Burns.

'If we are to be expunged as a Regt. [sic] it will be I think better to die game and not allow ourselves to be split up, and mutilated beyond recognition,' Burns wrote to one of his officers.[37] As determined as these words were, however, there was little that could be done to stop the GOC. Reductions in the military estimates by the government, for which he believed the Labor Party largely responsible, and 'General Hutton's action in making so many radical changes . . . has almost wrecked the whole business,' Burns despaired in July 1903. The Hunter Valley regiment 'would not amount to one good Squadron when brought together, though of course General Hutton can call it a Regiment, or Brigade, or anything he likes,' he concluded in disgust.[38]

Although upset by Hutton's proposals, the Lancers were not dealt with as harshly as other units. It was the established infantry regiments which suffered most as a result of the GOC's scheme. Once again, the primary cause of the trouble was the imperial function which Hutton envisaged but which he could not admit as the rationale for his reorganisation. A preponderance of mounted units were to be included in the field force and, as a result, infantry units would be disbanded to make way for them.

Hutton had drawn up a prescription for the new mounted regiments which went beyond mere considerations of efficient military organisation. It was his intention that the light horse would be comprised of Australians who had worked with horses throughout their lives. The suitability of such men for military operations had made a lasting impression on Hutton during his earlier command of the colonial forces of New South Wales. 'The mounted troops, Cavalry and Mounted Rifles, are recruited from the small farmers, the stock-men, and boundary riders, who, living in the saddle, seem to take naturally to their military duties,' Hutton had informed the British Military Society shortly after his return from Australia in 1896. In addition to their being '[f]ine horsemen', Hutton believed they were 'hardy, self-reliant, and excellent marksmen, . . . the *beau ideal* of Mounted Riflemen'.[39] This is why the GOC disapproved of the recruiting method used by the federal government to raise the 1st, 2nd, 3rd and 4th Battalions of Australian Commonwealth Horse for the Boer War. These units were raised before Hutton arrived in Australia by enlisting men in the metropolitan areas. The next four battalions were raised under Hutton's direction with care being taken to draw recruits from the rural areas who were, in the main, already members of mounted citizen units.[40] The GOC knew that the rural mounted units were comprised mostly of men 'employed in the agricultural or pastoral industries' and therefore proposed to continue to employ the same principles to raise new mounted regiments.[41] His attempt to raise the additional regiment on the Lancer remnant in the Hunter Valley is a practical example of this approach.

In conjunction with this plan to recruit experienced horsemen in rural districts, the GOC was also determined to increase the standard of training of the mounted force. Australia's new mounted regiments, Hutton had promised Brodrick, would be available for imperial service. To overcome the problem of limited training which he had noted during his initial inspections and to begin bringing the mounted force to an operational standard, the GOC increased its annual camp training from four days' duration to eight days.[42] Significantly, although Hutton had considered a similar measure for the field artillery, no other section of the military forces had its camp training increased.[43] The reason was almost certainly that the civil occupations of the majority of artillerymen precluded their attendance at camps of longer duration. Hutton was not oblivious to this problem. On the contrary, he advised 'that only officers and men should enrol themselves in Light Horse Regiments who can find time, by reason of their civil occupations, to attend for eight days per annum for consecutive and continuous instruction at a Camp of Training'.[44] As the GOC was aware, the longer duration camps suited those men involved in primary industry.[45] It did not concern Hutton that many men from other occupations would find

The GOC and the Australian Military Force

it difficult to participate in the camps. The indirect process of occupational selection accorded with his plan. Indeed, as the implementation of Hutton's scheme to raise eighteen light horse regiments proceeded, his preference for recruiting men involved in primary production became more apparent.

Part-time military service was popular in rural areas, largely because it was one way of relieving the boredom of country life. Yet most citizen soldiers throughout the country areas of Australia were members of infantry, not mounted, units. The reason was that to join a mounted unit a recruit had to provide his own horse and, in country towns especially, not all men were in a position to do so. In many instances it was not just a question of having access to a property on which a horse could be kept, but rather one of having sufficient financial means to buy and maintain the animal. And if they bought a horse, they could not use it to earn income in their civil occupations. As a result, mounted service was generally not appropriate for the tradesmen, school teachers, shopkeepers, labourers and bank clerks of the country towns.

This did not mean that all members of mounted units were wealthy men. Some were—especially the officers—and kept horses for recreation; some came from small properties where horse ownership was necessary for their livelihood; some were rural workers whose horses were supplied by their employers; and, in a few instances, some men simply borrowed a horse. But, as Hutton observed, most members of mounted units were engaged in agricultural or pastoral pursuits. In contrast with town-dwellers, horses were assets which helped such men earn their income. The two major arms of the military forces—infantry and mounted—therefore reflected the division in rural society of the town-dwellers and those who lived and worked on properties. It was a division which invited antagonism and, whether justified or not, encouraged the perception that, socially, the mounted service was a cut above its pedestrian counterpart.

The possibility that a commission agent of the rural town of Maitland, Captain William Markwell of the New South Wales Lancers, might be nominated as the commanding officer of Hutton's new mounted regiment, which was to be located in the Hunter Valley, prompted a fellow officer to register his concern confidentially with James Burns. The appointment 'would not be a success owing to [Markwell's] social position which he only holds thro' his connection with the Lancers', the officer informed Burns, adding: 'we had . . . previous experience . . . that placing a man at the head of a cavalry regiment . . . who is not on a social standing with other officers will never work.' If Markwell's appointment was confirmed then some officers would resign and other officers would refuse to serve under him, Burns was told. Such social qualifications did not, however, apply to the other major arm of the forces. As Burns' confidant informed him, 'it is different with an Infantry Regiment'.[46] The social perceptions

139

An Army for a Nation

Men of the part-time militia forces in Goulburn, New South Wales, in the 1890s. Rural infantry units like this were popular with townsmen because the men did not have to own a horse to be members. (NATIONAL LIBRARY OF AUSTRALIA)

and evaluations surrounding the two major arms of the forces were a virulent source of jealousy and friction.

Consequently, Hutton's plans to raise additional mounted regiments from men engaged in rural occupations promised to arouse deep resentment, especially since many established infantry units would be disbanded to compensate for the growth of the mounted force. Members of the disbanded infantry units would not only have to buy horses but also find a way around the additional barrier of extended-duration camps before they could join the new regiments, something their occupations generally did not permit. For many infantrymen it would mean the end of their military service. Implementation of Hutton's organisations was therefore a divisive issue for rural Australia.

Early signs of discontent arose in March 1903 in the Monaro district of southern New South Wales. A local building contractor, Lieutenant Herbert Mawson, had recently assumed command of the Cooma-based K Company, 2nd Infantry Regiment, but Army headquarters failed to promote him. Evidently, Hutton did not believe Mawson was a satisfactory officer for a new unit he planned to raise in the district.[47] The local newspaper, the *Cooma Express*, was upset and gave Mawson strong support. It reported that Army headquarters was attempting 'to foist upon the Cooma Company some of Hutton's hobble-de-hoy hoodlums from the ranks of Monaro's tinpot swelldom, as officers, over the heads of competent members of the Company who were honestly entitled to the positions'.[48] Further resentment

The GOC and the Australian Military Force

surfaced in the town when it was learned that Hutton planned to disband the local infantry unit and establish a squadron of light horse in the Monaro district with Cooma as the headquarters. But Hutton was unperturbed by the expressions of local concern. The GOC curtly dismissed them with the comment that he could 'quite conceive that this change is not consistent with the ideas of some of the existing members of the Infantry Company, more especially so if they are Townsmen'.[49]

A petition from Cooma residents, supported by the local member of parliament, Austin Chapman,[50] failed to prevent the closure of the 57-man infantry unit and the establishment of a mounted force in its place. The *Cooma Express* reacted bitterly and, displaying resentment aroused by social friction, criticised 'the Military Mogul Hutton's determination to kill the spirit of Volunteers in the Commonwealth amongst the classes from whose ranks the infantry are taken'. 'Aristocratic Hutton has an object besides military reform in his swelled noddle,' the newspaper warned. 'He desires, it is quite evident, to form swell companies, and for this reason he is determined to convert as many as is possible of the infantry companies into mounted Corps, where the common herd cannot hope to join.'[51]

Major Granville de Laune Ryrie, a grazier of Michelago and an officer in the 1st Australian Horse Regiment since his first appointment as a 2nd Lieutenant in 1898, supervised the recruiting of troops for the new mounted unit. One problem Granville Ryrie encountered was the selection of officers. He found that it was 'with the greatest difficulty that even one gentleman suitable for a commission [was] obtained at Cooma'.[52] It was not Herbert Mawson. Mawson's military career was at an end and he was placed on the unattached list of officers in July 1903. The new man appointed as an officer for the Cooma unit was Harold Ryrie, Granville's cousin and also a local grazier. Granville believed that no other resident of Cooma was suitable for appointment as an officer. He also rejected many applicants for enlistment in the ranks for the reason that they did not own a horse or were 'deemed ineligible as being too old or otherwise undesirable'. It was therefore decided that only one mounted troop, with an establishment of eighteen men, would be raised at Cooma.[53] As the *Cooma Express* fumed, the infantry company of some 60 men was being disbanded in favour of 'a dozen-and-a-half of tin-pot squatters and swell gents'.[54] Granville Ryrie recommended that a second troop could be raised in the nearby rural hamlet of Bredbo.[55] Like Cooma, Bredbo was on the railway line and was therefore accessible to visitors and instructors but, as Finn advised, Bredbo could also 'furnish a very suitable gentleman to command the troop'.[56] Hutton agreed. The two new troops would join with one at Bungendore and another at Michelago—both formerly of the 1st Australian Horse—and together they would form No. 2 Squadron, 3rd Australian Light Horse Regiment.[57] Granville Ryrie was promoted to the rank of lieutenant colonel and appointed as commanding officer of the new regiment.

There was 'too much of a disposition to give the "toney" classes the plums of the service,' Chapman complained to the House of Representatives as a result of the changes at Cooma. Men had to leave the military forces, he continued, because they were 'too poor to provide horses for themselves'.[58] Henry Willis, the federal member for the New South Wales rural seat of Robertson, made similar representations for the infantry units in the rural towns of Dubbo and Wellington. 'Practically they have been disbanded,' he protested, 'inasmuch as their members are unable to provide themselves with horses at their own expense.' Emphasising the waste, he added that all were competent horsemen and four or five of the men from Wellington had each served as infantrymen for nearly nineteen years.[59] One of them, Staff Sergeant Rose, had been winner of the rifle shooting competition for New South Wales in 1901 and 1902.[60]

The military authorities were not oblivious to the loss of experienced men. Major Maurice Hilliard, a young professional officer from the military district headquarters in Sydney, paid a visit to Wellington and, according to the *Wellington Gazette*, had the unpleasant task of telling 'his comrades that their services [were], to a great extent, dispensed with'.[61] Yet the changes continued and the protests persisted. In northern New South Wales the council clerk at Glen Innes pleaded in vain that the local infantry company of the 4th Infantry Regiment 'has been established some sixteen years and has always been kept up to its full strength and in a high state of efficiency'.[62] In southern Queensland, the member of federal parliament for the seat of Moreton, James Wilkinson, explained that the two companies of the 4th Darling Downs Infantry Regiment at Boonah and Lowood might be able to convert to mounted service but this would not, 'on account of the cost and inconvenience of keeping horses', be the case with the two companies at the coal-mining centre of Ipswich.[63]

The protests at the closure of infantry units in New South Wales and Queensland were also echoed in Victoria. In August 1903, Allan McLean, the member of federal parliament for the rural seat of Gippsland, drew Forrest's attention to the problems caused by the implementation of Hutton's organisation. Nearly 300 men from the Victorian Rangers would have to cease being infantrymen and become light horsemen. Like many of their counterparts throughout Australia, McLean continued, it was a conversion most of the men were unable to make because of the amount of time demanded for training and the requirement of horse ownership.[64] Yet the inevitable result had been contemplated by Hutton over a year previously when he had outlined his plans for his chief staff officer, Colonel John Hoad. The Rangers, Hutton confidentially informed Hoad in May 1902, would be 'either reconstructed into Light Horse or abolished altogether'.[65]

Only the imperial objective, still hidden, made good sense of Hutton's vigor in implementing these changes, and the full extent of the GOC's intentions were never explained to the government or the public. Politicians

The GOC and the Australian Military Force

like McLean could not understand why the men were being forced out of the military forces, especially since they were excellent horsemen and some 200 of them had served in South Africa.[66] As a result of McLean's complaint, the military district headquarters in Victoria reviewed the impact the proposed changes would have on the Rangers. There were four companies of the unit located at Echuca, Dandenong, Sale and Kerang with a total membership of 312 men. Enquiries revealed that less than 90 of the men would convert to light horse. The worst case was Echuca, where none of the 88 men in the company would become a light horseman.[67] It worried Hutton little. 'If the Company and Rangers at Echuca are not prepared to transfer their services to the Squadron of Light Horse allotted to that District,' the GOC observed, 'it will be better to allow them to dissolve.'[68] Brigadier Joseph Gordon, commandant of the forces in Victoria, anticipated a similar fate for the company at Kerang where only twelve of the 87 members would transfer.[69]

As in the case of Cooma, the misgivings of the local community were reported in a local newspaper, the *Kerang New Times*. Upset by the imminent closure of the Ranger company, the newspaper considered that the district could support both an infantry and a light horse unit. The company of Rangers should be retained for the townspeople of Kerang because there were 'plenty of farmers' sons, possessing mounts, in the locality ready and willing to join the mounted forces as opportunity offers', it reported.[70] Similar sentiments were expressed by another local newspaper, the *Kerang Observer*, which complained that, in addition to the initial expense of buying a horse, there was a continual commitment for feed and grooming. For these reasons, the newspaper reported, 'town residents, as a rule, find a bike a much more economical and useful method of locomotion than a saddle horse, and, if they join the mounted arm of the service they will have to keep a horse for that purpose alone'.[71]

However, the turmoil in the ranks of the rural infantry units was only one problem confronting the forces. In July 1903, another issue concerning the sensitive issue of pay suddenly erupted. In his report of April 1902 on Australian defence, the GOC had proposed that the field force would be comprised of militia who received pay for their service while the garrison force would be comprised of volunteers who received no pay.[72] It was a calculated decision which was obviously designed to enhance the efficiency of the field force at the expense of the garrison force. But pay served a vital function in the maintenance of an efficient citizen force in Australia. The Commonwealth was obliged to pay citizen soldiers amounts which were comparable with the rates received in their civil employment because a number of men had to pay a substitute to do their work when they were attending full-day, or even half-day, parades. If they were not paid then many soldiers would be out of pocket as a result of their military service.[73]

At the start of the 1903–4 financial year, the pay of members of those militia infantry units, which were now allocated to the garrison force, ceased, creating a serious morale problem. Yet it was obvious that the minister had not foreseen the problem. It was a further example of Forrest's failure to understand the full extent of the proposals which he had authorised the GOC to introduce. The issue was most acute in Western Australia, South Australia and Tasmania, where all citizen soldiers previously had received either pay or allowances.[74]

On 9 July Colonel Tom Price, the commandant of Queensland, sent a telegram to Army headquarters advising that 'serious opposition will follow and I doubt success' of changes which meant that pay had ceased for the 3rd and 5th Infantry Regiments of Queensland.[75] 'I do not like to prophecy [sic] evil,' the commandant of Western Australia similarly warned, 'but if a purely volunteer system is to be introduced for the infantry, I am afraid there will be very few of that arm in Western Australia, this opinion is shared by every Officer in the State.'[76] John Kirwan, federal member of parliament for Kalgoorlie, also protested to Forrest on behalf of the 5th Infantry Battalion of Western Australia—the Goldfields Battalion. The cessation of pay, Kirwan advised, would mean 'the death blow to our Battalion for our ranks are recruited from working miners and a good deal of expense is entailed by each man to keep up a state of efficiency'.[77] From South Australia there were more complaints. The commandant, Lieutenant Colonel John Lyster, informed Army headquarters that, with the exception of Adelaide, 'the principal Towns in this State do not contain a population who have either spare time or means to enable them to serve without remuneration'.[78] Indeed, the headquarters in Adelaide had already received a complaint from the commanding officer of the 1st Infantry Battalion at Gladstone informing it that men in his unit were 'wage earners who cannot afford to give their time without remuneration'.[79]

Taken by surprise, the minister sought an explanation from Hutton. 'The conversion of the infantry allotted to the Garrison forces throughout Australia to Volunteers,' the GOC responded to Forrest's request, 'was an essential of my Scheme of organization having in view the retrenchments desired by the Govt.'[80] But this was misleading advice. Hutton had proposed that the garrison force would be comprised of unpaid volunteers in April 1902, before the suggestion of financial reductions arose one month later. The minister's poor understanding of Hutton's scheme thus allowed the GOC to shift blame for the pay problem from himself to the government. Without questioning the advice given by Hutton, Forrest then tried to solve the problem. He decided that the two infantry regiments in Queensland would immediately have pay restored,[81] but the units in Western Australia and South Australia were not so fortunate.[82]

The decision not to restore pay to the two smaller states was influenced by the peculiarities of the financial arrangements between the Commonwealth and the states. The first federal government was firmly committed to a policy of imposing no taxes but relied on customs and excise duties for revenue. Previously, these duties had been the major source of revenue for the colonial governments, so under Section 87 of the Constitution, three-quarters of the net revenues from the duties raised in each state had to be paid by the Commonwealth directly to the state governments. From the remaining quarter of the revenue, the Commonwealth deducted amounts for federal services, including defence, with separate accounts being kept for each state. The residue was then paid to each state government for state development on a monthly basis under Section 89 of the Constitution. This was a vital issue, and without some such arrangement there could have been no federation.[83]

For the sake of federal harmony it was therefore prudent for the Commonwealth, by restraining expenditure on federal services, to return as much revenue as possible, particularly to the smaller, less-developed states. This was the policy pursued by the Treasurer, Sir George Turner.[84] For this reason, the federal government had given directions for defence expenditure to be minimised in South Australia, Western Australia and Tasmania during the previous financial year.[85] The unforeseen result of Hutton's plan not to pay members of the garrison force in Western Australia and South Australia was therefore upheld by the government. However pleasing this might have been for the governments in those states, for the citizen soldiers affected it was a provocative decision. Their interests had been ignored in favour of Commonwealth–state relations. But even worse treatment was handed out to the citizen soldiers of Tasmania. In this instance, cabinet agreed to a special request from the Tasmanian government not to pay any citizen soldier in that state—garrison force or field force—during the 1903–4 financial year.[86]

Like his mainland counterparts in Queensland, Western Australia and South Australia, the commandant of the forces in Tasmania, Lieutenant Colonel Ernest Wallack, was quick to protest. 'I have consulted Commanding Officers on this subject, and they are unanimous that, however willing the men may be to devote the necessary time, they simply cannot afford to do so, as it would mean a direct loss of income to them,' he wrote to Army headquarters. 'Many men can only get away for whole or half-day parades by paying for a substitute to take their place in factories, shops, or on farms; and this they are unable to do unless they receive pay for their military work.'[87] Understandably, the citizen soldiers of Tasmania were particularly resentful because they were treated differently from the soldiers in the other states where members of the field force received pay.[88]

Despite the protest from Wallack, the decision not to pay the forces in Tasmania was upheld. Forrest failed to protect the interests of Tasmania's citizen soldiers just as he had failed to defend the garrison force in Western Australia and South Australia from Hutton's scheme. In the case of Tasmania, the minister claimed, the decision not to pay the men was taken on the grounds of economy and the urgent plea of the Tasmanian government,[89] which was determined to gain the maximum revenue possible from the federal government. Forrest simply deferred in this matter to Sir George Turner and ignored the interests of the soldiers.[90] His acquiescence was incredible, especially since he was well aware of the necessity of pay to a large number of citizen soldiers. The decision taken for Western Australia, South Australia and Tasmania could only result in the deterioration of units in those states, increasing the despondency arising from Hutton's attack on the infantry units. Towards the end of 1903, therefore, the morale of the military forces was in decay throughout Australia.

The task facing Hutton on his assumption of the command of the Australian forces had not been simple. He first had to establish Army headquarters and then begin the long process of introducing a national organisation to what had been six separate colonial forces. At one level he was an undoubted success. He dealt promptly, energetically and effectively with the fundamental requirements of formal establishments, standardised training and uniform practices. To this extent, Hutton justified the decision of the Australian government to appoint an experienced military officer from Britain. But difficulties arose when Hutton confronted the insular outlook of some units; they were reluctant to take a broader, national perspective. On superficial issues, for example (as discussed above), Hutton compromised with the Lancers, allowing the unit to retain its name and the lance as an accoutrement but not as a primary weapon. Significantly, however, the far more radical matter of splitting the regiment and changing its tactical role was pushed through by Hutton regardless of the anguish of members. He was equally ruthless in dealing with the infantry units on which the brunt of his reorganisation fell.

The key to both his radical methods and his ruthless haste was the imperial objective—the obsession which Hutton so largely concealed from his Australian political masters. Motivated by the need to establish his mounted force for imperial operations, spurred on by the government's intention of reducing defence expenditure and knowing that his term of appointment would expire at the end of 1904, the GOC implemented his scheme with a haste and determination that accepted the risk of alienating a large number of men. In the brief period from January to September 1903, Hutton introduced sweeping changes which brought the forces to a state of trauma.

Yet the fault was not all Hutton's. Forrest was also to blame for the state of the forces in 1903. His inexperience, diffidence and, at times, indolence, made him a poor administrator of the defence portfolio. Hutton realised quickly that he could mislead Forrest with little difficulty. The ease with which the GOC blamed the government for the cessation of pay for the garrison force is a prime example. But as Hutton was to discover at the

The GOC and the Australian Military Force

end of Forrest's tenure of the defence portfolio, there were limits to the minister's malleability and patience. Forrest, obviously disturbed by the radical nature of developments within the military forces and by his own impotence, began to look for ways to relieve himself of his dependence on the GOC as his sole source of advice. Indeed, it was Forrest himself who finally lost patience and took the first small step in what would become a powerful parliamentary challenge to the excesses of the GOC.

8
The civil reaction: From GOC to military board, 1903–1905

The power and authority vested in the position of GOC were significant factors assisting the achievement of Hutton's imperial objectives in Australia. This important point had been discussed by Joseph Chamberlain and Hutton before Hutton's departure from London to take up his Australian posting. Concerned about constraints which might be placed on Hutton's authority, both men had feared that Australia might imitate the British model of a GOC's role, which left a commander-in-chief so constrained as to make him 'practically the Chairman of a Committee'.[1] It was clear to Hutton at least that if he was to implement his imperial scheme, he might have to find ways to exceed even the constitutional limits to his powers.

Hutton had come to Australia determined not to fail. Weighing heavily upon him was his promise to King Edward, Mr St John Brodrick and Lord Roberts to organise an Australian mounted force of 20 000 men for imperial operations. With characteristic determination he had planned at the outset to implement his scheme with or without the approval of the Australian government. It was a daring course of action but Hutton had decided to proceed 'at any cost' to himself.[2] However, as his radical organisation and his reforms began to alienate large numbers of people, it was at the cost of a mounting civil reaction to the extent of his power and authority. The way in which the tide was beginning to turn against Hutton was illustrated by the reaction to one of his decisions immediately before the annual camp of Easter 1903.

Without giving prior notice, Hutton placed a young professional officer from Army headquarters, Lieutenant Colonel George Lee, in command of a

The Civil Reaction

mounted militia brigade for the duration of the camp. Normally, the command would have gone to Lieutenant Colonel William Braithwaite of the Victorian Mounted Rifles, the senior militia officer. The militia officers were deeply upset at Hutton's action and an article condemning Lee's appointment was published in the *Herald*. The newspaper report challenged Sir John Forrest to protect the interests of citizen soldiers against 'the impudent claims of professionalism'. If this were not done, the paper warned, 'the Federal Parliament may just as well repeal all existing Defence Acts and Regulations, and proclaim a military dictatorship under Major-General Hutton'.[3]

The article enraged Hutton, especially since he suspected that a brother officer of Braithwaite, Lieutenant Colonel William Reay, was responsible for it. Knowing that Reay held a position on the staff of the *Herald*, Hutton sent for the officer so that he could question him. It was a threatening interview, but Reay, who was news editor, declined to confess any involvement with the article, or indeed, to provide any information about his professional position on the paper. Hutton resented Reay's determination not to submit to his military authority by disclosing information about his civil occupation and terminated the interview by relieving Reay of his military command, placing him 'on leave' and requesting his resignation from the forces.[4] It was a provocative act which inflamed the anger of militia officers.

The incident attracted a good deal of publicity, with Barton and Forrest being drawn into the controversy. Explaining the problem in a letter to the Prime Minister, Forrest maintained that Hutton had not followed the correct procedure because he had issued a general order for Lee's appointment on his own authority as GOC. Yet Lee's command of the militia brigade should have been approved by the Governor-General-in-Council before the general order was promulgated. Despite this breach, Forrest considered that the protest in favour of Braithwaite was unreasonable and supported the GOC's decision to appoint Lee, believing it would improve the standard of training at the Easter camp. Barton agreed with his minister but, in his written reply, reminded Forrest of the cabinet's view that 'exceptional tact and discretion were required' in the administration of citizen soldiers, 'especially during the inauguration of a new system'. He also had more important advice for Forrest. It seems that the Prime Minister had been stung by the *Herald*'s suggestion that Hutton might become a military dictator. In a careful explanation obviously designed for public consumption, Barton reminded Forrest that the powers of the GOC to issue general orders of this nature were circumscribed by the Constitution. It was a mistake, Barton continued, to assume that the role of the minister in relation to the command of the military forces was 'an empty form'.[5] The Prime Minister was anxious to dispel any perception that Hutton's powers were unrestrained. The letters by Barton and Forrest were therefore released to the press.

Hutton was angered when he read the letters exchanged by Barton and Forrest. To begin with, the GOC was unaware of their existence until a special reporter from the *Age* newspaper produced copies of them on his doorstep at 11.30 on the night before they were published. Confessing to Barton that he was 'astonished beyond measure' at this discourtesy, Hutton also expressed his concern that the letters implied that he had exceeded his powers as GOC in a disrespectful, if not negligent, manner.[6] The GOC then wrote to Forrest informing him that he was well aware of the limit to his powers as commander of the military forces under a constitutional government. 'In the absence of hard and fast Regulations I have however in this, and in similar instances,' Hutton wrote, 'to rely upon the Minister to whom I am responsible for directions when in his opinion approval of the Cabinet for any particular action must be obtained.' He reminded Forrest that he had previously shown him a list of all the senior appointments for the Easter camp during earlier discussions and that he had received the Minister's verbal approval. 'I assumed in the absence of any remark to the contrary, that in this instance Ministerial approval was all that was required to cover my action, more especially as the appointments [were] purely temporary, and strictly within the Regulations,' Hutton explained to Forrest.[7]

While Hutton maintained that he believed the verbal approval of the minister to be sufficient, there was no doubt in Forrest's mind that the appointments for the Easter camp required the approval of the Executive Council. As minister he would never approve the promulgation of a general order by the GOC until such formal approval had been given, Forrest explained to Barton in another—this time confidential—letter. Furthermore, while he could remember that Hutton had shown him a list of the camp appointments, he had paid little attention to them during the interview with the GOC because he had anticipated receiving them as recommendations for formal approval. 'I do not, however, remember anything being said as to Lt. Colonel Lee being junior to Lt. Colonel Braithwaite, or even the mention of the latter's name, or, the likelihood of any friction,' Forrest explained to the Prime Minister.[8]

The dispute over the Lee appointment strained the relationship between Forrest and Hutton. Anticipating this outcome, the Governor-General, Lord Tennyson, had written to Hutton at the height of the dispute. Tennyson informed Hutton that he believed Barton and Forrest would support him and that, probably, he could also expect support from the cabinet. But Tennyson was worried about the anger of the Victorian members of parliament— Braithwaite was a respected officer who had devoted a lot of his own time and money to the military forces. The Governor-General therefore counselled Hutton not to be too quick to blame Forrest. If either Forrest or Hutton were forced to resign over the issue, Tennyson was worried that imperial interests would suffer. '[P]ray be careful not to get backs of Forrest and Barton up now—else all the fat will be in the fire,' Tennyson warned

Hutton. 'If you went Ministers would take care not to have any other Imperial officer out even if they could have one for asking.' The Governor-General was emphatic and peremptorily informed Hutton: *'[I]t is your duty whatever happens—I feel convinced—to stay at your post.'*[9]

Despite Tennyson's advice, within a few weeks further difficulties arose between the minister and the GOC. In early May 1903, Hutton learned that, to save money, Forrest had decided to reduce his staff at Army headquarters by one officer. 'I am really not prepared to continue a sisyphus task in which I must fail unless I have assistance of an adequate degree,' Hutton complained bitterly to Tennyson. The GOC considered that he had never received 'any assistance whatever from the Minister or Government, but only consistent and persistent opposition'.[10] To Tennyson's annoyance, Hutton also sent a private letter of complaint to Forrest. 'Forrest is really distressed at your letter to him—doubting his efforts to help you,' Tennyson rebuked Hutton. The Governor-General issued a further warning to Hutton that serious difficulties could arise if he continued to write such letters to the minister.[11] But it was almost too late for such advice. Since March the minister had been trying, without success, to gain Hutton's response to the comments by the Colonial Defence Committee on the field force. In early July, the GOC was still evading Forrest's requests for information, but the minister had reached the limits of his patience. Signs of the deteriorating relationship between the two men surfaced in the Defence Bill which Forrest presented to parliament in July 1903.

Forrest included a provision in the Defence Bill for a board to advise the minister, reasoning that the GOC was currently the minister's sole military adviser and under such an arrangement the minister 'probably may not hear or see all that he would like'.[12] It was an unmistakable sign that Forrest did not trust Hutton completely. Not surprisingly, Hutton found this a disturbing development. When he first learned of it, he informed Forrest that 'the creation of a standing body of this nature [was] in every respect to be deplored', and recommended that the provision be removed from the Bill. He was especially worried that an advisory board might be the first step towards the establishment of some form of controlling council for the forces.[13] Certainly, the minister understood the reason for the GOC's concern. The advice provided by the board might clash with the authority of the general 'with the result that unpleasantness will be created and discipline probably impaired', Forrest noted, but he had made up his mind to proceed with the proposal.[14]

Forrest's board of advice did not go far enough for Samuel Mauger, the Protectionist member for Melbourne Ports. Mauger, who a few days earlier had expressed concern about a public statement by Hutton urging Australians to accept imperial defence responsibilities,[15] proposed the establishment of a council to control the forces rather than simply advise the minister. As Mauger explained it, his proposal was intended 'to a large extent [to take] the control of the forces out of the hands of the general officer commanding'. 'I do not want him to possess anything like the power which he now holds,' Mauger informed the House of Representatives. The forces in Victoria were in a state of 'seething discontent' and there was need for 'a radical change'.[16]

The House of Representatives rejected Mauger's proposal, but a similar suggestion also arose in the Senate. Senator Alexander Matheson proposed the establishment of a council of defence comprised of the minister, the GOC, the commander of the naval force, two members of the Senate and two members of the House of Representatives. He stated that his aims were the introduction of broader political influence into defence matters, the achievement of continuity in defence policy and the provision of more information for parliament because it was 'absolutely impossible for Parliament to get at the truth in connexion [sic] with defence matters under the existing system'.[17] Other senators, also intent on increasing parliament's control of the military forces, spoke in support of Matheson's proposal.

'[Hutton] came here imbued with Imperial traditions, he will leave our shores after a certain period, and take his place again in the Imperial Army,' Senator John Barrett observed. 'So far as I have been able to judge he has not shown that sympathy with the aims and aspirations of the Australian people which I should like to see.' Barrett was not the only senator who thought national interests were neglected by Hutton. 'It is remarkable what very little power Parliament has regarding the regulation of our military and naval affairs,' Senator Miles Staniforth Smith added. 'A clause such as Senator Matheson suggests will more accurately interpret Australian feeling than will an Imperial officer who believes only in professional soldiers.'[18]

Matheson's proposal was narrowly defeated,[19] only to be recommitted two weeks later. This happened after news reached Australia of the report of the Esher Committee appointed to examine Britain's conduct of the Boer War.[20] 'The report of the inquiry into the South African war has made thinking people shudder,' the *Age* newspaper observed. It had revealed considerable mismanagement and bungling in Britain's military affairs. The *Age* agreed with comments in the *London Times* that Britain needed a general staff, a 'brain of the army', which was engaged in the detailed work of planning and preparation for operations. But, significantly, the *Age* also noted that the Esher Committee had foreshadowed a reorganisation of the War Office along the lines of the Board of Admiralty.[21]

Armed with the knowledge that Britain was considering the establishment of a board or council to control its military forces, the Senate reviewed Matheson's proposal. 'In various parts of the world where there are military systems,' Senator William Higgs advised the Senate, 'we find that General Officers Commanding are being abolished in favour of Boards or Councils such as that suggested by Senator Matheson.' Examples were the United States, Germany, France, Switzerland and Japan, Higgs informed the Senate. Senator David O'Keefe added his belief that the position of GOC was inimical to a military force comprised of citizen soldiers. 'While our forces are under the supreme control either of Major-General Hutton . . . or of some other gentleman from the old country who has Imperial notions,' O'Keefe remarked, 'we are not likely to have such attention paid to our citizen soldiery as they deserve.' The debate illustrated that the mood of the Senate had changed marginally as a result of the report of the Esher Committee. After amending Matheson's proposal to reduce parliamentary representation from two members to one member from each House, the Senate narrowly carried an amendment to the Defence Bill to institute a Council of Defence.[22]

Back in the House of Representatives, the debate continued to rage about the method of managing the forces. Members were concerned about mounting evidence of widespread discontent in the ranks while Richard Crouch, the member for Corio, reported that Hutton had 'introduced a system of mounted infantry drill and [was] even training the infantry in that class of work'.[23] While never explaining his intentions to Australians, Hutton had decided to train the infantry regiments as a mounted force in order to provide the 20 000 horsemen whom he had promised to the British authorities. Harbouring suspicions about Hutton's intentions, Crouch came to the same conclusion as James Hume Cook who informed the House a few weeks later that 'by establishing and strengthening the light horse branch of the service, [Hutton] had an eye rather to the utilization of the service of Australians abroad than to any particular service they might render Australia'.[24] However, because Hutton failed to confess his imperial objectives, this remained a subject of conjecture. Of more immediate concern was the knowledge that all was not well in the forces. Responding to questions on the mood in the forces, Austin Chapman, who had assumed the portfolio of defence in recent weeks, acknowledged the serious morale problem but asked for more time 'to find out the cause of the friction'. This was a cautious statement by the minister, who had first-hand knowledge of part of the problem: his electorate of Monaro included Cooma and, six months earlier, he had delivered the petition on the closure of the local infantry company to Forrest. But now that he held the defence portfolio, it is obvious that Chapman wished to create the impression that he was being fair by taking a broad view of the problem and not simply reacting to the wishes of his constituents. Accepting Chapman's promise that he would not hesitate to make any changes necessary to rectify the problem, the House rejected the Senate's amendment for a controlling council in favour of a board of advice.[25]

With some recriminations, the Lower House's actions were subsequently accepted by the Senate. Provision to establish a board of advice for the minister rather than a controlling council was included in the *Defence Act* of 1903.[26] But some members felt that parliament should have introduced stronger measures and Senator O'Keefe warned that: 'If we find that in the future complaints arise similar to those which have been previously made, and there is evidence that the establishment of a Council of Defence will remedy the grievances, we can take action next session to bring such a body into existence.'[27] In October 1903, parliamentary opinion was thus in a state of precarious equilibrium on the question of controlling the military forces, but a series of incidents was soon to push parliament to make a decision.

On the evening of 9 November, Hutton spoke at a Lord Mayor's dinner in Melbourne. Towards the end of the speech, the GOC referred briefly to British recriminations over problems with the conduct of the Boer War. Hutton, not surprisingly, echoed a complaint by Wolseley that the lack of preparation for the campaign was due to excessive meddling in military matters by civilians.[28] As Hutton explained to the audience, the 'civilian had triumphed, and the needs of defence had been subordinated to political considerations'. Hutton then urged Australians to insist upon their military system being placed above party politics and personal interests.[29] Newspaper reports of the speech disturbed the new Prime Minister, Alfred Deakin, who was at the time travelling through rural New South Wales. Deakin, understandably, was offended by Hutton's suggestion that the military forces should be given a free hand and telegraphed Chapman from Glen Innes, asking him to look into the matter.[30] Hardly a momentous incident, it was a clear sign that the relations between parliament and the GOC were entering a new phase. It set the scene for an acrimonious dispute which erupted early in the new year.

One consequence of the enactment of the Defence Bill in late 1903 was the promulgation of military regulations. In January 1904, Chapman nominated the members of a committee to review the newly drafted regulations. While Hutton gave his concurrence to the minister's decision, the military commander was not prepared to accept one of Chapman's selections for the committee.[31] The offending member, Senator Lieutenant Colonel John Neild, was commanding officer of a Sydney-based infantry regiment.

The reason Hutton gave the minister for Neild's removal from the committee was that the standard of discipline in the senator's unit was not what it should be.[32] It was not the first time such a charge had been made;[33] Neild had long been a thorn in Hutton's side. He undoubtedly offended Hutton's military sensibilities—the senator wore a garibaldi beard and loud check suits—but, more importantly, Hutton took exception to statements on military matters that Neild occasionally made in the Senate. According to Neild, Hutton had twice suggested that he should submit his resignation from the forces as a result of such statements.[34] The last occasion was in September 1903, when he had drawn the Senate's attention to the low morale in the forces. 'Persons in high authority, seeking to achieve out-of-the-way results, may consider everything happy and satisfactory,' Neild had remarked, 'but from my knowledge of officers and men I can say positively that the Partially-Paid Forces are in an eminently discontented condition.'[35] As a result, Neild informed the Senate, there had been an alarming drop in membership of the military forces—figures showed a reduction of at least 25 per cent since 1901.[36] He blamed the halt on recruiting but, more significantly, he added that 'an extra number of men have left the force, and a great number have been discharged, while companies and corps have been broken up and disbanded'.[37]

The senator's public statements were a potential source of severe embarrassment for the GOC. Neild was a prominent member of the community and a senior officer in the citizen forces. Obviously, his opinion would have carried some weight in Australia. Hutton would also have been anxious about the likely impact of Neild's statements in Britain where he had been at pains to create a favourable impression of his work in Australia. In November, Hutton had written to Sir Arthur Bigge, private secretary to King Edward, informing him that his military reforms were proceeding well. 'You will, I am sure, be glad to hear with what satisfaction the new Scheme of Military Organisation for Australia has been received generally,' Hutton wrote. 'It has in fact simply astonished me to find such an excellent spirit permeating the whole Force in all the States which has acquiesced in such radical changes as few Troops have been subjected to since the Peninsular War.'[38] To avoid embarrassment, Hutton would have preferred Neild to keep quiet. Instead of silencing the troublesome senator, however, the GOC's actions in seeking his resignation from the forces and removing him from the committee to review the military regulations only provoked further comment under the privilege of parliament.

Early in March, Neild informed the Senate that the recently published military regulations were 'all wrong'. The senator then repeated earlier comments about the poor state of the military forces and their low morale. They had undergone a comprehensive change 'which was called reorganization, but which in many cases was disorganization', Neild told the Senate. The Lancer regiment had been split into two units which 'were greatly below strength' and the former commanding officer, James Burns, had given up 'in disgust'. It had simply not been possible to obtain the number of recruits in New South Wales to man the new organisation, the senator complained. Neild stopped short of blaming Hutton, but the imperial general was obviously the butt of the attack.[39]

Hutton was unable to tolerate Neild's use of parliament to taunt him; it inflamed his dislike for the institution. A week later, when the Minister for Defence asked the GOC to respond to statements on military subjects which emanated from the Senate and the Lower House, Hutton hit out. 'I will candidly confess,' he informed Chapman, 'that I find it difficult to reply to the comprehensive criticism by ill-informed Members of Parliament who have neither had the training nor possess the Military instincts to qualify them as critics in so difficult a profession as that of the Army.'[40] But Hutton had not finished yet. Within two weeks, Senator Neild was informed by district headquarters in Sydney that he had been relieved of his command pending his placement on the retired list of officers.[41]

Many senators were upset by Hutton's action. 'The Major-General might as well march his regiment into the Chamber and pitch us all out,' a deeply-offended Senator Andrew Dawson complained when he seconded Neild's successful motion to establish a Senate Select Committee to examine his sacking.[42] According to Neild, the GOC's action had offended parliamentary privilege. It was a serious charge and, as the subsequent examination revealed, it was not groundless. While the committee found in its report that Hutton had removed Neild from his command 'partly for military reasons', it also believed that the action was taken 'partly in consequence of speeches delivered in the Senate'. Furthermore, it considered that the GOC's 'comments or protests against Senator Neild's speeches . . . [could] . . . be regarded as an attempt to interfere with Senator Neild in the discharge of his duties as a Senator'. In the committee's opinion, however, Hutton's actions 'did not amount to intimidation'.[43] Despite this balanced, perhaps conciliatory, finding, the GOC's indiscretion in challenging the Senate's privilege would not have gone unnoticed by members and can hardly have helped his cause. It happened at a time when problems in the military forces were beginning to receive widespread attention.

In February, nearly 500 citizen soldiers out of a total of some 750 had failed to attend a parade in Hobart as a protest at their lack of pay—367 of them were absent without leave.[44] It was a deeply humiliating experience for Hutton and Chapman, especially since both men were present at the parade in their official capacities. However, Hutton's mortification turned quickly to uncontrollable anger when it was brought to his attention that many of the truant soldiers had attended as spectators, dressed in civilian clothes. While the commanding officer was reduced to weeping, Hutton, to the undoubted delight of the protestors, exploded in a public fit of rage.[45] To be fair, the lack of pay in this instance was no fault of Hutton, but his intemperate behaviour attracted intense interest, doing considerable damage to his reputation.

Reports of the incident spread quickly and the new Governor-General, Lord Northcote, wrote to Hutton asking whether the soldiers were protesting against the actions of the civil administration 'or your own as Commandant of the Federal forces'. Northcote also counselled Hutton that had he taken time to consider his reaction to the protest and not 'threatened punishment in a moment of personal irritation' then he believed the public would have given him its support.[46] Hutton's credibility had suffered as a result of his outburst and, obviously, the Governor-General was upset. In Britain, too, the authorities were starting to have serious doubts about the GOC's performance. In the month following the Hobart incident, Sir Arthur Bigge wrote to Hutton commenting that 'your letters are cheering' but 'lately we

The Civil Reaction

have been told that public opinion is not in sympathy with the Military movement, and that notably in Tasmania the volunteers did not turn out'.[47] Bigge's carefully chosen words can only have unsettled the GOC because they indicated that the King had been told of the problems in the Australian forces. Hutton was now under scrutiny at the highest levels in London. But his most pressing problems were local. The Hobart incident combined with the sacking of Neild worried an increasing number of Australians, giving currency to criticism of his performance as GOC and precipitating further searching questions about the state of the military forces.

The parade in Hobart, according to the *Bulletin*, featured 'a gaudy general, a gorgeous staff, and some purple language, but no soldiery'. Of particular concern to the journal was the recent outbreak of the Russo-Japanese war and the poor state of the Australian forces. 'If the enemy were to throw an invading force into Australia,' the *Bulletin* considered, obviously enjoying the opportunity to poke fun at the GOC, 'practically the only means of warding off the attack would be to mobilise General Hutton and launch him, armed with adjectives, against the foe.' On a more serious note the journal urged the introduction of military reforms which included 'Australian manufacture of Australian arms, universal liability to service, and the training of the army on Australian lines by Australian officers'. In this last measure, the *Bulletin*, yet unable to resist a further flourish of its irreverent humour, recommended '[t]he extension of the Undesirable Immigrants Act to all military instructors from abroad especially British officers'. Although superficially jocular, there was real concern underlying the *Bulletin*'s report.[48]

In a more subdued article in the next issue, the nationalist journal advocated the introduction of the Swiss military system which involved compulsory military training for all men on a part-time basis. In Switzerland, '[t]he army is the nation', the *Bulletin* said, concluding: 'So it should be in Australia'. The *Bulletin*'s call for 'root-and-branch reform' to remedy the rapidly dwindling size of the force[49] was corroborated a month later in April when further probing by Senator Neild revealed that the number of men in the forces was less than 19 000—compared with 29 000 at federation.[50] The move to review the method of managing the military forces was gathering momentum, placing Hutton under mounting pressure.

Struggling to shore up his military command in the face of probing by politicians and widespread dissatisfaction in the forces, Hutton was at pains to present an appearance of unity at Army headquarters. In February he had turned down an application for leave from Colonel John Hoad, his chief staff officer, informing him that he had 'said nothing to anyone' about your request because it would appear that you were 'deserting me and all the difficulties we are now weathering at a critical period of Australian military history'. Instead, he sent Hoad to Tasmania as temporary commander to resolve the problems which had arisen as a result of the reorganisation. It

An Army for a Nation

was a role which suited him. Since the establishment of Army headquarters, Hoad had become a trusted and experienced staff officer. Hutton had served with the Australian officer in the Boer War where he had been impressed by his 'honest and loyal hard work' and, when he had first learned of his appointment as GOC in Australia, he had told Hoad that he looked forward to having him on his staff. Indeed, the Australian officer had performed well in his senior appointment and, in July 1903, Hutton especially thanked him for 'many months of devoted hard work'. The secondment to Tasmania also produced good results and Hutton informed Hoad that the state Governor, Sir Arthur Havelock, 'had written to him in very high terms of his work'.[51] But it was on that very night—24 March 1904—that Hutton suddenly turned on Hoad.

At Ararat railway station, while travelling from Melbourne to Adelaide on the overnight express, the GOC was handed a telegram from the Minister for Defence, Austin Chapman, informing him that the government had selected Hoad for an attachment with the Japanese Army—he was to observe their military operations against Russia.[52] This news upset Hutton a great deal, primarily because the government had used its authority to make an important military appointment without consulting him. Hutton perceived this as a direct challenge to his own authority, undermining his command of the forces. Making matters worse, it seems that Hutton suspected that Hoad had been a party to discussions leading to the appointment. Where he had previously enjoyed the GOC's praise, Hutton now began to vilify Hoad, referring to him as that 'arch intriguer and soldier in buckram'.[53]

Early next morning, before the train arrived in Adelaide, Hutton sent a ciphered telegram to Chapman from Aldgate in the Adelaide Hills, claiming that Hoad had 'signally failed as Chief Staff Officer' and had neither the 'claims nor qualifications' to take up the Japanese appointment.[54] It was a deliberate attempt to discredit Hoad, but not simply because Hutton was miffed. 'My fear is that the prestige which Col. Hoad may acquire by being with the Japanese Army may enable his Labor and Socialistic views to place him in a position where he could do much harm if not upset the [imperial organization for the Australian military forces],' Hutton informed Major General Sir William Nicholson at the War Office, 'and indeed he may be able to do serious mischief in the relations of the Military Forces of the Commonwealth with the Imperial Army.'[55] Hoad, a man of nationalist sympathies, was suddenly seen as a threat to Hutton's imperial plans for the Australian forces. Even if the government did not establish a controlling committee for the forces, it had now occurred to Hutton that he might be replaced by Hoad as GOC. Either outcome was unacceptable to him. '[T]he control of the Military Forces if placed in the hands of a local officer, or in the hands of a Committee composed of local officers, must necessarily . . . be entirely subordinated to the local political and personal influences,' he wrote to Ommanney, informing him of his fears for imperial interests. [56]

The Civil Reaction

Failing to have Hoad's trip to Japan cancelled, Hutton still believed that all was not yet lost. But he did not appreciate the extent of the forces which were now mobilised against him. The day before the Senate agreed to establish the Select Committee to examine Senator Neild's charge, he wrote to Lord Tennyson, whom Northcote had recently replaced as Governor-General, expressing confidence that an imperial general would be appointed to succeed him as GOC. Nevertheless, he had recently become aware of mounting opposition from senior civilian staff in the Department of Defence. He informed Tennyson that 'there is a faction headed by Captain Collins [the Permanent Secretary] and other ignorant or malevolent people who would do away with an Imperial General and substitute a small committee controlled by and under the political party in power'.[57] On the same day he informed Ommanney that Australian officers did not possess 'the military judgements, or educational attainments' necessary to administer the Army. The local officers needed the support of 'the experienced influence and personal characteristics of an Imperial General'.[58] The position of GOC should be preserved, he believed, for the exercise of British influence on Australian military developments.

Hutton immediately attempted to use his influence to undermine the move to replace the GOC by a controlling committee. In his annual report to parliament on 1 May 1904, he argued strongly for a board not to manage the military forces but to co-ordinate the work of the military forces and the Civil Branch of the Department of Defence. This requirement, the GOC reported, was dictated by what he called 'the anxious endeavour' of the Civil Branch 'to resist expenditure of all kinds' even though such intransigence frequently placed defence interests in jeopardy. As paradoxical as Hutton's sudden support for a board might seem, the GOC was still determined to protect his position and power. He recommended that the minister should be president of the board and that the GOC should be vice-president. The five ordinary members of the board would include four senior military officers and the secretary of the department. Emphasising the limits to the board's authority, Hutton advised that it should not 'give decisions, but should merely record their views'. Any matters which normally fell within the jurisdiction of the GOC should not be discussed by this board 'unless [it was] invited to do so', he recommended. The GOC then turned his attention to the suggestion 'that a Committee or Army Council, following on the system recommended by Lord Esher's Committee, should be adopted for the Commonwealth' to replace the position of GOC. A controlling committee of that type, he advised, had no place in Australia. Australian officers did not have the experience and knowledge to sit on such a committee, Hutton reported. 'I see no alternative,' he concluded, 'than for the system now in force to be continued, at least for the present, and for the responsibilities of the General Officer Commanding, as defined in the Military Regulations under the *Defence Act* 1903, to be retained.'[59] As

Hutton wrote these words, however, the issue which would bring on the final rounds of the struggle for control of the forces was settling on the minister's desk.

Quite by chance, it was discovered that Hutton had sent a telegram in code to London. The implications worried Chapman and he requested a copy of the message from Hutton, at least insofar as it related to military business.[60] Responding to the request, Hutton confirmed that the message was certainly on a military subject but, as the telegram had been sent confidentially to the British Secretary of State for War, he was not prepared to provide a copy for the Australian minister.[61] Not to be deterred so easily, Chapman again requested a copy of the message,[62] but before he could take the matter further the Deakin government fell. Probably trying to take advantage of Chapman's demise, Hutton then informed Collins that he was still not prepared to provide a copy of the message because it would divulge 'the secret code' which had been given to him for 'communications direct to the War Office'.[63]

The new Labor Minister for Defence, Senator Andrew Dawson, was not about to let the matter die. He pressed Hutton, who was then touring northern New South Wales and Queensland, for a copy of the message. Only a few weeks earlier, Dawson had supported Neild's case in the Senate. Now he unambiguously informed Hutton in writing that his position as GOC made him a servant of the Australian minister, in this case Dawson himself. 'The right of the Minister to insist that all official communications as regards the Defence of the Commonwealth shall be submitted to him,' Dawson wrote to Hutton, 'cannot for a moment be questioned.'[64] Hutton, perhaps arrested by the stern tone of Dawson's minute, made no immediate public response. This uncharacteristically reserved approach was rudely interrupted, however, when, to Hutton's surprise, reports of the incident were published in the press and he was directed to return to Melbourne for an interview with the minister.[65] Suddenly Hutton was off-balance; his normal tactic of stone-walling ministers would not work on this occasion.

The GOC was in no doubt as to who was orchestrating the campaign against him. It was Collins. His contempt for the permanent secretary was apparent when he wrote to Lord Northcote charging that 'some malicious person in the civil system of Defence' had leaked the information to the press.[66] There can be little doubt that Hutton was correct in these deductions. The leak was certainly put to good use by the *Age* in parading the nationalist case for the abolition of the position of GOC. The Melbourne newspaper reported that, from the imperial perspective, Hutton was 'looked upon as a kind of military proprietor, holding authority delegated entirely by his superior officers at headquarters in London, and entrusted with the duty of keeping the Colonists in their proper places from a military standpoint'. Like almost all of the imperial officers who had come to Australia, the *Age* continued, Hutton gave his first allegiance to the War Office and felt obliged

The Civil Reaction

'only in a very secondary and subordinate sense . . . to consult the wishes of those who have engaged him and pay his salary'. As a result, the military authority considered itself to be 'quite separate from the civil authorities in Australia'. It was this very issue which Lord Esher's commission had addressed in Britain, the report noted. In conclusion, the *Age* consoled itself with the thought that the military forces would soon be controlled by a committee with the minister as president.[67] The newspaper report served notice on Hutton that he was losing the battle. There was only one way out of the immediate dilemma for him. He provided Prime Minister John Watson with a decoded copy of the offending telegram to the War Office.[68]

The reference by the *Age* to the impending establishment of a committee to control the forces was not speculation. The Watson Labor government held power only for the short period of four months, but before relinquishing office, Dawson submitted a report to parliament recommending the abolition of the position of GOC. Instead of a single senior commander, the Labor minister proposed to establish a Council of Defence to assist the government in developing defence policy and a Military Board to control and administer the forces. In his report, Dawson cited the precedent of Britain's recent abolition of the position of commander-in-chief as an obvious attempt to enlist conservative support for his suggestion to do likewise, but, unmistakably, he was motivated primarily by the peculiar difficulties being experienced in Australia.[69] This proposal was what Hutton feared most, and it came from a man whom he despised. Privileged by birth and marriage, Hutton held Dawson, a hard-drinking, poorly educated orphan from Brisbane,[70] in contempt. The GOC was especially embittered by Dawson's earlier outspoken opposition to Australian participation in the Boer War. At the outbreak of the war, Dawson had claimed that Australians who volunteered for service would be 'a mob of swashbucklers' with 'more of the dog nature [in them] than human nature'. Such comments disgusted Hutton and he now believed Dawson to be motivated by similar sentiments as Minister for Defence.[71]

The coded telegram incident was only one of several conflicts during Dawson's brief term as minister. Because the basis of the relationship between Dawson and Hutton was antagonism, and because of the deeper policy differences about national and imperial imperatives in defence planning, what might otherwise have remained minor administrative issues escalated quickly into a serious rift between the minister and the GOC. In May, Surgeon-General Williams, director general of medical services at Army headquarters, wrote to the secretary of the department on behalf of the GOC seeking approval for the expenditure of £15 to procure a pistol from London. The weapon was under consideration as the new pattern of service pistol for the Australian forces.[72] Responding to the request, Collins sought further justification for the purchase for the minister.[73] Not satisfied with the answer given by Williams, Dawson himself intervened with his opinion that it was 'very inadvisable to depart from the Imperial Service pattern' which was currently in service.[74] Hutton was resentful and personally wrote to the minister informing him that in his opinion £15 was an insignificant amount to spend on a trial pistol which he believed to be the best available. 'If the Government require any other opinion than mine upon a subject which for 25 years I have made peculiarly my own,' Hutton concluded in his letter to Dawson, 'I should advise their inviting opinions elsewhere as I am not prepared to submit further recommendations upon this subject.'[75]

The minister was offended by Hutton's provocative stand. 'I desire to point out,' he responded, 'that the GOC, whilst under engagement to this Government . . . will be expected to furnish such reports and information as may be called for by the Minister, and as may be in his power to supply.'[76] The relationship between Dawson and Hutton deteriorated rapidly. 'There appears to be no end to the points of difference which may arise between the Minister of Defence and Major-General Sir Edward Hutton,' the *Argus* observed as an introduction to a report on the pistol issue in July.[77] It was apparent that matters could not continue as they were. A major confrontation between the minister and GOC was averted only by the early demise of the Watson government in August. 'The General Officer Commanding and myself were unfortunately not in touch or in sympathy,' Dawson recorded on the day he left office.[78] The bickering between the minister and the GOC was viewed with interest by the public, their poor working relationship being the subject of several newspaper reports.[79]

Dawson was not the only threat to the survival of the position of GOC. Discontent was so widespread that the outcome was inevitable. Even Hutton had begun to face defeat. Significantly, in so doing he referred not to personal disagreements but to the primary policy issue of his hidden imperial scheme. 'Fostered by the Politicians, in and out of Parliament,' Hutton reflected, 'the Public and the Press were awakening to the fact that the policy upon which I was building their defence was not that of their own creation, and that no Government had ever publicly endorsed the principles laid down [in my original plans for organizing the forces].'[80]

In November, the principle of local control was enacted by the Reid–McLean government, a coalition of conservative Free Traders and Protectionists. The Minister for Defence, Lieutenant-Colonel James McCay, announced new measures to guide and control the defence forces. There had recently been a time of political turmoil in federal politics—three minority governments had been formed in the last twelve months—but McCay, who was an infantry officer in the militia, was careful to point out that the proposals he was about to announce were the result of work undertaken not only by himself, but also by his two predecessors in office, Chapman and Dawson. Subject to the approval of parliament, the development and implementation of defence policy, naval and military, would rest with a

The Civil Reaction

committee, the Council of Defence, which included the minister, the federal treasurer, an inspector-general of the military forces, a Naval director, a chief of the general staff and consultative members. Likewise the military forces would be administered by a committee, to be called the Military Board, of which the minister was chairperson. The position of GOC would no longer exist.[81]

Three senior military officers would hold seats on the Military Board. The chief of the general staff would be responsible for the supervision of defence schemes and intelligence matters. The deputy adjutant general would supervise personnel and transport. The third military member would be the chief of ordnance, who would be responsible for armaments and equipment. A civilian finance member and the Minister for Defence, who was the president or chairperson, completed the five-member board. It was envisaged that consultative members would be added as required. Significantly, the Military Board was conceived as a committee in which no military member was to enjoy supreme authority, perceived or endowed.[82] McCay left no doubt on this point when, at the inaugural meeting in January 1905, he instructed members that business was to be despatched in an informal fashion with members participating in discussions 'in a conversational manner without regard to individual seniority'. [83] Final authority in all matters before the board would rest with the minister.

McCay's decision to establish the Military Board was concerned fundamentally with gaining stronger parliamentary control over the affairs of the military forces, but it was more than a simple rejection of Hutton's autocratic style. The changes, as the minister explained, were a deliberate step towards adopting the Swiss military model for Australia because 'the Australian ideal is that our defence should be carried out by citizen forces'. Cabinet would be brought into 'more direct touch with the defence policy of Australia', and the implementation of the policy would be more sympathetic to parliament and the people.[84] But there was at the same time an emphatically nationalist dimension to the changes that McCay only hinted at when he spoke of introducing 'Australian feeling' to defence policy, and of dropping the practice of importing 'large numbers of officers from the Imperial Army'.[85] As Hutton feared, the introduction of the Military Board and the Council of Defence paved the way for national control of the Australian military forces.

Hutton's plans to create an imperial military force were beyond salvage. The Australian forces were in a state of disarray but, worse still for Hutton, the British authorities had also realised the hopelessness of his vision. Earlier attempts by Hutton to interest Brodrick's replacement as Secretary of State for War, Mr Arnold-Forster, in his plans for imperial military defence had been unsuccessful. Even a reminder by Hutton that it was the same scheme which he had presented to the Royal Colonial Institute in 1898, when Arnold-Forster had added his own 'powerful aid to the discussion that took place afterwards', had failed to elicit a response.[86] In August 1904, Hutton was advised that the Secretary of State for War had been too busy to read the papers which Hutton had sent him ten months earlier.[87] Hutton's dream of co-operative imperial defence was at an end.

Returning to the United Kingdom at the end of his appointment in December 1904, Hutton was ignored. In 1906, he complained to Sir George Clarke: 'I have no means of knowing the views or recommendations of the Imperial military authorities in London . . . as I have never received either directly or indirectly or privately, any communication upon the subject of Australia and Australian Defence from the military or colonial defence authorities since my return to England.'[88] He was never again consulted on the question of colonial or imperial defence. For the few remaining years of his military career he was given charge of administration in the Eastern Command and placed in command of the 3rd British Division. With the outbreak of World War I he was recalled from retirement to organise and command the 21st British Division, but in 1915 a riding accident brought a permanent end to his military service. Edward Hutton died in 1923.[89]

At the close of 1904, observers in Britain were uncertain about future military developments in Australia. Joseph Chamberlain, no longer Colonial Secretary, wrote to Lord Northcote in December informing him: 'We have left [the Australians] alone so long that the idea of contribution [to imperial defence] has not taken hold, and I am inclined to doubt whether we ourselves have gone the right way to secure a proper arrangement.'[90] Sir Montague Ommanney shared his former minister's opinion. In August 1904, Ommanney had informed Sir George Clarke that Britain's best hope in getting 'effective aid' from Australians was to encourage them 'to train, arm and equip their local forces so as to secure some small measure of efficiency and some sense of discipline'. 'We are a long way off even this modest standard and it will probably require a Jap invasion or some such salutary lesson to teach Australia that joining a rifle club is not all that is wanted to make a soldier,' Ommanney concluded.[91] Early in 1905, Chamberlain reached a similar conclusion, believing that the prospect of a Japanese victory in their war with Russia might produce more determined military developments in Australia.[92] Hopefully, Chamberlain thought, such developments might yet be turned to Britain's advantage, so assisting imperial defence requirements.

9
The creation of a national defence agenda: Alfred Deakin's plans for a national guard, 1905–1907

From 1905 to 1907 Australians developed a clear perception of the threat to their national security, dramatically despatching the uncertainties and confusion of previous years and promoting a national policy for the development of the defence forces. The incident which precipitated the radical change in Australian attitudes to defence was the resounding Japanese victory over the Russian navy in the Straits of Tsushima in May 1905. Suddenly, a general uneasiness about Asian designs on Australia gave way to the perception that Japan was the major threat to Australian security. Other worrying events, such as the renewal of the Anglo-Japanese treaty in 1905 and the withdrawal of the Royal Navy from the Pacific to the North Sea in response to the build-up in German naval strength, added to this anxiety about Australia's future well-being.[1]

On 12 June 1905, a few weeks after the Japanese victory over the Russian fleet, Alfred Deakin, formerly Prime Minister from September 1903 to April 1904 and now leader of the liberal-Protectionist group of federal parliamentarians, granted an interview to the *Herald* in Melbourne in which he proposed new directions and sounded a new urgency for the development of Australian defence. There was now an increased threat to the security of Australia, he told the newspaper, because of 'the striking growth of three new naval powers—the United States, Germany and Japan'. Australia was within striking distance of no less than sixteen foreign naval stations. 'As a fact,' Deakin stated suggestively, 'Japan is the nearest of all the great foreign naval stations to Australia.' He therefore urged the Australian public to take a greater interest in defence and advised them that 'the Commonwealth must be prepared to spend more liberally than it has ever done on its defence and defence force' in order to provide 'reasonable guarantees of safety to our ports, our cities, and our coasts'.[2]

Deakin confessed that he was not an expert in such matters, but he believed that the Australian forces were 'inadequate in number, imperfectly supplied with war *matériel*, and exceptionally weak on the naval side'. In an oblique reference to Major General Sir Edward Hutton's term as GOC, Deakin claimed that in recent years Australians had been preoccupied principally with questions relating to the organisation and control of the forces, but had largely ignored their efficiency. Although some remedial action was in hand, he observed that the field artillery was poorly equipped with guns and horses, suffered shortages of men and needed more intense training. The requirements of the infantry, Deakin noted, were 'pretty generally recognised'. Increased attention also had to be given to organising the supply of arms and ammunition from Australian sources and local railways needed extending to enhance the defence capability. Giving a clear indication of the degree of commitment which he thought was required, Deakin stated emphatically that he believed it was the duty of all able-bodied men to participate in defence.[3]

When the Reid–McLean government, a coalition of conservative Free Traders and Protectionists, collapsed a month after his interview with the *Herald*, Deakin was restored as Prime Minister. Among his political peers he was a man of uncommon talent, making him a dominant political figure in the first decade of the Commonwealth. Urbane, handsome and alert, Deakin was an intelligent, able administrator, practised in the art of compromise. He had integrity but could also relax his principles for political gain when the need arose; he knew that survival was the first lesson for a successful politician. But there was another noteworthy characteristic of Alfred Deakin. From the time he attended the Colonial Conference of 1887 as Victoria's principal representative, he was recognised in Britain as a colonial nationalist. Yet Deakin's pride in Australia was compatible with his pride in empire. He believed unwaveringly that Australians had a part to play in the development of imperial policy rather than subjugating national interests totally to those of Britain. During this, his second term in office which continued until November 1908 with the support of the Labor Party, Deakin also administered the Department of External Affairs.[4]

Having outlined his approach to defence in his interview with the *Herald*, Deakin now found himself with the responsibilities of formulating policy and implementing it. His first difficulty arose over a conflict of opinion among past and present senior service officers. In September 1904, the Reid–McLean government had requested British comments on a strategic analysis which had been undertaken by Hutton. In it the former GOC had assumed that acts of aggression against Australia would be either a small raid or an attack by a large well-equipped force. Originally, Hutton had discounted the probability of a determined attack on Australia but soon realised that the fear of invasion, whether real or imagined, would help him persuade the Australian government to establish and maintain a field force

The Creation of a National Defence Agenda

Sir Edmund Barton with Alfred Deakin. Barton was the first Prime Minister of the Commonwealth and Deakin was his Attorney-General. Deakin subsequently became Prime Minister on three occasions: 24 September 1903–27 April 1904; 5 July 1905–13 November 1908; and 2 June 1909–29 April 1910. It was during his second period as Prime Minister that Deakin provided the leadership to develop a national defence strategy for Australia. (NATIONAL LIBRARY OF AUSTRALIA)

---

of at least 20 000 men.[5] His difficulty was that this approach undermined the strategic policy of the British authorities who maintained that an invasion of Australia was not possible in view of the strength of the Royal Navy. In March 1903 Hutton had taken the Governor-General, Lord Tennyson, into his confidence, explaining that he felt compelled to offer advice contrary to the Colonial Defence Committee's policy because of the 'public feeling in Australia among a large section of the community'. If he had told Australians that an invasion was not possible, he had said, 'it would have been seized upon as an argument for the abolition of the Military forces altogether'.[6] Hutton had therefore justified maintenance of his field force, for which he actually had expeditionary functions in mind, by stimulating fear of an attack on Australia. Ironically, however, Hutton's contrived strategic analysis sounded increasingly convincing after May 1905.

Doubts about Hutton's modified strategic assessment arose in Australia at the end of 1904 in view of critical comments by Captain Creswell, the commanding officer of the Commonwealth naval forces. Using earlier edicts by the Colonial Defence Committee to support his own analysis, Creswell asserted that, even if sea supremacy were lost, Hutton's field force was not an appropriate defence force for Australia. 'No Field Force could be transported in time from Eastern to Western Australia, from Victoria to Queensland, to meet a threatened attack which might after all be a feint to uncover the desired position,' Creswell argued. In particular, as he noted, 'portions of units of the Field Force are as apart as Queensland, Tasmania and Western Australia'. The only other rationale for the field force was 'foreign service', Creswell pointed out, 'as a contribution to and acting with the Imperial forces'. Yet, he continued, the Australian *Defence Act* prevented deployment of the force in an overseas theatre, unless the members volunteered to serve abroad. Convincingly, Creswell argued that this was a significant limitation. Similar legislation prevailed in Britain in relation to its citizen militia, the naval commander explained, and only 9 per cent of its members had volunteered for service in the Boer War. In view of these considerations, Creswell asserted that the maintenance of the field force was 'a misdirection of Defence expenditure'. According to him, the defence of Australia demanded an enhanced naval capability so he recommended the establishment of a destroyer service in co-operation with the Admiralty and an expansion of the local naval forces.[7]

All these issues had been referred to the British authorities for advice by the Reid–McLean government.[8] Assuming office before Britain responded, Deakin too waited on the Whitehall strategists to comment on the difference of opinion before proceeding with any defence reforms. Yet the answer, when it arrived in Australia in the second half of 1905, only created further doubt and controversy.

The Colonial Defence Committee repudiated Hutton's military organisations and his strategic analysis. It reiterated its consistent claim that Australia should make defensive preparations for raids but not invasion because of the dominance of the Royal Navy. The establishment of the garrison force was therefore justified but Hutton's field force was neither appropriate nor necessary in the scheme of Australian defence. In the committee's words, the field force 'answers to no definite war requirement'. Yet, despite its rejection of Hutton's scheme, the committee still advised the Australian government to maintain a field force, although on a different scale and organisation to that envisaged by Hutton.[9]

In justifying its own proposal, the committee, like Creswell, criticised Hutton's organisation because it included brigades comprised of units drawn, in some cases, from four different states. But where Creswell had argued for disbanding the field force in favour of naval forces, the committee proposed, instead, that separate field forces be established in each state, or military district, arguing that the primary justification for these forces was their instructional value. They provided the opportunity to train soldiers for active field duties rather than sedentary garrison service, the committee advised, so creating a pool of trained personnel and appropriate equipment on which to build 'voluntarily enrolled forces' for deployment in the western

Pacific 'in certain contingencies'. Clearly, this was as close as the committee dared come to suggesting an expeditionary function because the Reid–McLean government had told it that no force would be maintained for any purpose other than local defence.[10]

The Colonial Defence Committee's comments placed Deakin in a quandary. His perception of the need to undertake a major review of the defence forces was inspired by the fear of invasion of Australia. Yet in its comments the committee discounted such a possibility and referred, in vague terms, to military operations in the Pacific region, suggesting that it had more extensive deployments in mind. From Deakin's point of view, it was unsatisfactory advice.

The inadequacy of the committee's opinion became more obvious in view of its comments on Creswell's proposal for the establishment of a destroyer service and the expansion of the local naval forces to defend Australia. 'The immense number of torpedo craft maintained by Continental Powers in European waters,' the committee informed the Australian government, 'compels us to keep the majority of our destroyers at home and in the Mediterranean.' For the same reason, the committee also rejected the Australian naval commander's suggestion to keep Royal Navy destroyers in Australian ports as a reserve for the China Station. 'Recent events in the Far East have rendered possible a considerable reduction of naval forces in that part of the world,' the committee asserted, referring to the victory of Britain's Japanese allies over the Russians. And, even if there were a change in the strategic outlook in the region, Hong Kong or Singapore were the most appropriate bases for reserve destroyers, the committee commented. There was also no reason for the Admiralty to maintain a force of torpedo craft and submarines in Australian ports. If Australians felt the need for such measures they should provide and maintain the force themselves, it was advised. Attempting to placate Australian fears for their security, the committee reminded the Australian government that there had been 'a substantial increase in the strength of the Imperial naval forces on the Australian Station' under the terms of the naval agreement. The committee therefore concluded that 'the *raison d'être* of the local naval forces, except for the minor services [of port defence] seems to have disappeared'.[11] There was obviously little comfort for Alfred Deakin in these comments.

Deakin believed that the requirements of Australian defence demanded an effective naval force operating under the control of the Commonwealth. In addition, he was convinced of the need for a military force but had doubts about how it should be structured to defend Australia. This proved to be a most difficult issue to resolve. Effectively, although it had other contingencies in mind, the Colonial Defence Committee's recommendations for the organisation of the local military forces did provide a realistic solution to the problem of local defence. Mobile citizen forces, organised and exercised on a district level but designed to operate in conjunction with strong static defences, were clearly an effective means of defending major ports and strategic centres. Indeed, ignoring questions of size and composition, the very rationality of this function also made it a convincing 'cover' for the expeditionary aspiration. But, despite such considerations, senior military officers in Australia added to Deakin's dilemma by disagreeing over this aspect of the Colonial Defence Committee's advice. Some officers supported the advice but others, who were quietly intent on preserving the national scale of Hutton's field force for its underlying expeditionary role, opposed it.

In an attempt to resolve the conflicting military opinion confronting him, Deakin cabled Sir George Clarke on 2 October, seeking his assistance.[12] The next day the Australian Prime Minister also wrote to Clarke, explaining his intention to introduce comprehensive measures for defending Australia. Already Deakin had decided that '[n]othing less than an adaption of the Swiss system of universal service' would be the basis of an effective national defence scheme. Deakin also told Clarke that the naval agreement with Britain was not popular, but it could be made so if the financial contribution resulted in naval developments which would be 'obviously Australian, visibly and concretely Australian in origin, but Imperial in end and value'. The local fortifications and their armaments were also 'hopelessly out of date'. 'We want new forts on a new plan with new armament manned by more permanent well-trained men and backed up by harbour boats of one or more types, with booms or mines . . . ,' Deakin explained. He wanted to develop a defence capability which would be effective 'even in the temporary absence' of the auxiliary squadron.[13]

Responding to Deakin's initial approach, Clarke recommended that the Australian Prime Minister refer the whole question of Australian defence to the Committee of Imperial Defence which had been established recently on the recommendation of the Esher Committee.[14] Chaired by the British Prime Minister, Lord Balfour, and with Clarke as its secretary, it provided a forum for those senior service officers and politicians who took a special interest in imperial defence. It was assisted in its deliberations by the original Colonial Defence Committee which was regarded as its sub-committee.[15] To assist in undertaking a comprehensive review, however, Clarke advised Deakin that detailed local knowledge of the layout of Australian harbours and the location of guns would be required. 'I would venture to suggest that the best course might be to send home Colonel Bridges with such information,' Clarke suggested. 'He is exceedingly well qualified for such a mission and he would incidentally learn a great deal which would be of value.'[16]

Lieutenant Colonel William Throsby Bridges was the chief of intelligence and a member of the Military Board. As a senior, experienced Australian artillery officer, he possessed a sound knowledge of Australian defence installations. Born in Greenock, Scotland, Bridges was the son of

The Creation of a National Defence Agenda

Major General Sir William Throsby Bridges. Bridges was the prime imperialist in the Australian Army. Appointed as the first Chief of the General Staff in January 1909, he became the commander of the Australian Imperial Force and of the 1st Australian Division at the beginning of World War I. Bridges was mortally wounded at Gallipoli on 15 May 1915. (ARMY OFFICE SECRETARIAT, AWM NEG. NO: AO2867)

William Bridges, an officer of the Royal Navy, and Mary Throsby, greatniece of Charles Throsby of Moss Vale, New South Wales. Educated in England, Throsby Bridges entered the Royal Military College, Kingston, in Canada where he intended to train for a commission in the Imperial Army. These aspirations were unfulfilled, however, when, for family reasons, he left Kingston in 1879 without completing the course and settled in Australia. In 1885 he took a permanent commission as an artillery officer in the military force of New South Wales.[17] As a junior officer, he had worked closely with Hutton during his colonial command in New South Wales and had been secretary to the meetings of the colonial commandants of 1894 and 1896 where Hutton had attempted to establish a federal military force. After federation, Bridges had assumed the important staff appointment of deputy assistant quartermaster general on Hutton's headquarters in Melbourne, being responsible for military organisations. He became Hutton's prime protégé in Australia. On returning to London after his Australian command, Hutton 'especially mentioned' Bridges to Colonial Secretary Sir Alfred Lyttelton and Sir Montagu Ommanney as one of the Australian officers who had taken 'a very prominent and leading part in carrying to a successful issue the various reforms'. 'He carried out all the details of my military reforms [of] 1902–04 and did invaluable service in that regard,' Hutton testified.[18]

Bridges was an officer who was sympathetic to the imperial view of defence and was well aware of the concealed expeditionary role which

Hutton envisaged for the field force. Indeed, it was his determination to preserve the force intact for this purpose which produced the intense conflict of opinion among senior Australian officers over the advice from the Colonial Defence Committee. Lieutenant Colonel George Kirkpatrick, an Imperial officer on the British general staff who arrived in Australia on a tour of inspection shortly after the Committee's advice was received, reported this conflict to Sir George Clarke.[19] According to Kirkpatrick, Bridges was 'to a great extent imbued with General Hutton's ideas' and so thought that the Colonial Defence Committee was 'wrong in recommending the substitution of District Field Forces for the Commonwealth Field Force'. Brigadier Harry Finn, the inspector-general, was an imperial officer but 'not a brainy man', Kirkpatrick continued, and he 'wobbled' in his opinion of the committee's advice. However, it was a different matter with the deputy adjutant general and senior military member of the Military Board, Colonel John Hoad. Kirkpatrick noted that he represented 'the Ultra-Australian party', was 'very powerful politically' and was known to be 'a violent opponent of General Hutton's'. Contrary to Bridges, Hoad believed that the committee's recommendations were 'thoroughly sound'.[20]

Although the disagreement between Bridges and Hoad would at times be motivated by personal ambition and cupidity, it was essentially a manifestation of the tension between national and imperial priorities for future defence developments in Australia. Yet, by the close of 1905, Bridges had learnt to be cautious by not being too forthright in arguing his case for the retention of Hutton's field force. In the aftermath of Hutton's period as GOC, it was a subject which aroused intense opposition. 'General Hutton's work here has raised much criticism on the one hand, and met with great admiration on the other,' Kirkpatrick explained to Clarke, 'but the net result has been a great deal of recrimination and heart burning . . . '[21] There was a strong belief that imperial influence in defence developments should be restricted in future and, as Deakin informed Clarke, an imperial officer would find his work 'much more difficult than you might suppose'.[22] It was therefore in the interest of the British authorities to cultivate a compliant Australian officer to plead their case. Bridges was the man selected for this role, explaining why Clarke was delighted to learn that Deakin had followed his advice and had nominated him as the military officer who would travel to London and assist the Committee of Imperial Defence in its review of Australian defence.[23] It was a choice which also pleased Kirkpatrick because he realised that if Hutton was called before the Committee of Imperial Defence for the review then 'the connection of his name with the matter might, to Australian eyes, be invidious'. But this did not necessarily mean that the former GOC's advice was not available to the committee. Kirkpatrick made a point of informing Clarke that 'Bridges may be relied upon to give evidence in support of General Hutton's views'.[24] Kirkpatrick had met Bridges a few days earlier in Melbourne and had realised that he was a reliable imperial ally. He had some long discussions with the Australian officer on the subject of uniformity in the military forces of the empire and had given him the 'notes as to what the General Staff at home would like done in the way of co-operation with them'.[25]

Bridges' determination to protect the military organisations introduced by Hutton had been evident at the earliest meetings of the Australian Council of Defence in 1905. He had seen immediately that Creswell's proposals to increase naval defence threatened to reduce military expenditure and lead to a review of military defence.[26] Responding bluntly to a question from Bridges on how much money would have to be transferred from military to naval expenditure, Creswell had stated: 'the money expended on the Field Force should be expended on a Naval Force'.[27] This had drawn a spirited defence of the field force from Bridges who had argued on the basis of the recommendations of the colonial commandants in 1894 and quoted from Hutton's paper on Australian defence of April 1902. He had then challenged the Council of Defence to explain how defence was to be provided 'after the destruction of the Military Forces, and before the completion of the proposed Naval Force'. To more telling effect, however, Bridges had managed to cast doubt on the validity of Creswell's financial estimates.[28]

Bridges' interest in preserving Australia's established military organisations did not escape Deakin's attention. The Australian Prime Minister wrote to Clarke prior to Bridges' appearance before the Committee of Imperial Defence and advised him that Bridges was 'only imperfectly in sympathy with some of our aims'. 'He was closely associated with Sir E. Hutton in preparing our present military organization,' Deakin informed Clarke, 'and is naturally biassed [sic] in respect to it or anything affecting a scheme for which he receives full credit in the force.'[29] These misgivings undoubtedly explain the careful wording of the written instructions given to the Chief of Intelligence before he left Australia. Bridges was informed that it was 'to be distinctly understood' that he was to assist the committee but he was 'not to furnish opinions'.[30] As a further precaution, Deakin also informed Clarke that if Bridges made any suggestions he had been instructed 'to make it clear that they are his opinions only and not those of his Minister or of our Government'.[31]

In the report produced on completion of the review, the committee ignored the reason for Deakin's anxiety and repeated the imperial dogma on the supremacy of the Royal Navy. In the worst case, an enemy raid on Australia would be limited to three or four cruisers and the landing party 'would usually not exceed 500 men', or in exceptional circumstances, the party 'might reach a total of 1000 men at the outside'. The committee therefore recommended a garrison force for local defence and a field force primarily for training purposes. Significantly, it did not see any requirement for garrison forces to include mobile elements because to do otherwise would have undermined the argument for maintaining an Australian field force. This was not a development which the Committee of Imperial Defence would have welcomed because it envisaged a special role for a separate, mobile force. Displaying a little more subtlety than the Colonial Defence Committee had done previously, it hinted that, in a great war, a power possessing naval supremacy might 'transfer the scene of the decisive land battles to foreign soil', and concluded that the main object of the field force organisation was to provide the basis for expansion in case of emergency. How the expanded force might be used was not spelt out, but the committee clearly had an imperial and expeditionary role in mind.[32]

An additional request from Deakin that the Committee of Imperial Defence should also comment on a proposal by Creswell for an Australian naval force of three cruiser destroyers, sixteen torpedo boat destroyers and fifteen torpedo boats for local defence was dealt with decisively. The proposal, which had been doomed from the outset, was dismissed.[33] Apart from the difficulties an Australian navy would pose for Britain's control of imperial defence, Bridges had undoubtedly told the committee that Creswell's suggestion almost certainly would be financed by a reduction in expenditure on the military forces and, as a result, would lead inevitably to the dismantling of the field force. Furthermore, Kirkpatrick had also taken the precaution of briefing Clarke on this vital point by sending him a copy of the minutes of the Australian Council of Defence meeting at which Bridges originally had challenged Creswell's proposal. Kirkpatrick, who probably had received the minutes from Bridges during their discussions in Melbourne, informed Clarke that on reading them 'it will be seen that the Naval Director's pleas for a local navy cannot hold water'.[34]

Creswell's suggestion invited opposition from imperialists because expenditure on naval forces would limit the funds available for the field force, undoubtedly threatening its existence. It is therefore not surprising that British strategists continued to remind the Australian government of the Royal Navy's supremacy while opposing the development of Australian naval defence. It was a sign of weakness, the committee contended in its response to Deakin's government, to use naval forces in a purely defensive line. 'Australia need not be reduced to such a role,' the committee advised, 'so long as she is a member of an Empire which is the strongest naval Power in the world, and which extends naval protection not only to the home land and to the most distant of the King's dominions beyond the seas, but also to all commerce sailing under the British flag.'[35] Disappointingly, all this advice did nothing to solve the problem of Australian defence as Deakin perceived it.

The Australian Prime Minister was upset by the apparent failure of the committee to recognise his concern for national security and to endorse his national defence aspirations. Writing anonymously in his role of special Australian correspondent in the *Morning Post*, Deakin criticised the committee's advice, particularly in relation to its decision 'to condemn any and every form of distinctively Australian naval defence'. 'What their Lordships forget is that our electors, who have to decide what they will do with their revenue, have no representation either on the Admiralty or in the Imperial Government and Parliament above it.' It was asking too much, the Australian Prime Minister contended, for the citizens of Sydney to rely totally 'upon a body of experts in London for the safety of our harbour and its commerce'. 'Self-respect, self-esteem, self-assertion, whatever name is given to it, a sentiment of the duty of self-defence, strong already, is growing stronger' and, as a result, the committee's advice would be ignored.[36] In his capacity as Prime Minister, Deakin turned to Australian resources to find a solution to the problem of national defence.

Deakin's Minister for Defence, Senator Thomas Playford, referred the advice from the Committee of Imperial Defence to Finn, Hoad and Lieutenant Colonel Havilland Le Mesurier, chief of ordnance on the Military Board, for comment. Yet he soon found that these men were not in agreement. While Finn and Le Mesurier responded favourably, Hoad was critical. First, the deputy adjutant general took issue with one of the committee's comments concerning the lack of uniformity in the coastal artillery. Hoad pointed out that for the last twenty years colonial governments, and since 1901 the Commonwealth government, had been guided in their selection of guns by imperial officers. The cost for this advice 'from Imperial Experts' amounted to something like £363 000 in pay and allowances alone, Hoad calculated. He also dismissed the committee's opinion that the only threat to Australia was a small-scale raid. He called this unrealistic, and asserted that 'in any event we should be prepared to defend ourselves'. Hoad therefore agreed with Deakin that Australia should prepare its defences to meet an attack. 'It seems that the right way now,' Hoad advised Playford, 'is to first discuss and decide the reasonable probabilities and the methods of attack on these shores then discuss and settle as far as possible what force or forces are reasonably required to meet and defeat such attack.' The principle to be kept in mind at all times, Hoad emphasised, was 'the Defence of Australian shores'.[37] As a result of these comments, the government appointed a committee of military officers with Hoad as president to comment formally on the report by the Committee of Imperial Defence.

In a matter of weeks the report was finished. While rejecting the strategic basis of the British report, the committee of officers did agree with the suggestion that the garrison force had no requirement for a mobile element. They also supported the recommendation that the field force should be retained, obviously to provide the necessary mobility and flexibility for effective defence. The brigade structure was therefore retained for the field force but it was modified to ensure that each complete brigade was composed of troops from a particular state.[38] Unlike the Committee of Imperial Defence, the committee of officers perceived the field force as an integral element in a national defence plan. In reaching this conclusion, the

An Army for a Nation

committee was obviously influenced by Hoad. To imperialists it was a clear sign that, under the Deakin government, officers of nationalist sympathy, like Hoad, might dictate Australian military developments and gradually insulate the forces from imperial influence.

A man of humble origins—the son of a one-time labourer and baker and apparently orphaned at 6—Hoad had enlisted in the Victorian militia in 1884 and had received a permanent commission in 1886.[39] During Hutton's term as GOC, Hoad had acquired a reputation as someone likely to threaten imperial interests in Australia although, ironically, his career had for a time owed much to Hutton's support. But it had been Hutton who had deliberately attempted to discredit Hoad with the object of destroying his chances of promotion. As GOC, Hutton had informed Major-General Sir William Nicholson at the War Office that the Australian officer had been 'quite incapable' as his staff officer in South Africa as well as being a 'hopeless failure' as his chief staff officer in Melbourne. Hoad lacked education, military knowledge and character, Hutton had continued.[40] Similar damning comments had also been made to the Minister for Defence, Austin Chapman, because Hutton had feared that Hoad might have replaced him as GOC or, alternatively, have gained a seat on the Military Board. Subsequently faced with the inevitable establishment of the board, Hutton had nominated Bridges for the principal military position and totally ignored the more senior Hoad.[41]

Hutton's vilification of Hoad had gained currency with imperial officers to the extent that Kirkpatrick confessed to Clarke that he was 'rather agreeably surprised' on meeting Hoad for the first time and spending Christmas with him in Melbourne in 1905. 'He seems a very intelligent, reflecting, but somewhat prejudiced man,' was Kirkpatrick's niggardly assessment.[42] But the fear remained that Hoad's nationalist outlook and his political influence might upset imperial plans. Hutton, therefore, was relentless in his attempt to stifle the Australian officer, especially since his earlier advice had been ignored and Hoad had been appointed to the Military Board. Writing from England in January 1906, Hutton expressed satisfaction to the Australian Governor-General, Lord Northcote, that the fundamental principles of the military organisation which he had established in Australia still 'have not been touched'. But future developments were uncertain, he warned. Northcote was advised that 'the best thing the Commonwealth can do is to put Colonel Hoad into Queensland' and ask for a British 'Colonel in the temporary rank of Major-General to replace him'.[43]

The accession of Australian officers of nationalist persuasion to positions of influence in the military forces was viewed with increasing concern in Britain. The indications that Deakin was moving towards the development of a national, and to some degree independent, defence policy added to these worries. New efforts were taken to assert British influence in Australia, but the Military Board was a difficult obstacle. With the Minister for

Defence as the president of the board and with three senior military officers and one senior public servant as its regular members, it was the body which formed the direct link between parliament and the forces. By constitution and character, the board, especially with Hoad as the senior military member, was not amenable to British control. This was precisely what Hutton had always feared. The only avenue through which Britain could reasonably hope to manipulate military developments was the position of inspector-general, which was to be vacated by Finn in December 1906. And even here there were difficulties.

Although senior in rank and precedence to all other officers, the inspector-general possessed no executive authority. His role was to inspect all aspects of the military forces, including equipment and defence installations, and to report annually to the Military Board.[44] However, at the beginning of May 1906, Clarke wrote to Deakin tactfully suggesting that the inspector-general's authority should be increased. He should 'be regarded as the servant of the Cabinet', Clarke advised, and while continuing to act as the 'eyes and ears of the Board', he should report directly to the minister rather than the board. In war, the inspector-general should become commander of the military forces while the principal military member on the board should become his chief of staff. It was a subject which he had thought much about, Clarke informed Deakin, and had 'come to the conclusion that it is most desirable that the Inspector General should be appointed from England or India for a term not exceeding four years'. 'There will always be some difficulty in selecting from the Australian Forces an I.G. who will command sufficient authority,' he reflected. Despite Clarke's interest in achieving greater efficiency for the Australian forces, there can be little doubt about his primary motive. The appointment of an imperial officer to a senior position with direct access to the minister was an attempt to circumvent the authority of the Military Board. Significantly, Clarke also handed a copy of this despatch to Bridges when he was in London assisting the Committee of Imperial Defence in its review of Australian defence.[45]

Clarke's advice was obviously designed to influence the Australian Prime Minister's selection of a replacement for Finn. But Deakin was in no mood for such counselling. On 7 June, the Governor-General, Lord Northcote, announced at the formal opening of parliament that the Deakin government had adopted a new policy in relation to the employment of imperial officers in the Australian military forces. 'Hereafter preference will be given to Australian officers and non-commissioned officers,' Northcote announced. Furthermore, he continued, the government would undertake a reorganisation of the military forces.[46] What this might entail was not explained but it was disclosed that the government was thinking of extending its cadet training scheme for youths who had left school. Clarke, for one, would have realised what this meant. Deakin had informed him earlier in the year that he intended to work towards the introduction of universal military training after the Swiss example by firstly developing cadet training.[47] It was disturbing news for imperialists because it confirmed their growing concern that Deakin was becoming more independent on the subject of defence. Not only was imperial influence on the wane but it seemed likely that the field force would be discarded in favour of an organisation designed specifically to fulfil the requirements of local defence.

The policy announcement evoked a tactless outburst from Finn. Writing to Playford the very next day, Finn expressed his belief that Australia should disband the Military Board and appoint an imperial officer as GOC to control and administer the forces. Australian officers did not possess sufficient knowledge to sit on the Military Board, Finn told Playford. Indeed, he was frankly disparaging about local alternatives. 'Surely no one who is qualified to judge,' he said, 'will assert that there are in Australia to-day three men, who in their combination can wisely be substituted for a General Officer of the wide experience and ability which many of the Imperial officers possess.' Realising how patronising this must sound, he conceded that imperial officers were preferable, 'not because of their greater natural endowments, perhaps, but because of the far greater experience and facilities for acquiring knowledge which they have had'. 'The advantages of having an Imperial officer at the head of the Forces, who would be less trammelled by private and political influence, is worthy of much consideration,' Finn continued. Failing such an arrangement, he recommended that an 'Imperial Inspector-General' should be appointed as 'President of the Military Board, or at any rate, Vice-President' and also act as 'adviser to the Minister for Defence'. This would avoid what Finn thought was an anomalous situation where the inspector-general was 'practically under the control of the Military Board'. Then, in a move to influence his imminent replacement, Finn added that the government should continue to appoint imperial officers as inspectors-general while Brigadier Joseph Gordon and Colonel Hoad, either one a likely successor for Finn, 'should be sent to England and India for at least one year, to gain experience and knowledge in the most up-to-date administration and training in all their details'.[48]

It seems that, in addition to wishing to have an imperial officer replace him as inspector-general, Finn also wanted to stem the growing interest in a scheme of compulsory military training for Australia. Not only had Deakin intimated to Clarke that he favoured introduction of such a scheme but he had also taken the more positive step of instructing Bridges to proceed to Switzerland after his appearance before the Committee of Imperial Defence to inspect and report on the Swiss scheme of compulsory military training.[49] Undoubtedly, these issues were in Finn's mind when he wrote to Playford.

Playford ignored Finn's advice. The government policy announced by the Governor-General was upheld. In September, Hoad was promoted to the rank of brigadier and, during Finn's absence on leave, was appointed temporarily to the position of inspector-general. However, for the period of

The Creation of a National Defence Agenda

his temporary appointment, Hoad still retained his permanent position on the Military Board. 'Imagine Hoad as IG with a seat on the Board,' was Clarke's disparaging comment to Hutton. 'Playford's starting to build afresh with hopelessly incompetent architects!'[50] To Clarke's further disappointment, in January 1907, Hoad was promoted to the rank of major-general and confirmed as Finn's successor as inspector-general, so relinquishing his appointment to the Military Board.[51] One of the worst fears of imperialists had thus been realised. For the first time since federation, the senior military appointment was held by an Australian officer of nationalist sympathies.

Yet Finn's own achievements had been prodigious and it had been during his period as inspector-general that the infrastructure for Australia's military forces finally began to take rational shape. Indeed, Finn's attempt to convince the minister to abandon the Military Board and to introduce administration through a GOC failed not simply because it was such an obvious attempt at imperial manipulation, but for the fundamental reason that the new administrative arrangements had proved to be so successful in enabling a reformist government to exert its influence on the forces. No longer could a government be misled and confused by a recalcitrant GOC. Ironically, one important reason for the efficacy of the new system was the single-minded perseverance Finn had displayed in his two-year appointment as inspector-general.[52] The comprehensive nature of the information provided for the Military Board by the inspector-general established the basis on which the government could begin to implement its policy in the forces. 'The Military Board system has the advantage of the Minister of Defence having frequent opportunities, as President of the Military Board, of conferring with the Heads of Departments, and thus being brought closely into touch with responsible Officers,' Playford reported enthusiastically to parliament. He believed that the system of administration allowed decisions to be taken more quickly, reducing the amount of correspondence and achieving a substantial degree of continuity.[53]

During 1905 the board had completely reviewed and authorised publication of regulations and standing orders for the forces. It had approved the placing of orders for 8000 magazine rifles and 2000 rifle barrels as maintenance stocks. It had examined the production capacity of the Colonial Ammunition Company at Footscray, Victoria, and had noted that it could produce 18 million small arms rounds annually. Following the board's negotiations with the company, a reserve of ammunition components had also been established to ensure some continuity of supply during an emergency. Orders had been placed for the field artillery to be equipped to a total strength of sixty 15 pounder and 18 pounder guns. A reserve of ammunition for field and garrison artillery had been established and action had been taken to have harnesses, saddlery and ammunition waggons manufactured in Australia. Where possible, orders had also been placed on local suppliers to provide enough camp equipment for the entire force and to provide medical equipment. Arrangements had been made for the local manufacture of transport waggons and ambulances for the Medical Corps, and standard forms of contract were drawn up by the Military Board to facilitate the supply of equipment in each state.[54] It was a deliberate policy of the Military Board to pursue the local supply of war *matériel* to encourage the development of Australia's defence infrastructure. The final objective was succinctly enunciated by Hoad as inspector-general when he commented on the government's subsequent decision to establish small arms and cordite factories in Australia. Such initiatives, Hoad hoped, would 'eventually render the Commonwealth independent of overseas supplies for the whole of its Warlike Stores, including guns and ammunition'.[55] As Deakin had indicated in his interview with the representative from the Melbourne *Herald*, his government was intent on building the Australian defence capability from local resources where possible.

While Deakin was introducing his comprehensive program to develop the Australian forces, the British authorities continued to grapple with the issue of imperial defence. Giving new impetus to their military endeavours was the British General Staff, whose creation had been one of the important Army reforms following the recommendations of the Esher Committee. The Secretary of State for War, Richard Burdon Haldane, carefully explained the benefits of the new body to colonial representatives at the Colonial Conference of April 1907. Flanked by Sir Neville Lyttelton, the chief of the general staff, Sir William Nicholson, the quartermaster general, and Sir George Clarke, Haldane described the General Staff as the brain of the Army. It brought together a group of competent officers whose military knowledge and experience meant that military undertakings and developments could be given new purpose and direction. They 'constituted the nucleus of a serious and thoughtful military school', Haldane told participants. Illustrating the point, the General Staff had produced four papers to be considered at the conference.[56]

The first paper discussed the military aspects of imperial strategy. The pre-eminent role of the Royal Navy was acknowledged, but it was considered that something more would be required 'to bring a great war to a successful conclusion'. The Staff envisaged a situation where combined military action would be necessary and therefore indicated the advantage in having 'a system of military organization capable of being readily assimilated to that of the many other contingents which would compose the Imperial army'.[57] Recognising that most of the military forces throughout the empire were confined to their local areas, the Staff counted on men volunteering for imperial military service when the crisis arose. Such an arrangement introduced an element of uncertainty into planning, but it was considered that the existence of the General Staff provided the means of resolving the problem. It was a body which would eventually 'embrace officers from all parts of the Empire', forming 'a bond of union in regard to military thought throughout its length and breadth'.[58] The second paper prepared by the General Staff therefore addressed the question of assimilating war organisations throughout the empire. Uniform organisations, standard nomenclature and common administration and supply systems operating on British methods were considered desirable.[59] The third paper emphasised the need to adopt standard equipment because it was considered essential that small arms, machine guns and ammunition were of a common pattern.[60] With this object in mind, the fourth paper urged that the self-governing dominions should order their ordnance stores, particularly arms and ammunition, through the War Office.[61]

The suggestion that the General Staff would become the means of integrating the military forces of the empire was taken up by Haldane. The General Staff, the Secretary of State for War told the conference, should become an imperial organisation. 'My main purpose in addressing the Conference,' Haldane explained, 'is to suggest for your acceptance the opinion that the General Staff which we have created at home and which is in its infancy should receive as far as possible an Imperial character.'[62] By accepting colonial officers as members and sending imperial officers in exchange to fulfil similar functions in the colonies and dominions, an integrating influence could be imposed on imperial military efforts. The important object, Haldane thought, was to inspire a school of imperial thought in which members shared similar traditions, viewed the problems of strategy from the same perspective and operated according to standard principles and theories.[63]

Participants at the conference were enthusiastic about Haldane's proposal to give an imperial dimension to the General Staff. Deakin, for example, asserted that '[a]ny proposition which would extend its activities or permit us to share them, would be heartily welcomed in the Commonwealth'.[64] But it became clear, when Haldane put a resolution to the conference to establish an Imperial General Staff, that support was not unqualified and participants were quick to circumscribe its role. 'We have no Imperial Army', Sir Frederick Borden, Minister of Militia and Defence in Canada, stated bluntly. Therefore, while there was agreement among participants on a conceptual basis, Borden was worried that some Canadians 'may be somewhat sensitive about being committed . . . to something like an obligation'. Attempting to relieve such anxiety, Haldane explained that the 'General Staff is a purely advisory body'. Yet other participants, including Deakin, shared Borden's concern and the Australian Prime Minister successfully amended the resolution to ensure that the Imperial General Staff could offer advice on military training, education and organisation only at the request of the respective governments.[65] The colonial participants did not want the Imperial General Staff to be in a position to exert control over their military forces. Clearly, Deakin perceived it solely as a body of informed military advice.

Despite Haldane's assurances that the Imperial General Staff would simply dispense advice to colonial governments, behind the benevolent façade was a more intrusive motive. On the day before the conference discussed defence, the Secretary of State for War had decided to exercise caution in his approach to imperial military objectives. He was therefore content to introduce and promote the concept of the Imperial General Staff as an advisory body, but it was clearly only an initial step designed to win approval from participants. A more forthright proposal by Clarke which would have sought agreement from participants that the self-governing colonies were obliged to give military assistance to the empire in addition to defending their own territories was rejected by Haldane.

'Mr Haldane has seen the enclosed and thoroughly sympathises with the proposal,' Clarke was informed before the conference sat to discuss defence, 'but he thinks on the whole that it will be best in the first instance to put one resolution only, and that relating to a General Staff system for the Empire as a whole.'[66] In his subsequent address to the conference, Haldane therefore only hinted that colonial military forces should incorporate a force for local defence and a separate expeditionary force for imperial service.[67] However, the real motive behind the Imperial General Staff was discussed more openly in a paper prepared by the British General Staff after Haldane's amended resolution had been approved. It postulated that imperial defence, unlike local defence, called for offensive operations and combined military action throughout the empire. 'This ideal can only be fully realized when all the parts are organized and trained by one brain, and in the modern army that brain is the General Staff,' it was asserted.[68]

Haldane's decision to reject Clarke's proposal for a military commitment by the colonies displayed sound judgement. A proposal by Dr Smartt, representing the Cape Colony, for each colony to establish a military force for imperial service when required by Britain failed to get any support when it was put to the conference.[69] Knowing that Smartt would make such a proposal, Thomas Ewing, who had replaced Playford as Minister for Defence in January 1907, had advised Deakin before he left Australia that '[t]he Military Board considers that the proposal to form an Imperial Guard for service outside Australia does not appear to come within the scope of what is generally understood as the policy of Australia on Defence matters'.[70] Deakin obviously agreed and remained silent while other participants opposed Smartt's resolution.

The Australian Prime Minister had come to the conference believing that, as well as building national defence, Australia had a part to play in the development of imperial policy. Deakin therefore submitted a resolution to the conference for the colonies to be represented permanently on the Committee of Imperial Defence. Another Australian resolution called for the provisions of the naval agreement to be reconsidered.[71] However, the ensuing discussions on these two issues only convinced Deakin that Australia

The Creation of a National Defence Agenda

had little chance of influencing imperial defence policy and practice. He gained small satisfaction when the British Prime Minister agreed that a colonial representative could sit with the Committee of Imperial Defence, but only when the committee discussed matters submitted by that colony.[72] Failing to achieve permanent representation on the committee, Deakin hoped that this new arrangement would at least overcome such problems as those recently encountered by Australia where the committee's deliberations were, in his words, 'most admirably drafted from a general point of view, without meeting some of our particular difficulties at that time'.[73] The British position on the naval question, however, left little room for any satisfaction.

Lord Tweedmouth, the First Lord of the Admiralty, informed the conference, while referring to the financial contributions from Australia and New Zealand under the terms of the naval agreement, that Britain was 'willing to take in kind what has been paid in hard cash'. No doubt existed in Tweedmouth's mind how such naval resources would be controlled. 'There is one sea, there is one Empire and there is one Navy,' Tweedmouth announced, 'and I want to claim in the first place your help, and in the second place authority for the Admiralty to manage this great service without restraint.' Naval strategy, naval command and the distribution of ships were to be determined by the Admiralty alone, Tweedmouth informed the conference. However, the colonies were encouraged to maintain small craft such as submarines and torpedo boats for coastal protection. While these vessels would provide some defence against sudden, unpredictable raids it is clear that Tweedmouth believed that, in the event of prolonged hostilities, they would be incorporated within imperial squadrons and would be subject to British control. In Deakin's opinion, therefore, there was only one acceptable conclusion and that was the cancellation of the naval agreement and the establishment of an Australian flotilla of destroyers and submarines, but not as Tweedmouth had recommended.[74] The Australian Prime Minister made this clear when he discussed the issue with Admiralty officials outside the Conference forum. 'I went on to insist that these submarines and destroyers, built, manned, and maintained at the sole expense of the Commonwealth, must remain under the control of the [Australian] Government,' Deakin informed the House of Representatives after his return to Australia. 'Their distribution would be entirely subject to that Government at all times.'[75]

Responding to Haldane's call for uniformity under the guidance of the Imperial General Staff, Deakin also took the opportunity to inform the conference that he believed there were limits to the application of British military doctrine throughout the empire. Australian defence, for example, presented unique military problems not encountered in Britain and Europe. Therefore, British military practices and training had to be modified for Australian requirements. Australian officers were also chosen from all social classes and most of them, like the ordinary soldiers, worked for their living at other occupations. 'They devote their spare hours to defence purposes and that earnestly, as well as most generously,' Deakin asserted, 'becoming more effective in fact than they might appear to be, judging them merely by the tests of military parades.' Australians were beginning to realise that they had been too slavish in following the British military model and had concentrated too much on getting the soldiers 'upon parade, in exact line, at the exact angle, with the proper cap and belt'.[76] So Deakin indicated a refreshing willingness, as he had in many other areas, to adapt standard practices to satisfy a unique national requirement.

The Australian Prime Minister's determination to serve the interests of national defence was also demonstrated when he skilfully rejected the General Staff's proposal for the War Office to organise the supply of war *matériel*. 'Our position at the other side of the globe, surrounded by alien races to whom we cannot look for aid or assistance in this matter,' Deakin argued, 'and far from any sources of supply of arms and material of war is very different [from other members of the Empire, such as Canada] and we feel its urgency.' However, when he proceeded to point out that the War Office had failed to provide a satisfactory supply of small arms in the past, he offended Haldane. The reason for the failure, the Secretary of State for War interjected, was probably the excessive demand for small arms during the Boer War. 'Exactly,' was Deakin's immediate response, 'you are always ready to execute orders when neither of us is under pressure.' The War Office 'looks after itself before it looks after us', the Australian Prime Minister charged. Consideration was therefore being given to the building or leasing of an ammunition factory in Australia 'to make us independent' for 'any of the reasonable requirements of war'.[77] Alfred Deakin left the Colonial Conference of 1907 determined to develop Australian defence along national lines.

Deakin was now convinced that the centrepiece of his defence plans was the introduction of universal training on the Swiss model. As revolutionary as such a scheme would be for Australia, it required solid support from the electorate. Yet the federal election of 1906 had not given a majority to any of the three main political groups or parties. Deakin's Protectionists retained office until 1908 only with the support of Labor. This meant that universal training could be introduced only after popular agreement and broad political support had been achieved. As early as January 1906 Deakin had informed Clarke that the cadet movement was the starting-point for the process leading to the achievement of his ultimate goal. 'The Senior Cadets will be splendid recruits almost efficient in early manhood,' Deakin had planned. 'Then we hope to weed out the ineffectives from our Rifle Clubs, add drill and camps of exercise so as to bring in a large body of men—in the country especially.' In time the growing body of men 'will be numerous enough to help us as electors to get universal service legalised', Deakin had calculated.[78] Indeed, the government had already begun to pay clothing allowances and capitation allowances to school cadet units and senior cadets.[79] As a result of these policies, the total number of cadets and senior cadets increased from 14 723 at the end of 1906 to 22 901 at the end of 1907.[80]

Interest in universal, or compulsory, military training was also promoted by the Australian National Defence League which was established in New South Wales in September 1905. An important pressure group, from the very beginning it attracted a range of interested membership from state and federal politics, the churches, the universities, the trade unions, business and the military forces. Owing much to the untiring work of Colonel Gerald Campbell, the establishment of the first branch was followed by a Victorian branch later that same year.[81] The league played a prominent role in keeping the issue of compulsory military service in public view, promoting debate and gradually winning converts. In July 1908, delegates at the Fourth Commonwealth Political Labor Conference also adopted compulsory service as party policy.[82] With support from two major political groups and increasing public approval, the future of universal training was assured.

Initially, Deakin adopted a low public profile on the subject of compulsory service. He had sent Bridges to Switzerland without any fanfare to inspect and report on the Swiss scheme of compulsory military training. Remarkably, the special attraction such a scheme held for him was explained more revealingly in correspondence with Rose Scott, a leading suffragette and foundation president of the Peace Society of New South Wales. Inspired by notions of international liberalism, the society was formed in November 1907 to oppose the influence of the National Defence League in lobbying for compulsory service. 'I have written to no one else as earnestly or as often as to you upon this great issue,' Deakin informed Scott and proceeded to share ideas which he had never raised in correspondence with Clarke. An army enlisted on a compulsory, universal basis in a democratic community, Deakin reasoned, would be less likely to be motivated by the undesirable excesses of militarism than one comprised purely of a select number of volunteers. This was especially so, Deakin thought, because Australian women had received the vote in 1902 and, with the lives of their sons at stake, would be 'very sensible of the risks they run if they prod the horns of war'. It suggested strongly that Deakin was thinking in terms of a purely defensive scheme. Indeed, he explained to Scott, perhaps displaying naive optimism, that 'when a whole people solemnly, I hope piously, with no aim but *self defence*, prepares for emergencies they pray may never occur, you have I believe and will have a spirit of patient self restraint and self confidence which will make for amity'.[83] In late 1907, after his return from the Colonial Conference and the submission of Bridges' report on his Swiss inspection, Deakin was ready to declare publicly his intentions. By that time the electorate had been exposed to debate on the subject for more than two years and Australians appeared ready to build their national defence capability.

In December 1907, Deakin delivered a major statement to the House of Representatives on the subject of his government's defence policy. 'There was a time, not long since, when it was confidently maintained that Australia was outside the area of the world's conflicts, and might regard in comparative quietude any hostile movements in other parts of the globe,' he began. 'That comfortable outlook has long since passed away.' Deakin then proceeded to set out his solution to the problems of Australian defence. In a speech of strong nationalist appeal, he announced his intention to seek cancellation of the naval agreement and to proceed with the establishment of an Australian naval service. To begin with, he planned to establish a naval capacity which would complement shore defences and keep the major harbours open in war. 'Hereafter,' Deakin explained, 'we shall also provide other and more powerful vessels for coastal defence.' The new vessels would be ordered overseas, but he hoped they could eventually be built locally. With Australian crews they would soon contribute to the defence of the empire. Clarifying what he meant by this last point, Deakin informed the House that local defence was imperial defence 'at a particular spot, but none the less Imperial on that account'.[84] In Deakin's opinion, therefore, Australia's contribution to imperial security would be the strengthening of its own defence.

Turning to the military forces, Deakin outlined the deficiencies of the current system of voluntary enlistment. In numbers of enlisted men, he believed, the forces were 'absurdly weak'. There were nearly 1 million men of military age in Australia but only 22 000 men in the forces. Furthermore, the average time in the ranks was only eighteen months, 'so frequent are the incomings and outgoings'. It was also an expensive force to maintain and the amount of money required to expand the force on the existing pattern was prohibitive. Deakin therefore proposed a system of compulsory training. 'We propose a system of universal training, in order to form a National Guard of Defence, in which every young man in the Commonwealth shall be required to serve during his nineteenth, twentieth, and twenty-first years,' Deakin informed the House. Each young man would have to spend an average of sixteen days annually, 'not in drill-rooms or on parade-grounds, but in local camps, devoted wholly and solely to continuous practical instruction'.[85]

It was a calculated decision by the Prime Minister to reject the ritual usually associated with military forces and to concentrate instead on producing an effective fighting force. Existing drill books were to be amended to include only sufficient drill to move troops on the march; otherwise the drills would be restricted to those relating to operational procedures. There would be one standard uniform on free issue, a move intended to ensure that the principle of promotion on merit would work effectively; the requirement for officers to buy expensive uniforms had often prevented capable men from accepting a commission. Swords and other accoutrements were

The Creation of a National Defence Agenda

also to be removed from dress regulations unless they satisfied some practical purpose.[86] 'Whether [Australian soldiers] will attain the standard of European nations in regard to the minutiae of deportment or parade, or the precision of their movements, I do not know,' Deakin informed the House. 'But what we do know of our countrymen entitles us to feel well assured that at the end of that period they will suffice in all that is material.'[87]

Deakin also intended to 'greatly enlarge the Cadet system' as an integral part of the scheme of military training.[88] All youths aged 12 to 18 would undergo compulsory training as cadets or senior cadets where they would be taught the basic drills to be used by the Australian forces and become proficient in the use of small arms. After receiving this basic training and on turning 18 years of age they would progress into the ranks of the national guard where their training would be 'restricted to the practice of military operations in the field'.[89] Emphasising the practical nature of the proposal, Deakin explained that members of the military forces would not be employed in clerical roles. 'We want our soldiers for soldiers' service, not for indoor work,' he said. When the scheme had been operating for a period of eight years Deakin calculated that Australia would have over 200 000 men available 'with full provision for arms, ammunition, and equipment for field artillery and cavalry, organized for service within the Commonwealth'.[90]

Each infantryman—about three quarters of the total force—would be equipped with a rifle, a bayonet and scabbard. 'We have satisfied ourselves, after careful inquiry,' Deakin continued, 'that they can be made here cheaper than they can be purchased abroad.' It was planned to commence manufacture at the rate of 20 000 rifles each year. Infantrymen would also be equipped with a sling, a water bottle, a great coat, a blanket, a waterproof sheet, mess tins and a haversack. 'All these will be made locally,' Deakin announced. The 60 guns of the artillery would also be increased gradually to 240 guns with 16 new guns being bought each year. The associated waggons and limbers were already being manufactured in Australia. There would be an ammunition factory, a cordite factory and possibly a rolling-mill to manufacture cartridge cases. A general staff would also be established to complement the work of the newly established Intelligence Corps which was gathering information and maps for 'operations in any part of the Commonwealth'. A Corps of Signallers had been established early in 1906 and the existing Medical Corps was to be augmented by a medical reserve comprised of medical practitioners, students and chemists. 'We are at the very beginning of a period of development which I trust will be as thorough and complete as that of Japan,' the Prime Minister stated. And so Deakin announced the comprehensive and far-reaching plans to develop Australian defence. It was a scheme which he hoped would achieve high standards of service to which ordinary citizens could aspire. 'Speaking for myself, I am content to trust the Australian people,' Deakin stated. 'I believe they are not

An Army for a Nation

only fitted to serve, but to command, and to rival in the arts of war, so far as they can be practised in times of peace, any of like experience against whom they may be pitted.'[91]

As imperialists had feared, the introduction of universal training posed a threat to Hutton's military organisation and the imperial aspirations on which they were based. Although Deakin envisaged that the national guard would be capable of mobile operations, it was because he believed that Australians not only had to protect the centres of population but also 'the great unoccupied parts of this immense continent'. The ethos of the national guard was exclusively national defence. As Deakin stated, his government was 'not preparing for any expeditionary adventures outside Australia'.[92] It was therefore no longer paramount that the Australian forces should develop completely along the lines of the British forces. As Deakin had already indicated, there were compelling reasons why the Australian forces should develop unique procedures to meet local conditions, both natural and social. Yet another significant obstacle in the way of imperial aspirations was the compulsory enlistment of the national guard. The provisions of the *Defence Act* meant that overseas service could only be undertaken on a voluntary basis and, while the field force was still recruited by voluntary enlistment, there was some chance that a large number of men in the force would do so, thus preserving the essential form of the force for an expeditionary role. Taking this view, Hutton had sustained himself with the belief that in an emergency 'the major part, if not the whole of the Field Force will volunteer for service abroad'.[93] However, the compulsory enlistment of Australian soldiers under Deakin's scheme raised doubts about such a probability in the future.

Hutton had tried to avert such an outcome. As early as January 1906, he had written to Deakin from England informing him that he was opposed to compulsory military service by citizen soldiers in peace. This unsolicited advice was probably prompted by the knowledge that Deakin had given instructions to Bridges in the previous month to examine and report on the Swiss scheme (there can be little doubt that Bridges wrote immediately to Hutton telling him of this ominous development). Compulsory service should only be implemented in war, Hutton asserted.[94] However, while the former GOC was obviously aware of the direction in which the Australian Prime Minister was heading, he had no hope of changing Deakin's mind. Faced with the inevitable introduction of compulsory service, Hutton also wrote to Forrest trying to undermine the basis of Deakin's defence policy. He informed the former Minister for Defence that he understood that it was 'no doubt the product of the instinct for creating a Nation, which shall at the earliest possible moment be capable of standing alone, and of facing the other Powers whose interests are concerned in the Pacific'. 'A noble ambition, but premature, I submit,' Hutton concluded, 'so long as the Mother Country holds the supremacy of the Seas.'[95]

The Creation of a National Defence Agenda

While he shared Hutton's concern about the introduction of compulsory military training, Bridges did not dare state his opposition as bluntly as Hutton had. Only in the opening paragraph of his report on the Swiss military system had the chief of intelligence subtly attempted to arouse opposition to the scheme. Switzerland had proved that democratic government and an efficient military system were not incompatible, Bridges had announced, but he also had drawn attention to the potentially unpopular aspects of the scheme in which 'every man either serves in the army or pays a direct tax towards its maintenance'. By contrast he observed, in 'most, if not in all, Anglo Saxon countries, the army only affects the majority of the people indirectly'.[96]

Not surprisingly, Bridges was dismayed by Deakin's statement to the House of Representatives in December 1907. He immediately despatched a transcript to Hutton, telling his former GOC that 'you will be no more pleased than I am'. The Chief of Intelligence was also upset because Deakin had not referred his plans to the Military Board, nor had he sought the board's advice on his proposals. There can be little doubt that the Prime Minister took this action because he knew that Bridges, who sat on the Military Board, was not sympathetic to his national aspirations. Instead, the Prime Minister had selected another proponent of universal training, Major James Legge, to work directly under his Minister for Defence, Thomas Ewing, to formulate his military proposals. Bridges was upset at his own impotence. 'I have up to the present been able to still maintain your principles of organization,' Bridges informed Hutton despondently after Deakin's statement, 'but I cannot answer for the future.'[97]

From 1905 to 1907 Australians reacted to the perception that their interests and security in the southwest Pacific were under threat, especially from Japan. It was a perception which was not shared by Britain. The Colonial Defence Committee and the Committee of Imperial Defence failed to acknowledge the strategic assessment which increasingly worried Australians. To revise their opinions, the two committees would have cast doubt on the first plank of imperial defence policy by raising difficult questions about the invincibility of the Royal Navy. It was simply not an alternative for the Whitehall strategists and would have confirmed Australian determination to develop a national defence capability which included enhanced naval defence, undoubtedly at the expense of the military forces. The issue was further complicated for Britain because imperial strategy in the southwest Pacific rested on Britain's alliance with Japan, the major source of Australian anxiety for their security. Sensing that imperial policy and their national interests were diverging, Australians moved with remarkable speed to mobilise national resources to develop their defence capability.

The War Office, however, would not easily relinquish their objective of harnessing the military capacity of the empire for concerted imperial operations. It would simply fall back on a more indirect approach.

Confronting the reality of colonial nationalism, the War Office no longer proposed the direct involvement of colonial troops in its imperial plans. Instead, it chose to influence and encourage colonial military developments along imperial lines. Standard procedures, organisations and equipment were the preparatory stages for future imperial emergencies. The Imperial General Staff, operating in an advisory capacity, was as close as the colonies would come to participation in imperial military involvement in peace. But at the close of 1907, Australia was on the verge of implementing comprehensive plans of national military development, thus fulfilling the prescription Alfred Deakin had outlined in his interview with the *Herald* more than two years earlier. Although he acknowledged a commitment to the security of the empire, the major interest Deakin had in military developments was the direction of Australian manpower and industry towards a national defence strategy.

10
Bridges, Hoad and the convergence of policy, 1908–1909

In developing the plans for the introduction of universal military training and the establishment of a national guard during 1908, Prime Minister Alfred Deakin and his Minister for Defence, Thomas Ewing, did not consult the Military Board. Apparently this decision was taken because they realised that the chief of intelligence on the board, Colonel William Throsby Bridges, was not sympathetic to their aims but, rather, was intent on protecting and preserving the military organisation introduced during Hutton's term as GOC. Ewing, a liberal Protectionist whose judgement was highly valued by Deakin, had long been convinced that Asia posed the prime threat to Australian security and was an avid proponent of compulsory military training.[1] Instead of consulting the senior officers in the Army, he had selected Major James Legge, a former barrister who had taken a permanent commission in 1894, to draw up the plans and legislation for the scheme.[2] Understandably, it was a decision which failed to please members of the Military Board,[3] but Ewing explained to parliament in September 1908 that he felt justified 'in obtaining information and assistance from any source'. As for the members of the Military Board, Ewing continued, they were free to offer advice to the Minister 'but not control him'. The introduction of universal training was a question of policy, Ewing concluded, and therefore it 'must remain under the control of Parliament and cannot be relegated to any Board'.[4]

The tension between Ewing and the Military Board over the introduction of universal training had been but thinly veiled. The members of the board resented Ewing's public reminder of their subservient role. The minister's action emphasised the sudden decline in the status and influence of the military since the abolition of the position of GOC. As Sir John Forrest commented in October 1908, since Major-General Sir Edward Hutton had relinquished his command in 1904, Australians had handed over

Sir Thomas Ewing. Ewing was Deakin's Minister for Defence from 23 January 1907 to 13 November 1908. (NATIONAL LIBRARY OF AUSTRALIA)

their forces to 'a Board, of which, so far as I know very little has since been heard'. They 'have no personality', he added.[5] It was a situation which also worried board members and, in July of the same year, they noted, lamenting their lack of recognition, that they had never received an invitation to a state function in Victoria where they were located. As 'the chief Military Administration of the Commonwealth Forces', the Military Board complained, official representation at such functions was its due.[6] At a deeper level however, the three military members of the board resented Ewing's actions because they were opposed to the military reforms proposed by Deakin and Ewing. Their attitude was undoubtedly influenced by the senior military member, Bridges, whose views were those of an imperialist temporarily frustrated in the aftermath of Hutton's failure. Significantly, it was left to a civilian—the finance member Mr Ferguson—to prompt the board to record its approval of the introduction of universal training as a step towards improved Australian defence.[7]

Bridges was in no position to oppose Ewing openly, and had become quite despondent about his impotence in influencing military developments. Indeed, since returning from his appearance before the Committee of Imperial Defence in London and his inspection of the Swiss military system, the chief of intelligence had been attempting to gain an increase to his power and authority in Australia. Yet it is equally apparent that Ewing was determined to curb Bridges' aspirations, thus explaining the minister's readiness to assert his authority over the Military Board. The old tensions between imperialist and nationalist priorities were being resolved, at least in the short term, through the eclipse of imperial influences.

In February 1907, Bridges wrote to Ewing informing him that work in the department of the Chief of Intelligence had increased to such an extent that he required assistance. The problem should be considered in conjunction with reforms in the central administration of the military forces, he counselled Ewing.[8] Two months later he recommended to the minister that a chief of the general staff, or CGS, should be appointed in place of the chief of intelligence, and that a fourth military member should be added to the Military Board to perform the duties of quartermaster general. Furthermore, Bridges wanted Ewing to approve the establishment of a general staff operating under the authority of a CGS. He believed that this would achieve the desirable goal of stronger central control over the six military districts and improved military efficiency. To support his argument, he also advised Ewing that the appointment of a CGS had been the initial intention of James McCay, the Minister for Defence who instituted the Military Board. Indeed, the appointment was considered 'necessary' by Sir George Clarke, Bridges had concluded.[9]

While Bridges did cite Clarke's support for the appointment of a CGS, he did not inform Ewing that his other recommendations were also based on a paper Clarke had given to him when he was in London.[10] Perhaps the Minister realised this because Clarke had also sent a copy of the same paper to Deakin. Nevertheless, Ewing was unimpressed by Bridges' advice, believing there were more urgent defence problems to be resolved. He was concerned that no plans for mobilisation or local defence had been developed and, emphasising the lack of preparation, noted that 'there were few reliable maps, even of the most important localities'. These were the important national defence issues which Ewing commended to Bridges for his immediate attention. As for the recommendations made by the chief of intelligence, the minister decided that he would wait until he had more experience in administering defence 'before sanctioning any important permanent arrangements'.[11] It was not so much a specific rejection of the CGS proposal as a subtle reminder to Bridges that the minister intended to maintain tight control over military developments.

It was perhaps also evidence of Ewing's disinclination to elevate one senior military officer to a position of pre-eminence as CGS. The proposal raised those sensitive questions of civil–military relations which had led to the institution of the Military Board in the first place. Yet Bridges was correct when he drew Ewing's attention to McCay's initial intention to designate one member of the Military Board as CGS. In November 1904, when McCay had first published his proposal to institute the board, he had envisaged that the CGS would be the principal military member.[12] However, when he promulgated the order to convene the board in January 1905 there was no CGS listed among the members. Instead, the closest functional equivalent to a CGS was designated the chief of intelligence with responsibility for the supervision of defence schemes and intelligence matters. The position was also listed as second in precedence to the deputy adjutant general, who supervised personnel, equipment and transport.[13] The third military member of the board was the chief of ordnance who was responsible for armament and the supply of stores and equipment. A civilian finance member and the Minister for Defence, who was the president, completed the five-member board.

It seems that, on reflection, McCay had decided against appointing a CGS because the appointment would institute a degree of military authority which a cautious civil administration was not prepared to accept. His decision to institute the Military Board was, after all, a reaction to Hutton's excesses. The minister might also have looked to Britain where the CGS enjoyed pre-eminent status and authority among senior military officers. It was a prestigious appointment. Significantly, the Australian Military Board was conceived as a means of stripping power from the senior military authority by abolishing the position of GOC, sharing his function among a group of military officers and imposing tight civil control. But, despite McCay's edict that no military member was to enjoy pre-eminent authority in the operation of the board, the reality of military rank and seniority could not be ignored completely. Therefore, it seems probable that McCay's decision was influenced also by consideration of the personalities involved. If McCay had proceeded with his initial proposal, Bridges, because of his function, would have become the CGS while the more senior Colonel John Hoad would have been appointed deputy adjutant general. Yet overriding all other considerations for the Deakin administration in 1907 was the vital issue of Bridges' imperial outlook. In attempting to develop a national defence strategy, Deakin and Ewing would not have wanted to give such a man pre-eminent status in military affairs, explaining the terms of the minister's rebuff to Bridges' proposal to appoint a CGS. The senior officer was left in no doubt that national requirements were the first priority for defence.

In December 1907, ten days after Deakin announced that a general staff would be established in Australia, Bridges gained recognition from the Military Board that, according to War Office definition, his appointment as chief of intelligence was the only General Staff appointment in the Commonwealth.[14] Six months later, in June 1908, he presented a submission to the Military Board based on the paper which Clarke had given him on the subject of reforming the central administration of the Australian forces. It was more comprehensive than his initial approach to Ewing of the previous February but the recommendations were the same. This time Bridges made no secret of the origin of his suggestions which, he claimed, would bring Australia into line with similar arrangements for the British Army Council and the Canadian Militia Council.[15]

While it was not stated by Bridges, clearly the object of his submission was not just the achievement of greater efficiency in the command and control of the Australian forces. The longstanding imperial agenda was also at work. His suggested reforms followed the imperial pattern because they were designed to prepare a functional Australian command arrangement which could easily key into the imperial network of the Imperial General Staff and so promote the development of an imperial force. To be effective, it was essential to reform the committee-like approach to military administration which existed in Australia by introducing a more direct command structure ready to respond to directions from London.

In his submission, Bridges argued that the Military Board and the headquarters staff in each military district should be organised like the staff of a military headquarters operating in the field. In relation to the Military Board, this was a distinct break with the initial concept which inspired it. He rejected the administrative committee for a functional command arrangement with enhanced central control over units and formations in the districts. 'The duties [of the board] should be grouped in natural divisions and not according to the predilection of individuals,' he argued. Accordingly, there should be a fourth military member added to the board. Two of the military members would then share responsibility for the administration and maintenance of the forces: the adjutant general would supervise manpower and discipline and the quartermaster general would supervise equipment and transport. A third member, the old chief of ordnance, should retain responsibilities for the supply of stores and equipment and the supervision of armament but he should be designated the master general of the ordnance to conform with British and Canadian practice. The remaining military position would evolve from the appointment already held by Bridges and would 'supervise the training and preparation of the forces for war and . . . study military schemes'. According to Bridges, imperial conformity demanded that this officer should be designated the CGS, but he noted that Ewing 'feared some trouble might arise by the introduction of the title'. Attempting to elicit a favourable response from the minister, Bridges claimed that failure to use it would create confusion throughout the empire.[16] It was perhaps an indication that the imperial objective for military organisation was becoming less controversial that he felt confident in using such an argument, but events were to show that in this Bridges, like Hutton before him, was being rather too sanguine.

To reassure the minister, Bridges asserted that the introduction of his suggested reforms would not establish a hierarchy of authority among military members of the board. But this was an unconvincing statement. Bridges well knew that his suggestions were designed to create a dominant military appointment with authority over vital questions which determined the operational and organisational ethos of the military forces. The remaining military appointments on the suggested board were designed to assist the achievement of these objectives and necessarily assumed supporting, or subservient, roles. The misleading nature of Bridges' submission was clearly revealed in Clarke's paper which, unwisely, Bridges had included with his own submission. Clarke had taken care to explain that, because of his special responsibilities, the CGS 'must necessarily be the premier Military Member of the Board, and, if it is thought necessary to accentuate his position as such, he should be given temporary rank'.[17] It is unlikely that Clarke failed to appreciate the promise a pre-eminent position on the Military Board held for imperial interests if the incumbent was an imperial officer, or an Australian officer like Bridges. There can be little doubt that Clarke sought more than organisational changes in the Military Board but also wanted Bridges promoted to the position of CGS.

Ewing, convinced that greater efficiency in the administration and control of the forces would be achieved, approved the functional changes and the addition of a fourth military member to the board as Bridges had suggested. But, significantly, the minister still refused to agree to designate the position occupied by Bridges as CGS. It was a question which he would address when progress had been made with the introduction of universal military training, he declared.[18] Ewing obviously wished to deny Bridges the kudos of assuming the title of CGS, being worried about additional influence Bridges might acquire. Since Hoad had left the board in January 1907 to become the Inspector-General, Bridges had become unobtrusively the dominant military member of the Board. 'Col. [sic] Bridges is doing excellent work and quietly he is achieving a great deal,' Captain Cyril Brudenell White, Hutton's former *aide-de-camp* in Australia and now a staff officer under Bridges at Army headquarters, assured Hutton in May 1908. 'His influence with the Board is most beneficial.'[19]

As subtle as Bridges' influence might have been, it had not escaped Ewing's attention and obviously worried him. In March 1908, during a meeting of the Military Board, it was decided to break with previous practice by submitting two annual reports: one from the military members and another from the civilian finance member.[20] 'I induced [Major John] Parnell and [Colonel Ernest] Wallack to join me in a Joint Annual Report which they were very willing to do, since I undertook to write it,' Bridges confided to Hutton. But the result was a critical report which was not well received by Ewing. 'It made the Minister very angry,' Bridges informed his former GOC, 'and he threatened to dismiss us and appoint Hoad GOC and held him up as a model for us to copy.' As a result of Ewing's outburst, Parnell and Wallack withdrew their support from the report, leaving Bridges to submit it on his own.[21] The following month Ewing decided that Bridges' appointment would not be designated as the CGS for the time being, a decision which suggested that the minister might have been preserving the prestigious appointment for Hoad.

Certainly the direction of Bridges' leadership was clear—and in clear contrast to Hoad's nationalist priorities. With the assistance of Brudenell White, he used his influence in the routine business of the Military Board and Army headquarters to serve imperial interests. For example, in Decem-

Bridges, Hoad and the Convergence of Policy

ber 1907 the board approved his recommendation to print and distribute to the military forces 600 copies of the papers prepared by the British General Staff for the Colonial Conference of 1907. These were the papers which advocated the development of standard imperial procedures for the military forces of the empire and laid the foundation for the development of the Imperial General Staff, which Brudenell White hoped, in writing to Hutton, would be 'the first step to Imperial military consolidation'.[22] Bridges also endeavoured to preserve Hutton's organisation for the field force—'all Hoad's efforts have altered it very little', Brudenell White assured Hutton. And, because military organisations were the responsibility of Bridges at Army headquarters, Brudenell White told Hutton that he 'need not fear any stupid alterations which are preventible'.[23] Bridges could also use his influence to improve the standard of military training—'particularly if they make him chief of the genl. Staff', Brudenell White continued in his correspondence with Hutton. 'Training is one urgent need and for this we require as you say Sir, good British officer comdts. in each state.' But the young Australian officer's ability to assist the chief of intelligence at Army headquarters came to an end late in 1908 when he received a posting order as a junior staff officer at the War Office. Initially Brudenell White was disappointed, informing Hutton that he would rather remain in Melbourne because he was 'very anxious to have a humble share in the working out of your plans for the Austn. forces'. However, he consoled himself with the thought that in London he could contribute to the development of the Imperial General Staff. 'I am glad if I am to be a humble agent for its furtherance!' Brudenell White confessed to Hutton.[24]

Despite the assistance and support of men like Brudenell White, Bridges knew that the real threat to the development of an expeditionary force in Australia was universal military training. He feared that Hutton's field force would not survive its introduction, and to his disappointment, he was powerless to prevent the Deakin government proceeding with the scheme. The legislation was introduced to the House of Representatives by Ewing on 29 September 1908.

Ewing's Bill, as he informed the House, was virtually the same in principle and 'almost every detail' as Deakin had foreshadowed in his major defence statement of the previous December.[25] Training would be compulsory for youths from the age of 12 until they turned 18, either at school or after leaving school. Their commitment would amount to 52 one-hour sessions and four one-day sessions each year. On reaching 18 years of age, youths would be enrolled in the defence forces—some would be allocated to the Navy but the majority would fill the ranks of the military force to be known as the National Guard. The young men would then undergo compulsory training until they reached the age of 26. Most members of the forces would receive training of eighteen days' duration each year during the first three years of their service. During each of the subsequent five years these men would train for seven working days. The remaining men, who would be allocated to the more technically demanding areas of the military forces—the artillery and the engineers—would receive more rigorous training. Their annual commitment would be 28 days for the first five years and seven days for the last three years. Employers would face prosecution and fines if they dismissed or penalised trainees, or docked their wages.[26]

In defending the government against the emotive charge that it was introducing conscription, Ewing pointed out correctly that the *Defence Act* of 1903 already empowered the government to conscript men of military age to defend Australia in the event of invasion. 'If the Government or this Parliament permitted the manhood of Australia to engage unprepared in the defence of the country,' Ewing argued persuasively, 'they would simply send them to the shambles, to be destroyed by men who had made use of their period of preparation.'[27] On this basis, the government justified compulsory enlistment, or conscription, for military and naval training.

Ewing's Bill exemplified a new mood in Australian politics, a mood inspired by fears for national security sufficiently strong to dispel the liberal aversion to militarism and compulsion of earlier years. Indeed, the Minister for Defence publicly rejected the opinion of the Committee of Imperial Defence that Australia needed only to prepare defences against raids 'of some thousand men with a few unarmoured cruisers'. 'If that were all we had to fear we might almost hope to cope with it by means of the police,' Ewing claimed. Contrary to the long-held British opinion, it was his belief that Australia was 'in more danger of absolute destruction than . . . any other part of the British Empire', and that the Commonwealth therefore had to develop its national defence. Ewing, like many of his fellow countrymen, was influenced by racial images of predatory Asians, but he perceived also the bias in imperial defence policy. The strength of the Royal Navy was obviously on the wane, he believed, and, in the event of war, it would be deployed mainly in protecting 'the heart of the Empire—the "power-house of the line"—to hold it intact against invasion and to so arrange that the food supplies of Great Britain shall continue without stint'. Hence the need for Australia to look after itself. Yet, in stating the case for Australian defence, the minister did not advocate complete independence from Britain. The preservation of Australian security by the measures which he proposed, Ewing concluded, was not only a national, but also an imperial, obligation.[28] Realising the need for self-reliance in defence, these men also had to contend with the strength of the imperial attachment. Therefore, like Deakin, he claimed that improved Australian defence was in itself a contribution to imperial security.

Despite his testimony of imperial loyalty, Ewing was inspired chiefly by nationalist sentiment. While it was not explained during the minister's speech, the Defence Bill incorporated a most important aspect of Deakin's

Bridges, Hoad and the Convergence of Policy

Senator George Foster Pearce. As Minister for Defence in the Fisher Labor government, Pearce gave the British Chief of the Imperial General Staff, General Sir William Nicholson, an undertaking on 17 June 1911 that that he would begin preparations for Australia to provide an expeditionary force for a war which was expected in 1915. Pearce never disclosed this undertaking to the Australian people. (NATIONAL LIBRARY OF AUSTRALIA)

earlier statement on defence: the government had no intention of maintaining an organised force in Australia for an expeditionary role. As well as retaining the original provision in the *Defence Act* of 1903 which denied a government the power to despatch forces outside Australia, Ewing's Bill envisaged that volunteers for overseas service would join the Imperial Army individually and not serve as members of a distinct Australian force. The implications for Hutton's field force were obvious. Furthermore, the Bill laid the groundwork for imperial officers serving in the Australian forces to be subject to Australian legislation.[29] It was undoubtedly provisions like these which alarmed Bridges. Writing to Hutton on the day on which Ewing introduced his legislation, he observed despondently that the only hope lay in parliament's rejection of the Bill. Otherwise, he told Hutton, 'the mischief will be done and our existing forces destroyed'. A dejected Bridges believed there was little chance that the government could be diverted from its goal and, he concluded pessimistically, 'it seems doubtful if they will be put out of office'.[30]

Almost without warning, Bridges and Hutton received a reprieve. After barely commencing its passage through parliament, Ewing's Defence Bill became irrelevant. On 6 November 1908, Andrew Fisher, who had become leader of the Labor Party when Watson had retired earlier in the year, withdrew support from the Deakin government, not for any one reason, and not because of Ewing's Bill, but as a result of several minor issues of difference. As a result, Fisher formed the second federal Labor government.

It is not hard to imagine the sense of relief with which Bridges would have viewed the demise of the Deakin government. If it did not mean the final scrapping of universal military training, at least it ended a difficult relationship with Ewing. Ewing's successor as Minister for Defence, Senator George Foster Pearce, initially little known, turned out to be much less threatening than Ewing. He had left school at the age of 11, trained as a carpenter, and made his living as an itinerant worker and prospector before entering politics. Having no military experience and lacking in formal education, Pearce, an otherwise capable man, was poorly prepared for his portfolio.[31] He needed the advice and support of experienced men and, although Ewing had advised him that Bridges was 'an impossible man', the new minister put his trust in the military officer. 'I pointed out to him that I had no military experience and asked him for his advice in such circumstances as to my future actions,' Pearce wrote of his early relationship with Bridges.[32] The Chief of Intelligence could hardly believe his good fortune. In December, the month after Pearce assumed office, the Military Board endorsed a submission by the adjutant general that Bridges' position on the board as chief of intelligence should be redesignated as CGS. Unlike Ewing, Pearce gave his immediate agreement.[33] It is doubtful whether the new minister realised that he had presided over more than a change in military title. But, as a result, Bridges and other imperialists certainly anticipated increased authority in defeating nationalist influence on the development of the military forces.

At the time of Bridges' appointment as the CGS, Hoad was in London. He had arrived there over three months earlier, in mid-September 1908, with instructions from Deakin to discuss the establishment of the Imperial General Staff with the staff at the War Office.[34] Hoad was obviously an officer whom Deakin felt he could trust to protect Australian interests, but, in the opinion of Bridges, who was more attuned to the imperial aspirations behind the Imperial General Staff, it was, as he informed Hutton, 'hard to conceive a worse selection for such work'.[35]

The instructions which Deakin had given Hoad—a copy was also sent to the British authorities[36]—spelt out the broad policy of the Australian government in relation to its military forces. Significantly, the Imperial General Staff scheme was now perceived by Deakin not only as a source of informed military advice but also a means of representing Australian defence interests in Whitehall. Therefore, Hoad was instructed to inform the British authorities of the requirements of Commonwealth defence 'from an Australian point of view'. He was to explain the sentiments 'animating Australia in such matters' while pointing out that the defence policy of Australia, 'as expressed in the Commonwealth *Defence Act*', gave the government 'authority only for the raising and maintenance of troops for the defence and protection of the Commonwealth'. He was briefed to explain to the British authorities that Australians were permitted to serve outside the Commonwealth on a voluntary basis, but he was to reiterate emphatically that the Australian military forces were only 'organized for Home Defence'.[37]

In the interests of diplomacy, an attempt was made to dilute the national emphasis in Hoad's instructions by noting that Australian participation in the Boer War was evidence 'that Australians are prepared to voluntarily take their part anywhere in the Defence of the Empire'. Furthermore, after the instructions had been drafted in the Department of Defence, one additional provision appeared in the final copy, presumably added by Deakin. But it was not a primary instruction. The Australian officer was empowered to *'discuss the desirability* of initiating a scheme for ultimately uniting the forces of Great Britain and the Colonies in one general bond for common defence—bearing in mind the foregoing conditions'.[38] Clearly, this statement would appeal to the British authorities and so strengthen Hoad's position in his dealings with them. But, at the same time, its addition was more than a diplomatic concession: it added a sense of imperial balance to the national accent of the initial draft and was not inconsistent with Deakin's idealistic view of Australia's role in the empire. The Australian Prime Minister was committed to the ideal of imperial unity, but he believed strongly that it should not be to the detriment of national integrity. Australia, in Deakin's view, should participate in the determination of imperial defence and foreign policy and not just accept domination from London.[39] However, as co-operative as this approach was, it was still perceived in London as a threat to British control.

Arriving in London two months before the fall of the Deakin government, Hoad was welcomed with open arms by War Office officials. Not only was Australia the first member of the empire to take a positive step towards co-operating in the development of the Imperial General Staff, but Hoad's instructions, despite enabling him only to *'discuss the desirability'* of uniting the forces of the empire, held great promise for Britain's defence planners. Brudenell White, who had already assumed his appointment on the staff at the War Office, was resentful, but was also, it seems, puzzled as a result of the attention Hoad received. Sharing his feelings with Bridges, Brudenell White believed that the British authorities had 'erred in overdoing their part—there was no need to make so much fuss of him'. The senior Australian officer was given audiences with the King and the Prince of Wales. He was also 'chief spokesman at the Canada Club dinner' and, as Brudenell White's comments suggest, was obviously enjoying the attention. Hoad was 'certainly pushing', Brudenell White noted, and 'he has been continually in evidence'.[40]

Brudenell White noticed another important aspect of Hoad's behaviour in London. The senior Australian officer gave the impression that he expected to be appointed as the first CGS in Australia. Indeed, it is likely that Hoad had been promised the appointment by Ewing before he left Australia, a promise consistent with the minister's refusal to appoint Bridges to the position. 'I have not the least doubt in my mind that the gentleman means to be C.G.S.,' Brudenell White informed Bridges before news of Bridges' appointment reached London. 'I am wondering what then is to be your fate?' The antagonism between Hoad and Bridges had its origins in their different views of Hutton's proposals for the Australian forces and, in Brudenell White's opinion, the extent of the disagreement meant that Bridges would be unable to work under Hoad if he were appointed CGS. He therefore told Bridges that he was unable to 'see how you are to be got out of the way'. 'I do not think we can expect much assistance from these people here,' Brudenell White observed astutely of the War Office staff, 'they will give in on any personal matter in order to secure a favourable reception for their broad principles.' Clearly, the establishment of the Imperial General Staff was more important to them than the welfare of Bridges and, certainly, Hutton's long-forgotten and irrelevant scheme. Given the encouraging signs emanating from Australia and Hoad's co-operative mood, Bridges suddenly assumed less importance in Whitehall. Brudenell White became concerned for the welfare of his former master. 'I am not speaking with any inner knowledge,' he told Bridges, 'but if you were offered an appointment here, would you like it?' Bridges could then leave Hoad in Australia as CGS 'to work out his own Salvation, and await the end of his first period,' Brudenell White suggested.[41] The young Australian officer could not have foreseen the remarkable and sudden turn of events in Australia which saw the demise of the Deakin government and the appointment of Bridges as the CGS.

In December 1908, three months after Hoad's arrival in London, the British CGS, General Sir William Nicholson, released the War Office paper on the establishment of the Imperial General Staff. Although it appeared over Nicholson's signature, Major-General Sir Douglas Haig, as Director of Staff Duties, was chiefly responsible for its composition.[42] Drawn up on the basis of the decision by the Colonial Conference of 1907 to establish an informed consultative body of military opinion for the empire, it was, in reality, a blueprint for the development of the imperial military force which Britain had been working towards since the Carnarvon commission of 1879. The introductory section of the paper claimed that defence of the empire had to be considered on two levels. The first requirement was that local defence arrangements should enable 'each particular division of the Empire to secure itself against reasonable initial contingencies' but, Haig observed, 'no organization for defence can be regarded as adequate or complete which does not contemplate offensive action'. There was therefore a second requirement of imperial defence which would enable the military forces of the empire to combine for concerted offensive operations. Concentration, Haig noted, was a 'fundamental principle of war, and the existence of different schools of thought in an army is fatal to such combination'. 'The ideal to be arrived at,' he concluded in his introduction, 'is that all divisions of a military force should be capable of acting in war as parts of a whole.' The Imperial General Staff provided the means of achieving this end.[43]

A central element of the organisation would be located in London, 'working directly under the Chief of the Imperial General Staff'. It would 'consider and draw up plans for the defence of the Empire as a whole . . . study and formulate broad principles of general application, and . . . collect and disseminate general information.' Local branches would also be established in each of the regular garrisons, in India and in the self-governing dominions. 'But,' Haig noted, 'the Imperial General Staff must be an entity; therefore, these local branches must form part of one whole, springing from the central body.' It would be regarded as a large organisation with a central body and branches 'stretching out to all the various units of an army'. A local section in each dominion, comprised of dominion officers, would have 'a Chief at its head' and representatives in the elements of the local forces in the various regions. It would deal with questions of local defence as well as the supervision of training in accordance with the policy of the War Office. The chief of the local section, Haig believed, would be the 'adviser of his own Government as well as the head of all General Staff Officers in his section whether at his headquarters or with the troops'.[44]

The relationship between the central section at the War Office and local sections in the dominions was obviously a difficult area and ran the risk of inflaming nationalist sensibilities. Haig was unable to ignore the problem. To start with he believed that the organisation should be 'built up gradually' under 'the more or less direct supervision of the Chief of the Imperial General Staff'.[45] Yet, once established, Haig confessed that the relationship between the central chief and the regional chief could entail further difficulties. In view of the conditions determined by the colonial representatives at the 1907 conference, he had no alternative but to admit that the central chief would be unable to issue orders to the local chiefs. To overcome this difficulty, Haig proposed various methods of ensuring that a standard imperial doctrine was established and disseminated by 'close and frequent personal communication between the centre and the branches . . . to prevent the initiation and growth of divergent opinion'. The selection, education and training of imperial and dominion officers before appointment to the General Staff were therefore paramount. Attendance at the British staff college, Camberley, was to be considered a necessity not only to ensure that officers had been educated 'up to a certain common standard of military knowledge' but had 'become imbued with the requisite uniformity of thought and practice'. To consolidate the process of indoctrination, staff officers from local sections would occasionally be appointed to the central section, forming a direct link with their regional sections. Frequent conferences would also be held.[46]

Haig's paper was motivated by a sense of urgency because, as he noted in its introduction, in the near future there would be 'a great development in the potential military resources of the Empire'.[47] The British General Staff obviously had one eye on the progress towards the introduction of universal military training in Australia. Similar developments were also imminent in New Zealand. As Haig put it, the Imperial General Staff had to be inaugurated 'without any avoidable delay' because there were 'cases where the oversea Dominions are contemplating a considerable expansion of their military forces on new principles'. It was therefore of paramount importance, he concluded, that 'the military forces of the Empire should not be allowed to develop on divergent and independent lines, but on common and approved principles as regards organization and training'.[48] What was being proposed in Haig's lengthy paper was stated more succinctly in the covering letter from the Army Council to the Colonial Office, a copy of which subsequently arrived in Australia. It was recognised, the Army Council explained, that the self-governing status of the dominions permitted no guarantees or commitments for the supply of contingents of specified strength or composition in the event of war, but, as happened in South Africa, they were assured that such support would be forthcoming. The council therefore suggested that, in organising for their local defence, the dominions should give consideration to the preparations required for 'a situation in which [they] desired to give effective military service in association with the troops of the Mother Country'. It advocated the development of two separate elements in dominion military forces, one for local defence and the other 'designed for the service of the Empire as a whole'. 'Such a contingency has been kept in view in the accompanying paper,' the council concluded.[49]

Notwithstanding the comments by the Army Council, the chief military architect of universal training in Australia and now quartermaster general on the Military Board, James Legge, quickly deduced the British General Staff's true objective and exposed the difficulties when he examined Haig's paper. 'Carefully worded though it is,' Legge noted, attributing authorship to Nicholson as the signatory, 'an analysis of the memorandum shows that, interleaved in the recommendation of the C.G.S. is much that was not asked for by the resolution of the Imperial Conference.' To start with, Legge questioned the compatibility of the proposed imperial organisation with the practice of democratic government. The Imperial General Staff was clearly an imperial instrument with the capability of influencing the development of local military forces but without responsibility to the electorate. The British CGS had also been vague in his choice of words in certain areas. For example, Legge continued, the development of 'general principles' on which the military forces should be built might 'be taken by the War Office to cover discussion of and advice on larger matters, such as whether the organisation and training of the troops should be for Imperial Service abroad, or primarily, for Australian Defence'.[50]

The British CGS had clearly assumed that the forces of the empire would be combined into one imperial force, but the Australian people had not been consulted on the issue, Legge charged. Furthermore, he pointed out that Britain had developed a force of 500 000 men for home defence but 300 000 of them—the militia—were not liable to serve outside Britain. Therefore, he asked, 'why should the Citizen Forces of Australia be liable to service abroad when those of Great Britain are not?' Somewhat tongue-in-cheek, he attempted to absolve Nicholson from blame by observing that the paper might cause 'a strong suspicion to arise that he has been speaking not on his own opinions, but those of his Government'. When examined in conjunction with the comments by the Army Council, the British CGS's intention was clear, Legge concluded. 'By all means let us have an Imperial General Staff, to attain uniformity of military methods,' he recommended, 'but the ideas of Imperial Co-operation, so plainly suggested for acceptance in the letter of the Army Council [and the CGS's paper] need to be understood and accepted advisedly, or expressly reserved for further consideration.'[51]

It seems that Legge's trenchant criticism of aspects of Haig's paper made Pearce think again about the Imperial General Staff. At first the minister had accepted what the British General Staff had proposed,[52] but he soon changed his mind. Undoubtedly influencing Pearce's thinking was a British proposal he had seen a month earlier, designed to give Britain full control of dominion troops in time of war. The British authorities wanted the Australian *Defence Act* amended because, while it placed Australian soldiers on active service under the British *Army Act*, it did so only insofar as it was 'not inconsistent with the local law'. If this qualification was removed, the British authorities reasoned, then they would have control of Australian troops as if they 'belonged to the regular forces [of Britain]'.[53] However, when this proposal was placed before the Military Board in January 1909, Pearce balked, deferring a decision. Yet, determined to have the *Defence Act* amended, Bridges used all his influence to achieve a positive response from Pearce at the next meeting, two weeks later.[54] 'The D.M.O. [Director of Military Operations] seemed pleased at the action which you have managed to get the Board to take,' Brudenell White wrote enthusiastically from the War Office.[55] But it was too early to consider the matter settled. At the end of February, when Pearce considered Haig's paper in conjunction with Legge's comments, he obviously realised that the two issues were directly related. Not only was the *Defence Act* never amended, but Pearce withdrew his initial, uncritical acceptance of Haig's paper, voicing his concern at the suggestion that the dominions should commit themselves to military developments with the object of undertaking imperial operations. Specifically, he was worried that participation in the Imperial General Staff scheme, as Haig had proposed 'might be construed into a willingness on our part to assist in the formation and provision of expeditionary forces not designed for local defence, but possibly and conceivably for the carrying into effect of some Imperial policy, in the shaping and deciding of which Australia and other Colonial Dominions had been given no voice'.[56] Prime Minister Andrew Fisher agreed with Pearce and informed the British authorities that participation in the Imperial General Staff scheme was not to be considered as a binding commitment by Australia to develop any special forces for service either outside, or indeed within, Australia.[57]

Remarkably, Hoad, ardent nationalist and member of the Australian Natives Association, embraced Haig's paper on the Imperial General Staff. Indeed, when Pearce pressed Hoad for his comments on the paper, he replied from London that he had given his assistance in the final stages of its composition and therefore concurred 'with [the] general principles enumerated'.[58] The Secretary of State for War, Richard Burdon Haldane, had discussed a draft of Haig's paper with Hoad and Sir Frederick Borden of Canada in December, presumably testing its acceptability from a dominion perspective. As a result, amendments suggested by Hoad and Borden were included in the paper before it was released.[59] It was a remarkable turnaround for the senior Australian officer. Hoad's rise to prominence and his rapid promotion to senior rank under the Deakin government had largely been the result of his nationalist stance on defence. Of course, he had not seen Legge's specific comments on Haig's paper, but he had professed similar sentiments over a long period of time. Indeed, in certain circumstances, the senior Australian officer had and would continue to express them, but in London Hoad supported Haig's proposals.

Responding formally to Haig's paper, Hoad cast aside the primary elements of the instructions which had been given to him by Deakin and proceeded to outline plans for the Australian forces which were hand-in-glove with the British proposals. In his opening paragraph, he acknowledged that the Australian forces were 'maintained and organized primarily with a view to safeguarding Australia from any reasonably probable form of attack' but this was his only, hollow concession to the expressed policy of the Deakin government, which had fallen two months earlier. 'The object of any military organisation in Australia may . . . be considered of a two-fold nature,' Hoad wrote. One object of Australian military forces, he continued, was 'the security of the Commonwealth against all reasonable contingencies or until such time as the naval and military resources of the Empire can be concentrated at the decisive point or points'. The other object was the ability of the Australian force to combine with the other forces of the empire for 'efficient co-operation in the event of more extensive undertakings being necessary'. These results, Hoad believed, would be achieved by Australian participation in the Imperial General Staff as Haig had indicated.[60] Although not yet aware of the concern expressed by Fisher and Pearce, Hoad had given a clear signal to the War Office that he was prepared to co-operate in their proposals. Nicholson, therefore, could not have been more pleased when he read Hoad's report. The Australian officer's proposals appeared 'to be in full accordance with the general principles propounded in the War Office paper, and to call for no remarks from me', the British CGS commented.[61]

Brudenell White was sceptical about Hoad's apparent new-found sense of imperial co-operation. 'These good folk here think they have converted him from anti-educational, anti-imperial and republican sentiments,' Brudenell White reported to Bridges, believing that Hoad's new mood would not last. But his pessimism was not shared by the War Office officials, perhaps because they had seen more often than Brudenell White how totally personal ambition and flattering professional patronage could transform more abstract commitments. 'They smile at me when I say that the assumed air of conversion will only last until he crosses the 5 fathom line [after his departure from England],' he told Bridges.[62] The staff at the War Office remained quietly confident about future developments, despite Brudenell White's doubts about the strength of Hoad's imperial conviction. Certainly, they did not share the fear of Hutton, Bridges and Brudenell White about the introduction of universal military training. As Haig had indicated in his paper on the Imperial General Staff, Britain had every reason to support the introduction of schemes like compulsory military training so long as the developments proceeded along what Haig called 'common and approved principles as regards organization and training'.[63] Obviously, the War Office staff had more confidence than Brudenell White in retaining Hoad's co-operation. 'They have erred however with their eyes open,' Brudenell White wrote to Bridges in disgust, 'and I have been quite persistent in urging the danger of lending support to any of H___'s projects. They are however so pitiably afraid of doing anything to retard the progress of the Imperial Genl. Staff that they will expose their souls to any risk!'[64]

There can be little doubt that Hoad jettisoned his nationalist principles and supported Haig's proposals because of personal ambition. One month before he had finished his report on Haig's paper, news reached London that Bridges had been appointed as CGS in Australia. 'It has caused a little consternation here as Gen. Hoad seemed quite certain, apparently, that if there was to be a General Staff, he would be chief,' White told Bridges. 'It will be rather interesting now to see what tactics will be employed—and I opine that they will have to be masterly to replace you.'[65] Retaliating quickly, Hoad seized Haig's proposal for the local CGS to be the primary military adviser and head staff officer in the local forces. In his report, Hoad recommended adoption of this proposal in Australia. Cleverly, he also proposed that military inspections of a special nature, such as those concerned with major camps and manoeuvres, should be undertaken by the CGS or a senior staff officer appointed by him especially for the task. The more routine inspections of military administration should be undertaken by members of the Military Board, he recommended.[66] Hoad did not spell out the implications, but the introduction of these recommendations in Australia would effectively abolish the position of inspector-general which he currently occupied. With such an outcome, Hoad, as the senior Australian officer with the rank of major-general, would inevitably be appointed to the senior staff appointment occupied by Bridges, who held the rank of colonel. Hoad therefore had one good reason to sanction Haig's proposals and, discreetly, Nicholson added his support.

In his comments on Hoad's report, the British CGS agreed with the recommendation for the Australian CGS but, diplomatically, left it to the Australian authorities to decide on the inspection function.[67] Five years earlier, Nicholson had described Hoad as 'an officer of inferior education and small military capacity' without ever having met him.[68] It was a judgement which was clearly influenced by Hutton's advice to Nicholson of 1904 when Hutton had decided to denigrate Hoad, whom he perceived as a nationalist threat to his imperial scheming.[69] But, after meeting Hoad in London in the winter of 1908, Nicholson changed his opinion of the Australian officer. He now described him as 'personally pleasant, good tempered and obliging; and [furthermore] he possesses tact and knows how to keep in touch with the leaders of political parties in his own country'.[70] Nicholson seemed satisfied that imperial military plans would be secure with Hoad as CGS in Australia.

The object of Hoad's scheming did not escape the attention of Bridges in Australia. He wrote immediately to Pearce pointing out that the introduction of Hoad's recommendations would mean 'by inference that the appointment of Inspector General should be abolished'. Bridges also opposed Hoad's recommendation for the CGS to become the head staff officer and the chief military adviser to the minister, describing it as 'a radical and detrimental change'. Arguing his case, he maintained the illusion that there was no hierarchy among the senior officers on the Military Board with each enjoying access to the minister. 'An appointment will be created with the power of a General Officer Commanding but without responsibility,' the CGS informed Pearce.[71] Obviously, Bridges wanted arrangements to stay as they were, so permitting him to remain in the prestigious staff appointment. But the minister was unsure of what he should do and sought the opinion of the other members of the Military Board.[72]

In their responses, the military members of the board were unanimous and echoed Bridges' warning. The CGS would assume pre-eminent power and status if Hoad's recommendations were implemented, and they opposed such an outcome.[73] The acting secretary of the Department of Defence, Samuel Petherbridge, who probably was unaffected by the loyalties and undercurrents in the military camp, alone supported Hoad's recommendation. He informed Pearce that, after close observation of the Military Board in operation, he had come to the conclusion that 'no matter how many members are actually on the Board and notwithstanding the accepted theory that each member is responsible to the Minister for matters connected with his own department, in actual practice it almost invariably means that the member with the strongest personality becomes (perhaps unconsciously) the member from whom the Minister obtains the advice he values most and thus becomes practically the Minister's chief adviser'.[74] The military members could not have been unaware of this reality but became accomplices of Bridges in denying it. While Bridges' motive is clear, there are a number of reasons which might have influenced the other members. Among them are loyalty to Bridges; personal dislike of Hoad and his scheming; the loss in perceived status which each of them would suffer if the CGS was formally recognised as the paramount military appointment and the ministerial adviser; and, perhaps in the case of Legge, fear of what might happen to universal military training if either Hoad or Bridges acquired inordinate authority.

Confronted with conflicting recommendations and advice, Pearce attempted to resolve the issue as amicably as he could. He removed Bridges from the office of CGS after a tenure of less than five months but decided to send him to London as one of the Australian representatives at an Imperial Conference on Defence to be held later in the year. After the conference, he was to assume a staff appointment at the War Office as the first Australian representative on the nascent Imperial General Staff.[75] Bridges' departure from high military office was perhaps made easier by the knowledge that the Fisher government had arranged for him to be appointed as a Companion of the Most Distinguished Order of Saint Michael and Saint George at Buckingham Palace. But it was still inadequate compensation for Bridges. Before he left Australia, he obtained a written understanding from Pearce that he would be reappointed as CGS on his return.[76]

With Bridges out of the prime staff position, the way was clear to appoint Hoad as CGS. But, initially, Pearce contemplated not giving him a seat on the Military Board in view of the proposal to establish the Imperial General Staff. 'I think this is wise,' he told Fisher, 'because if we were to connect that position with the Military Board we would be connecting up Imperial control with our local administration.'[77] His comments illustrated a determination to protect the national forces from direct imperial influence but they also indicated Pearce's failure to understand the operation of the Military Board. Originally conceived as an administrative committee, it had, in fact, developed into a functional command headquarters, especially since Ewing had approved the realignment of functions and roles of members on the recommendation of Bridges. It was inconceivable that the CGS would not sit on the board. This was obviously brought to the tyro minister's attention, because he changed his mind one week later, deciding that Hoad *would* be given a seat on the board. At the same time, probably attempting both to accede to the wishes of the other military members and to maintain ministerial control, he still promoted the misconception that the Military Board was a committee. In appointing Hoad as the CGS, Pearce decreed that appointments to the board were 'not intended to convey any positions of superiority and, as at present, each member will be primarily and directly responsible to the Minister for the Department assigned to him'.[78]

Bridges had every reason to be despondent as he prepared to leave Australia for London in mid-1909. Apart from the injury to his personal pride at being ousted from the prime staff appointment so quickly, there were also doubts whether the new CGS would serve the imperial cause as effectively as he had done. With the pliable Pearce as minister, Bridges had been in an excellent position to exercise imperial influence. Yet there were also political developments afoot. Although Brudenell White was 'praying hard that the Labor Ministry may remain,'[79] within days of Bridges' departure the three separate non-Labor political factions, which had developed in federal politics, united as the Fusion ministry, so removing Fisher's government from power. Alfred Deakin was again Prime Minister of Australia, but this time imperialists had little to fear.

The international situation had changed since Deakin's previous tenure in the office. Early in 1909, while Fisher's government was still in power, the imperial dimension in Australian defence considerations had received a new emphasis. On 19 March the *Age* had revealed that, according to statements by Britain's Prime Minister Asquith and the First Lord of the Admiralty, Reginald McKenna, Germany's battleship building program threatened the supremacy of the Royal Navy. It was believed possible that Germany might possess more heavy battleships than Britain by 1912. Australia was caught up in the empire-wide panic of the dreadnought crisis: 'that period of temporary hysteria', as William Morris Hughes referred to it a few months later.[80] The impulsive response by New Zealand was to offer Britain the gift of a dreadnought. Fisher resisted pressure to do likewise but the state governments of New South Wales and Victoria, spurred on by imperial fervour, offered to share the cost on a *per capita* basis if the Commonwealth failed to do so.[81]

The Labor Prime Minister had been prepared to acknowledge that Australian naval forces, such as they were, would be placed at the disposal of Britain in an emergency but, otherwise, he believed that local resources should be directed towards enhancing Australian defence.[82] As a first step towards an Australian fleet, Fisher's government had already decided before the dreadnought crisis erupted to place orders for two destroyers to be built in Britain and a third to be assembled locally from British components. At the height of the crisis in late March, Fisher delivered a major statement on national defence policy at Gympie, a small town in the centre of his electorate of Wide Bay. The Labor government was committed to the introduction of compulsory military training, the building of an Australian navy and the development of a local munitions industry, he said.[83] There would be no gift of a dreadnought to Britain. But while Fisher resisted the temptation to be swept up in the imperial hysteria, others succumbed.

The proposal to donate a dreadnought found support among conservative politicians in Australia. Deakin, whose attention had been occupied recently by the problem of uniting the three non-Labor groups in federal parliament, was not prepared to oppose the suggestion. He had decided to play the part of a political opportunist. Perhaps without conviction, he therefore declared his agreement with the dreadnought proposal, hoping to win the approval of conservative politicians. But his decision disappointed at least one of his liberal supporters. 'I was rather sorry to get your wire yesterday saying that you are keen on the Dreadnought offer,' friend and confidant Arthur Jose wrote to Deakin from Sydney at the beginning of April.[84] Jose, a journalist and historian,[85] seems to have sensed that Deakin's decision was politically expedient, but tried tactfully to inform Deakin that he had erred.

There were many Australians who, like Jose, supported the development of Australian defence within the imperial framework, but not by paying tribute to Britain. It was their belief that the 'best help the colonies can give is the strengthening of their own defences,' as Jose, a founder of the Sydney branch of the Australian National Defence League, assured Deakin. But the offer of a dreadnought, he argued, was 'irrelevant to local defence', 'fostered by people who are against local defence', and, furthermore, was 'a positive harm to local defence, because it withdrew funds which are needed for that purpose'.[86]

The view expressed by Jose faced a conservative political challenge. Before the month had ended, he was again writing to Deakin bemoaning the recent development that the 'question of Australia's contribution to the defence of the Empire seems to have become so much a matter of party controversy'. The Sydney journalist was upset that 'hot-headed and narrow-minded' politicians had made the issue 'a test, purely for electioneering purposes, of loyalty to the Empire, and should be able to import the cries of "loyalty" and "disloyalty" into local quarrels which are sure to be fought out bitterly not long hence'. It was disappointing for Jose to contemplate such an outcome, but he conceded that it appeared 'inevitable' as he looked forward 'with great misgiving to seeing the Empire degraded to a party catchword'.[87] Degradation or not, the dreadnought crisis was a catalyst in mobilising a conservative political reaction in Australia to embrace imperial defence policy.

A few weeks later a political platform for a federal liberal party was adopted at a meeting in Victoria. Its defence plank was the development of 'the Australian Naval and Military Forces by means of Universal Training commenced in the schools, and a Commonwealth Coastal Defence'.[88] As foremost liberal politician, Deakin negotiated with the other two non-Labor factions, the corner party led by Sir John Forrest—essentially a group of deserters from Deakin's Protectionist Party who had objected to reliance on Labor's support—and the direct-opposition led by Joseph Cook, attempting to define common ground for a political fusion. It was Cook's group of conservative Free Traders who proved most difficult. In dealing with them, the defence plank underwent a subtle change in emphasis. Deakin explained to them that the liberal defence policy embraced local defence—he referred to it as 'Imperial defence here'—as a first priority and 'then elsewhere upon some constitutional plan'.[89] Deakin's careful choice of words and the promise of further imperial developments, albeit hedged by constitutional considerations, struck a deliberate note of conciliation for conservative members of Cook's faction, a note which also held special appeal for the ears of Forrest. At a final meeting between the leaders of the three factions on the morning of 25 May it was noted that the liberal defence plank would 'stand almost untouched'. But there was an ominous addendum: on matters of defence, Australia was 'to be put in touch with British Naval and Military authorities'.[90]

That afternoon, at a meeting of Deakin's liberal group, Sir William Lyne was driven to anger and despair at the imminent fusion with the parties led by Cook and Forrest. 'We are asked to join men who will hoodwink us in carrying out our programme,' Lyne thundered. 'If the Party does the thing contemplated we will go down, down, down as conservatives!'[91] But Deakin was not to be diverted; it appeared to some that he was prepared to pay any price to become Prime Minister again. When the basis of fusion was published four days later, it was clear that the imperial connection had not been overlooked. The naval and military forces were to be developed 'with the advice and assistance of the Admiralty and War Office, by means of universal training, commenced in the schools, and a Commonwealth coastal defence [would be established] . . . ' Furthermore, the new political group declared that it would 'recognise our Imperial responsibilities'.[92] This basis of agreement, Governor-General Lord Dudley observed when he informed Lord Crew, secretary of state for the colonies, was an 'interesting statement'.[93]

By mid-1909, national influence over Australian military developments was in decline. As a result of imperial manipulation, Australia had established the dominant military appointment of CGS. It was a vital achievement because, in a hierarchical authoritarian organisation like the Army, it provided an effective means of introducing and disseminating standard doctrine throughout the rank and file. As CGS, Bridges subsequently used his influence with ease to serve imperial objectives. The kudos associated with the prestigious appointment also laid ambitious men open to manipulation. Hoad, the avowed nationalist, was seduced easily into apostasy by the opportunity of becoming CGS. Thereafter, with the debate over the position of CGS resolved in favour of the imperialists and with Australia's willingness to participate in the Imperial General Staff scheme, British military doctrine and practice quickly and easily assumed dominance in the forces. As Haig had realised in arguing the case for the Imperial General Staff, the

Bridges, Hoad and the Convergence of Policy

achievement of imperial military objectives meant that dominion forces 'should not be allowed to develop on divergent and independent lines'. As far as the military forces were concerned, the plan espoused by Deakin in December 1907 to adapt comprehensively military developments to national requirements and conditions had already been despatched to oblivion.

The final phase of the imperial campaign now lay in the more intractable, less predictable arena of Australian politics. Presenting far more obstacles than the military forces, victory depended largely upon the absolute strength of imperial ideology rather than direct imperial manipulation. But, by May 1909, there were clear signs that the tide was on the turn. Since the 1880s Australian politicians had occasionally talked of support for Britain during war but they had given no undertakings. The basis of agreement which brought the Fusion government to power therefore seemed to promise a more substantial commitment to imperial defence and was undoubtedly viewed with some satisfaction in London. How this commitment developed after May 1909 will be the theme of the final chapter.

11
The achievement of the imperial objective, 1909–1914: An Australian imperial force

On becoming Prime Minister for the third time on 2 June 1909, Alfred Deakin had to choose representatives to attend an Imperial Conference on Defence called at the height of the dreadnought hysteria. As the conference was due to begin in London in late July, he had little time to ponder, and decided quickly to uphold an earlier decision by Senator George Pearce, the Minister for Defence in the former government, to send Colonel Bridges and Captain Creswell as service representatives. The selection of an appropriate member to represent his government demanded a little more care, however. Despite his considerable experience at such conferences, Deakin himself was in no position to attend—more pressing problems confronted him in Australia, not the least being the consolidation of his own position as Prime Minister. Leadership of the fusion which included Joseph Cook's conservative Free Trade Party and Sir John Forrest's independent conservatives was no easy task for the former liberal Protectionist. Deakin wrote to his sister at this time informing her that 'behind me sit the whole of my opponents since Federation'.[1] Finally, it was announced that Justin Foxton, the federal member for Brisbane since 1906 and a colonel in the militia, had been selected.[2]

This was a remarkable choice, and one undoubtedly influenced by the new political order, an order in which Joseph Cook had become Minister for Defence. Foxton, a solicitor by profession, had been active in Queensland politics for 21 years. He had no political experience in the imperial forum but, like other conservatives, was an avowed imperialist whose personal views on Australian defence diverged markedly from those of Deakin. The magnitude of this divergence was starkly illustrated when he gave an interview to the Australian press on the announcement of his selection.

Australia should have a navy, Foxton asserted, but 'we must be, for very many years, dependent on Great Britain'. Therefore, he believed that, in building its own naval force, Australia 'should co-operate . . . in every way possible with the navy of Great Britain'. His views on the Australian military forces were the same. 'Whatever the nature of our organisation on land, and the extent to which we carry compulsory training, or set it aside,' Foxton told the press, 'the idea should be, in my opinion, to enable our troops, with the least amount of friction, to take the field side by side with the British troops.' There should be 'complete and harmonious relations between the land forces of the mother country and of Australia', he concluded.[3] Although Foxton would soon be forced to qualify his position, it was nevertheless significant that, after 30 years in the shadows of imperial planning, the imperial objective could now be stated boldly by a representative of the Commonwealth government! It illustrated how the fusion of the conservative parties had strengthened the hand of Australian imperialists.

The prospect that Foxton would attend the Imperial Conference alarmed some of Deakin's traditional liberal supporters. Foxton was known as an outspoken opponent of universal military training and as an imperialist, and his statement to the press provoked a nationalist reaction. What, Deakin was asked by fellow Victorian liberal Charles Carty Salmon, 'has become of the Defence policy we have been advocating, fighting for and getting our friends to subscribe to?'[4] Foxton was obviously the wrong man to represent Australia at the conference because Salmon believed emphatically that 'Australia is entitled to play a leading part and to define rather than merely acquiesce'. How could Foxton play such a role? Salmon wondered. 'That the position you gave the Commonwealth at the Imperial Conference [of 1907] can be maintained by a man with Foxton's political past and recent declarations cannot for a moment be even suggested,' he concluded in disappointed resignation.[5]

Salmon's indignation at Foxton's selection was echoed in the *Age*. The newspaper noted in its editorial comment that Foxton had told the press 'very frankly and candidly more than enough to show that his personal opinions are quite unrepresentative of public opinion in the Commonwealth'. The militia colonel obviously believed that the military forces should be 'trained wholly and solely for foreign service', a proposal the *Age* believed to be 'absolutely repugnant to Australian sentiment'. In sending a 'declared opponent of the national policy' to the Imperial Conference, it was 'quite inevitable' that 'his personal views will color [sic] his representations'. The *Age* therefore stated that it was 'essential that Mr Deakin should reconsider his position'.[6]

The day the critical comments appeared in the *Age* editorial Foxton again spoke to the press, attempting, as he explained it, 'to correct some quite erroneous deductions from my replies yesterday'. To start with, he said that he supported the establishment of an Australian navy for

An Army for a Nation

co-operation 'with the British fleet *on this coast*'. His qualification was a belated attempt to emphasise that the navy would operate as a national defence force and not embark on imperial operations in distant seas. In relation to the military forces, Foxton asserted, the 'co-operation of the land forces with those of the Empire' to which he had referred entailed nothing more than Australia's participation in the Imperial General Staff scheme. The Australian military forces would be trained from 'first to last for the effective defence of this country' but, resorting to a Hutton-like argument, he concluded: 'if Australia can be defended at any time outside her borders, so much the better for her'.[7]

Despite Foxton's inference that he had been incorrectly reported, his latest explanation was an obvious retreat from his initial statement. The reason for his public change of mind was that he had just emerged from a meeting of cabinet where he had been instructed on the government's defence policy. 'The upshot,' Deakin remarked, 'is that Mr Foxton is now fully informed of the views of the Government *as a whole*.' On this occasion, nationalist sentiment had reasserted itself within the cabinet. It was a pleasing result for the *Age*, which observed that Foxton's personal views 'have not been altogether in accord with those now voiced by a majority of the Cabinet, but there should be no confusion in the delegate's mind as to what is expected of him'.[8]

While Deakin was occupied finalising the Australian position for the Imperial Conference, Lord Crew, the Colonial Secretary, requested Whitehall officials to prepare for the conference by considering 'the best means of securing the co-operation of the self-governing Dominions in the Defence of the Empire'. All the old difficulties were addressed in the subsequent review as the British position was prepared. How could the dominions contribute? How would the self-governing status of the dominions be reconciled with British command of an imperial force in war? What were the best means of facilitating the exchange of officers, or of giving advice to ensure efficiency in the local forces?[9] Deakin was asking a great deal of Foxton to expect him to protect national interests in the face of the persuasive arguments being developed by the British authorities. As Carty Salmon had pleaded with the Prime Minister, it was not simply Foxton's utterances on which his attitude should be judged, but 'his demeanour—which was always suggestive'.[10]

The major reason for calling the conference was naval defence. Preliminary discussions on this subject were held in the Foreign Office. Here the Australian representatives, along with the Canadians, expressed their intentions of laying the foundations of their own national fleets. The British officials concurred, but emphasised that dominion naval personnel should be trained and disciplined under regulations similar to those of the Royal Navy, so permitting the interchange of personnel and, ultimately, combined operations. 'While laying the foundations of future Dominion navies to be

An Australian Imperial Force

maintained in different parts of the Empire,' the Admiralty discussion paper noted, 'these forces would contribute immediately to Imperial defence.' In further discussions at the Admiralty, Foxton and Creswell agreed that the Australian unit should be considered a part of a planned British Pacific fleet. In peace the unit would be controlled by the Commonwealth government but, the Admiralty noted, the dominion governments recognised that in war their naval units should be placed at the disposal of the Admiralty to be controlled by Britain.[11] This was a distinct change from the conference of 1907 when Deakin had told Admiralty officials that Australia's naval forces would remain under Australian control at all times.[12]

Military questions were discussed separately at the War Office where the British CGS, General Sir William Nicholson, presented papers which had been written by the general staff under his direction. In preparing for the conference, Nicholson had decided that Britain's best hope for the future lay in encouraging the dominions to establish common organisations and procedures. Suggestions to interchange units with the object of achieving integration were no longer considered practical because they aroused nationalist suspicion, inviting opposition. Indeed, Nicholson believed that Britain had gone 'as far as we prudently can do by inviting the Dominions to assimilate their military organizations and General Staff system to ours, and by offering facilities for the training and interchange of General Staff officers'.[13] He therefore decided to continue with this policy. His proposals included the introduction of standard British military organisations and training, standard transport arrangements and standard patterns of weapons and equipment, as well as a commitment to the continuing development of the Imperial General Staff. Bridges and Creswell, who represented Australia at the War Office meeting, and the representatives from Canada, New Zealand and South Africa agreed. Furthermore, they took the unprecedented step of agreeing that should a dominion provide an expeditionary force for imperial operations then it would include its own logistic support elements, making it a complete combat force.[14]

The results of the War Office discussions were subsequently endorsed by the main conference and the Committee of Imperial Defence. Encouraged by this outcome, the British authorities were now more confident and openly discussed their ultimate objective. While acknowledging that each dominion was autonomous in such matters, it was concluded that 'should the Dominions desire to assist in the defence of the Empire in a real emergency, their forces could be rapidly combined into one homogeneous Imperial Army'. Of course this depended on the implementation of the agreed measures well before the crisis broke and, realistically, Prime Minister Asquith sounded a note of caution. The resolutions, he informed the Commons after the conference, had 'no binding force unless and until submitted to their various Parliaments'.[15]

Asquith's challenge to dominion parliaments to demonstrate the strength of their commitment to imperial defence objectives held special relevance for Australia. The most significant military agreement at the conference concerned the possible provision of an expeditionary force for imperial service; all the other military points of agreement were subservient to this central objective. But, despite the results of the conference, it was not clear where the Fusion government stood on the issue. Deakin's attempt to pull Foxton into line before his departure for London was an indication of the underlying tension within the ranks of the government on the defence question. The defence policy of the last Deakin government had been motivated primarily by a Pacific-based strategic outlook which made local defence its first priority. It had not been prepared to give a firm commitment to imperial defence beyond limited participation in the Imperial General Staff and had indicated that it intended to develop military doctrine and organisations to meet the unique requirements of Australian defence. Significantly, Deakin had deliberately ruled out any preparations for an expeditionary force[16] and had left to Australians, as individuals, the option of volunteering for imperial military service. Now that Deakin's tenure of office depended on men more attuned to imperial aspirations, there were clear signs of a shift towards involvement in imperial defence strategies, but it was not yet certain which line the government would ultimately take and whether a more substantial undertaking would be given to Britain.

The direction in which the Fusion government was heading on this question was illustrated more clearly in the month following the Imperial Conference when Joseph Cook rose in the House of Representatives to introduce a Defence Bill incorporating the long-promised defence reforms. In his introduction, Cook maintained that the provisions contained in his Bill were urgent. The public would 'not much longer brook delay in connexion [sic] with reforming the defence of Australia', he contended. 'Every nation is arming to the teeth,' he warned, 'and there seems to be a mad race between the nations of the world as to who shall get the best engines of destruction and who shall be able first to be in the field when the great arbitrament of war is resolved to.' With such developments at hand, it was his intention that Australia would become 'a buttress to the Empire, instead of a burden'. Australia was, he continued, 'the most distant, the richest, and, at the same time, the most vulnerable part of the British Empire'. While Germany was an obvious cause for concern for Britain, the United States and Japan were more likely threats to Australia. As both these nations had significant naval forces operating in the Pacific, he believed that the Pacific had become as important as the Mediterranean and the Atlantic in terms of naval defence. Cook therefore endorsed the agreement reached at the Imperial Conference for Australia to participate in the planned British Pacific fleet. Australia's contribution would be an armoured cruiser of the *Indomitable* class, three unarmoured cruisers of the *Bristol* class, six destroyers of the improved *River* class and three submarines.

Like Deakin and Ewing, Cook said that the rationale for his defence policy was a Pacific-based strategy. But this, it seems, was simply a hollow concession to government members who were proponents of a national defence strategy, for it soon became clear that Cook was thinking along quite different lines. Self-reliance was not a feature of the defence policy he was developing. Confirming the undertaking given by the Australian representatives at the Imperial Conference, he declared that the Australian naval unit 'of course, will pass under Imperial control whenever required for war service'. Cook said that Australians had to determine 'what is our duty as an integral portion of the Empire'. His Bill set the stage for Australia to embrace the imperial defence strategy.[17]

Turning to the military forces, Cook stated that it was the government's intention to create 'a national army, well balanced in all its parts, and complete so far as human ingenuity can make it'. It would be comprised of 'infantry, artillery, light horse, engineers, signallers, telegraphists, army service corps, and army medical corps in their due and proper proportions'. He then announced that the government would proceed with the introduction of compulsory military training but, in a cardinal departure from the original Deakin–Ewing plan, there would be no single force organised as a national guard. The primary component of Cook's scheme would be a militia force recruited for the most part on a voluntary basis and maintained as 'a first line field force'. It would be developed from the existing militia force by increasing its size 'to war strength . . . with much improved organization'.[18] But what part would be played by the scheme of compulsory military training? According to Cook's plan, the major role of the scheme would be the provision of a recruiting pool of trained men for the first-line field force. Compulsory trainees would also be allocated to the first-line field force in their final year of training. Although there were some similarities, on the fundamental issue of force structure Cook's proposal was therefore significantly different from that originally planned by Deakin and Ewing.

Training under the compulsory scheme was to be organised along the lines of the original Deakin scheme. Youths aged 12 to 18 would be trained in school and senior cadet corps. On turning 18, the cadets would undergo more advanced, compulsory training in brigade level organisations. For the first year of this advanced training they would be organised into units which conformed with the military organisations of the first-line field force. This force would be considered to be a second-echelon fighting force. However, for the second year of their compulsory adult training they would be absorbed into actual units of the field force. This final year of training was designed to encourage the young men to enlist voluntarily in the field force when they turned 20 and their compulsory training obligation ceased. Men who had completed their compulsory training and who elected not to join the field force remained under an obligation until they reached the age of 26 and, along with members of rifle clubs, would constitute a third echelon, or reserve, force. Within seven or eight years of commencement, Cook estimated, the scheme would produce '206 000 well drilled and thoroughly trained men'.[19]

Cook denied members of the House a clear, concise explanation of his proposals. Furthermore, he introduced his Bill on a suspension of standing orders before the opposition had a chance to examine it. However, he did circulate a memorandum to members containing a brief description of the proposed scheme, but it failed to spell out all that Cook had in mind.[20] There can be little doubt that the minister's address and his methods were designed to cloud what was essentially a radical departure from the original universal training scheme envisaged by Deakin and Ewing. The former proposal was designed to produce a national fighting force for the defence of Australia but Cook's scheme was designed to produce a smaller, self-contained force for more flexible purposes. What Cook described as the first-line field force was intended to be an expeditionary force.

This became clear when, later in his address, he raised the subject of an expeditionary force. With a hesitancy induced by the controversial nature of the subject, he explained: 'The bill will provide us also, if necessary—I hope we may never have to do it—[with] an expeditionary force for immediate despatch overseas or elsewhere whenever the Government of the day feel themselves under an obligation to send the force.' This statement perplexed Andrew Fisher, the leader of the opposition. One constant feature of the ongoing defence debate in Australia was that overseas service would be undertaken only on a voluntary basis. It was well known that the *Defence Act* denied a government the power to deploy troops outside Australia. Raising the subject of an expeditionary force in conjunction with compulsory military training therefore confused Fisher and he sought immediate clarification by interjecting: 'Would that mean reswearing the men?'

'I am going to get the men ready,' Cook responded dismissively. 'All these special matters can be considered afterwards.' Jumping to the minister's assistance, James Fowler volunteered: 'An expeditionary force would be required even for some parts of Australia.'

'Exactly,' Cook agreed, evidently hoping the matter was settled. However, the opposition leader was not to be fobbed off so easily. 'But the Minister spoke of a force to be sent outside Australia,' he persisted.

'An expeditionary force in every sense of the term would be required if we had to send troops *up North*,' an unsettled Cook answered evasively, trying to divert attention from overseas service. 'Our scheme in this respect is capable of systematic expansion.'

Fisher was not happy with this answer. 'Does the honourable gentleman mean that the men could be sent abroad without being resworn?' he asked.

'I tell the honourable member candidly that if these men are wanted for overseas service, in the defence of Empire, no Government of the

Commonwealth worthy of the name would hesitate to send them,' was Cook's final retort.[21]

Despite Fisher's probing, it seems that the opposition never fully understood Cook's plans for the field force. A few weeks later William Morris Hughes referred to the exchange between the minister and leader of the opposition because he, too, was puzzled about Cook's intentions. The confusion in the mind of the opposition had probably deepened because by this time they had examined Cook's Bill and they could see that he had not included a provision which would empower a government to order troops overseas.[22] Yet, as Hughes pointed out, Cook's original statement to the House inferred that he was contemplating a departure from the 'basic principle' that compulsory training was for 'home defence only'. Explaining his own reservations about such a development, Hughes said he was happy for Australians to defend the empire but not as 'pressed men'.[23]

Responding to Hughes, Cook again resorted to evasion and failed to state clearly what he had in mind.[24] Yet, despite his reticence, it seems clear that the Minister for Defence was attempting to combine the two schemes of compulsory training and voluntary service to ensure that his first-line field force could be mobilised as an expeditionary force. Cook was obviously confident that most men would volunteer for overseas service when the time came and therefore no increase to government power was required. But it is probable that he had no alternative—Deakin would have been unlikely to give his blessing to compulsory overseas service. And even if he had achieved Deakin's agreement, there was no urgent need to take the politically risky course of legislating for such power at this time.

Cook's Bill enjoyed a good reception. Foxton told newspaper reporters in London that he thought this would be the case 'for the public think we have a possible danger in the future. One cannot say what danger, but the feeling exists.'[25] An editorial in the *Age* echoed similar fears when it commented that the additional defence expenditure associated with Cook's Bill 'cannot be considered an extravagance in a world that is going mad in preparation for a mammoth war'. The newspaper was satisfied that the Bill had at last presented Australia with a scheme of 'National defence'. Yet the *Age*, in what appears to be the only adverse comment by a major Australian newspaper, took exception to Cook's statement that Australia had been a burden on the empire. 'We are a part of the Empire and must take our share of the responsibility of Imperial wars,' the *Age* believed. But it then revealed what it thought Australia's contribution to such a war should be when it supported the establishment of an Australian navy. What was needed was 'a navy strong enough, in conjunction with our land forces, *to make our coasts secure* against the one danger which must confront us on the outbreak of any war between Great Britain and a naval Power'. The *Age* was therefore upset by Cook's declaration that from the outbreak of war the Australian naval unit would be subject to British control. This indicated that the government did not have a policy of its own, the newspaper continued, 'but that it is waiting to adopt the scheme which may have been framed in London'. Certainly, the *Age* conceded, 'from an Australian point of view' it might be expedient to place the local force under British control, but only on a temporary basis. To give control of Australian naval forces to Britain automatically and without question on the outbreak of war was not acceptable but, the newspaper noted sourly, this had 'always been a part of the policy of the anti-Australian party'. Notwithstanding the possibility of granting temporary control to the Admiralty, the *Age* concluded that 'the first, last and middle of the Defence policy we are now entering on must be Australian defence, not Imperial defence. It is Australian defence as a part of the Empire.'[26]

Despite its vehement conclusion, the *Age* editorial failed to address the full implications of Cook's Bill and his stated policy, especially in relation to his intention to prepare an expeditionary force. Perhaps the newspaper had erred in its analysis of the Bill and the minister's speech. After all, Cook had not spoken with absolute clarity and he had resorted to a certain amount of evasion when dealing with questions. Interestingly, the *Sydney Morning Herald* editorial, which discussed the new Defence Bill, made no comment about its imperial thrust nor expressed any nationalist misgivings, only noting certain aspects of the training regime which it heralded.[27] Yet the vital issue of the metamorphosis in Australian defence policy did not escape the attention of newspapers in Britain.

According to the *Evening Standard*, Cook's Bill displayed 'a newer and better understanding' which was 'destined to render the Empire a true and tremendous hegemony'. 'Thus magnificently is the Commonwealth setting itself to discharge its Imperial obligations,' trumpeted the *Observer*. 'The contagion will doubtless spread to the other dominions of the King.' The *Pall Mall Gazette* was also warm in its praise, noting that Australia was about to establish 'a fleet which will materially affect the balance of power in the Pacific, and an army which not even the greatest military Power will be able to regard as a negligible quantity'. The *Daily Mail* proclaimed that the Bill would provide '375 000 men and 13 ships for the Empire', while the *Standard* noted with satisfaction that it was evidence that the important decisions taken at the Imperial Conference were being implemented. 'A new era has been inaugurated, which will make 1909 memorable in the annals of the Empire,' the *Daily Chronicle* announced. 'The Australian scheme happily combines the principle of nationalism with Imperial co-operation.' Noting these comments by the British press, the *Sydney Morning Herald* did not think it an exaggeration to comment that 'Britain Eulogises Scheme'.[28] Against this wave of imperial fervour the comments by the *Age* suddenly seemed insignificant, isolated, *passé*.

Although Cook's Bill was enacted on 13 December 1909,[29] it was not proclaimed until 1 January 1911 and then only after being the subject of certain amendments which had been suggested by Field Marshal Lord Kitchener. The eminent British military authority had been invited to inspect and comment on Australian defence preparations by the Fusion government within days of its assumption of power.[30] Apparently forewarned, Kitchener had already discussed such a visit with Sir George Clarke before Deakin's initial inquiry on the availability of the senior officer arrived in London. Realising that it presented an ideal opportunity to influence Australian military developments, Kitchener was quick to accept the invitation when it arrived.[31] The Australian government therefore decided to await Kitchener's comments before proceeding with the scheme which it had devised.

Cook claimed credit for Kitchener's visit to Australia. 'For two years I sought on every suitable occasion to get the Government of the day to invite Lord Kitchener to Australia,' the Minister for Defence announced publicly. 'And when I discussed the matter with the Prime Minister he at once fell in with the idea.'[32] Deakin undoubtedly perceived the immediate benefit of gaining the public blessing of the popular Kitchener for compulsory military training. It was a splendid opportunity for an astute politician to convince the electorate that the government's defence initiatives were soundly based. Indeed, this was undoubtedly a paramount consideration in Deakin's mind because Kitchener was to arrive in Australia in late December 1909, two weeks after the closing session of the third parliament of the Commonwealth. A federal election was due in the new year. Of lesser importance, Kitchener could also have a positive influence on conservative waverers within his own government who were not wholehearted in their support for compulsory service. In this regard, the *Age* noted sarcastically that conservatives 'enthusiastically supported the proposal to invite Lord Kitchener . . . for no doubt they expected that his counsel would follow the lines of their old fashioned Tory prejudices'.[33]

Deakin's official invitation to Kitchener was carefully worded; he was requested to inspect 'our forces and fixed defences in order to advise this Government upon the best means of developing and perfecting the land defence of the country'.[34] More than anyone, Deakin would have wished to avoid any suggestion that Kitchener was working to an imperial design because it could easily offend his traditional supporters, producing a backlash on election day. It is easy, therefore, to assume that Kitchener came to Australia simply to review and report on the local defence capability. Significantly, however, the British authorities harboured no doubts about the prime purpose of Kitchener's visit. Richard Haldane, Secretary of State for War, announced in Bradford that 'we are within sight—and, indeed something more than within sight—of common plans, which will unify the forces of the Crown throughout the whole of the Empire. [W]herever the theatre of war may be . . . we should have the forces of the Empire so organised that they can be concentrated wherever the field may be, and that plans for our mutual defence may be worked out by one Empire, one whole.'

Kitchener was going to Australia and then to New Zealand 'to work out the details', Haldane concluded.[35]

Kitchener arrived in Darwin on the Dutch steamer *Vanouthoorn* on 21 December 1909 accompanied by Colonel George Kirkpatrick, his staff officer, and Captain Fitzgerald, his *aide-de-camp*. Immediately, he transferred to the waiting British warship *Encounter* where he was greeted by the CGS Major-General John Hoad.[36] It was the start of a demanding seven weeks of inspections of units and installations in each state and an exhausting series of social commitments. Despite Deakin's initial assurances to the stern but shy Kitchener that 'there will be little "fuss" apart from your military inspections',[37] at the end of his visit Kitchener confessed to a friend that it had been 'rather hard work, not so much from the military point of view, but on account of the innumerable receptions by mayors, and those sort of people'.[38] Everywhere the visiting officer went he was besieged by toadying officials and adoring crowds; he was venerated to the point of adulation. His name, it was exclaimed by the *Sydney Morning Herald*, had 'become a household word, . . . associated with stirring scenes in the military history of the Empire'.[39] He was a soldier of legendary status. One British officer in Australia at the time believed Kitchener was 'the greatest Englishman that had ever visited the country' and observed that Australians 'mobbed him wherever he went and *fêted* him to an alarming extent'.[40] As he moved southward on his tour of inspection, so the intensity of public excitement increased.

When his train arrived at Central Railway Station, Sydney, in early January, he was met by a crowd of 10 000, 'one mass of people, anxious to get a glimpse of the hero of Omdurman and Atbara'. The arches and supports of the station were draped with palms and greenery; flags and bunting added colour, while barricades kept back the crushing crowd. Suddenly, he stepped from the train on to a crimson carpet to be recognised in an instant by the excited public. They cheered as one voice. 'Tall, well set up, and military-looking, Lord Kitchener has a typically British face, florid, with brown moustache, and keen blue eyes,' wrote an admiring reporter from the *Sydney Morning Herald*. An official party greeted the distinguished visitor but, as the reporter noted, at the entrance to the station six young cadets had also formed up as 'a diminutive unofficial self-constituted guard of honour'. The boys stood stiffly at attention 'hoping yet fearing that they might attract the notice of the great Kitchener'. [41] It seems that all of Sydney waited expectantly for any word the taciturn soldier might utter.

The morning's newspaper had prepared Sydneysiders for the visit. The editorial in the *Herald* declared that Kitchener had come for 'Business, Not Ceremony' and counselled Australians to take a broad view of the requirements of defence. Australia had to think of itself 'as an integral part of the Empire with issues of life and death waiting upon the decision of Britains

An Australian Imperial Force

Lord Kitchener walking out of Sydney's Central Railway station on 5 January 1910 during his visit to inspect the Australian military forces. The railway station had been decorated with flags, bunting and palms and a crimson carpet had been laid for the distinguished visitor. The official party includes *(from left to right)* Mr Joseph Cook, Minister for Defence, Lord Kitchener, Admiral Sir Richard Poore, Mr Charles Lee, the acting State premier, Major General John Hoad CGS, the stationmaster and Brigadier Joseph Gordon. (AUSTRALIAN WAR MEMORIAL, AWM NEG. NO: P595/174/05)

---

beyond the seas'. The inspection, the editorial advised, was being undertaken 'not so much for Australia's sake as for the good of the Empire'. Australians might view their forces in isolation 'but Lord Kitchener himself is probably regarding Australia as a detail in the great scheme of a coming world war'.[42] If this were so, he gave no hint when he spoke at a Lord Mayor's banquet in the Town Hall that night.

Kitchener spoke only a few words on the defence of Sydney Harbour because he said it was an important naval base. Complete security of the harbour, he told guests, could only be obtained by efficient fixed defences, supported by mobile land forces.[43] However, when he addressed a state dinner in Parliament House three nights later he was a little more expansive and recalled that New South Wales had provided contingents for the Sudan Campaign and the Boer War. In the event of another war he therefore did not have the slightest doubt that 'we shall see the New South Wales lads shoulder to shoulder with us . . . '[44] The assembled diners greeted his words with enthusiasm.

One week later Kitchener was in Melbourne where he was welcomed officially at a dinner by the federal government. In proposing a toast to the distinguished guest, Deputy Governor-General Lord Chelmsford said that he hoped one result of the visit would be a defence force 'fully armed and equipped'. 'If that be the result it will be fraught with great benefit not to Australia but to the Empire at large,' Chelmsford said. Supporting the toast, Prime Minister Deakin made no mention of possible imperial benefits arising from the development of Australian defence forces but, instead, echoed the words of his official invitation to Kitchener by making only a brief reference to national requirements. The defence of Australia, Deakin told guests, posed 'a grave problem indeed for a small population to retain a vast territory at a very long distance from the centre of the Empire'. Responding to the toast, Kitchener also made no reference to imperial defence but repeated Deakin's comment about sparse population.[45]

If Kitchener had come to Australia with plans for developing the military forces for imperial operations, it was not being stated publicly by himself or the government. Yet one month later, when his visit was in its final days and his report was being prepared for submission to the government, the *Age* published an article which, while not nominating its source, claimed that it was 'now admitted' that Kitchener's mission in Australia was concerned as much with the development of an imperial field force as it was with giving advice to the local defence authorities. The article commented that Kitchener needed more time to complete his report because he was developing a 'plan by which he proposes to fit in the compulsorily trained Australian citizen "defence" army of the near future into the great scheme which aims at the creation of an "Imperial Field Force" which shall be available for "offence" as well as "defence" '. He intended to provide a 'great reserve of Australian soldiers', the article continued, 'which can be fitted easily and swiftly into the secret plans of the War Office'. According to an unofficial source, who was described as a 'well known British military writer', the War Office planned to establish an imperial force of nineteen divisions and nineteen mounted brigades. The combined contribution to this force from Australia and New Zealand would be one division and two mounted brigades.[46]

Deakin and Cook wasted no time in responding to the article in the *Age*. The very next day the newspaper reported that the Prime Minister and the Minister for Defence refuted its claims and denied 'that Lord Kitchener's mission has anything to do with any suggested Imperial field force'. They expected him 'to deal mainly with Australian forces formed strictly for the purposes of Commonwealth defence'.[47] Clearly, the stated expectations of the Australian authorities were quite different from those of Richard Haldane.

As might be expected, Kitchener's report, which proposed a scheme of compulsory military training and organisation, was well received in Austra-

The people of Melbourne turn out to see Lord Kitchener proceed along Collins Street in a horse-drawn carriage, early in 1910. Kitchener, who had been invited to Australia to inspect the military forces, was on his way to Government House, Melbourne. (AUSTRALIAN WAR MEMORIAL, AWM NEG. NO: P595/174/48)

lia. He had been accepted as the supreme authority on military matters; his word was beyond dispute. Even the *Age* was content, commenting that 'no patriotic Liberal will cavil at the scheme'. The reason was that the newspaper believed it was 'essentially an Australian scheme. It has been based on our requirements.' Kitchener's proposal would enable Australians to defend themselves from attack. Furthermore, he had 'taken it for granted' that Australians could implement and operate the scheme 'without external aid'. It was especially pleasing for the Melbourne newspaper to find that the report contained not even 'the slightest hint of an opinion that we should revert to the discredited old custom of importing general or other officers'.[48]

But was the *Age* correct in believing that Kitchener's report was concerned with local defence? Was the newspaper also correct in assuming that Kitchener had intended that Australians would develop their defence forces without influence from outside? An analysis of the report and the implications reveals that the *Age* was wrong on both these vital issues. The newspaper, and presumably many Australians, failed to understand

Kitchener's real designs and also underestimated his skill and ability to influence politicians.

It was easy to conclude, as the *Age* had done, that Kitchener's scheme was concerned primarily with local defence. Not only was his report entitled 'Defence of Australia' but Deakin and Cook had assured the public that Kitchener's mission had nothing to do with developing an imperial field force. And, if that was not enough, readers of Kitchener's report could see that, for the first time since the inspection by Major-General Sir James Bevan Edwards in 1889, an imperial representative had admitted that an invasion of Australia was possible. In the strategic assessment at the beginning of his report, Kitchener claimed that, because of Australia's remote location, it was quite possible that an enemy could launch a major operation against Australia before the Royal Navy could concentrate its forces and assert control. This was contrary to all previous advice from the Colonial Defence Committee and the Committee of Imperial Defence. Indeed, it appeared that Kitchener had confirmed Deakin's earlier conclusion that Australia needed to develop a self-reliant defence strategy. Accordingly, Kitchener recommended that the Australian military forces should have the strength and organisation to combat an invasion.[49] This was undoubtedly the principal reason for the *Age*'s glowing report on Kitchener's recommendations.

In his report, Kitchener supported the introduction of compulsory military training for cadets and young men. School cadets aged 12 to 14 years would undergo 120 hours of training each year, calculated on the basis of half an hour of drill each schoolday. Senior cadets aged 14 to 18 years and recruits aged 18 to 19 years would receive sixteen days' training annually, with recruits spending half this time in camp. In a departure from Cook's scheme, Kitchener then recommended an increase to the upper age of trainees from 20 to 25 years, thus producing a substantial increase in the number of men of prime military age in the military force. He estimated that this would produce a trained force of 80 000 citizen soldiers who would attend an annual camp of six days' duration.

For training purposes, his scheme divided Australia into 215 areas, each providing a proportion of a fighting unit and each being supervised by a training and administration officer who would be trained at a proposed Australian military college. He calculated that two training areas from the cities, or three from the country districts, would combine to produce one battalion with supporting arms organised on the basis of Imperial Army establishments. By identifying fighting units with districts, he believed that healthy rivalry would be easy to encourage, enhancing *ésprit de corps* and enlisting community support. The result would be a more efficient body of troops. In total he estimated that the scheme would produce a force of 84 battalions of infantry—the equivalent of 21 brigades, 28 regiments of light horse, 49 four-gun field batteries, 7 four-gun heavy and howitzer batteries, 7 communication companies and 14 field engineer companies.

Kitchener's report became the blueprint for Australian military developments but as a defence scheme it was sadly lacking. Certainly, he laid down an outline for establishing and training combat units comprised of citizen soldiers, but he provided practically no information on the development and composition of logistics units. Other vital issues also were not addressed. He failed to establish a concept of operations for the military force. He simply claimed that Australia should prepare for a possible invasion but he had not suggested how an invading force might be constituted or where it might land. His training areas were determined by relating population distribution to the requirements of standard imperial establishments, primarily the infantry battalion; he made no attempt to determine whether unique tactical organisations should be developed to defend strategic points of importance. Apart from a brief criticism of the lack of a standard railway gauge between the states, he also ignored important questions concerning the local infrastructure, especially the ability to support military operations from local resources. Furthermore, while he mentioned the requirement for military district headquarters in each state, they were only to fulfil administrative functions for units in those districts. Significantly, he failed to mention the fundamental necessity of establishing operational headquarters, either at the brigade or divisional level. Nowhere did he state the composition of these important bodies. His failure to deal adequately with this issue was, it seems, an oversight for brigade headquarters but not for divisional headquarters. He mentioned that a citizen officer might rise to command a brigade but this was the limit in Kitchener's mind because elsewhere in the report he stipulated that the highest rank for a citizen officer would be colonel, the rank worn by a brigade commander. Likewise, he recommended that the highest rank for a permanent officer would also be colonel. Therefore, if his recommendations were followed, there would be no Australian generals and, consequently, no Australian divisional commanders. Yet he did not explain where the commanders and staff of higher operational formations, such as divisions, would come from in case of war.[50]

Overall, Kitchener's recommendations would not produce a defence scheme. They would not even produce a viable military force, only a collection of units or, with the addition of appropriately staffed headquarters, a collection of independent brigades organised on the imperial pattern. Significantly, the only justification he had offered for introducing imperial standards of organisation and equipment was to comment enigmatically that the best defence was achieved 'generally by taking the offensive'. In this respect, Kitchener's scheme looked like Hutton's earlier proposals which were designed to deliver an offensive blow outside Australia. But this was

A horse-drawn Maxim machine gun being moved at the commencement of a military exercise held to coincide with the inspection by Lord Kitchener in 1910. The exercise was held at Flat Rock Crossing, NSW. (AUSTRALIAN WAR MEMORIAL, AWM NEG. NO: P595/174/21)

not the only similarity. Like Hutton, Kitchener also recommended a reduction in the daily rate of pay for private soldiers from 8 shillings to 4 shillings. The citizen soldier 'must remember that he is discharging a duty to his country, and that the pay he receives is not a wage but an allowance to assist him in the discharge of his duty', he reported. [51] Yet it seems that these patriotic sentiments were not the real reason for Kitchener's recommendation. There can be little doubt that this was the latest attempt by an imperial officer to remove what the War Office perceived as a possible source of friction when Australians served alongside more lowly paid troops from Britain. Therefore, when Kitchener's recommendations and comments are considered in conjunction with Haldane's earlier statement in Bradford about the purpose of his visit, one is drawn to the conclusion that the primary object of Kitchener's report was the organisation of a number of Australian units which would combine as brigades under the command of British generals and staff for imperial operations.[52]

Yet, if Kitchener was not primarily concerned with the defence of Australia, as the title of his report suggests, why did he overturn imperial policy and base his recommendations on a strategic assessment that Australia had to prepare for a possible invasion? The answer to this question, it seems, was that it provided a powerful stimulus for Australians to establish a strong military capability, a capability which Kitchener undoubtedly intended for use on imperial operations. Without questioning this aspect of his report, Australians accepted Kitchener's recommendations as a significant contribution to the development of their national security, making the visit a highly successful imperial exercise. With only minor exceptions such as his recommendation to reduce the pay of private soldiers, Kitchener's report was accepted and, where necessary, amendments were made to the universal training legislation of December 1909.[53]

However, in his report, Kitchener did more than lay down the framework of a scheme of compulsory training and organisation. He also took deliberate steps to draw Australia more deeply into the imperial military network, primarily by controlling the training of future Australian Army officers. In this regard, he followed the advice of Major-General Sir Douglas Haig when, in advocating the development of the Imperial General Staff, he had pointed to the necessity of Britain ensuring that officers throughout the empire had been educated 'up to a certain common standard of military knowledge', becoming 'imbued with the requisite uniformity of thought and practice'[54] Accordingly, Kitchener recommended the establishment of an Australian military college to train officers for appointments as instructors and administrators in the training areas and as staff for positions on the Imperial General Staff. Graduates of the college would constitute an exclusive Staff Corps: Kitchener recommended that no officer already serving should be admitted as a member. The Staff Corps should be 'entirely drawn from the Military College', he advised. In his subsequent report to the government of New Zealand, he also recommended that their officers be trained at the same college. Training would be based on stringent standards of discipline and efficiency and any political interference in the management of the college 'should be strictly avoided', he suggested. The director of this college 'must be a man of exceptional qualifications, well educated, and accustomed to do his duty fearlessly and thoroughly'.[55] When asked by Cook whom such a man might be, Kitchener nominated Bridges.[56]

Kitchener favoured Bridges because he was a trusted imperialist. Shortly after it had been announced that Kitchener was to visit Australia, Bridges, who was on his way to London to take up his appointment on the Imperial General Staff, had written to Kitchener's staff officer, Colonel George Kirkpatrick. It was their first meeting in Melbourne in December 1905 which led to Bridges' recruitment by Sir George Clarke as an agent for the imperial cause in Australia. Although the precise contents of Bridges' 1909 letter to Kirkpatrick are not known, Kirkpatrick's response is suggestive. 'Please regard the contents of this letter as absolutely for your own personal information,' Kirkpatrick had replied to Bridges, 'I read extracts of your letter . . . to Lord K. who desired me to tell you that he was "exceedingly interested in your views".'[57] Encouraged by this response, Bridges had written another letter, undoubtedly arming Kitchener with first-hand information on affairs in Australia. Kirkpatrick found this letter 'most interesting' and, because it had been decided that he would accompany Kitchener on his visit to Australia, he had encouraged the Australian officer to continue the liaison. Kirkpatrick had told Bridges that he would 'look forward to hearing from [him] frequently'.[58]

The appointment of Bridges as the commandant of the new military college was a significant achievement for the imperial cause. Immediately, Bridges approached the War Office to select imperial officers for appointment as instructors at the college. These dealings were executed by private letter for the obvious reason that the Minister for Defence had directed that, in accordance with government policy, the college appointments would be made on a competitive basis after calling for applications from Australia, New Zealand, Canada and the United Kingdom. But, despite the intentions of the Australian government, the British military authorities were determined to exploit the appointment of Bridges for their own purposes. If the right men were not chosen as college staff, Brigadier Lancelot Kiggell, Director of Staff Duties at the War Office, informed Bridges, then 'our Imperial G. S. scheme will get on the rocks'.[59] Acceding to the wishes of Whitehall, Bridges never seriously considered any of the formal applications for the major appointments. For example, an application from Lieutenant Colonel James Legge, director of operations at Army headquarters, holder of three degrees from the University of Sydney and an experienced campaigner from South Africa, was ignored. As a result of Bridges' private dealings with the War Office, the senior military appointments of director of instruction and instructor of military engineering were filled by two imperial officers. The only Australian appointed was a retired officer who taught mounted drill.[60] Therefore, as far as Australia and New Zealand were concerned, the first step in Haig's plan for the War Office to control the education of military officers had been taken. The next step entailed sending them to the British staff college, Camberley, where they would receive more specialised staff training. 'All you local section people must hurry up in producing good men to go through the Staff College,' Kiggell informed Bridges, 'or we shall be on our beam ends for P.S.C. men to fill all the posts they are wanted for.'[61]

Although these were important achievements for the exercise of British influence in Australian military developments, there was one more obstacle which could effectively upset War Office plans. John Hoad had recently replaced Bridges as CGS and it is clear that he was still not completely trusted by imperialists. It is also evident that Bridges was still smarting over Hoad's successful scheming which had resulted in his removal from the premier military appointment. In the letters they exchanged before Kitchener's visit, Kirkpatrick and Bridges discussed Hoad's appointment as CGS with concern. Presuming that another officer would be appointed to replace Hoad as Inspector-General, Kirkpatrick observed that the 'selection will have to be very careful because if you don't get the right man the cause

An Australian Imperial Force

will be badly set back'.[62] These fears were obviously shared by Kitchener because, in his report, he recommended an increase to the power and authority of the position of inspector-general. Instead of working under the direction of the Military Board where Hoad was the senior military member, Kitchener recommended that the Inspector-General should be directly responsible to the minister. Furthermore, he recommended that the Inspector-General should be president of the promotion board for officers above the rank of major and that he should advise on the qualifications required by field officers for appointment as commanders of battalions, regiments, brigades and districts.[63] When it approved these recommendations, the government made the future incumbent of the position of Inspector-General the most influential officer in the Army. Kitchener's final coup was delivered when he successfully convinced the government that Kirkpatrick, his own staff officer, should be appointed to the position. Yet it was not announced publicly until after the elections of 13 April 1910 in which Deakin's Fusion government suffered a resounding defeat, giving Labor a clear majority in both Houses. However, not wishing to become involved in any controversy, the new Labor government left it to Joseph Cook, the minister responsible for the appointment, to make the announcement.[64] Nevertheless, privately, there were misgivings. The new government considered rescinding the decision but accepted the advice of its Attorney General, William Morris Hughes, that the Commonwealth had already completed a contract with Kirkpatrick and was bound to honour the appointment.[65]

There was a mixed reaction to Kirkpatrick's appointment. 'Saturated with the Conservative idea that everything that is good must come from abroad,' the *Age* reported indignantly, 'Mr Joseph Cook's last act of defence administration has been to announce the appointment of Colonel Kirkpatrick, of the Imperial army, as Inspector-General of the Commonwealth military forces.' The Melbourne newspaper labelled the appointment as a 'Military Scandal' whereby the 'anti-Australian Minister' Cook 'intended to swamp the whole department with imported officers'.[66] Similarly, the Sydney *Worker* reported that '[t]he amazing crookedness of the whole business is proved by the secrecy with which it has been engineered'.[67] By contrast, the conservative *Daily Telegraph* thought 'Australia was fortunate in being able to secure such an officer' because he was 'thoroughly *au fait* with Lord Kitchener's scheme for the defence of Australia'.[68] However, none of the newspapers associated Kirkpatrick's appointment with the increased powers which Kitchener had recommended for the position.

With Andrew Fisher's Labor Party triumphant, it fell to Senator George Pearce as incoming Minister for Defence to implement Kitchener's recommendations. It was an outcome which Kitchener had anticipated. During his visit to Australia, he had requested the Governor of Western Australia, Sir Gerald Strickland, to arrange a meeting with Pearce.[69] 'I received a summons to attend at State Government House at 11 a.m. on a given date,' Pearce recalled in later life. 'At 10.55 a.m. I reported there and was shown into a room. Punctually at 11 a.m. the door opened and in strode Kitchener, who shook hands with me and said, "Sit down, please".' Confessing no interest in politics, Kitchener had then said that he had been advised that should there be a change of government after the elections then Pearce would be the new Minister for Defence. 'There are some things that I am telling [Mr Cook] which I will not put in my report,' he had told Pearce, 'I have the minister's permission to tell them to you. Would you like to hear them?' With Pearce's concurrence, Kitchener had then told the Labor senator how to manage the transition from the old voluntary militia system to the new scheme of compulsory military training. Having done this, he had then proceeded to give Pearce his assessment—good and bad—of the capabilities of certain Australian officers. Indeed, Kitchener also had submitted a formal report to the government about some officers—'the misfits and the inefficient', as Pearce recalled. The Labor senator remembered that Bridges had been mentioned especially by Kitchener as a good officer. Bringing the meeting to a close, Kitchener had given Pearce the chance to clarify any doubts still in his mind. 'Then he rose abruptly,' Pearce recalled, 'held out his hand, said good-bye and our interview was over.'[70]

As Minister for Defence, Pearce, undoubtedly following Kitchener's advice, had decided to retain the existing militia force for the time being. Furthermore, he had also reached an important conclusion on future developments. The military force developed as a result of Kitchener's recommendation, Pearce contended, would have the responsibility of local defence but '[w]e also have to bear in mind that we are part of the British Empire [and] may be called upon, willy nilly, to bear the consequences of our Imperial connexion [sic]'.[71] Yet, although Pearce did not mention it, a fundamental difficulty remained. The *Defence Act* still denied an Australian government the power to send troops overseas, posing a problem for units raised on a compulsory basis. Without an amendment of the Act, the new units would be limited to service in Australia. The voluntarily enlisted militia force clearly provided an immediate solution to this problem; questions of its possible metamorphosis into an expeditionary force were perhaps best left until an actual crisis sparked imperial fervour in Australia. Yet in the long term the voluntary militia would cease to exist due to natural attrition and the units raised under the compulsory scheme would have to provide the overseas force. At this stage Pearce clearly was not sure how to resolve this issue. Clearly, Fisher's Labor government stood on the brink of some important decisions on Australian defence policy. In the meantime, problems were beginning to arise in the senior ranks of the military forces over important aspects of Pearce's administration of the portfolio.

One Australian officer at Army headquarters was not pleased with recent developments in the military forces, particularly the recent changes to the

An Australian Imperial Force

original concept of universal military training. In November 1910, Legge tendered his resignation as director of operations. An officer of considerable ability, Legge had been selected in 1907 by Thomas Ewing, Minister for Defence in Deakin's government, to become the chief military architect of the universal military training scheme. He had continued to work on the scheme for another three successive governments and, from 1908, also had held a position on the Military Board. By the end of 1910 he was tired, mentally and physically, but he was also deeply disappointed. On the eve of the introduction of the universal military training scheme, it had become clear that the control of the Australian military forces had fallen into the hands of imperialists. The emerging national strategy which had inspired Deakin's defence initiatives was moribund.

In tendering his resignation, Legge drew the minister's attention to the demise of national influence over the military forces. A major cause was the appointment of imperial officers to key positions while other officers, like Legge, were being overlooked because they were Australian. Foremost among Legge's complaints was the appointment of Colonel George Kirkpatrick as Inspector-General. In Legge's opinion the problem was compounded by then promoting Kirkpatrick to the rank of major-general —Australians advertised 'our assumed universal inferiority by giving such officers higher "Local Rank" ', Legge told Pearce. But, more to the point, Legge believed that Kirkpatrick had acquired inordinate power through his influence over Pearce. For example, at Kirkpatrick's request the minister had directed that the Inspector-General be given a copy of all submissions and papers considered by the Military Board. It was a direction which had already prompted the board to register its formal disapproval.[72] But Pearce was content with the arrangement and had on several occasions overruled the board's decisions on the advice of Kirkpatrick. It had obviously become a contentious issue at Army headquarters. In his resignation, Legge told the minister that not only had the imperial officer interfered with Legge's own work on universal training but he had also eclipsed the authority of the Military Board. As Legge told Pearce, the members of the Military Board had been reduced 'to a species of head clerks of the I.G. . . . [who had] all the powers and none of the responsibilities of a General Officer Commanding'. Furthermore, he also informed Pearce that Bridges was proceeding to appoint instructors for the military college from Britain while ignoring applications from Australian officers like himself. After alerting Pearce to the increasing strength of British control of the forces, Legge reminded Pearce of a recent comment by General Sir William Nicholson, advising dominion governments to guide their military developments into 'correct channels from the outset'. 'I had hoped that the "channels" referred to were going to be Australian made, and that Australian aspirations would have done the guiding,' Legge concluded pointedly.[73]

Legge's submission upset Pearce. The minister reminded the officer that he was 'not allowed . . . to criticise and reflect upon the administration and policy of the Minister' while tendering a resignation. Pearce directed Legge to withdraw his submission.[74] In this way he effectively silenced Legge, for he realised that the issues raised by him would be controversial. There can be little doubt that public disclosure of comments from a senior, informed source like Legge would have mobilised a wave of nationalist sentiment and revived the earlier public outcry over the appointment of Kirkpatrick. Yet the minister was not only trying to avoid such an outcome. Pearce condoned the rise of imperial influence in the military forces because he, too, had become committed to imperial defence objectives.

While Pearce was dealing with Legge, staff at the War Office were considering ways to tie down the dominions to firm military commitments. It was acknowledged that military uniformity was being secured gradually throughout the empire, a development which was enhanced by the advent of the Imperial General Staff and, for Australia and New Zealand, by the Kitchener recommendations. This was therefore no longer considered a problem. The major concern of the War Office was that military assistance from the dominions would come only as men volunteered when the crisis broke. Something more predictable was needed: the strength of the assistance should be known in advance. Yet, barring imperial federation or a formal agreement with the dominions, there seemed to be no easy solution which satisfied the constitutional rights and political realities in the dominions. One possible solution, it was suggested, was that the central section of the Imperial General Staff should notify local sections of War Office requirements, thereby permitting them to devise local schemes 'for overcoming the difficulty, by no means insuperable, that only a proportion of citizen forces will be available for oversea service'.[75]

Such were the issues pondered by Brigadier Henry Wilson, director of military operations at the War Office, as he worked out proposals to be put to dominion representatives at the Imperial Conference of 1911. However, one suggestion appealed especially to him. He thought it might be possible to define the theatres and times for which assistance might be required from the dominions. Developing this idea, he considered that each of the dominions might have 'certain natural spheres of action peculiar to itself'. Wilson wrote to General Sir William Nicholson explaining that: 'Thus, we might say to Australia that for the present any forces she was prepared to lend for oversea operations would in all probability not be sent further west than Capetown, further to the north than Egypt, the north-west frontier of India, Singapore or Hong Kong, or employed for some minor operations such as the capture of some outlying coaling stations belonging to the enemy. But the real truth of the matter is, that in order to get full value out of such assistance as the Dominions may elect to give us, their troops should be placed under the orders of the War Office (C.I.G.S.) and made available for

An Australian Imperial Force

The Military Board outside Army Headquarters, Melbourne, in 1910. *Rear, from left*: Lieutenant Colonel J. G. Legge, Commander S. A. Petherbridge (Civil Member), J. B. Laing (Finance Member), Lieutenant Colonel R. Wallace; *front*: Major-General J. C. Hoad (CGS), Senator G. F. Pearce (Minister for Defence), Colonel E. T. Wallack. (ARMY OFFICE SECRETARIAT)

service in any part of the World.'[76] In this manner Wilson planned to draw the dominions into an unlimited imperial commitment.

Wilson's notion of dominion spheres of action met with approval from British strategists and was included in a paper presented to the Imperial Conference in 1911. But, as Nicholson explained to Haldane during its preparation, the Committee of Imperial Defence had requested the War Office 'to make it somewhat vague and we have therefore avoided details'.[77] Despite this advice to take care in its preparation, Haldane thought the paper was still 'a little too strong for the sentiment of some of the Dominions',[78] and ordered a revision. One subsequent amendment indicated clearly the cautious approach being taken. Where the document had stated originally that: 'The four great Dominions to which the Mother Country will naturally turn in time of emergency lie at a distance . . . ', it now stated that: 'The four great Dominions which will turn to the Mother Country, or to which the Mother Country may turn, for help in time of emergency lie at a distance . . . '[79]

As a result of such bowdlerisation, the document given to participants at the conference was quite innocuous and provided little information apart from floating the principle behind Wilson's suggestion. Members of the empire were so scattered throughout the world, the paper suggested, that they could easily provide each other with support. The result would be that 'Australian forces might not be able to reach Egypt in time to take part in a decisive action, but reinforcements from India might do so provided they started in anticipation of relief by troops coming from the Commonwealth'. It was concluded that each of the dominions had 'certain natural spheres of action', but no attempt was made to define them.[80] The desirable goal of mutual support among members of the empire therefore became the camouflage for British plans, plans which for at least two years had contemplated combined imperial operations against Germany.[81] Since 1909, Wilson had been preparing for a contingency in which a British expeditionary force would join with French forces in Belgium against a German advance.[82] However, reflecting the prescription to be vague, the paper concluded that '[i]t does not seem advisable to discuss in any detail these spheres of action here and now. They will more properly form the subject of consideration by the Imperial and local General Staffs whose function it is to discuss such detailed matters.'[83] Wilson's plan had therefore been grafted on to the suggestion that the network of the Imperial General Staff should be utilised to handle the military details, thereby hopefully escaping the attention of dominion governments.

Australia was represented at the 1911 Imperial Conference by Prime Minister Andrew Fisher, Minister for Defence Senator George Pearce and Minister for External Affairs Egerton Batchelor. Being the first time that ministers of a Labor government had attended a conference, Pearce noted that 'there was a great curiosity and I sensed some trepidation as to what our attitude on Imperial questions would be'.[84] However, there was no need for concern by the British authorities. While the position of the Labor cabinet, determined before the Australian representatives left Melbourne, made no specific commitments, it was not a radical nationalist departure from previous Australian policy. The Australian naval force would be developed with advice and assistance from the Admiralty during peace, and in war the dominions should be 'trusted in the exercise of their judgment [sic] to give full weight to the claims that such a contingency would make for general assistance and co-operation'. Cabinet supported Australian participation in the Imperial General Staff, the training of Australian officers at the imperial staff colleges at Camberley and Quetta and the continued exchange of military officers.[85] But this was as far as it intended to go. Pearce told the *Times* on his arrival in London that the Australian Labor Party believed 'that Australia must first be able to defend herself before she could consider her share in a general Imperial defence scheme'.[86] Although it did not reflect the degree of imperial enthusiasm displayed by men like

An Australian Imperial Force

Cook and Foxton, the public face of Labor's policy was similar to the position adopted by earlier Australian governments.

Soon after their arrival, the Australian representatives attended a special meeting. 'We were invited to a secret session with Ministers only present,' Pearce recalled. 'There we listened to an address by the Foreign Secretary [Sir Edward Grey] in which he gave us all the confidential information from Europe as to what was going on.' It made such an impression that, according to Pearce's recollection some 40 years later, the three of them came 'unanimously to the opinion that a European war was inevitable and that it would probably come in 1915 when the preparations that Germany was making would be complete'.[87]

As a result of what they learned about the situation in Europe, the three decided that Australia should 'push on with all possible speed' with defence preparations.[88] Deakin's advice, given to the Labor ministers before they left for the conference, was ignored or probably forgotten. Speaking from the opposition benches, Deakin had claimed that the Foreign Secretary, as a matter of practice, took greater interest in Europe and Asia than in Australia. He had asked the Australian representatives 'to impress upon their colleagues at the Conference that Australia, in spite of herself, is being forced into a foreign policy of her own because foreign interests and risks surround us on every side. A Pacific policy we must have.'[89] However, Pearce, like Sir Edward Grey, was more impressed with the European situation.

During the Imperial Conference a separate committee of interested members met twice at the War Office to discuss military defence. At the second of these meetings, presided over by Nicholson, the subject of the War Office paper on military co-operation was raised. Pearce, who had already studied the paper, explained that the Australian government was constrained by the *Defence Act* which prevented its sending any soldiers overseas. However, he reassured the committee that support would come from Australia because a considerable number of men would volunteer for such service. 'As that is so,' he continued, to the undoubted surprise of the senior War Office staff, 'it seemed to us that our local General Staff ought to know what is in the minds of the Imperial General Staff as regards what use such forces should be put to so that they could be employed in their various Dominions in arranging schemes for mobilisation or transportation of the troops, and so that they would be guided in the preparation of such a scheme by the general idea that the Imperial Staff had as to the use to which such troops could be put.' The vague nature of the War Office paper, Pearce thought naively, was attributable to uncertainty in the minds of the British staff, so he sought Nicholson's opinion on whether the paper provided sufficient basis for adequate planning by dominion staffs.[90]

Sir Frederick Borden of Canada, who also attended the War Office

The Imperial Conference of 1911 in London. It was at this Conference that the secret undertaking was given for Australia to provide an expeditionary force in the event of war. Prime Minister Asquith of Britain is seated in the centre of the front row. Prime Minister Andrew Fisher of Australia is seated second from the extreme right in the same row. Senator George Pearce is standing in the second row, second from the left in front of the pillar. (NATIONAL LIBRARY OF AUSTRALIA)

meeting, was more guarded than Pearce. A long-serving Minister for Militia and Defence, Borden pointed out that at the previous conferences in 1907 and 1909 agreement had been reached on military standardisation and commitments, although unspecified, had been given on the general defence of the empire. 'Now it seems to me that that is enough, and I should very much prefer, as far as I am concerned, that we should not do anything more,' Borden emphasised. 'I think that is sufficient.' But Pearce persisted, not wanting to drop the subject. Since those conferences Australia also had taken action to standardise organisations and equipment, he said, adding that now 'there is something more than that to be done'. He went on to call for 'the preparation of schemes of mobilisation by the local sections of the Imperial General Staff in order to enable that uniformity to be availed of'.[91] Thus Pearce committed Australia to future imperial undertakings without question, breaking previously untouched ground in Australia's relationship with Britain. With the co-operation of the other dominion representatives, Pearce wanted to secure 'a general understanding—there does not need to be any resolution—that the local section of the Imperial General Staff are to work along those lines'. This statement at least satisfied Borden. It gave the Canadian the opportunity to avoid giving an unconditional undertaking, leaving the initiative in dominion hands.[92]

An Australian Imperial Force

Whether Nicholson was forewarned of Pearce's remarkable offer is not clear, but the Chief of the Imperial General Staff was not about to let the matter die. Nicholson pressed Pearce so that there could be no dispute about the nature of the agreement about to be reached. His understanding of Pearce's position was that, although the Australian forces were raised and maintained for local defence, Pearce had decided that they would in future also have an expeditionary role. Nicholson understood that the Australian minister would therefore return to Australia and direct his General Staff to 'work out a scheme so that, if the Government of Australia so desires, they will have preparations made for mobilising a certain proportion of their force to proceed to certain ports for oversea action'. Where the force would be used, Nicholson noted, 'we cannot tell', although he had 'some idea where, it might be used'. Nicholson wanted the new development to be shrouded in secrecy, obviously because he did not want to mobilise nationalist opposition in the dominions. 'It is much better to hold our tongues about it and not say anything according to the old Persian proverb "What two ears only hear, God himself does not know",' Nicholson suggested. 'Therefore in those matters we do not say anything and nobody else knows about it.' To confirm Nicholson's understanding of the agreement, Pearce acknowledged that the Australian general staff would send the plans to the War Office when completed.[93] This was exactly what Nicholson wanted.

'I think it is much better we should do this thing quietly without any paper on the subject,' Nicholson suggested, 'because I am sure in some of the Dominions it might be better not to say anything about preparations.' 'It gives mischievous people an opportunity to talk,' Borden jumped in. 'I quite recognise that,' Pearce acknowledged, joining the conspiracy, 'and I suppose we have as large a proportion of that kind of people in Australia as there are anywhere else.' Pearce therefore agreed that information concerning the undertaking should be suppressed. Nicholson then suggested that the War Office paper be withdrawn. 'Suppressed or withdrawn—I would hope so,' Borden concurred. Pearce agreed but insisted that the paper was being withdrawn '[o]n the understanding that it will be acted upon'.[94] These exchanges, indicative of the kind of clandestine imperial scheming which had gone on for decades, now heralded a new element: the dominion politicians specifically responsible for defence were participants for the first time. No report of these discussions was ever published in the proceedings of the conference.

Pearce never spoke openly of his undertaking to provide an expeditionary force for Britain. On the contrary, he contrived to mislead the public. Speaking at a charitable function in Brunswick after his return to Australia, he told his audience that his recent trip to London had convinced him that Australia's future would be determined primarily by the nations to the north rather than by any group of European powers. After leaving London he had travelled through Europe and Russia before spending some time in Japan.[95]

It had been an educational experience for the untravelled Pearce and, as he claimed, it had made him realise Australia's proximity to Asia. It took only eight days to go from Japan to Australia, he said, but Europe was a month away. Thus Pearce tweaked the sensitive nerve of Australia's fear of Japan. Continuing in this vein, he told his Brunswick audience that, while the aims of the Labor Party were peaceful, he believed preparations for war were urgent. Few would argue with Pearce's stated perception of the threat to Australian security: fear of a Japanese invasion had been the rationale for the introduction of universal military training from the outset. It was the same fear that Kitchener counted on to encourage Australians to press on with the introduction of the scheme. However, perhaps some were curious about Pearce's haste. Certainly, questions were being asked about the priorities for defence expenditure. Only a week earlier, Pearce had had to defend the government from a newspaper charge that it was not spending sufficient money to build drill halls for the cadets who had commenced their compulsory training on 1 July. Responding, he explained that it 'was endeavouring to grapple seriously with the question of providing the war equipment necessary for our troops'. 'It is essential that those who would have to fight in case of war should have the means wherewith to take the field,' he said. Therefore, if it came to a choice between drill halls and war equipment, 'there can be only one answer as to which is to take first place'.[96] Apparently accepting Pearce's explanation, Australians remained unaware of the real object of the preparations which were underway.

Commencing in 1911, Fisher's government made significant increases to defence expenditure by approving a special vote of £600 000 in addition to the normal budget allocation. Machinery was acquired and installed in the small arms factory at Lithgow. The cordite factory at Maribyrnong was developed as a small munitions plant. Woollen mills were established at Geelong and clothing factories were brought into production at South Melbourne. A harness and saddlery factory was also established at Clifton Hill. At the Royal Military College, Duntroon, the training of officer cadets from Australia and New Zealand began under the supervision of Bridges. Yet, despite further questions from newspapers and political opponents about the extent of defence expenditure, Pearce's undertaking to the senior War Office staff remained a secret.[97]

On the same day that Pearce spoke at Brunswick, the Literary Societies of Victoria and South Australia conducted a debate in Adelaide on the subject of 'Should Australia hold herself bound to take part in any war in which Great Britain might become involved'. The host team argued the affirmative case and won by a score of 239 points to Victoria's 220.[98] But a debate quarantined within the forum of a literary society was one thing and an unrestrained, public discussion of a potentially controversial issue quite another. Judging by the comments Pearce had made to Nicholson in London, it seems clear that Pearce believed that, although many Australians

An Australian Imperial Force

would support preparations for direct military involvement with Britain, others, perhaps more likely to be among Labor constituents, would not. Pearce, and obviously Fisher, realised that a debate on such an issue could threaten the survival of their Labor government, especially since the electorate was adjusting with some reluctance to the realities of universal military training for Australian youth. The advent of the new scheme was undoubtedly a major reason for Pearce's and Fisher's reticence. Some 92 000 boys from 12 to 17 years of age had commenced training in 1911 and each successive year would produce a new batch of 12-year olds for the scheme which was designed to produce fully trained recruits by the time they turned 18.[99] While many members of parliament, newspaper editors, leaders of public opinion and trade union officials were in favour of compulsory training, it soon became evident that a great many Labor voters and a number of more conservative Australians were not.[100] Politically, it was prudent to avoid risk by using the defence of Australia as a cover until the outbreak of war when it was expected that a wave of imperial patriotism would swamp any opposition to military service and training. In the meantime, planning was well advanced at Army headquarters.

In August 1913, the Australian General Staff reviewed proof copies of secret plans which they had compiled under the title of the 'General Scheme of Defence'. Included in its pages were the results of a considerable amount of staff work which detailed the steps and procedures for Australia to go to war. Information on internal transport arrangements, the location of telegraphic stations, climate and demography were included along with comprehensive military plans covering organisations, dispositions and staff responsibilities. The strength of the military forces required by Australia, the staff calculated in the section dealing with strategic considerations, must not be less than 100 000 men. A proportion of these men was required to secure naval bases and harbours as well as 'to maintain public confidence and national credit'. 'The remainder,' the paper continued, 'must be left free to form a field army capable of acting as a mobile expeditionary force.' A defensive attitude of 'a purely passive nature' was, according to the general staff document, 'the most ineffectual method of employing an army as an instrument of policy'. Therefore, 'the whole of the Australian Military Forces are . . . being uniformly enrolled, organized, and equipped in order that any subdivision thereof may be able to assume the offensive'.[101] The staff considered that the term 'Expeditionary Force' could be used instead of 'Field Army', because the defence of Australia might necessarily mean overseas service and they anticipated that the statutory restrictions on deployment of the force would be lifted. In the meantime, they were considering ways in which a 'special expeditionary force for employment in an Imperial undertaking' could be raised by voluntary enlistment.[102] In addition to Pearce's interest in promoting such plans, Kirkpatrick, who had become the sole general in Australia with the premature death of Hoad in

October 1911, had also put pressure on the Australian CGS, Brigadier Joseph Gordon, to prepare for military operations overseas.[103] Britain's long-cherished imperial goals were now formally incorporated in the plans of the Australian General Staff, an achievement which Governor-General Lord Denman was quick to bring to the attention of the British authorities.[104]

Behind the formal plans, however, were more detailed preparations which had been initiated in October 1912, apparently at the suggestion of Gordon,[105] with the concurrence of Pearce.[106] Prime Minister Andrew Fisher and Prime Minister William Massey of New Zealand had agreed with a recommendation from Pearce that a conference should be organised for Gordon and the New Zealand CGS, Major-General Alexander Godley, to discuss co-operative defence arrangements.[107]

Convened in Melbourne in mid-November 1912, Pearce attended the opening session of the conference, telling Gordon and Godley of his gratitude that both Australia and New Zealand 'recognized their common interests and realized the necessity of joint action'. Giving a clear indication of the type of co-operation he had in mind, Pearce asked the two senior military officers to suggest ways of overcoming statutory limitations in both countries which gave a government 'no power to employ the respective forces oversea unless they voluntarily agreed so to serve'. Pearce appreciated the highly controversial nature of the subject and indicated that their suggestions 'must not do violence to the feelings of the people which had originated the restrictive clauses'.[108] As a precaution, he instructed the conference secretary, Brudenell White, to keep the notes on plans to contribute an Australian force for overseas service most strictly to himself.[109] Yet the minister's ultimate objective was stated clearly. He stipulated that he wanted a solution to the problem posed by the restrictive legislation because, as he told Gordon and Godley, it made it very difficult 'to promise a definite quota to augment an Imperial expeditionary force'. Despite Pearce's concern, Gordon reassured the minister that the important issue was the early preparation of mobilisation plans because 'the rest might safely be left to the spirit of the British people'. Obviously, there was a degree of uncertainty, Gordon continued, thus presenting some difficulties for the operational plans of the Imperial General Staff in London but he thought that 'their knowledge would let them realize that . . . they were only taking slight risks'. Pearce accepted this advice and then withdrew, gratified 'at finding the Conference unanimous on broad principles'.[110]

The major recommendation agreed on by Gordon and Godley after two days of discussions was that Australia and New Zealand should prepare plans to form a composite expeditionary force, enlisted on a voluntary basis. The force would be either a division of some 18 000 men, with Australia supplying about two-thirds of its strength, or a mounted force of four brigades, three being Australian. The two senior officers recommended that detailed planning should be undertaken by the general staffs of Australia and

20 000 youths undergoing compulsory military training in the Universal Military Training scheme march along Hunter Street, Sydney, in May 1913. The young trainees in this parade were probably senior cadets aged fourteen to seventeen.
(NATIONAL LIBRARY OF AUSTRALIA)

New Zealand on the basis of direct correspondence because they were integral elements of the Imperial General Staff. It was also recommended that New Zealand should procure its arms, ammunition and equipment from Australia's newly established munitions factories.[111] Fisher agreed and informed Massey accordingly in January 1913 with the reasonable qualification that these preparations were not to be construed as a binding commitment for an Australian government to despatch the expeditionary force.[112] That final decision would be made when the time arrived. In the meantime, Brudenell White, as a staff officer at Army headquarters, prepared the necessary plans which would eventually be implemented in August 1914.[113]

The question of whether sufficient volunteers would come forward remained unanswered for the time being, but, as Gordon had reassured Pearce, there were grounds to be confident. Writing to Hutton two months later, Brudenell White told his old master of progress in compulsory military training which had been operating for some two years. According to Brudenell White, the attitude of the young soldiers was 'quite good' and they had performed 'wonderfully well' at their recent camps. The training of young officers had 'greatly improved' and they had greater knowledge of tactical principles, devoting themselves to study 'much harder than would be readily believed!' Brudenell White was encouraged by what he saw. 'What has been done in this country, in a military sense, is really quite

An Army for a Nation

Above and below Men of the 2nd Infantry Brigade and the 4th Light Horse Regiment, 1st Australian Division, parade through the streets of Melbourne on 25 September 1914. The men had been enlisted, equipped and organised in a period of some six weeks from the declaration of war on 4 August. Without the preparations which had begun some three years earlier this would not have been possible. (NATIONAL LIBRARY OF AUSTRALIA)

wonderful,' White enthused to Hutton. 'The Labour [sic] Party certainly deserve great credit for it. At the back of everything too there is a remarkably strong vein of Imperialism. Could you see the Imperialism evident in much that we have in hand now you would be quite astonished.' White thought it was all the more remarkable because, as he noted, 'the Labour Party Platform is not Imperialistic nor do they look favourably upon what they call . . . "militarism" '.[114] Despite Brudenell White's approbation, the growing imperial enthusiasm was not enough for Fisher. He still exercised caution in his public statements. Four weeks after Brudenell White wrote to Hutton, Fisher told Australians during the delivery of his party's policy speech for the 1913 elections that a Labor government would co-operate with the dominions and Britain for 'the protection of British interests *in the Pacific*'. He made no mention of possible military involvement in Europe.[115] Yet Joseph Cook, who had assumed leadership of the Fusion Party on the retirement of Deakin due to poor health, did not feel as constrained as his political opponent. He declared that when the empire was at war, 'Australia, as part of the Empire, is also at war; and it is no evidence of jingoism to recognise this plain, naked and salient fact'. 'Above all else, we must not leave the Dominions in danger of dismemberment by one swift blow at the centre of the Empire,' he said. 'Along these fundamental lines our present defence schemes should proceed, aiming at common standards and common preparations for the defence of the whole.'[116]

Cook's party won the election by the narrowest possible margin of one seat but, facing a substantial Labor majority in the Senate, the new government was virtually powerless. At Cook's behest the Governor-General granted a double dissolution in mid-1914. Australians were again at the polls but, during this campaign, war suddenly threatened to erupt. Speaking at Colac four days before its outbreak, a more confident Fisher could now pledge his party's unrestricted support for Britain, if necessary, to the 'last man and the last shilling'.[117] It was a popular declaration. But it made little difference that Labor won the September elections with a comfortable majority in both Houses. When the recruiting depots opened there was no shortage of men eager to enlist, so fulfilling the claim that Australians would stand by Britain in the event of war. The preparations, which had begun three years earlier, meant that the men could be organised, equipped and ready for departure within six weeks. Indeed, in his official history of the war, Dr Charles Bean reported the common belief that 'no troops ever went to the front more generously equipped than this first Australian contingent'. The only remaining question was who would command the force. A suggestion by Bridges that Edward Hutton should be offered the top appointment was turned down by the government. Instead of Hutton, the government wanted an Australian officer as its commander and chose Bridges. On 1 November 1914, the convoy of ships carrying the Australian Imperial Force sailed from Albany headed for Europe.[118]

Appendix I
Ministries: Commonwealth of Australia, 1901–1914

Barton Ministry, 1 January 1901 to 24 September 1903
Minister for Defence: Sir James Dickson 1 January 1901 to 10 January 1901; Sir John Forrest 17 January 1901 to 7 August 1903; Senator James Drake 7 August 1903 to 24 September 1903.

Deakin Ministry, 24 September 1903 to 27 April 1904
Minister for Defence: Austin Chapman

Watson Ministry, 27 April 1904 to 18 August 1904
Minister for Defence: Senator Andrew Dawson

Reid–McLean Ministry, 18 August 1904 to 5 July 1905
Minister for Defence: James McCay

Deakin Ministry, 5 July 1905 to 13 November 1908
Minister for Defence: Senator Thomas Playford 5 July 1905 to 11 January 1907; Sir Thomas Ewing 23 January 1907 to 13 November 1908.

Fisher Ministry, 13 November 1908 to 2 June 1909
Minister for Defence: Senator George Pearce

Deakin Ministry, 2 June 1909 to 29 April 1910
Minister for Defence: Joseph Cook

Fisher Ministry, 29 April 1910 to 24 June 1913
Minister for Defence: Senator George Pearce

Appendix I

Cook Ministry, 24 June 1913 to 17 September 1914
Minister for Defence: Senator Edward Millen

Fisher Ministry, 17 September 1914 to 27 October 1915
Minister for Defence: Senator George Pearce

Appendix II
Chiefs of the General Staff
1909–1914

Colonel W. T. Bridges, 1 January 1909 to 25 May 1909
Major General J. C. Hoad, CMG, 26 May 1909 to 30 May 1911
Lieutenant Colonel F. A. Wilson, DSO (Acting), 1 June 1911 to 10 May 1912
Brigadier General J. M. Gordon, CB, 11 May 1912 to 31 July 1914
Colonel J. G. Legge, CMG, 1 August 1914 to 19 May 1915

Notes

Introduction

1 C. E. W. Bean *Official History of Australia in the War of 1914–1918*, UQP edn, Vol. I 'The Story of ANZAC' St Lucia, 1981, pp. 3, 8, 27
2 *ibid.*, p. 27. *Note*: I have emphasised *'in case either were invaded'*.
3 *ibid.*, pp. 11, 28, 63. *Note*: I have emphasised *'against the chance'*.
4 *ibid.*, pp. 15–16
5 *The Defence of Australia 1987* Presented to Parliament by the Minister for Defence the Honourable Kim C. Beazley, MP, March 1987, Australian Government Printing Service, Canberra, 1987
6 Bean 'The Story of ANZAC', pp. 14–17. *Note*: I have emphasised *'perfectly definite'* and *'united'*.

Chapter 1

1 *Official Year Book of The Commonwealth of Australia* No. 2, 1909, Section XXVIII, Part 1.1, Military Defence—Historical Outline, pp. 1075–81
2 T. B. Millar 'History of Defence Force of The Port Philip District and Colony of Victoria 1836–1900', MA thesis, University of Melbourne, 1957, pp. 72–80, MSS 998, AWM; *ibid.*, p. 80
3 *Official Year Book of The Commonwealth of Australia* No. 2, 1909, Section XXVIII, Part 1.1, Military Defence—Historical Outline, pp. 1075–81
4 *ibid.*; Millar p. 84; D. H. Johnson *Volunteers at Heart: The Queensland Defence Forces 1860–1901* UQP, St Lucia, 1975, p. 6; G. F. Wieck *The Volunteer Movement in Western Australia 1861–1903* Paterson Brokensha P/L, Perth, pp. 22–5
5 K. Sinclair (ed.) *A Soldier's View of Empire: The Reminiscences of James Bodell 1831–92* 1982, Bodley Head, London, pp. 125–6
6 L. Barton *Australians in the Waikato War 1863–1864* 1979, Library of Australian History, Sydney, pp. 15–16; Australian Enlistments 1863–1864, p. 52
7 Millar, pp. 119–20; Johnson *Volunteers at Heart* pp. 67–70

8 R. C. Thompson *Australian Imperialism in the Pacific: The Expansionist Era 1820–1920* MUP, Melbourne, 1980, pp. 58–9, 84–5
9 Meaney *The Search for Security in the Pacific* Appendix 1 'Australian Colonies: Defence Forces, 1870–1900' pp. 268–9
10 W. Calder *Heroes and Gentlemen: Colonel Tom Price and the Victorian Mounted Rifles* Jimaringle Publications, Melbourne, 1985, p. 19; P. V. Vernon (ed.) *The Royal New South Wales Lancers 1885–1960* Royal New South Wales Lancers, Sydney, 1961, pp. 3–5
11 Chauvel to Lieutenant T. W. White, 24 June 1932; Chauvel to Mr R. Peacock, 4 July 1932 *Chauvel Papers* Defence Regional Library, Campbell Park
12 K. S. Inglis *The Rehearsal: Australians at War in the Sudan 1885* Rigby, Sydney, 1985, p. 21
13 *ibid.*, pp. 53, 73–4
14 Thompson *Australian Imperialism in the Pacific* pp. 65, 92
15 Meaney *The Search for Security in the Pacific* p. 30
16 Parkes to Gillies, 30 October 1889, in H. Parkes *Fifty Years in the Making of Australian History* Longmans, London, 1892, pp. 586–9
17 Thompson *Australian Imperialism in the Pacific* p. 103
18 B. Disraeli, quoted by H. E. Egerton in *A Short History of British Colonial Policy* Book IV, 'The Period of the Zenith and Decline of *Laissez Aller* Principles—1861–1885', 3rd edn, Methuen, London, 1910, p. 362
19 First Report of the Royal Commissioners appointed to inquire into the Defence of British Possessions and Commerce Abroad: together with the Minutes of Evidence and Appendix, 3 September 1881, Commission of Appointment, p. iii, Cab 7/2, PRO
20 Second Report of the Royal Commissioners appointed to inquire into the Defence of British Possessions and Commerce Abroad: with Appendix, 28 March 1882, paras. 25–7, p.6; Appendix No. 4, Inclosure 1 in No. 4, Australia—Report on Colonial Defences by Wm. F. Drummond Jervois, 29 November 1879, Government House, Adelaide, para. 27, p. 80
21 *ibid.*, para. 27, p. 6; paras. 129(b)–31, p. 34; para. 105, p. 20; paras. 115–16, 119, 119A, pp. 30–1
22 Third and Final Report of the Royal Commissioners appointed to inquire into the Defence of British Possessions and Commerce Abroad, 22 July 1882, para. 166, p. 30, Cab 7/4, PRO; Colonial Defence—Précis of Important Events connected with the Question of the Employment of Colonial Military Forces on Imperial Service, CDC, 29 June 1909, para. 2, p. 1, Cab 11/125, PRO
23 D. C. Gordon *The Dominion Partnership in Imperial Defence* John Hopkins Press, Baltimore, 1965, p. 98
24 Colonial Forces—Memorandum, 21 June 1886, Henry Thring, Cab 11/125, PRO
25 Gordon *The Dominion Partnership in Imperial Defence* p. 106
26 R. Jones 'Tryon in Australia: The 1887 Naval Agreement' *Journal of the Australian War Memorial* No. 10, April 1987, pp. 45, 49–50
27 M. Dunn *Australia and the Empire: From 1788 to the Present*, 1984, Fontana/Collins, Sydney, pp. 62–3
28 Colonial Defence—Précis of Important Events connected with the Question of the Employment of Colonial Military forces on Imperial Services, Colonial Defence Committee, 29 June 1909, paras. 4, 5, p. 2, Cab 11/125, PRO
29 *BPP* Vol. 56, July 1887, C.5091, Proceedings of the Colonial Conference 1887, p. 26
30 *ibid.*, pp. 292–3, 362

Notes

31 *BPP* Vol. 49, C. 6188, Correspondence Relating to the Inspection of the Military Forces of the Australasian Colonies by Major-General J. Bevan Edwards, No. 1, War Office to Colonial Office, 5 April 1889, p. 87 and No. 10, Lord Knutsford to the Governors of the Australasian Colonies, 17 June 1889, pp. 89–90
32 L. Trainor 'British Imperial Defence Policy' *Historical Studies* Vol. 14, No. 54, April 1970, p. 207
33 *Age* 2 August 1889, Melbourne, p. 9; *Advertiser* 15 August 1889, Adelaide, p. 5
34 *Brisbane Courier* 13 July 1889, Brisbane, pp. 5, 15 July 1889, p. 4
35 *Sydney Morning Herald* 22 July 1889, Sydney, p. 8, 29 July 1889, p. 6
36 *Age* 2 August 1889, Melbourne, p. 5, 12 August 1889, p. 5
37 *Advertiser* 15 August 1889, Adelaide, p. 5, 26 August 1889, p. 6
38 *BPP* C. 6188, No. 11, Edwards to Lord Carrington, 9 October 1889, pp. 91–4; Edwards to Sir W. C. F. Robinson, 9 October 1889, pp. 95–7; Edwards to Earl of Kintore, 9 October 1889, pp. 101–4; Edwards to Sir Robert Hamilton, 9 October 1889, pp. 99–101; Edwards to Sir Napier Broome, 9 October 1889, pp. 104–5; Edwards to General Sir H. W. Norman, 9 October 1889, pp. 97–9
39 *ibid.*, Proposed Organisation of the Military Forces of the Australian Colonies, pp. 106, 108
40 *ibid.*, pp. 105–6
41 *ibid.*, pp. 106, 109
42 *ibid.*, pp. 105–6
43 *ibid.*, Enclosure in No 12, Proposed Organisation of the Military Forces of the Australasian Colonies, Reports by Major-General J. Bevan Edwards CB—Remarks by Colonial Defence Committee, pp. 114–16; CDC Remarks No. 40R, 16 May 1890, Part 1, Cab 9/1, PRO
44 CDC Remarks No. 40R, pp. 116–17
45 J. Bevan Edwards 'Australasian Defence' *Proceedings of the Royal Colonial Institute* Vol. XXII, 1890–91, pp. 202, 211, 217
46 *ibid.*, pp. 197–8, 203, 205, 206–7
47 *ibid.*, pp. 205, 210
48 J. Bevan Edwards 'Australasian Defence' p. 196; T. A. Coghlan *Labour and Industry in Australia: From the First Settlement in 1788 to the Establishment of the Commonwealth in 1901* Vol. 4, Oxford University Press, London, 1918, p. 2336
49 Norris *The Emergent Commonwealth* pp. 111–12
50 J. Bevan Edwards 'Australasian Defence' p. 196
51 Norris *The Emergent Commonwealth* p. 109
52 H. Parkes *The Federal Government of Australasia—Speeches delivered on various occasions* November 1889–May 1890, Turner & Henderson, Sydney, 1890, pp. 3–6
53 *Age* 15 October 1889, Melbourne, p. 4
54 *Sydney Morning Herald* 17 October 1889, Sydney, p. 6
55 *Brisbane Courier* 18 October 1889, Brisbane, p. 4
56 Letter by Dingo, in *Bulletin* 24 August 1889, Sydney, p. 5
57 *Bulletin* 31 August 1889, Sydney
58 *Official Record of the Proceedings and Debates of the National Australasian Convention* Sydney, March–April 1891, pp. lxi–lxii, & p. 11–12
59 Meaney *The Search for Security* p. 34

Chapter 2

1. 'Defence of Australia' lecture by Major-General Tulloch, CB, Military Commandant of Victoria, Melbourne, 1891, ANL
2. Report of the Royal Commission appointed to Inquire into the Military Service of New South Wales—Appointed June 10, 1892, in *New South Wales Defence Schemes, 1863–1892* pp. 7, 8, 24, AWM Library 301.011
3. Sir George Clarke, quoted by L. Trainor, in 'British Imperial Defence Policy' *Historical Studies* Vol. 14, No. 54, April 1970, p. 210
4. Ralph Thompson, War Office, to Under Secretary of State, Colonial Office, 11 March 1893, NSW No. 4208, CO 201/614, ANL
5. A. J. Hill, 'Hutton, Sir Edward Thomas Henry [1848–1923]' *ADB* Vol. 9, Melbourne, 1983, pp. 415–18; W. Perry 'Military Reforms of General Sir Edward Hutton in New South Wales 1893–96' *The Australian Quarterly* December 1956, p. 66; Cutting from *Colonial Military Gazette* 15 July 1893, and cutting from *Sydney Mail* 15 July 1893 *Hutton Collection* Vol. 6, Australian Newspapers 1893–94, ff. 46, 44; cutting from *Sydney Morning Herald* 23 October 1895, *Daily Telegraph* no date, *Morning Post* 14 December 1895 *Hutton Collection* Vol. 7, Australian Newspapers 1894–95, f. 118, Ms. 1215, ANL
6. Confidential—Memoranda of Conversation between Hon. Robert Meade CB—Permanent Under Secretary for the Colonies and Colonel E. T. H. Hutton ADC 9 March 1893 in Colonial Office *Hutton Papers* Vol. I, Add. Ms. 50078, ff. 251–2, BL
7. Chandran Jeshurun 'The Anglo-French Declaration of January 1896 and the Independence of Siam' *Journal of the Siam Society* July 1970, vol. 58, Part 2, pp. 107–10
8. Hutton to Sir Henry Norman, 4 July 1894 *Hutton Papers* Vol. V, Add. Ms. 50082, ff. 229–30, BL
9. Memoirs of Lieutenant-General Sir Edward Hutton, Ch. XIII *Hutton Papers* Vol. XXXV, Add. Ms. 50112, ff. 211–17, BL
10. Cutting from *Sydney Illustrated News, Hutton Collection* Vol. 6, Australian Newspapers 1893–94, f. 24, Ms. 1215, ANL
11. *Sydney Morning Herald* 30 May 1893, Sydney, p. 5
12. *Bulletin* 21 March 1896, Sydney, p. 10
13. Manuscript note by Hutton *Hutton Collection* Vol. 6, Australian Newspapers 1893–94, f. 58, Ms. 1215, ANL
14. *Sydney Morning Herald* 5 June 1893, Sydney, p. 5
15. Cutting from *Sydney Illustrated News* no date, f. 24; cutting from *The Australian Star* 7 July 1893, f. 36 *Hutton Collection* Vol. 6, Australian Newspapers 1893–94, Ms. 1215, ANL
16. Cutting from *Town and Country* no date, f. 33; cutting from *Sydney Illustrated News* June 1893, f. 26, *ibid.*
17. Memoirs of Lieutenant-General Sir Edward Hutton, Ch. XIII *Hutton Papers* Vol. XXXV, Add. Ms. 50112, ff. 211–17, BL
18. Cuttings from *Sydney Morning Herald* 15 May 1894; *Daily Telegraph* 12 May 1894 *Hutton Collection* Vol. 6, Australian Newspapers 1893–94, Ms. 1215, ANL
19. Cutting from *Daily Telegraph* 21 June 1893 *Hutton Collection* Vol. 6, Australian Newspapers 1893–94, f. 33, Ms. 1215, ANL
20. Hutton to Principal Under Secretary with enclosed memorandum, 16 June 1893 *Hutton Papers* Vol. VII, Add. Ms. 50084, ff. 196–8, BL; Cutting from *Sydney*

Notes

Morning Herald 26 June 1893, *Hutton Collection* Vol. 6, Australian Newspapers 1893–94, f. 34, Ms. 1215, ANL

21 Cutting from *Daily Telegraph* 2 June 1893, *Hutton Collection* Vol. 6, Australian Newspapers 1893–94, f. 24, Ms. 1215, ANL
22 Hutton to HRH Duke of Cambridge, 18 September 1893 *Hutton Papers* Vol. 1, Add. Ms. 50078, ff. 82–5, BL; for problems in the artillery: Hutton to Peacocke, 19 May 1894 *Hutton Papers* Vol. X, Add. Ms. 50087, ff. 81–3, BL
23 Cutting from *Colonial Military Gazette* 15 April 1896, *Hutton Collection* Vol. 8, Australian Newspapers 1895–96, f. 70, Ms. 1215, ANL
24 Cuttings from *Sydney Morning Herald* 9 September 1893, 11 September 1893; *Daily Telegraph* 11 September 1893, 12 September 1893, *Hutton Collection* Vol. 6, Australian Newspapers 1893–94, ff. 65–6, Ms. 1215, ANL
25 Cutting from *Daily Telegraph* 19 September 1893, *ibid.*, f. 69
26 Cutting from *Star* 4 October 1893, *ibid.*, f. 70
27 Cutting from *Evening News ibid.*, f. 76
28 Cutting from *Daily Telegraph* 13 October 1893, *ibid.*, f. 74
29 Cutting from *Evening News* 14 October 1893, *ibid.*, f. 74
30 Cutting from *Daily Telegraph* 24 July 1893, *ibid.*, f. 48
31 Cutting from *Daily Telegraph* 27 July 1893, *ibid.*, f. 50
32 *Sydney Morning Herald* 10 July 1893, p. 5, & 11 July 1893, p. 3
33 *Bulletin* 15 July 1893, Sydney, p. 12
34 Letter by Verite, 20 July 1893, in cutting from *Daily Telegraph* 22 July 1893 *Hutton Collection* Vol. 6, Australian Newspapers 1893–94, f. 54, Ms. 1215, ANL
35 Chandran Jeshurun 'The Anglo-French Declaration of January 1896 and the Independence of Siam' *Journal of the Siam Society* July 1970, Vol. 58, Part 2, pp. 111–12
36 Cutting from *Evening News* 26 July 1893, *Hutton Collection* Vol. 6, Australian Newspapers 1893–94, f. 52, Ms. 1215, ANL
37 *ibid.*
38 Cutting from *Bulletin* 12 August 1893, *Hutton Collection* Vol. 6, Australian Newspapers 1893–94, f. 54, Ms. 1215, ANL
39 *Sydney Morning Herald* 19 August 1893, Sydney, p. 7
40 *Sydney Morning Herald* 21 August 1893, Sydney, p. 3
41 Cuttings from *Newcastle Morning Herald* and *Miners' Advocate*, 21 August 1893 *Hutton Collection* Vol. 6, Australian Newspapers 1893–94, f. 61, Ms. 1215, ANL
42 Cutting from *Daily Telegraph* 21 August 1893, *ibid.*, f. 58
43 Cuttings from *Newcastle Morning Herald* and *Miners' Advocate*, *ibid.*, f. 60–1
44 Introductory address by Major-General E. T. H. Hutton, Chairman, to Lecture XX, 30 August 1893, *Journal and Proceedings of the United Service Institution of New South Wales for the Year 1893* Vol. V, pp. 13–15
45 Hutton to Principal Under Secretary with enclosed memorandum, 16 June 1893 *Hutton Papers* Vol. VII, Add. Ms. 50084, ff. 196–8, BL
46 Hutton to Principal Under Secretary, 27 September 1893 *Hutton Papers* Vol. VII, Add. Ms. 50084, ff. 199–201, BL
47 Notes regarding my interview with Sir George Dibbs, Premier of New South Wales, 13 November 1893 *Hutton Papers* Vol. VII, Add. Ms. 50084, ff. 203–4, BL
48 *Daily Telegraph* 4 November 1893, Sydney, p. 9
49 Notes regarding my interview with Sir George Dibbs, Premier of New South Wales, 13 November 1893 *Hutton Papers* Vol. VII, Add. Ms. 50084, ff. 203–4, BL

50 *ibid.*
51 *Daily Telegraph* 4 November 1893, Sydney, p. 9
52 Private and confidential—Resume of a personal interview between Sir George Dibbs and Major-General Hutton, at the Colonial Secretary's Office, Sydney, on 13th November, 1893, at 8 pm, Mr Crichett Walker, Principal Under Secretary being present, *Hutton Papers* Vol. VII, Add. Ms. 50084, ff. 205–10, BL
53 Hutton to Dibbs, 1 February 1894, ff. 211–12; Note by Hutton, Hobart, 18 February 1894, f. 213 *Hutton Papers* Vol. VII, Add. Ms. 50084, BL
54 Report and Summary of Proceedings Together with Appendices and Minutes of the Federal Military Conference Assembled at Sydney to Consider a General Scheme of Military Defence Applicable to the Australian Colonies and Tasmania, Sydney, October 1894, Minutes and Summary of Proceedings, p. 18, AWM Folio Pamphlet Collection No. 301.013, Queensland Defence Reports, Box No. 49A, AWM
55 *Sydney Morning Herald* 26 January 1894, Sydney, p. 6; *Daily Telegraph* 26 January 1894, Sydney, p. 4
56 Parkes to Hutton, 26 January 1894 *Hutton Papers* Vol. VII, Add. Ms. 50084, ff. 168–9, BL
57 Hutton to Parkes, 28 January 1894, ff. 170–1, *ibid.*
58 Parkes to Hutton, 30 January 1894, ff. 172–3, *ibid.*
59 Parkes to Gillies, in H. Parkes *Fifty Years in the Making of Australian History* London, 1892, pp. 586–9
60 Hutton to Duke of Cambridge, 14 February 1894 *Hutton Papers* Vol. I, Add. Ms. 50078, ff. 86–8, BL
61 Hutton to Duke of Cambridge, 27 August 1894, ff. 96–9, *ibid.*
62 Defence Scheme of New South Wales, by Major-General E. T. H. Hutton, 1 September 1894, Sydney, 1894, ANL
63 Report and Summary of Proceedings . . . of the Federal Military Conference, October 1894, Minutes & Summary of Proceedings, Minute by G. H. Reid, 23 October 1894, with cabinet approval, p. 17
64 *ibid.*, p. 19
65 *ibid.*, pp. 19–25; Report of Military Conference, held at Sydney, 24 October 1894, Sydney, 31 March 1895, Australian Federal Defence, Part I, Appendix A, pp. 5–6, ANL
66 Report and Summary of Proceedings . . . of the Federal Military Conference, October 1894, Minutes and Summary of Proceedings, p. 25, AWM; Report of Military Conference . . . , Sydney, 31 March 1895, Australian Federal Defence, Part I, Appendix A, para. 8, p. 7, ANL
67 Report and Summary of Proceedings . . . of the Federal Military Conference, October 1894, Minutes and Summary of Proceedings, p. 34, AWM
68 Australian Federal Defence, Amended 12 February 1896, Part I, General Scheme of Defence, para. 8, p. 9, ANL
69 Report and Summary of Proceedings . . . of the Federal Military Conference, October 1894, Minutes and Summary of Proceedings, p. 35, AWM
70 Hutton to Sir Henry Norman, 4 July 1894 *Hutton Papers* Vol. V, Add. Ms. 50082, ff. 229–30, BL
71 Report of a Military Conference, Sydney, 31 March 1895, Australian Federal Defence, Part II, Draft Federal Defence Agreement, Section A, Federal Defence Force of Australia—Terms of Agreement for Formation and Maintenance, para. 10, p. 25, ANL

Notes

72 Report of a Military Conference, Sydney, 31 March 1895, Australian Federal Defence, Part II, Draft Federal Defence Agreement, Section A, Federal Defence Force of Australia—Terms of Agreement for Formation and Maintenance, para. 19, p. 27, ANL
73 *Sydney Morning Herald* 25 October 1894, Sydney, p. 4
74 Report of a Military Conference, Sydney, 31 March 1895, Australian Federal Defence, Part II, Draft Federal Defence Agreement, Section A, Federal Defence Force of Australia—Terms of Agreement for Formation and Maintenance, para. 18, pp. 26-7, ANL
75 Hutton to Peacocke, 20 May 1895 *Hutton Papers* Vol. X, Add. Ms. 50087, ff. 113-14, BL
76 Hutton to Cambridge, 20 January 1895 *Hutton Papers* Vol. I, Add. Ms. 50078, ff. 111-12, BL
77 *NSWPD* Vol. LXXIII, 16 October 1894, Mr Griffith, p. 1363
78 Hutton to Peacocke, 21 October 1894 *Hutton Papers* Vol. X, Add. Ms. 50087, ff. 86-7, BL
79 Report and Summary of Proceedings . . . of the Federal Military Conference, October 1894, Minutes and Summary of Proceedings, p. 26
80 *QPD* Vol. LXV, 2 October 1891, pp. 1363-5
81 Report and Summary of Proceedings . . . of the Federal Military Conference, October 1894, Minutes and Summary of Proceedings, p. 27
82 Report of a Military Conference, Sydney, 31 March 1895, Australian Federal Defence, Part II, Draft Federal Defence Agreement, Section A, Federal Defence Force of Australia—Terms of Agreement for Formation and Maintenance, para. 8, p. 25, ANL
83 *ibid.*, p. 23
84 Report of Summary of Proceedings . . . of the Federal Military Conference, October 1894, Minutes and Summary of Proceedings, p. 33, AWM
85 *Sydney Morning Herald* 31 January 1895, Sydney, p. 5
86 *Sydney Morning Herald* 2 February 1895, Sydney, p. 9
87 Peacocke to Hutton, 8 May 1895 *Hutton Papers* Vol. X, Add. Ms. 50087, ff. 101-4, BL
88 Nathan to Hutton, 27 November 1895 *Hutton Papers* Vol. X, Add. Ms. 50087, ff. 150-4, BL
89 Hutton to Nathan, 5 January 1896 *Hutton Papers* Vol. X, Add. Ms. 50087, ff. 158-63, BL
90 Australian Colonies and Tasmania, Report of Federal Military Conference—Remarks by the Colonial Defence Committee, New South Wales No. 9052, 21 November 1895, Cab 11/23, PRO; Remarks by CDC, No. 119R, 21 November 1895, Part 1, Cab 9/1, PRO
91 Hutton to Nathan, 5 January 1896 *Hutton Papers* Vol. X, Add. Ms. 50087, ff. 158-63, BL
92 Hutton to Nathan, 19 January 1896 *Hutton Papers* Vol. X, Add. Ms. 50087, ff. 164-5, BL
93 Australian Federal Defence, Amended 12 February 1896, Part II, Federal Defence Agreement, Section A, Federal Defence Force of Australia—Terms of Agreement for Formation and Maintenance, para. 8(1), p. 17, ANL
94 *ibid.*, para. 2, p. 15
95 *ibid.*, para. 2, p. 15
96 *Sydney Morning Herald* 6 March 1896, Sydney, p. 5; Australian Colonies and Tasmania—Report of Inter-Colonial Military Committee, January 1896, CDC Minute No. 72M, 20 July 1896, Cab 8/1, PRO

An Army for a Nation

97 Confidential Memorandum of a Conversation between Sir Robert Meade Permanent Under Secretary of State for the Colonies and Colonel Hutton May /1/96 Upon his return from Commanding Troops in New South Wales *Hutton Papers* Vol. 1, Add. Ms. 50078, ff. 253–5, BL

Chapter 3

1 P. H. Colomb 'The Functions of the Navy and Army in the Defence of the Empire' *Royal United Service Institution Journal* Vol. XL, July–December 1896, pp. 1424, 1447, 1448, 1450, 1459
2 Calculated from information provided in B. R. Mitchell and P. Deave *Abstract of British Historical Statistics* 'Gross Public Expenditure—UK 1801–1939', Public Finance 4, Cambridge, 1962, pp. 397–9
3 Miles (J. Maurice) 'Where To Get Men' *Contemporary Review*, Vol. LXXXI, January 1902, pp. 79, 86
4 Wolseley to Permanent Under Secretary of State for War, 22 February 1896, file no. 266/104, WO 32/6357, PRO
5 Colonial Defence, Confidential Memorandum by the CDC, No. 57M, 19 May 1896, Cab 8/1, PRO; a copy of the same Memorandum, Cab 11/118, PRO; also *Hutton Papers* Vol. X, Add. Ms. 50087, ff. 173–6, BL
6 ibid.
7 ibid.
8 Circular, enclosing Memorandum No. 57M, by J. Chamberlain, Secretary of State for the Colonies, 6 July 1896, Cab 11/118, PRO
9 J. Chamberlain, quoted by R. R. James in *The British Revolution: British Politics 1880–1939* Methuen, London, 1978, p. 170
10 *ibid.*, pp. 167–70; B. Tuchman *The Proud Tower: A Portrait of the World Before the War 1890–1914* Hamish Hamilton, London, 1966, pp. 55–7
11 Colonial Premiers and Colonial Defence, 1897, Secret Memorandum by the CDC, No. 106M, 12 June 1897, Cab 8/1, PRO
12 Proceedings of a Conference between the Secretary of State for the Colonies and the Premiers of the Self-Governing Colonies, At the Colonial Office, London, June and July 1897, Memorandum 31 July 1897, p. 7, ANL
13 *ibid.*, pp. 7–8
14 *ibid.*, pp. 8–9; Colonial Defence, Précis of Important Events connected with the Question of the Employment of Colonial Military Forces on Imperial Service, CDC, 29 June 1909, para. 6, p. 2, Cab 11/125, PRO
15 Report of a Conference between the Right Hon. Joseph Chamberlain MP, and the Premiers of the Self-Governing Colonies of the Empire, June and July 1897, p. 107, AA, CP 103/12, Bundle 1. *Note*: I have emphasised '*not*'
16 Proceedings of a Conference Between the Secretary of State for the Colonies and The Premiers of the Self-Governing Colonies, At the Colonial Office, London, June and July 1897, Memorandum 31 July 1897, p. 18, ANL
17 Report of a Conference between the Right Hon. Joseph Chamberlain, MP, and the Premiers of the Self-Governing Colonies of the Empire, June and July 1897, pp. 94–6, CP 103/12, Bundle 1, AA
18 B. K. de Garis, 'The Colonial Office and the Commonwealth Constitution Bill', in A. W. Martin (ed.) *Essays in Australian Federation* MUP, Melbourne,

Notes

1969, pp. 94–6; C. Cuneen, 'The Role of Governor-General In Australia, 1901–27', August 1973, PhD thesis, Australian National University, p. 53
19 Cuneen, 'The Role of Governor-General In Australia, 1901–27', p. 55
20 Comments on the draft constitution by John Anderson, Chief Clerk Australian Section, 19 June 1897, with minutes by John Bramston, Assistant Under Secretary of Australasian Affairs, S.A. No. 12012, 7 June 1897, CO 13/152(1), ANL
21 *ibid.*, Minute by Joseph Chamberlain, 29 June 1897
22 de Garis, 'The Colonial Office and the Commonwealth Constitution Bill', p. 98
23 *ibid.*, p. 121
24 Chamberlain to Reid, July 1897, S.A. No. 12012, 7 June 1897, CO 13/152(1), ANL
25 Memorandum B, Australian Constitution Bill—Notes on Suggested Amendments, p. 3, S.A. No. 12012, 7 June 1897, CO 13/152(1), ANL
26 Draft of Federal Constitution 1897, Section 68, S.A. No. 12012, 7 June 1897, CO 13/152(1), ANL
27 Memorandum A, Australian Federal Constitution—Suggested Amendments, Clause 68, p. 2, S.A. No. 12012, 7 June 1897, CO 13/152(1), ANL
28 A. Todd *Parliamentary Government in the British Colonies* 2nd edn, Longmans Green, London, 1894, p. 17
29 Memorandum 091/2153 by J. Scott, DJAG, with agreement by F. H. Jeune, JAG, 9 June 1899, Australian General No. 15890, CO 418/6, ANL; D. C. Gordon *The Dominion Partnership in Imperial Defence* John Hopkins Press, Baltimore, 1965, pp. 128–30
30 General Sir Henry Norman, comments recorded in *Proceedings of the Royal Colonial Institute* Vol. XXIX, 1897–98, London, 1898, p. 250
31 Memorandum B, Australian Constitution Bill—Notes on Suggested Amendments, p. 5, S.A. No. 12012, 7 June 1897, CO 13/152(1), ANL
32 de Garis, 'The Colonial Office & the Commonwealth Constitution Bill', pp. 112–13
33 A Deakin, in *Official Record of the Debates of the Australasian Federal Convention* 3rd edn, Vol. II, Melbourne, 1898, p. 2252
34 J. Quick and R. R. Garran *The Annotated Constitution of the Australian Commonwealth* Angus & Robertson, Sydney and Melbourne, 1901, Section 281, p. 713
35 Minute by E. F. W., 24 March 1898, Vic. No. 6391, CO 309/147, ANL
36 Brassey to Chamberlain, 23 August 1897, Appendix, to Australia—Mounted Rifles for Imperial Service in War, Secret Memorandum by the CDC, No. 122M, 8 December 1897, Cab 8/1, PRO; No. 126M. 25 February 1898, Cab 8/2, PRO; Defence forces and Defences (Memorandum by Colonial Defence Committee), 30 March 1901, *CPP*, 1901–2 Session, Vol. II, No. 31, 'Defence force and Defences (Memorandum by CDC)', para. 12, p. 116
37 Australia—Mounted Rifles for Imperial Service in War, Secret Memorandum by the CDC, No. 122M, 8 December 1897, Cab 8/1, PRO
38 Australia—Mounted Rifles for Imperial Service in War, Secret Memorandum by the CDC, No. 126M, 25 February 1898, Cab 8/2, PRO
39 M. Nathan, Secretary, CDC, to Wingfield, Colonial Office, 16 July 1898, Australia General No. 15929, CO 418/5, ANL
40 Australia—Colonial Troops for Imperial Service in War, Secret Memorandum by the CDC, No. 144M, 11 July 1898, Cab 8/2, PRO
41 Wingfield, Colonial Office, to Under Secretary of State, War Office, 24 October 1898, file no. 266/36, WO 32/6365, PRO; Draft-E.W. [Wingfield] to

Under Secretary of State, War Office, 24 October 1898, Australia General No. 23201, CO 418/5, ANL
42 Wolseley to Permanent Under Secretary, War Office, 4 August 1898, file no. 266/34, WO 32/6365, PRO
43 Minute by Evelyn Wood, Adjutant-General to Commander-in-Chief, 3 November 1898; Minute by Wolseley to Permanent Under Secretary, 4 November 1898; Minute by Lansdowne, Secretary of State for War, 9 November 1898, file no. 266/36, WO 32/6365
44 G. F. Wilson, War Office, to Under Secretary of State, Colonial Office, 25 November 1898, file no. 266/36, WO 32/6365, PRO; Australia General No. 26837, CO 418/5, ANL
45 Lord Salisbury, quoted by A. L. Kennedy, in *Salisbury 1830–1903: Portrait of a Statesman* Murray, London, 1953, p. 277
46 Memoirs of Lieutenant-General Sir Edward Hutton *Hutton Papers* Vol. XXXVI, Add. Ms. 50113, f. 94, BL
47 E. T. H. Hutton 'A Co-operative System for the Defence of the Empire' *Proceedings of The Royal Colonial Institute* Vol. XXIX, 1897–98, p. 234 and f. 2
48 Memoirs of Lieutenant-General Sir Edward Hutton *Hutton Papers* Vol. XXXVI, Add. Ms. 50113, f. 92, BL
49 Hutton 'A Co-operative System for the Defence of the Empire' p. 224, pp. 232, 258
50 Memoirs of Lieutenant-General Sir Edward Hutton *Hutton Papers* Vol. XXXV, Add. Ms. 50112, ch. XIII, ff. 211–17, BL
51 Memoirs of Lieutenant-General Sir Edward Hutton *Hutton Papers* Vol. XXXVI, Add. Ms. 50113, f. 93, BL
52 Hutton 'A Co-operative System for the Defence of the Empire' p. 231
53 *ibid.*, pp. 244–5, pp. 247, 249–50, 252–4, 256
54 *ibid.*, pp. 244, 246–7, 251
55 *ibid.*, p. 244–5, 247–8, 256
56 *ibid.*, pp. 245, 250, 253
57 J. H. Knox, War Office, to Under Secretary of State, Colonial Office, 22 July 1898, Australia General No. 16748, CO 418/5, ANL
58 Note by J. C. [Joseph Chamberlain], 12 November, Australia General No. 12990, CO 418/5, ANL
59 Draft Colonial Office to Canada, NSW, Victoria, New Zealand, Queensland, South Australia, Western Australia, Tasmania, Cape Natal, 3 August 1898, Australia General No. 12990, CO 418/5; a copy of the same letter, Cab 11/124 PRO; Colonial Defence—Précis of Important Events connected with the Question of Employment of Colonial Military Forces on Imperial Service, CDC, 29 June 1909, para 8, p. 3, Cab 11/125, PRO
60 Opinion by Isaac Isaacs, Attorney General, Crown Law Office, 23 March 1899, Vic. No. 12916, CO 309/148, ANL
61 Governor, Western Australia, to Chamberlain, 24 June 1899, covering comments by Chippindall, Commandant, 7 June 1899, WA No. 19406, CO 18/226, ANL
62 Gormanston to Colonial Office, 22 September 1898, covering Premier to Gormanston, 13 September 1898, Tas. No. 24505, CO 280/401, ANL
63 Governor, South Australia, to Chamberlain, 8 October 1898, SA No. 25602, CO 13/153, ANL
64 Minute by J. A. [John Anderson], 15 November 1898, *ibid.*

Notes

65. Lamington to Secretary of State for the Colonies, 21 December 1898, Qld No. 2416, CO 234/67, ANL
66. Hampden to Chamberlain, 21 November 1898, covering French to Permanent Under Secretary, 29 September 1898, NSW No. 29192, CO 201/624; Beauchamp to Chamberlain, 15 June 1899, NSW No. 19405, CO 201/625, ANL
67. Minute E. H. M. [Marsh] to Sir E. Wingfield, 25 July 1899, NSW No. 19405, CO 201/625, ANL
68. Minute by J. A. [John Anderson], 4 July 1899, Australia General No. 15890, CO 418/6, ANL
69. Minute J. A. [John Anderson] to Cox, 26 July 1899, NSW No. 19405, CO 201/625, ANL
70. J. E. Clauson to Marsh, 15 September 1899, NSW No. 19405, CO 201/625, ANL
71. Brassey to Chamberlain, 5 April 1899, covering R. Collins, Secretary for Defence, to the Hon. the Premier, 29 March 1899, Vic. No. 6391, CO 309/147; Beauchamp to Chamberlain, 15 December 1899, covering Major-General G. A. French to The Principal Under Secretary, 25 November 1899, NSW No. 2410, CO 201/625, ANL
72. Mr Reid, 7 March 1899, *NSW PD*, 1st Session 1899, 21 February–30 March 1899, Vol. XCVII, p. 411
73. F. Wilkinson *Australian Cavalry: The New South Wales Lancer Regiment and First Australian Horse* Angus & Robertson, Sydney and Melbourne, 1901, pp. 18–20
74. J. H. Knox, War Office, to Under Secretary of State, Colonial Office, 30 November 1898, NSW No. 27114, CO 201/624, ANL
75. Darley, Lieutenant Governor of NSW, to Chamberlain, 8 March 1899, NSW No. 9475, CO 201/625, ANL
76. Draft–H.B.C., Colonial Office, to Under Secretary of State, War Office, 7 July 1899, NSW No. 17284, CO 201/625, ANL
77. Telegram Beauchamp to Colonial Office, 9 July 1899, NSW No. 17790, CO 201/625, ANL
78. Telegram Governor, Vic., to Colonial Office, 5 July 1899, Vic. No. 17285, CO 309/148, ANL
79. Minute for E. W. [Wingfield] 10 July 1899, and minute by J. C. [Chamberlain] 10 July 1899, NSW No. 17790 CO 201/625; C. N. Connolly 'Manufacturing "Spontaneity": The Australian Offers of Troops for the Boer War' *Historical Studies* Vol. 18, No. 70, April 1978, pp. 106–17
80. Telegram Governor, NSW, to Colonial Office, 12 July 1899, NSW No. 18083, CO 201/625, ANL
81. Telegram Governor, NSW, to Colonial Office, 14 July 1899, NSW No. 18303, CO 201/625, ANL
82. Telegram Governor, NSW, to Colonial Office, 21 July 1899, NSW No. 19112, CO 201/625, ANL
83. Telegram Governor, NSW, to Colonial Office, 14 July 1899, NSW No. 18303, CO 201/625, ANL
84. Text of Telegram J. C. [Joseph Chamberlain] to Government, NSW, 15 July 1899, NSW No. 18303, CO 201/625, ANL. *Note*: I have emphasised '*if made spontaneously*'.
85. Connolly 'Manufacturing "Spontaneity" ', p. 113
86. *ibid.*, pp. 112–13

87 Telegram Beauchamp to Chamberlain, 3 October 1899, NSW No. 27052, CO 201/625, ANL
88 L. M. Field *The Forgotten War: Australian Involvement in the South African Conflict of 1899–1902* MUP, Melbourne, 1979, Appendix C—Details of Contingents, pp. 193–6. *Note*: Figures for nurses provided by Ms J. Bassett from her study into Australian Army nursing. The figures include 41 enlistees in official contingents but, in addition, at least another 23 nurses joined units in South Africa.
89 N. Meaney *The Search for Security in the Pacific 1901–14*, Sydney University Press, Sydney, 1976, Appendix 1—Australian Colonies: Defence Forces, 1870–1900, pp. 270–1
90 Major-General French to the Right Hon. the Premier, Sydney, 8 May 1900, in Papers Relating To A Conference Between The Secretary of State for the Colonies and The Prime Ministers of Self-Governing Colonies—June to August, 1902, London, 1902, Summary of Proceedings of the Colonial Conference, Appendix V(2)—Major-General French's Defence Scheme (Australia's Mounted Men), p. 62; Defence Forces and Defence (Memorandum by CDC), 30 March 1901, *CPP* 1901–2 Session, Vol. II, No. 31, para. 12, pp. 116–17
91 French to Lord Lansdowne, 1 May 1900, file no. 091/2180, WO 32/8302
92 Wolseley to Permanent Under Secretary, 7 June 1900, file no. 091/2180, WO 32/8302
93 Memorandum—Australia: Colonial Troops for Imperial Service in War, M. Nathan, Secretary CDC, 26 January 1900, Cab 11/121, PRO
94 Nathan, Secretary CDC, to Sir E. Wingfield, 2 February 1900, NSW No. 24346, CO 201/625, ANL
95 Draft J. C. [Joseph Chamberlain] to Beauchamp, 7 February 1900, NSW No. 24346, CO 201/625, ANL
96 Confidential Memorandum, Colonial Co-operation in Imperial Defence, M. Nathan, Secretary, CDC, 16 August 1900, Cab 11/121, PRO
97 Possible Methods of Employing Troops from the Self-Governing Colonies in a Great War, no date, Cab 11/121, PRO
98 Confidential Memorandum, Colonial Co-operation in Imperial Defence, M. Nathan, 16 August 1900, Cab 11/121, PRO
99 *Sydney Morning Herald* 2 January 1901, Sydney, p. 9
100 *Sydney Morning Herald* 2 January 1901, Sydney, p. 12

Chapter 4

1 R. Norris *The Emergent Commonwealth—Australian Federation: Expectations and Fulfilment 1889–1910* MUP, Melbourne, 1975, p. 107
2 Return—Showing Strength and Yearly Cost of the Military Forces on 1st March, 1901, 30 June 1902, CRS B168, file no. 02/4127, AA; *CPP*, 1901–2 Session, Vol. II, No. A13, 'Defence Forces of Commonwealth', p. 47
3 Norris *The Emergent Commonwealth* pp. 119–20
4 *CPD* Vol. II, p. 2159
5 F. K. Crowley 'Forrest, Sir John' *ADB* vol. 8, Melbourne, 1981, pp. 544–51
6 Forrest to Chamberlain, 21 January 1901 *Chamberlain Papers* JC 14/1/1/11, BU
7 Crowley 'Forrest, Sir John' *ADB* Vol. 8, pp. 544–51

Notes

8 Australia, Report of the Military Committee of Inquiry, 1901, Remarks by CDC, No. 297R, 14 August 1902, CO 26420, pp. 1–5, AWM 3, file no. 207/1/20, Bundle 11, Item 03/142, AWM; Cab 9/5, PRO
9 *ibid.*, p. 1; Report of the Military Committee of Inquiry, 1901, Part I—General, p. 1, AWM 3, file no. 207/1/20, Bundle 11, Miscellaneous, AWM
10 *CPP*, 1901–2 Session, Vol. II, No. A7, 'Further Report of the Federal Military Committee, 1901' para. IV, p. 67
11 Report of the Military Committee of Inquiry, 1901, Part 1—General, p. 1
12 Papers Relating to a Conference between the Secretary of State for the Colonies and the Prime Ministers of Self-Governing Colonies—June to August, 1902—Summary of Proceedings, Appendix V(2) Major-General French's Defence Scheme (Australia's Mounted Men), French to Premier, NSW, 8 May 1900, pp. 62–3
13 French to 'My Lord', 1 May 1900, file no. 091/2180, WO 32/8302, PRO
14 Undated draft letter to French, with manuscript minute: '. . . seen and agreed to by C in C, L. [Lansdowne]', with approval by Chamberlain and Cabinet—See: minute Robert Herbert to Lord Lansdowne, 21 June 1900, file no. 091/2180, WO 32/8302, PRO
15 Commonwealth Defence Bill, drafted by the Federal Military Committee, 1901, pp. 38–41, BML
16 *ibid.*, pp. 43–4
17 The *Commonwealth Constitution Act* Section 119, p. 23, *CA*, Vol. I, 1901–2
18 Commonwealth Defence Bill, drafted by the Federal Military Committee, 1901, pp. 36, 39–41, 44
19 *ibid.*, pp. 37, 42–3, 45
20 *ibid.*, pp. 37–8, 40–1, 63, 65
21 'Further Report of the Federal Military Committee, 1901', Appendix 1, p. 72; the Parliament of the Commonwealth, 1901, House of Representatives, Commonwealth Defence Bill—1901, p. 2, PL
22 'Further Report of the Federal Military Committee, 1901', Appendix 1, p. 72
23 Constitution Act, Section 68, p. 15; Section 63, p. 14
24 'Further Report of the Federal Military Committee, 1901', Appendix 1, p. 70
25 J. Quick and R. R. Garran *The Annotated Constitution of the Australian Commonwealth* Angus & Robertson, Sydney and Melbourne, 1901, pp. 707, 713
26 A. Deakin, in *Official Record of the Debates of the Australasian Federal Convention*, 3rd edn, Vol. II, Melbourne, 1898, p. 2252, ANL
27 'Further Report of the Federal Military Committee, 1901', Appendix 1, p. 70
28 Forrest to Minister of Defence, New South Wales, 27 February 1901, together with instruction by Forrest of 1 March 1901, CRS A6, Item 01/866, AA
29 Barton to Forrest, 2 April 1901, *ibid.*
30 'Further Report of the Federal Military Committee, 1901', Appendix 1, pp. 71–3
31 *ibid.*, p. 11
32 Australian Federal Defence, Amended 12 February 1896, Part II, Federal Defence Agreement, Section A, Federal Defence Force of Australia—Terms of Agreement-Formation and Maintenance, p. 17, ANL
33 'Further Report of the Federal Military Committee, 1901', Appendix 1, p. 70
34 *ibid.*, para. II, (c), (4) and (5), p. 66
35 *CPD* Vol. II, pp. 2161–2, 2172
36 *ibid.*, pp. 2163–4; Commonwealth Defence Bill—1901, Section 15, p. 4, PL
37 *CPD* Vol. II, p. 2162
38 *ibid.*, p. 2165; Commonwealth Defence Bill—1901, Section 16, p. 4, PL

39 Commonwealth Defence Bill, drafted by the Federal Military Committee, 1901, para. 29(2), p. 43, BML
40 *CPD* Vol. II, p. 2165; Commonwealth Defence Bill—1901, Section 10, p. 3 and Section 17, p. 4, PL
41 Commonwealth Defence Bill—1901, Section 31, p. 7 and Section 36, p. 8, PL
42 *CPD* Vol. II, p. 2168
43 *ibid.*, p. 2169; Commonwealth Defence Bill—1901, Section 49, p. 10, PL
44 *CPD* Vol. II, p. 2169; Commonwealth Defence Bill—1901, Section 48, p. 9 and Section 50, p. 10, PL
45 *CPD* Vol. II, pp. 2169, 2171; Commonwealth Defence Bill—1901, Section 52, p. 10 and Section 111, p. 22, PL
46 L. Hunt 'Hackett, Sir John Winthrop' *ADB* Vol. 9, Melbourne, 1983, pp. 150–3. *Note:* Hackett was not knighted until 1911.
47 Forrest to Chamberlain, 21 January 1901 *Chamberlain Papers* JC 14/1/1/11, BU
48 Forrest to Chamberlain, 24 August 1901 *Chamberlain Papers* JC 14/1/1/13, BU
49 *CPD* Vol. III, pp. 2990, 3292
50 G. Souter *Lion and Kangaroo—Australia: 1901–1916, The Rise of a Nation* Collins, Sydney, 1976, f. 3, p. 68
51 *Age* 25 July 1901, Melbourne, p. 5
52 *CPD* Vol. III, Sir William McMillan pp. 3302–3, Mr Fowler p. 3434, Mr J. Cook pp. 3527, 3528, 3532, Mr Salmon pp. 3417, 3418, 3419, Mr Conroy pp. 3537, 3538, Sir John Quick p. 2968, Mr McDonald pp. 3519, 3522, Mr G. Edwards pp. 2977, 2979, 2981, Mr Page p. 3324, Sir Edward Braddon p. 3200, Mr Kirwan p. 3525, Mr McLean p. 3204, Mr Higgins pp. 2991, 2996, Mr Wilks pp. 2984, 2987, Mr R. Edwards p. 3598, Mr Spence p. 3595, Mr A. Groom p. 3592, Mr H. Cook pp. 3311, 3312, 3313, Mr Mauger p. 3320, Mr Reid pp. 3104, 3105, Mr Hughes pp. 3295, 3298, Mr Wilkinson p. 3214, Mr Piesse p. 3438, Mr Watkins pp. 3435, 3438, Mr Sawers pp. 3517, 3518, Mr Brown p. 3539, Mr Barton p. 3605, Mr Watson p. 3192
53 *ibid.*, Sir John Quick pp. 2968–9; Mr Watson p. 3194
54 *ibid.*, Mr Wilkinson p. 3214, Mr R. Edwards p. 3598, Mr Kirwan p. 3525, Mr McDonald p. 3519, Sir William McMillan p. 3302, Mr Higgins pp. 2991, 2996, Mr Sawers p. 3517, Mr Hume Cook p. 3311, Sir Edward Braddon p. 3200
55 *ibid.*, Mr Hughes p. 3295
56 *ibid.*, Mr Hughes p. 3297, Mr McCay pp. 3205–3206, Mr Salmon p. 3417, Sir John Quick pp. 2970, 2971, 2972, Mr Paterson p. 3543, Mr G. Edwards p. 2980, Mr Page pp. 3326, 3327, Mr Knox p. 3305, Mr Thomas p. 3315, 3316, Sir Edward Braddon p. 3201, Mr Kirwan p. 3526, Mr Ronald p. 3423, Mr McLean p. 3204, Mr Wilks p. 2987, Mr R. Edwards p. 3597, Mr Solomon pp. 3596, 3597, Mr A. Groom p. 3592, Mr Reid p. 3102, Mr Wilkinson pp. 3211, 3214, Mr Fuller p. 2966, Mr Watkins pp. 3435, 3438, Mr Brown p. 3540
57 *Age* 25 July 1901, Melbourne, p. 5
58 S. Encel 'The Study of Militarism in Australia' *The Australian and New Zealand Journal of Sociology* Vol. 3, No. 1, April 1967, p. 3; S. P. Huntington *The Soldier and the State* Belknap Press, Cambridge, Mass., 1957, pp. 155–7
59 *CPD* Vol. III, Mr Mauger p. 3320, Mr Joseph Cook p. 3528, Mr Reid p. 3107, Mr McDonald pp. 3519–20, Mr Watson p. 3192, Mr Spence p. 3595, Mr G. Edwards p. 2979

Notes

60 *Age* 23 July 1901, Melbourne, p. 5; *Sydney Morning Herald* 23 July 1901, Sydney, p. 5; *ibid.*, 24 July 1901, p. 6; *Argus* 23 July 1901, Melbourne, p. 6
61 *Bulletin* 20 July 1901, Sydney, p. 7
62 P. Weller (ed.) *Caucus Minutes 1901–1949* Vol. I, 1901–1917, MUP, Melbourne, 1975, pp. 56–7
63 *CPD* Vol. III, Mr McDonald pp. 3522–3 (Labor), Mr Conroy p. 3536 (Free Trade), Mr Watson p. 3192 (Labor), Mr Reid p. 3106 (Free Trade), Mr Spence p. 3595 (Labor), Mr Thomas p. 3318 (Labor), Mr Hughes p. 3298 (Labor), Mr Wilkinson p. 3212 (Independent Labor), Mr Wilks p. 2986 (Free Trade), Mr Mauger pp. 3320–4 (Protection)
64 *ibid.*, Mr Paterson p. 3545 (Independent), Mr Page p. 3325 (Free Trade), Mr Crouch pp. 2962–3 (Protection), Mr Knox p. 3307 (Free Trade), Mr McCay p. 3206 (Protection), Mr McLean p. 3204 (Free Trade), Mr G. Edwards p. 2979 (Free Trade), Mr Higgins p. 2995 (Protection), Mr Fowler p. 3433 (Labor), Mr Salmon p. 3419 (Protection), Mr Cruickshank p. 3428 (Protection)
65 *ibid.*, Mr Winter Cook p. 3191, Sir William McMillan p. 3303
66 *ibid.*, Mr Higgins pp. 2991–2, 2995
67 *ibid.*, Mr Higgins and Mr Barton p. 2992
68 Australia—Organization of Defence Department and Constitution of Headquarters Staff, Memorandum by CDC, No. 266M 30 July 1901, CRS A8, Item 353/01, AA
69 Forrest to Prime Minister, 18 April 1901, CRS A2657/ T1, *MBPHI*, Vol. I, AA
70 *CPD* Vol. II, p. 2173
71 'Further Report of The Federal Military Committee, 1901' See Note, p. 66
72 Australia—Organisation of Defence Department and Constitution of Headquarters Staff, Memorandum by CDC, No. 266M
73 *CPD* Vol. IX, Mr Barton p. 11238 and Vol. XII, Senator O'Connor, p. 16594

Chapter 5

1 Percentage calculated from information provided in B. R. Mitchell and P. Deave *Abstract of British Historical Statistics* Cambridge University Press, Cambridge, 1962, pp. 397–9
2 T. Pakenham *The Boer War* Weidenfeld and Nicholson, London, 1979, p. 572
3 Reports from Commissioners, Inspectors and Others; Forty-one Volumes: War in South Africa (Royal Commission), Session 2 February 1904–15 August 1904, Vol. 33, para. 148, p. 80, ZHC 1/6718, PRO; *BPP*, vol. 40, 1904, Cd. 1789 'Report of His Majesty's Commissioners Appointed to Inquire Into the Military Preparations and Other Matters Connected with The War in South Africa' para. 148, p. 80
4 Hutton to Kitchener, 31 May 1900 *Hutton Papers* Vol. IX, Add. Ms. 50086, ff. 312–3, BL
5 Record of Interview—Rt Hon. Joseph Chamberlain—Secretary of State for the Colonies (including an interview with Balfour), 1 March 1900 *Hutton Papers* Vol. I, Add. Ms. 50078, ff. 155–9, BL
6 Interview between Rt Hon. Joseph Chamberlain S of S for the Colonies and Colonel Hutton in his Private Room, House of Commons, Monday August (n.d.) 5.30 pm, 1898 *Hutton Papers* Vol. I, Add. Ms. 50078, ff. 168–71, BL
7 Record of Interview—Rt Hon. Joseph Chamberlain, 1 March 1900 *Hutton Papers* Vol. I, Add. Ms. 50078, ff. 155–9; Hutton to Balfour, 27 June 1904 *Hutton Papers* Vol. I, Add. Ms. 50078, ff. 160–3, BL

An Army for a Nation

8 Memorandum by G. S. Clarke 'The Militia' no date, Cab 18/23, PRO
9 Record of Interview—Rt Hon. Joseph Chamberlain, 1 March 1900 *Hutton Papers* Vol. I, Add. Ms. 50078, ff. 155–9; Hutton to Balfour, 27 June 1904 *Hutton Papers* Vol. I, Add. Ms. 50078, ff. 160–3, BL
10 *General Hutton's Letters to His Wife* Ms. 1215, Letter No. VII, Bloemfontein, 7 April 1900, pp. 26, 28, ANL
11 Hutton to Lansdowne, 5 October 1900 *Hutton Papers* Vol. VIII, Add. Ms. 50085, ff. 13–14, BL
12 Hutton to Rt Hon. St John Brodrick, 30 January 1901 *Hutton Papers* Vol. VIII, Add. Ms. 50085, ff. 15–29; Hutton to Brodrick, 30 July 1902 *Hutton Papers* Vol. VIII, Add. Ms. 50085, ff. 37–40, BL
13 Hutton to Rt Hon. St John Brodrick, 30 January 1901 *Hutton Papers* Vol. VIII, Add. Ms. 50085, ff. 13–14, BL
14 *ibid.*
15 Confidential Memoranda of a Conversation between Sir Robert Meade, Permanent Under Secretary of State for the Colonies and Colonel Hutton, 1 May 1896, Upon his return from Commanding Troops in New South Wales *Hutton Papers* Vol. I, Add. Ms. 50078, ff. 253–5, BL
16 Hutton to Rt Hon. St John Brodrick, 30 January 1901 *Hutton Papers* Vol. VIII, Add. Ms. 50085, ff. 13–14, BL
17 *BPD* Fourth Series, 28 February 1901 to 14 March 1901, Vol. XC, pp. 1075–6
18 E. T. H. Hutton 'The Evolution of Mounted Infantry' *The Empire Review* Vol. I, No. 4, May 1901, pp. 373–9
19 *CPP* 1901–02 Session, Vol. II, No. 31 'Defence Forces and Defences (Memorandum by Colonial Defence Committee)' p. 117; Chamberlain to Hopetoun, 6 September 1901, with attachment 'New Zealand–Colonial Co-operation in Imperial Defence' CDC Memorandum, No. 271M, 2 August 1901, CRS A8, Item 01/285[1], AA
20 Hopetoun to Chamberlain, 3 May 1901, p. 51, 13 June 1901, p. 55, 7 August 1901, p. 66, 7 August 1901, p. 67, 22 August 1901, p. 70, 11 September 1901, p. 74, 17 September 1901, p. 75, 24 September 1901, p. 76, 10 October 1901, p. 78, 12 November 1901, p. 89, 15 November 1901, p. 91, AA, CRS 78/9, Vol. 1, Copies of Secret and Confidential Despatches, Recorders and Acknowledgements from the Governor-General; Hopetoun to Barton, 2 August 1901 *Barton Papers* MS 51/1/809–810, ANL; Sir Ian Hamilton for Lord Roberts to Chamberlain, 31 July 1901 *Chamberlain Papers* JC11/28/4 BU; Decypher to Telegram from Governor-General Australia, Hopetoun, 6 August 1901 *Chamberlain Papers* JC 11/28/9, BU
21 Roberts to Lord Monk-Bretton [John William Dodson, Principal Private Secretary to Secretary of State for Colonies 1900–03], 7 August 1901 *Chamberlain Papers* JC 12/28/12, BU
22 *CPD* Vol. VI, 2 December 1901, Mr Barton, p. 8064
23 R. A. Preston *Canada and 'Imperial Defense'* University of Toronto Press, Toronto, 1967, pp. 233–59; D. Morton, *Ministers and Generals* University of Toronto Press, Toronto, 1970, pp. 133–62; R. G. Haycock *Sam Hughes* Wilfred Laurier University Press, Canada, 1986, pp. 69–79
24 Copy—Laurier to Minto, 7 November 1899 *Hutton Papers* Vol. III, Add. Ms. 50080, f. 21, BL
25 Haycock *Sam Hughes* p. 79
26 Minto to Hopetoun, 15 December 1901 *Hopetoun House Manuscripts* mfm M936, Reel No. 1, ANL

Notes

27 Hamilton to Hutton, 13 January 1902 *Hutton Papers* Vol. IX, Add. Ms. 50086, ff. 376–7, BL
28 Chamberlain to Hopetoun, 15 January 1902 *Hopetoun House Manuscripts* mfm M936, Reel No. 1, ANL
29 Secret—Notes on Interview between the Rt Hon. Joseph Chamberlain, Secretary of State for the Colonies and Major-General Sir Edward Hutton, Comg. (Elect) Military Forces of Australia, Colonial Office, 1.30 p.m., 19 December 1901 *Hutton Papers* Vol. I, Add. Ms. 50078, ff. 236–41, BL
30 *ibid.*
31 *ibid.*, see note on f. 241
32 There is no comprehensive record of the discussion at the meeting. A list of points raised by each participant is in Memo of Interview, 11.30 a.m., 21 December 1901 *Hutton Papers* Vol. V, Add. Ms. 50082, ff. 3–6. Hutton subsequently referred to the undertaking given at this meeting to raise 20 000 Australian mounted troops for imperial service in correspondence with Brodrick and Nicholson: Hutton to Brodrick, 18 August 1903 *Hutton Papers* Vol. VIII, Add. Ms. 50085, ff. 41–3, BL; Hutton to Nicholson, 23 July 1902 *Hutton Papers* Vol. IX, Add. Ms. 50086, ff. 251–7, BL
33 Narrative of Lieutenant-General Sir Edward Hutton's Command in Australia 1901–04, Period VIII *Hutton Papers* Vol. XXXVI, Add. Ms. 50113, f. 208, BL
34 Hutton to Ommanney, 8 April 1902 *Hutton Papers* Vol. I, Add. Ms. 50078, ff. 262–8, BL; Hutton to Ommanney, 6 August 1902 *Hutton Papers* Vol. I, Add. Ms. 50078, ff. 269–76, BL
35 Hutton to Ommanney, 3 February 1902 *Hutton Papers* Vol. I, Add. Ms. 50078, f. 259, BL
36 Hutton to Ommanney, 24 February 1902 *Hutton Papers* Vol. I, Add. Ms. 50078, ff. 260–1, BL
37 *Sydney Morning Herald* 19 February 1902, Sydney, p. 4; *Age* 18 February 1902, Melbourne, p. 5; *Argus* 19 February 1902, Melbourne, p. 6. *Note*: Hutton placed a copy of the *Argus* article in his scrap-book and underlined Barton's statement on overseas service in red. See *Hutton's Newspaper Cuttings*, 1900–04, Ms1215, p. 65, ANL
38 *Sydney Morning Herald* 19 February 1902, Sydney, p. 4
39 *Age* 18 February 1902, Melbourne, p. 5
40 Hutton to Ommanney, 24 February 1902 *Hutton Papers* Vol. I, Add. Ms. 50078, ff. 259–61, BL
41 Hutton to Brodrick, 24 February 1902 *Hutton Papers* Vol. VIII, Add. Ms. 50085, ff. 31–2, BL
42 Hopetoun to Barton, 29 April 1902 *Hopetoun House Manuscripts* mfm M936, Reel No. 1, ANL; a copy of the same letter in *Barton Papers* Ms 51/1/954a–962a, ANL
43 Hutton to Brodrick, 18 August 1903 *Hutton Papers* Vol. VIII, Add. Ms. 50085, ff. 41–3, BL
44 *Age* 13 February 1902, Melbourne, p. 5; *Age* 14 February 1902, Melbourne, p. 5
45 *Age* 14 February 1902, Melbourne p. 5
46 Barton to Hopetoun, 18 February 1902 *Hopetoun House Manuscripts* mfm M936, Reel No. 1, ANL
47 Hopetoun to Barton, 14 February 1902 *Barton Papers* Ms 51/1/918–920, ANL
48 *Bulletin* 22 February 1902, Sydney, p. 6

49 Hutton to Duke of Cambridge, 29 April 1902 *Hutton Papers* Vol. I, Add. Ms. 50078, f. 138, BL
50 Hutton to Nicholson, with notes added by Hutton, 10 March 1903 *Hutton Papers* Vol. IX, Add. Ms. 50086, ff. 273–6, BL
51 Hutton to Tennyson, 3 October 1903 *Hutton Papers* Vol. V, Add. Ms. 50082, ff. 46–53; Hutton to Ommanney, 23 December 1903 *Hutton Papers* Vol. I, Add. Ms. 50078, ff. 283–5, BL
52 Hutton to Bigge, 6 September 1902 *Hutton Papers* Vol. I, Add. Ms. 50078, ff. 16–18, BL
53 Chamberlain to Hopetoun, 6 September 1901, and minute Hopetoun to Barton, 8 October 1901, with attachment 'New Zealand—Colonial Co-operation in Imperial Defence' CDC Memorandum, No. 271M, 2 August 1901, CRS A8, Item 01/285[1], AA
54 *Sydney Morning Herald* 13 March 1902, Sydney, p. 7
55 M. Chamberlain 'The Wilmansrust Affair: A Defence of the 5th Victorian Mounted Rifles' *Journal of the Australian War Memorial* No. 6, April 1985, pp. 47–55
56 General Beatson, quoted by G. Souter in *Lion and Kangaroo* Collins, Sydney, 1976, pp. 59–60
57 Copy—Minute for the Right Honourable the Prime Minister of the Commonwealth of Australia by the Governor-General, 7 November 1901, CRS B168, file no. 1902/919, AA
58 Copy of telegram, Governor-General to Secretary of State for Colonies, 3 October 1901; Copy of reply by Secretary of State for Colonies, 5 November 1901, CRS B168, file no. 1902/919, AA
59 Barton, Department of External Affairs, to Governor-General, 30 November 1901, CRS B168, file no. 1902/919, AA
60 Kitchener to Governor-General, 7 February 1902, CRS B168, file no. 1902/919, AA
61 Hutton to Secretary, Department of Defence, 27 March 1902, AWM 3, file no. 207/1/20, Bundle 1, Item 02/673, AWM
62 Brodrick to Chamberlain, no date, and minuted note by Chamberlain, 21 February 1902 *Chamberlain Papers* JC 11/8/95, BU
63 Brodrick to Kitchener, 22 February 1902 *Kitchener Papers* PRO 30/57, Vol. 22, ff. 500–2, PRO
64 Hutton to Brodrick, 7 April 1902 *Hutton Papers* Vol. VIII, Add. Ms. 50085, ff. 33–4, BL
65 *Age* 3 April 1902, Melbourne, p. 5. *Note:* The *Age* reported that Mrs Handcock had five children. According to F. M. Cutlack *Breaker Morant: A Horseman Who Made History* Ure Smith, Sydney, 1962, p. 97, there were three Handcock children.
66 *CPD* Vol. IX, Mr Isaacs, Mr Barton, 2 April 1902, pp. 11250–1
67 Hopetoun to Barton 3 April 1902 *Barton Papers* Ms 51/1/945–946, ANL
68 Commonwealth Defence Bill—1901, Part V, Section 86, p. 17, PL
69 Hutton to Clarke, 7 October 1906 *Hutton Papers* Vol. V, Add. Ms. 50082, ff. 363–4, BL
70 Clarke to Hutton, 17 January 1902 *Hutton Papers* Vol. V, Add. Ms. 50082, ff. 265–8, BL
71 *CPP* 1901–2 Session, Vol. II, No. A36, 'Minute Upon the Defence of Australia, by Major-General Hutton, Commandant' 7 April 1902, pp. 53–5
72 Hutton to Brodrick, 7 April 1902 *Hutton Papers* Vol. VIII, Add. Ms. 50085, ff. 33–4, BL

Notes

73 Hutton to Ommanney, 8 April 1902 *Hutton Papers* Vol. I, Add. Ms. 50078, ff. 262–8, BL
74 'Minute Upon the Defence of Australia, by Major-General Hutton, Commandant' 7 April 1902, pp. 55–6
75 R. Norris *The Emergent Commonwealth* MUP, Melbourne, 1975, p. 124. Norris states: 'To this end garrison troops should man the fixed defences and a mobile field force should be created to concentrate at any threatened point'.
76 Clarke to Hutton, 11 March 1902 *Hutton Papers* Vol. V, Add. Ms. 50082, ff. 277–8, BL. *Note*: Clarke said that soldiers might not like being members of a 'passive' force, but he also recommended not using the word 'active'.
77 *CPP* 1903 Session, Vol. II, No. 38, 'Military Forces of the Commonwealth: Scheme of Organization of, into a Field Force (for Interstate or Commonwealth Defence), and into Garrison Troops (for Local or State Defence)', pp. 99–115
78 Clarke to Hutton, 11 March 1902 *Hutton Papers* Vol. V, Add. Ms. 50082, ff. 277–8, BL
79 'Minute Upon the Defence of Australia, By Major-General Hutton, Commandant' 7 April 1902, pp. 54–5
80 Hutton to Nicholson, 23 July 1902 *Hutton Papers* Vol. IX, Add. Ms. 50086, ff. 251–7, BL
81 Notes on basis of Hutton's scheme of organisation for the military forces, CRS B168, file no. 02/2688 [folder 2], AA; 'Defence Force and Defences (Memorandum by Colonial Defence Committee)' 30 March 1901, p. 111
82 Hutton to Minister of Defence, 22 November 1902, Part II, 'Future Expenditure on the Military Forces' with Schedules A to D, Section 5, CRS B168, file no. 02/2688 [volume], AA
83 'Minute Upon the Defence of Australia, By Major-General Hutton, Commandant' 7 April 1902, p. 55
84 E. T. H. Hutton, 'A Co-operative System for the Defence of the Empire' *Proceedings of the Royal Colonial Institute* Vol. XXIX, 1897–98, London, 1898, p. 232
85 General Officer Commanding to Minister of State for Defence, 25 April 1902, CRS B168, file no. 02/688, AA
86 Hutton to Brodrick, 7 April 1902 *Hutton Papers* Vol. VIII, Add. Ms. 50085, ff. 33–4, BL
87 General Officer Commanding to Minister of State for Defence, 25 April 1902, para. 7, p. 3, CRS B168, file no. 02/2688, AA
88 'Minute Upon the Defence of Australia, By Major-General Hutton, Commandant', Section III, para. D, p. 57
89 General Officer Commanding to Minister of State for Defence, 25 April 1902, para. 4, p. 1, CRS B168, file no. 02/688, AA
90 Hutton to Nicholson, 23 July 1902 *Hutton Papers* Vol. IX, Add. Ms. 50086, ff. 251–7, BL
91 'Military Forces of the Commonwealth: Scheme of Organization, into a Field Force (for Interstate or Commonwealth Defence), and into Garrison Troops (for Local or State Defence)', pp. 95–121
92 'Minute Upon the Defence of Australia, by Major-General Hutton, Commandant' 7 April 1902, p. 56
93 Hutton to Brodrick *Hutton Papers* Vol. VIII, Add. Ms. 50085, ff. 41–3, BL
94 Hutton to Nicholson, 23 July 1902 *Hutton Papers* Vol. IX, Add. Ms. 50086, ff. 251–7, BL

An Army for a Nation

95 Hopetoun to Barton, 29 April 1902 *Hopetoun House Manuscripts* mfm M936, Reel No. 1, ANL; copy of the same letter *Barton Papers* Ms 51/1/954a–962a, ANL
96 *ibid.*
97 *CPD* Vol. IX, 29 April 1902, Sir John Forrest, p. 12092
98 'Minute Upon the Defence of Australia, By Major-General Hutton, Commandant' Part III, para. D, p. 57 and Part VIII, p. 59
99 *CPD* Vol. IX, 29 April 1902, Sir Edward Braddon p. 12094, Mr Watson p. 12096, Mr Conroy p. 12105, Mr Batchelor p. 12109, Mr McCay p. 12113, Mr Glynn p. 12119, Mr McLean p. 12126, Mr G. Edwards p. 12121, Mr Watkins p. 12124, Mr McDonald pp. 12128–9, Mr Higgins p. 12129, Mr Spence p. 12132, Mr Salmon p. 12138, Mr Poynton p. 12144, Mr Wilks p. 12138, Mr Knox p. 12140, Mr Fowler p. 12141
100 *ibid.*, Vol. XII, 2 October 1902, Mr McCay, p. 16364; Vol. XVI, 11 September 1903, Mr Sydney Smith, p. 5045
101 *ibid.*, Vol. IX, 29 April 1902, Sir John Forrest, p. 12120
102 Forrest Collins, 2 May 1902, CRS B168, file no. 1902/2441 [19], AA
103 *Bulletin* 3 May 1902, Sydney, p. 7
104 *CPD* Vol. XVI, 11 September 1903, Mr Sydney Smith, p. 5045
105 *ibid.*, Vol. IX, 29 April 1902, Mr Watson p. 12101, Mr Glynn pp. 12101, 12118, Sir Edward Braddon p. 12094, Lieutenant Colonel McCay p. 12116, Mr Spence p. 12134, Mr Higgins p. 12129. See also: Mr Sawers p. 12102, Mr Conroy p. 12103
106 *Sydney Morning Herald* 6 May 1902, Sydney, p. 5

Chapter 6

1 Bigge to Hutton, 17 July 1902; Hutton to Bigge, 6 September 1902, ff. 13–18; Hutton to HRH The Duke of Connaught, 29 April 1902, f. 63; Hutton to Duke of Cambridge, 29 April 1902, f. 138; Hutton to Ommanney, 8 April 1902, ff. 262–8 *Hutton Papers* Vol. I, Add. Ms. 50078, BL; Hutton to Brodrick, 7 April 1902 *Hutton Papers* Vol. VIII, Add. Ms. 50085, ff. 33–4, BL; Hutton to Dilke, 29 April 1902 *Dilke Papers* Vol. XLIV, Add. Ms. 43917, ff. 103–4, BL
2 Nicholson to Hutton, 10 June 1902 *Hutton Papers* Vol. VIII, Add. Ms. 50085, ff. 212–15, BL
3 Papers Relating to a Conference between the Secretary of State for the Colonies and the Prime Ministers of the Self-Governing Colonies, June to August 1902, Appendix: 'The Organisation of Colonial Troops for Imperial Service by Lieutenant-Colonel E. A. Altham', ANL
4 Nicholson to Commander-in-Chief, 16 December 1901, file no. 091/2236, WO 32/8303, PRO
5 Roberts to Secretary of State, 31 December 1901, file no. 091/2236, WO 32/8303, PRO
6 Minute by St J. B. [Brodrick], 12 February 1902, and Wilson to Under Secretary of State, Colonial Office, 19 February 1902, file no. 091/2236, WO 32/8303, PRO
7 H. Bertram-Cox to Under Secretary of State, War Office, 6 May 1902; Minute by Altham to DGMI [Nicholson], 8 May 1902, file no. 091/2245, WO 32/8305, PRO
8 Colonial Troops for Imperial Service in War, Confidential Memorandum by the CDC, No. 293M, 13 June 1902, Cab 8/3, PRO

Notes

9 Hutton to Ommanney, 24 February 1902 *Hutton Papers* Vol. I, Add. Ms. 50078, f. 259; Hutton to Brodrick, 24 February 1902 *Hutton Papers* Vol. VIII, Add. Ms. 50085, ff. 31–2, BL
10 Confidential Memorandum by the CDC, No. 293M, 13 June 1902, Cab 8/3, PRO
11 Altham to PUS [Permanent Under Secretary], 27 June 1902; H Bertram-Cox to Under Secretary of State, War Office, 26 June 1902; E. W. D. Ward to Under Secretary of State for the Colonies, 28 June 1902, file no. 091/2242, WO 32/8304, PRO
12 Barton to Chamberlain, 9 June 1902 *Chamberlain Papers* JC 17/2/4, BU
13 Barton to Chamberlain, 19 June 1902 *Chamberlain Papers* JC 17/2/6, BU
14 Chamberlain to Brodrick, 25 July 1902 *Chamberlain Papers* JC 17/1/3, BU
15 Forrest to Chamberlain, 24 August 1901 *Chamberlain Papers* JC 14/1/1/13, BU
16 Chamberlain to Brodrick, 25 July 1902 *Chamberlain Papers* JC 17/1/3, BU
17 Text of telegram, no date, Sir Edmund Barton's London Telegrams (24 June–16 August 1902), CP 103/12, Bundle 5, AA
18 Papers Relating to a Conference Between the Secretary of State for the Colonies and The Prime Ministers of the Self-Governing Colonies, June to August 1902, pp. 26–30, ANL
19 *ibid.*, pp. 30–1
20 Brodrick to Chamberlain, 11 August 1902 *Chamberlain Papers* JC 17/1/9; Colonial Conference 1902, Abstract, Tenth Day, Monday 11 August 1902, 'The Imperial Reserve' *Chamberlain Papers* JC 17/1/1, BU
21 Colonial Conference 1902, Abstract, Tenth Day, Monday 11 August 1902, 'The Imperial Reserve' Note by J. C. [Joseph Chamberlain] *Chamberlain Papers* JC 17/1/1, BU
22 Papers Relating to a Conference Between the Secretary of State for the Colonies and The Prime Minister of the Self-Governing Colonies, June to August 1902, pp. 30–1, ANL; Colonial Defence—Précis of Important Events connected with the Question of the Employment of Colonial Military Forces on Imperial Service, Secret Memorandum by the CDC, 29 June 1909, para. 12, p. 4, Cab 11/125, PRO; *Age* 28 July 1902, Melbourne, p. 5; *Argus* 28 July 1902, Melbourne, p. 5
23 Papers Relating to a Conference Between the Secretary of State for The Colonies and The Prime Ministers of the Self-Governing Colonies, June to August 1902, Draft Naval Agreement pp. 22–4; Barton to Secretary to Lord Commissioners of the Admiralty, 25 September 1902, p. 22, ANL
24 Forrest to Chamberlain, 24 August 1901 *Chamberlain Papers* JC 14/1/1/13, BU
25 Forrest to Chamberlain, 18 September 1902, and enclosed newspaper cutting: *Montreal Daily Star*, 9 September 1902 *Chamberlain Papers* JC 17/2/7, BU
26 Chamberlain to Forrest, 12 October 1902 *Chamberlain Papers* JC 17/2/7, BU
27 Forrest to Chamberlain, 24 November 1902 *Chamberlain Papers* JC 17/2/9, BU
28 Chamberlain to Forrest, 1 April 1903 *Chamberlain Papers* JC 18/2/7, BU
29 *Brisbane Courier* 28 July 1902, Brisbane, p. 4
30 *Argus* 29 July 1902, Melbourne, p. 4
31 *Age* 29 July 1902, Melbourne, p. 4
32 *Advertiser* 30 July 1902, Adelaide, p. 4
33 *Sydney Morning Herald* 28 July 1902, Sydney, p. 6
34 *Bulletin* 9 August 1902, Sydney, p. 9

35 *Age* 29 July 1902, Melbourne, p. 6
36 *CPD* Vol. XII, 25 September 1902, Mr Page, pp. 16126–7
37 *ibid.*, Vol. XII, 24 September 1902, Sir William Lyne, p. 16020
38 Secretary, Department of Defence, to General Officer Commanding, 6 August 1902, CRS B 168, file no. 02/2688 [folder 2], AA. *Note:* Barton kept Cabinet informed of developments at the Colonial Conference, especially his rejection of overseas service for colonial forces as part of an imperial reserve. See Sir Edmund Barton's London Telegrams (24 June–16 August 1902), CP 103/12, Bundle 5, AA
39 General Officer Commanding to Secretary, Department of Defence, 11 August 1902, CRS B 168, file no. 02/2688 [folder 2], AA
40 Hutton to Brodrick, 30 July 1902 *Hutton Papers* Vol. VIII, Add. Ms. 50085, ff. 37–40, BL. See also Hutton to Duke of Connaught, 4 August 1902, f. 64, and Hutton to Ommanney, 6 August 1902, ff. 269–76 *Hutton Papers* Vol. I, Add. Ms. 50078, BL
41 Hutton to Ommanney, 23 December 1902 *Hutton Papers* Vol. I, Add. Ms. 50078, ff. 281–2, BL
42 Hutton to Ommanney, 18 March 1903 *Hutton Papers* Vol. I, Add. Ms. 50078, ff. 288–98, BL
43 Hutton to Brodrick, 30 July 1902 *Hutton Papers* Vol. VIII, Add. Ms. 50085, ff. 37–40, BL
44 *ibid.*
45 Hutton to Ommanney, 2 June 1903 *Hutton Papers* Vol. I, Add. Ms. 50078, ff. 301–3, BL. See also Hutton to Ommanney, 4 June 1904 *Hutton Papers* Vol. I, Add. Ms. 50078, ff. 312–13, BL
46 Hutton to Ommanney, 6 August 1902 *Hutton Papers* Vol. I, Add. Ms. 50078, ff. 269–76, BL
47 Hutton to Ommanney, 23 December 1902 *Hutton Papers* Vol. I, Add. Ms. 50078, ff. 281–2, BL
48 Hutton to Ommanney, 23 December 1902 *Hutton Papers* Vol. I, Add. Ms. 50078, ff. 283–5, BL
49 Hutton to Ommanney, 18 March 1903 *Hutton Papers* Vol. I, Add. Ms. 50078, ff. 288–98, BL
50 Hutton to Ommanney, 23 December 1902 *Hutton Papers* Vol. I, Add. Ms. 50078, ff. 281–2, BL
51 N. K. Meaney *The Search for Security in the Pacific 1901–14* Sydney University Press, Sydney, 1976, p. 66; C. Cunneen *King's Men: Australia's Governors-General from Hopetoun to Isaacs* George Allen & Unwin, Sydney, 1983, p. 46
52 Australia—Minute upon Defence by General Officer Commanding the Military Forces, Confidential Remarks by the CDC, No. 301R, 22 October 1902, Cab 9/5, PRO
53 *ibid.*
54 Meaney *The Search for Security in the Pacific 1901–14* p. 66
55 Ommanney to Hutton, 20 November 1902 *Hutton Papers* Vol. I, Add. Ms. 50078, ff. 277–80, BL
56 *ibid.*
57 Hutton to Tennyson, 10 March 1903 *Hutton Papers* Vol. V, Add. Ms. 50082, f. 83, BL
58 Secret note by T [Tennyson], 1 March 1903 *Hutton Papers* Vol. V, Add. Ms. 50082, f. 66, BL

Notes

59 Secretary, Department of Defence, to General Officer Commanding, 6 March 1903; Bridges to Secretary, Department of Defence, 14 March 1903, CRS B168, file no. 02/2688 [folder 6], AA
60 Hutton to Forrest, 20 March 1903 *Hutton Papers* Vol. VII, Add. Ms. 50084, ff. 281–2, BL
61 Hutton to Ommanney, 1 April 1903 *Hutton Papers* Vol. I, Add. Ms. 50078, f. 300, BL
62 Hutton to Tennyson, 10 March 1903 *Hutton Papers* Vol. V, Add. Ms. 50082, f. 83, BL
63 General Officer Commanding to Minister for Defence, 9 May 1903, CRS B168, file no. 02/2688 [folder 6], AA
64 General Officer Commanding to Minister for Defence, 4 June 1903, CRS B168, file no. 02/2688 [folder 1], AA
65 Minister for Defence to Secretary, Department of Defence, 23 June 1903—referred to General Officer Commanding, 23 June 1903, CRS B168, file no. 02/2688 [folder 1] and a copy of the same minute, file no. 02/2688 [folder 6], AA
66 General Officer Commanding to Secretary, Department of Defence, 1 July 1903, CRS B168, file no. 02/2688 [folder 1] and a copy of the same minute, file no. 02/2688 [folder 6], AA
67 *CPD* Vol. XIV, 16 July 1903, Sir John Forrest, pp. 2268–9
68 Secretary, Department of Defence, to General Officer Commanding, 3 July 1903, CRS B168, file no. 02/2688 [folder 6], AA
69 General Officer Commanding to Minister for Defence, 8 July 1903, CRS B168, file no. 02/2688 [folder 6], AA
70 *CPD* Vol. XIV, 16 July 1903, Sir John Forrest, p. 2268
71 *CG No. 35* 25 July 1903, pp. 387–402
72 General Officer Commanding to Minister for Defence, 8 July 1903, CRS B168, file no. 02/2688 [folder 6], AA
73 *CPP* 1903 Session, Vol. II, No. 37 'Annual Report Upon the Military Forces of the Commonwealth for the Period January, 1902–30th April, 1903' Part III, p. 85
74 Draft Defence Bill by E. T. H. [Hutton], 25 February 1903, Section 4—Interpretation *MBPHI* Vol. I, Clauses 35, 44, and explanatory notes, CRS A2657/ T1, AA
75 *CPD* Vol. XIV, 16 July 1903, Sir John Forrest, pp. 2265–6
76 *ibid.*
77 *ibid.*, p. 2266
78 General Officer Commanding to Minister for Defence, 6 July 1903, para. III, p. 2, AWM3, file no. 03/341, AWM; for original copy *MBPHI* Vol. I, CRS A2657/ T1, AA; General Officer Commanding to Minister for Defence, 25 May 1903 *MBPHI* Vol. 1, CRS A2657/ T1, AA
79 General Officer Commanding to Minister for Defence, 6 July 1903, pp. 3–4; *CPP* 1903 Session, Vol. II, No. 37, Part III, pp. 85–6
80 *CPD* Vol. XIV, 16 July 1903, Sir John Forrest, p. 2272
81 *CA* Vol. II, No. 20 of 1903, Defence, Clause 4, p. 110; *CPD* Vol. XIV, 16 July 1903, Sir John Forrest, pp. 2269–70
82 *CA* Vol. II, No. 20 of 1903, Defence Division 2, Clause 33, p. 114, and Part IV, Clauses 59–60, p. 117
83 *ibid.*, Part III, Division 1, Clause 31(2), p. 113; *CPD* Vol. XV, 5 August 1903, pp. 3086–92

84 *CPD* Vol. XV, 5 August 1903, pp. 3124–6; *CA* Vol. II, No. 20 of 1903, Defence, Part III, Division 3, Clause 49, p. 116
85 *CA* Vol. II, No. 20 of 1903, Defence, Part III, Clause 53; Part X, Clause 117, p. 128
86 *CPD* Vol. XV, 6 August 1903, pp. 3221–4. *Note*: Australian forces remained subject to the provision of the British *Army Act*, 1881, while on active service until 1985, 30 years after Britain repealed the Act. See S. G. Thompson 'An Officer and a Gentleman' *Law Society Journal* May 1985, pp. 306–7
87 Hutton to Ommanney, 19 August 1903 *Hutton Papers* Vol. I, Add. Ms. 50078, ff. 304–5, BL
88 Hutton to Brodrick, 18 August 1903 *Hutton Papers* Vol. VIII, Add. Ms. 50085, ff. 41–3, BL
89 Narrative Lieutenant-General Sir Edward Hutton's Command in Australia 1901–04, Period VIII *Hutton Papers* Vol. XXXVI, Add. Ms. 50113, f. 212, BL
90 Hutton to Minister of Defence, 6 July 1903, AWM 3, file no. 03/341, p. 4, AWM
91 Hutton to Ommanney, 19 April 1904 *Hutton Papers* Vol. I, Add. Ms. 50078, ff. 309–11, BL
92 Narrative of Lieutenant-General Sir Edward Hutton's Command in Australia, 1901–1904, Period VIII *Hutton Papers* Vol. XXXVI, Add. Ms. 50113, ff. 217–20, BL
93 J. P. Lehmann *The Image of Japan: From Feudal Isolation to World Power 1850–1905* George Allen & Unwin, London, 1978, p. 147
94 Narrative of Lieutenant-General Sir Edward Hutton's Command in Australia, 1901–1904, Period VIII *Hutton Papers* Vol. XXXVI, Add. Ms. 50113, f. 218, BL
95 Tennyson to Hutton, 6 May 1903, and Fanshawe to Tennyson, 5 May 1903 *Hutton Papers* Vol. V, Add. Ms. 50082, ff. 93–6; Forrest to Hutton, 11 May 1903 *Hutton papers* Vol. VII, Add. Ms. 50084, f. 294, BL
96 Hamilton to Hutton, 25 December 1903 *Hutton Papers* Vol. IX, Add. Ms. 50086, ff. 388–9; Hutton to Hamilton, 2 February 1904 *Hutton Papers* Vol. IX, Add. Ms. 50086, ff. 395–6, BL
97 Brodrick to Hutton, 12 November 1903 *Hutton Papers* Vol. VIII, Add. Ms. 50085, ff. 45–7, BL
98 Roberts to Hutton, 12 October 1903 *Hutton Papers* Vol. VIII, Add. Ms. 50085, ff. 229–34, BL

Chapter 7

1 *CPP* 1903 Session, Vol. II, No. 37 'Annual Report Upon the Military Forces of the Commonwealth for the Period January 1902–30th April, 1903, By Major-General Sir Edward Hutton' Part I, Section I, p. 62
2 *ibid.*, Appendix A, pp. 88–9
3 *ibid.*
4 Hutton to Forrest, 14 November 1902 *Hutton Papers* Vol VII, Add. Ms. 50084, ff. 264–5, BL
5 'Annual Report Upon the Military Forces of the Commonwealth for the Period January 1902–30th April 1903' Part 1, Section 17, p. 71; *CPP* Vol II, 1904 Session, No. 25 'Military Forces of the Commonwealth of Australia—Second

Notes

Annual Report By Major-General Sir Edward Hutton' Part 1, Section 15, p. 292

6 Clarke to Chirol, 27 March 1902 *Sydenham Papers* Vol I, Add. Ms. 50831, ff. 73–8, BL

7 'Annual Report Upon the Military Forces of the Commonwealth for the Period January 1902–30th April 1903' Part I, Sections 13, 17, pp. 69, 71; *Sydney Morning Herald*, 6 December 1902, Sydney, p. 11

8 *Note*: Although many workers under Federal and State awards achieved annual holidays over the years it was not until 1944 that all workers in New South Wales were guaranteed an annual paid holiday of two weeks. This was the first State to legislate for annual holidays for all workers. *The Statutes of New South Wales (Public & Private) Passed During the Year 1944 Annual Holidays Act* No. 31, 1944, pp. 276–85; *NSWPD* Session 1944–45, Second Series, Vol. 176, 5 December 1944, Mr McKell, p. 1547

9 'Annual Report Upon the Military Forces of the Commonwealth for the Period January 1902–30th April 1903' Part I, Section 17, p. 71

10 ibid., Part I, Sections 8, 9, 11, 14, pp. 66–9

11 ibid., Part I, Sections 3, 5, 6, pp. 63, 65; 7 *CG* No. 65, 21 November 1903, pp. 865–7

12 'Military Forces of the Commonwealth of Australia—Second Annual Report', Part II, Sections 21, 22, 23, pp. 295–6

13 'Annual Report Upon the Military Forces of the Commonwealth for the Period January 1902–30th April 1903', Part I, Section 7, p. 65

14 Military Forces of the Commonwealth, General Orders, 1902, No. 104(2), 8 July 1902

15 Hutton to Minister of Defence, 12 January 1904, and Hutton to Secretary of Defence, 24 March 1904, AWM 3, file no. 3/1902, AWM

16 Proceedings of Military Board, 1921, Vol. II, Meeting No. 23, 27 May 1921, Agenda No. 352/1920, CRS A 2653/1, AA. *Note*: Formation of Army Ordnance Corps approved by G. F. Pearce, Minister for Defence, on 25 July 1921.

17 Collins, Secretary Department of Defence, to GOC, 28 November 1902, CRS B168, file no. 02/2688, AA; GOC to Minister for Defence, 4 June 1903, CRS B168, file no. 02/2688 AA (folder 1)

18 *Argus* 10 December 1902, Melbourne, p. 7

19 Rushall to McCulloch, Minister of Defence, Victoria, 20 December 1900, AWM 3, file no. 02/479, AWM

20 Rushall, OC Melbourne Cavalry, to AAG and CSO, Victoria, 10 August 1903, CRS B168, file no. 1902/1631, AA

21 ibid., Minute by Hutton to DAG, 9 September 1903. *Note*: Hutton's minute was written in large, red manuscript across Rushall's letter.

22 Hutton to Secretary of Defence, 20 October 1903, CRS B168, file no. 1902/1631, AA

23 *CPD* 1901–2 Session, Vol. IX, 30 April 1902, Mr Watson, p. 12099

24 Principles of Drill, Tactics and Organization Necessitated By the Latest Military Experience, Issued with GO No. 96 of 27th June, 1902, under cover of Hutton to Secretary of Defence, 25 June 1902, CRS B168, file no. 02/2688, AA

25 Hutton to Burns, 25 August 1902 *Vernon Papers*

26 Burns to Hutton, 5 September 1902 *Vernon Papers*

27 Hutton to Burns, 5 September 1902 *Vernon Papers*

28 Capt J. M. Purves to Burns, 15 December 1902 *Vernon Papers*

29 John See, Premier and Chief Secretary, to Prime Minister, 15 November 1902, CRS A8, file no. 02/2688, AA
30 Hutton to Secretary of Defence, 9 December 1902, CRS A8, file no. 02/2688, AA
31 Confidential Memo of Commanding Officers, New South Wales Lancer Regiment, 21 December 1902 *Vernon Papers*
32 Hutton to Roberts, 19 August 1903 *Hutton Papers* Vol. VIII, Add. Ms. 50085, ff. 226–8, BL. *Note:* Hutton refers to two Lancer Regiments. Both these Regiments were formed from the NSW Lancers in 1903.
33 Hutton to Burns, 25 August 1902 *Vernon Papers*
34 Hutton to Deputy Adjutant General, 14 May 1902, AWM 3, file no. 02/1236, AWM
35 Burns to Captain Bowman, 4 September 1902 *Vernon Papers*
36 Unsigned copy of a letter with no date to Colonel Burns. It has been assumed that Bowman was the author *Vernon Papers*; Captain Purves to Burns, 15 December 1902 *Vernon Papers*
37 Burns to Captain Bowman, 24 November 1902 *Vernon Papers*
38 Burns to Captain Bowman, 27 July 1903 *Vernon Papers*
39 Lieutenant-General Sir Edward Hutton's Memoirs *Hutton Papers* Vol. XXXVI, Add. Ms. 50113, ff. 66–7, BL
40 'Annual Report Upon the Military Forces of the Commonwealth for the Period January 1902–30th April 1902', Part I, Section 15, pp. 69–70, and Appendix C, pp. 92–4
41 *ibid.*, Part II, Section 23, p. 74
42 *ibid.*, Part II, Section 23, p. 76
43 'Military Forces of the Commonwealth of Australia—Second Annual Report', Part I, Section 10(c), p. 289
44 *ibid.*
45 'Annual Report Upon the Military Forces of the Commonwealth for the Period January 1902–30th April 1903', Part II, Section 23, p. 76
46 An unsigned copy of a letter with no date to Colonel Burns. The copy refers to 'Your letter of 11th Inst . . .' and addresses issues raised in another letter, Burns to Captain Bowman, 11 August 1902 *Vernon Papers*. It has therefore been assumed that Bowman was the author of the unsigned copy.
47 Finn to DAG, 24 June 1903; Hutton to Secretary of Defence, 13 May 1903, CRS B168, file no. 02/2688[4], AA
48 *Cooma Express—Monaro & Southern Districts Advertiser* Cooma, 12 May 1903
49 Hutton to Secretary of Defence, 9 March 1903, CRS B168, file no. 02/2688[4], AA
50 Chapman to Forrest, 7 May 1903, and Petition from 140 Cooma residents, presented to Forrest by Chapman on 16 April 1903, CRS B168, file no. 02/2688[4], AA
51 *Cooma Express—Monaro & Southern Districts Advertiser* Cooma, 12 May 1903
52 Brig. H. Finn to DAG, 18 December 1903, CRS B168, file no. 02/2688[4], AA
53 Brig. H. Finn to DAG, 18 December 1903, CRS B168, file no. 02/2688[4], AA
54 *Cooma Express—Monaro & Southern Districts Advertiser* Cooma, 12 May 1903

Notes

55 Brig. H. Finn to DAG, 18 December 1903, CRS B168, file no. 02/2688[4], AA
56 Finn to AQMG, 1 October 1903, CRS B168, file no. 02/2688[4], AA; Finn to Deputy Adjutant General, 28 October 1903, AWM 3, file no. 02/1710, AWM
57 Hutton to Secretary for Defence, 6 November 1903, CRS B168, file no. 02/2688[4], AA; copy of the same minute in AWM 3, file no. 02/1710, AWM
58 *CPD* Vol. XV, 5 August 1903, Mr Austin Chapman, p. 3121
59 *ibid.*, 5 August 1903, Mr Henry Willis, p. 3121
60 *Wellington Gazette* 3 September 1903, Wellington
61 *ibid.*, 6 August 1903
62 Veness, council clerk, municipality of Glen Innes, to W. Sawers, 4 April 1903, CRS B168, file no. 02/2688[4], AA
63 J. Wilkinson, MP, to Secretary, Department of Defence, 7 August 1902, CRS B168, file no. 02/2441[8], AA
64 *CPD* Vol. XV, 3 August 1903, Mr McLean, p. 3120
65 Hutton to Deputy Adjutant General, 14 May 1902, AWM 3, file no. 02/1236, AWM
66 *CPD* Vol. XV, 3 August 1903, Mr McLean, p. 3120
67 J. M. Gordon, Victorian Commandant, to DQMG, 29 August 1903, CRS B168, file no. 02/2688[5], AA
68 Hutton to Secretary of Defence, 12 September 1903, CRS B168, file no. 02/2688[5], AA; Hutton to Secretary of Defence, 11 September 1903, AWM 3, file no. 03/1348, AWM
69 J. M. Gordon, Victorian Commandant to DQMG, 29 August 1903, CRS B168, file no. 02/2688 [5], AA
70 Copy of article published in *Kerang New Times* 22 September 1903, CRS B168, file no. 02/2688 [5], AA
71 Copy of article published in *Kerang Observer* 12 September 1903, CRS B168, file no. 02/2688 [5], AA
72 *CPP* 1901–2 Session, Vol. II, No. A36, 'Minute Upon the Defence of Australia, by Major-General Hutton, Commandant', 7 April 1902, Section II, pp. 55–6
73 *CPP* 1901–2 Session, Vol. II, No. A19, 'Report and Appendices Prepared By the Commonwealth Defence Pay Committee, Assembled at Sydney, New South Wales' 1 August 1901, Part 1—Military Forces, No. 4—Pay of Militia Officers, Non-Commissioned Officers, and Men, p. 85
74 Hutton to Minister for Defence, 22 November 1902, covering Part II, 'Future Expenditure on Military Forces' Section 5, CRS B168, file no. 02/2688 (volume), AA
75 Telegram, Col T. Price to Lt. Col Bridges, HQ Melbourne, 9 July 1903, CRS B168, file no. 02/2688 [5], AA
76 Extract of report by commandant, Western Australia, in J. C. Hoad, DAG and CSO, to Secretary for Defence, 13 August 1903, CRS B168, file no. 02/2688, AA
77 J. W. Kirwan, MP, to Minister of Defence, 11 July 1903, CRS B168, file no. 02/2688 [5], AA
78 Lt. Col. Lyster, commandant South Australia, to DAG, 17 July 1903, CRS B168, file no. 02/2688[5], AA
79 A. C. Catt, OC, 1st Battalion Reserve, to DAG, Adelaide, 1 July 1903, CRS B168, file no. 02/2688 [5], AA
80 Minute No. 3 by Forrest, 11 July 1903, and Minute No. 4 by Hutton to Sec. of Defence, 24 July 1903, CRS B168, file no. 02/2688 [5], AA
81 Minute No. 6 by Forrest, 3 July 1903, CRS B168, file no. 02/2688 [5], AA

82 Secretary, Department of Defence, to J. W. Kirwan, MP, 22 July 1903; Minute No 4. by Secretary, Department of Defence, to GOC 10 August 1903, CRS B168, file no. 02/2688[5], AA
83 G. Sawer *Australian Federal Politics and Law 1901–29* MUP, Melbourne, 1956, Chapter 1, Section IV, pp. 26–8; The Commonwealth of Australia Constitution Act, 9 July 1900, Chapter IV, Sections 87 & 89 *CA* Vol. I, 1901–2
84 Sawer *Australian Federal Politics and Law 1901–29* pp. 26–28
85 Hutton to Secretary of Defence, 12 June 1902, para. H, p. 2, AWM 3, file no. 02/1121, AWM
86 Diary of Sir Edmund Barton, Entry for 1 July 1903 *Barton Papers* Ms. 51/2/951, ANL
87 Lt. Col. Wallack, Senior Officer Commanding CMF Tasmania, to AQMG, Melbourne, 13 July 1903, CRS B168, file no. 02/2688, AA; *CPP* 1903 Session, Vol. II, No. 48, 'Military Forces: Tasmania (Correspondence Concerning Position Under Re-Organization Scheme)' p. 154
88 Wallack to DAG, Melbourne, 10 August 1903, CRS B168, file no. 02/2688, AA; 'Military Forces: Tasmania', p. 157
89 Minute No. 5 by Forrest, Tasmania—Pay for Camps and Daylight Parades, 30 July 1903, CRS B168, file no. 02/2688, AA; 'Military Forces: Tasmania', p. 156; *CPD* 1903 Session, Vol. XV, 5 August 1903, Sir John Forrest, p. 3084
90 *CPD* Vol. XX, Mr Watson, 20 July 1904, p. 3393

Chapter 8

1 Secret Notes of an Interview between the Rt Hon. Joseph Chamberlain, Secretary of State for the Colonies and Major-General Sir Edward Hutton, Comg. (Elect) Military Forces of Australia, Colonial Office, 1.30 p.m., 19 December 1901 *Hutton Papers* Vol. I, Add. Ms. 50078, ff. 236–41, BL
2 Narrative of Lieutenant-General Sir Edward Hutton's Command in Australia 1901–04, Period VIII *Hutton Papers* Vol. XXXVI, Add. Ms. 50113, f. 208, BL
3 *Herald* 18 March 1903, Melbourne, in CRS B168, file no. 1903/849[3], AA
4 The Case of Lieut-Colonel Reay (Commanding 2V.M.R.)—Details of questions of the General Officer Commanding and Lieut-Colonel Reay's replies, 20 March 1903; J. C. Hoad, DAG and CSO, to Brigadier General Commanding Commonwealth Forces of Victoria, 21 March 1903, CRS B168, file no. 1903/849[3], AA
5 Minute from Minister of Defence to Prime Minister; Minute from Prime Minister to Minister of Defence, in *Age* 3 April 1903, Melbourne, p. 5
6 Hutton to Barton, 3 April 1903 *Hutton Papers* Vol. VII, Add. Ms. 50084, ff. 25–7, BL
7 Hutton to Minister of Defence, 3 April 1903, CRS B168, file no. 1903/849[3], AA
8 Forrest to Rt Honourable the Prime Minister, 3 April 1903, CRS B168, file no. 1903/849[3], AA
9 Tennyson to Hutton, 26 March 1903 *Hutton Papers* Vol. V, Add. Ms. 50082, ff. 86–7, BL
10 Hutton to Tennyson, 4 May 1903 *Hutton Papers* Vol. V, Add. Ms. 50082, f. 92, BL
11 Tennyson to Hutton, 6 May 1903 *Hutton Papers* Vol. V, Add. Ms. 50082, ff. 93–4, BL

Notes

12 *CPD* Vol. XIV, 16 July 1903, Sir John Forrest, p. 2276
13 Hutton to Minister of Defence, 6 July 1903, p. 7, AWM 3, file no. 03/341, AWM
14 *CPD* Vol. XIV, 16 July 1903, Sir John Forrest, p. 2276
15 *ibid.*, Vol. XV, 13 August 1903, Mr Mauger, p. 3547; *Argus* 12 August 1903, Melbourne, p. 4
16 *CPD* Vol. XVI, 21 August 1903, Mr Mauger, p. 4061
17 *CPD* Vol. XVI, 11 September 1903, Senator Matheson, pp. 4976–8
18 *ibid.*, Senator Barrett, p. 4983, Senator Staniforth Smith, p. 4985
19 *ibid.*, p. 4991
20 *ibid.*, Vol. XVII, 1 October 1903, pp. 5639, 5641, 5642
21 *Age* 29 September 1903, Melbourne, p. 5
22 *CPD* Vol. XVII, 1 October 1903, Senator Higgs, pp. 5640–1, and Senator O'Keefe, pp. 5642, 5648
23 *ibid.*, 14 October 1903, Mr Crouch, p. 6121
24 *ibid.*, Vol. XXIII, 15 November 1904, Mr Hume Cook and Mr Crouch, pp. 6932; Vol. XXIV, 25 November 1904, Mr Hume Cook, p. 7519
25 *CPD* Vol. XVII, 14 October 1903, Mr Chapman, pp. 6126, 6134
26 *CA* Vol. II, 1903, No. 20, Defence Act, Part II, Section 28, p. 113
27 *CPD* Vol. XVII, 16 October 1903, Senator O'Keefe, pp. 6237–8
28 W. S. Hamer, *The British Army: Civil Military Relations 1885–1905* The Clarendon Press, Oxford, 1970, p. 181
29 *Age* 10 November 1903, Melbourne, p. 5; *Argus*, 10 November 1903, Melbourne, p. 6
30 Telegram, Deakin to Chapman, 12 November 1903, CRS B168, file no. 03-6238, AA
31 Telegram Hutton to Chapman, 22 January 1904, CRS B168, file no. 02/963[5], AA
32 Telegram, Hutton to Chapman, 23 January 1904, CRS B168, file no. 02/963[5], AA
33 M. Rutledge 'Neild, John Cash' *ADB* Vol. 10, Melbourne, 1986, pp. 672–3; St George's English Rifle Regiment, Case of Sergt G. A. King, CRS B168, file no. 03/4672, AA; *Sydney Morning Herald* 23 March 1903, Sydney, p. 5
34 *Age* 21 April 1904, Melbourne, p. 8; *CPD* Vol. XVIII, 20 April 1904, pp. 1109–10
35 *CPD* Vol. XVII, 23 September 1903, Senator Lt. Col. Neild, p. 5383
36 *ibid.*, Vol. XV, 12 August 1903, pp. 3397–8
37 *ibid.*, Vol. XVII, 13 October 1903, Senator Lt. Col. Neild, p. 6006
38 Hutton to Bigge, 11 November 1903 *Hutton Papers* Vol. I, Add. Ms. 50078, ff. 26–8, BL
39 *CPD* Vol. XVIII, 3 March 1904, Senator Lt. Col. Neild, pp. 47–54
40 Hutton to Minister of Defence, 14 March 1904, CRS B168, file no. 02/2688 (folder 3), AA
41 Neild to Dawson, 7 May 1904, CRS B168, file no. 03/4672, AA
42 *CPD* Vol. XVIII, 20 April 1904, Senator Dawson pp. 1107, 1113–14, Senator Lt. Col. Neild, pp. 1106–13, 1121
43 *Journals of the Senate* 1904, Vol. I, Report, 20 October 1904, p. 564
44 Proceedings of a Court of Enquiry assembled at Hobart on 11 February 1904, CRS B168, file no. 1904/1253, AA
45 Hutton to Northcote, 8 February 1904 and 15 February 1904 *Hutton Papers* Vol. V, Add. Ms. 50082, ff. 123–7, BL

46 *ibid.*, and Northcote to Hutton, 15 February 1904 *Hutton Papers* Vol. V, Add. Ms. 50082, ff. 123–7, BL
47 Bigge to Hutton, 19 April 1904 *Hutton Papers* Vol. I, Add. Ms. 50078, ff. 37–8, BL
48 *Bulletin* 17 March 1904, Sydney, p. 8
49 *Bulletin* 24 March 1904, Sydney, p. 9
50 *CPD* Vol. XVIII, 13 April 1904, pp. 833–5
51 Extracts from Private Letters from Major-General Hutton to Colonel Hoad, Re application by Colonel Hoad for leave, 16 February 1904; South Africa—10 August 1900; From London, 26 November 1902 (This year is incorrectly recorded. It should be 1901.); In writing of the Scheme of Organization having been approved—27 July 1903; Re command in Tasmania—24 March 1904, CRS B168 , file no. 1904/32[8], AA
52 Copy of telegram, Chapman to GOC, 24 March 1904, CRS B168, file no. 04/32[3], AA
53 Hutton to Tennyson, 19 April 1904 *Hutton Papers* Vol. V, Add. Ms. 50082, ff. 103–4, BL
54 Copy of telegram, Hutton to Minister for Defence, 25 March 1904, CRS B168, file no. 04/32[3], AA
55 Hutton to Nicholson, 8 April 1904 *Hutton Papers* Vol. IX, Add. Ms. 50086, ff. 303–4, BL
56 Hutton to Ommanney, 19 April 1904 *Hutton Papers* Vol. I, Add. Ms. 50078, ff. 309–11, BL
57 Hutton to Tennyson, 19 April 1904 *Hutton Papers* Vol. V, Add. Ms. 50082, ff. 103–4, BL
58 Hutton to Ommanney, 19 April 1904 *Hutton Papers* Vol. I, Add. Ms. 50078, ff. 309–11, BL
59 *CPP* 1904 Session, Vol. II, No. 25 'Military Forces of the Commonwealth of Australia—Second Annual Report with Appendices by Major-General Sir Edward Hutton' 1 May 1904, Part II, Section 26, pp. 297–9
60 Copy of Telegram, 19 February 1904, with minute by Collins, 20 April 1904, CRS B168, file no. 04/2278, AA
61 Minute by Hutton, 21 April 1904, on Copy of Telegram, CRS B168, file no. 04/2278, AA
62 Minute by Chapman, 22 April 1904, on Copy of Telegram, CRS B168, file no. 04/2278, AA
63 Hutton to Secretary of Defence, 6 May 1904, CRS B168, file no. 04/2278, AA
64 Confidential minute by Dawson, 12 May 1904, CRS B168, file no. 04/2278, AA
65 Hutton to Northcote, 31 May 1904 *Hutton Papers* Vol. V, Add. Ms. 50082, ff. 129–34, BL
66 *ibid.*
67 *Age* 26 May 1904, Melbourne, p. 4
68 Hutton to Watson, 31 May 1904 *Hutton Papers* Vol. VII, Add. Ms. 50084, ff. 65–6, BL
69 *CPP* 1904 Session, Vol. II, No. 58, 'Defence Forces of the Commonwealth—Memorandum by a Committee in Regard to the Command and Administration of the Military and Naval Forces; Together with Memorandum Thereon by Senator Hon. A. Dawson, and Major-General Sir E. T. H. Hutton', p. 361
70 D. J. Murphy 'Dawson, Andrew (Anderson)' *ADB* Vol. 8, Melbourne, 1981, pp. 244–245

Notes

71 *Hutton's Newspaper Cuttings* 1900–1904, p. 151, Ms. 1215, ANL. *Note:* In October 1899, Dawson, then a member of the colonial parliament in Queensland, had spoken in disparaging terms about men who might volunteer for service in the Boer War. Hutton preserved a copy of Dawson's comments in his private papers and noted that this 'will give some idea of the man and of his opinions'. Armed with this knowledge 'The principles underlying his administration of the Mil. Forces of the Commonwealth will be understood', Hutton concluded.
72 W. D. Williams for GOC to Secretary for Defence, 10 May 1904, CRS B168, file no. 03/4592, AA
73 Collins to GOC, 18 May 1904, CRS B168, file no. 03/4592, AA
74 Minute by A. Dawson, Minister of State for Defence, 7 June 1904, CRS B168, file no. 03/4592, AA
75 Hutton to Minister of Defence, 21 June 1904, CRS B168, file no. 03/4592, AA
76 Minute by Dawson, 28 June 1904, AA, CRS B168, file no. 03/4592
77 *Argus* 18 July 1904, Melbourne, p. 5; *Sydney Morning Herald* 19 July 1904, Sydney, p. 4
78 Dawson to Secretary, Department of Defence, 18 August 1904, CRS B168, file no. 03/4592, AA
79 *Age* Melbourne, 25 August 1904, p. 5, and 26 August 1904, p. 5; *Argus* 26 August 1904, Melbourne, p. 9; *Sydney Morning Herald* 27 August 1904, Sydney, p. 11
80 Narrative of Lt–Gen Sir Edward Hutton's Command in Australia: 1901–04, Period VIII *Hutton Papers*, Vol. XXXVI, Add. Ms. 50113, f. 223, BL
81 *CPD* Vol. XXIII, 2 November 1904, Mr McCay, pp. 6383–96
82 *CPP* 1904 Session, Vol. II, No. 51 'Defence Forces—Memorandum By The Minister for Defence On the Administration and Control Of' p. 358
83 Military Board Proceedings, 1905–07, Vol. I, Meeting of 12 January 1905, pp. 1–2, CRS A2653, AA
84 *ibid.*, pp. 6385–8
85 *ibid.*, pp. 6388–93
86 Hutton to Arnold–Forster, 12 October 1903 *Hutton Papers* Vol. VIII, Add. Ms. 50085, ff. 63–6, BL
87 Arthur Norris to Hutton, 9 August 1904 *Hutton Papers* Vol. VIII, Add. Ms. 50085, ff. 69–70, BL
88 Hutton to Clarke, 7 October 1906 *Hutton Papers* Vol. V, Add. Ms. 50082, ff. 363–4, BL
89 A. J. Hill 'Hutton, Sir Edward Thomas Henry' *ADB* Vol. 9, pp. 415–18
90 Chamberlain to Northcote, 23 December 1904 *Northcote Papers* PRO 30/56/1, ff. 23–7, PRO
91 Ommanney to Clarke, 1 August 1904, Cab 17/77, PRO
92 Chamberlain to Northcote, 18 January 1905 *Northcote Papers* PRO 30/56/1, ff. 29–32, PRO; copy of the same letter in *Chamberlain Papers* JC 20/1/1, BU

Chapter 9

1 N. Meaney *The Search for Security in the Pacific, 1901–14* Sydney University Press, Sydney, 1976, pp. 120–1

2. *CPP* 1905 Session, Vol. II, No. 31 'The Defence of Australia (Statement By The Honourable Alfred Deakin, MP)' communicated to *The Herald*, 12 June 1905, pp. 315–17
3. *ibid.*
4. R. Norris 'Deakin, Alfred' *ADB* Vol. 8, Melbourne, 1981, pp. 248–56
5. CDC Remarks, No. 377R, 'Defence Scheme (Draft Chapter 1), September 1904' 17 July 1905, Appendix I, Enclosure—Defence Scheme for the Commonwealth of Australia, pp. 5–7, Cab 9/8, PRO
6. Hutton to Tennyson, 9 March 1903 *Hutton Papers* Vol. V, Add. Ms. 50082, ff. 75–80, BL
7. CDC Remarks, No. 377R, Appendix II, Enclosure—Remarks by Captain Creswell, CMG, upon the Defence Scheme for the Commonwealth of Australia, Chapter 1, 3 December 1904, pp. 9–13, Cab 9/8, PRO
8. *ibid.*, Appendix I, Northcote to Secretary of State for the Colonies, 8 September 1904, p. 5
9. CDC Remarks, No. 377R, pp. 1–2
10. *ibid.*
11. *ibid.*, pp. 3–4
12. Deakin to Sir George Sydenham Clarke, 2 October 1905, Cab 17/48, PRO; copy of the same cable in *Deakin Papers* Ms. 1540/15/3520, ANL
13. Deakin to Clarke, 3 October 1905 *Deakin Papers* Ms. 1540/15/3522, ANL; Extract of a Letter from Mr Deakin, 3 October 1905, Cab 17/48, PRO
14. Cable Clarke to Deakin, 5 October 1905 *Deakin Papers* Ms. 1540/15/3524–3525; Clarke to Deakin, 6 October 1905 *Deakin Papers* Ms. 1540/15/3526, ANL; Note by Clarke referring to cabled reply to Deakin of 5 October 1905 written on Deakin to Sir George Sydenham Clarke, 2 October 1905; Extract from letter to Mr Deakin sent 6 October 1905 G. C. [George Clarke] Cab 17/48, PRO
15. CID—Memorandum as To The Functions of The Committee of Imperial Defence, March 1907, Cab 17/77, PRO
16. Clarke to Deakin, 6 October 1905 *Deakin Papers* Ms. 1540/15/3526, ANL; Extract from letter to Mr Deakin sent 6 October 1905 G. C. [George Clarke], Cab 17/48, PRO
17. C. D. Coulthard-Clark 'Bridges, Sir William Throsby' *ADB* Vol. 7, pp. 408–11
18. Hutton to Ommanney, 12 May 1905 *Hutton Papers* Vol. I, Add. Ms. 50078, ff. 314–17, BL
19. Diary of a Journey to Australia: December 1905–January 1906, by Lt. Col. G. M. Kirkpatrick, General Staff, Entry for 22 December 1905, p. 19, Cab 11/25, PRO
20. G. M. Kirkpatrick to My dear Colonel [Clarke], 26 December 1905, Cab 17/48, PRO
21. G. M. Kirkpatrick to My dear Colonel [Clarke], 26 December 1905, Cab 17/48, PRO
22. Deakin to Clarke, 8 January 1906 *Deakin Papers* Ms. 1540/15/3549–51, ANL
23. Clarke to Deakin, 10 November 1905 *Deakin Papers* Ms. 1540/15/3533–5; Clarke to Deakin, 5 January 1906 *Deakin Papers* Ms. 1540/15/3547–8, ANL
24. G. M. Kirkpatrick to My dear Colonel, 26 December 1905, Cab 17/48, PRO
25. Diary of a Journey to Australia: December 1905–January 1906, by Lt. Col. G. M. Kirkpatrick, General Staff, Entry for 23 December 1905, p. 19, Cab 11/25, PRO

Notes

26 Council of Defence, No. 1, Development of Defence Forces, II, 'Memorandum by the Director of Naval Forces submitted to the Council of Defence, 12th May, 1905' pp. 4–6, AWM 113, MH 1–2, AWM
27 *ibid.*, III, Answers to questions put to the Director of Naval Forces by the Chief of Intelligence, Question No. 1, 1 June 1905, p. 7
28 *ibid.*, IV, 'Memorandum by the Chief of Intelligence submitted to the Council of Defence, June, 1905', pp. 9–11
29 Deakin to Clarke, 8 January 1906 *Deakin Papers* Ms. 1540/15/3549–3551, ANL
30 Instructions to Lieut-Colonel W. T. Bridges, RAA, Chief of Intelligence, by Collins with approval by Playford, 21 December 1905, MP84, file no. 1856/2/13, AA; see also G. M. Kirkpatrick to My dear Colonel, 26 December 1905, Cab 17/48, PRO
31 Deakin to Clarke, 8 January 1906 *Deakin Papers* Ms. 1540/15/3549–3551, ANL
32 Report of the Committee of Imperial Defence upon a General Scheme of Defence for Australia, B173 CA6, file no. S 06/46, AA; copy of the same report in *CPP* 1906 Session, Vol. II, No. 62, pp. 165–178; Australia—General Scheme of Defence, Memorandum by the CDC, No. 362M, 15 May 1906, Cab 8/4, PRO
33 Northcote to Secretary of State for Colonies, 3 January 1906, and enclosure, Deakin to Governor-General, 28 December 1905, Cab 17/48, PRO
34 G. M. Kirkpatrick to My dear Colonel, 26 December 1905, Cab 17/48, PRO
35 Report of the Committee of Imperial Defence upon a General Scheme of Defence for Australia, B173 CA6, file no. S 06/46, AA
36 A. Deakin *Federated Australia: Selections from Letters to the* Morning Post *1900–1910* MUP, Melbourne, 1968, No. 83, Australia Wants A Navy, pp. 190–2
37 Minute No. 1, no date, by T. Playford; Minute No. 3, H. Finn to Secretary, 18 August 1906; Le Mesurier to Minister, 21 August 1906; Notes on Report of Imperial Defence Committee (4OC), J. C. Hoad, 9 August 1906, B173 CA6, file no. S 06/58, AA
38 *CPP* 1906 Session, Vol. II, No. 87 'Report of Committee of Officers Appointed By the Minister of State for Defence to Consider and Report upon The General Scheme of Defence of Australia as Submitted by The Committee of Imperial Defence' p. 205; for allocation of Brigades to States, CG No. 52, 5 October 1907, p. 1231
39 W. Perry 'Hoad, Sir John Charles' *ADB* Vol. 9, Melbourne, 1983, pp. 311–12
40 Hutton to Nicholson, 8 April 1904 *Hutton Papers* Vol. IX, Add. Ms. 50086, ff. 303–4, BL
41 Hutton to Minister of Defence, 6 September 1904 *Hutton Papers* Vol. VII, Add. Ms. 50084, f. 380, BL
42 Kirkpatrick to My dear Colonel, 26 December 1905, Cab 17/48, PRO
43 Hutton to Northcote, 24 January 1906 *Hutton Papers* Vol. V, Add. Ms. 50082, ff. 151–2, BL
44 *CPP* 1906 Session, Vol. II, No. 43 'Annual Report for the Year 1905 By The Inspector-General, Major-General H. Finn' Introductory Remarks, p. 121
45 Private—Note of Central Administration, Etc., by G. S. Clarke, 1 May 1906—Copy Sent to Mr Deakin, 3 May 1906, Cab 17/48, PRO; copy of the paper in *Sydenham Papers* Vol. VI, Add. Ms. 50836, ff. 78–84, BL. *Note*: A note is enfaced on the copy in the *Sydenham Papers*: 'Sent to Mr. Deakin. Given to Colonel Bridges'.
46 *CPD* Vol. XXXI, 7 June 1906, Governor-General, pp. 6–8

47 Deakin to Clarke, 8 January 1906 *Deakin Papers* Ms. 1540/15/3549–3551, ANL
48 *CPP* 1906 Session, Vol. II, No. 109 'Administration and Control of the Military Forces By a Board. (Minute By Major-General H. Finn)' 8 June 1906, pp. 161–2
49 Instructions to Lieut-Colonel W. T. Bridges, by Collins and approved by Playford, 21 December 1905, MP 84, file no. 1856/2/13, AA
50 Clarke to Hutton, 9 October 1906 *Hutton Papers* Vol. V, Add. Ms. 50082, ff. 365–6, BL
51 *CPP* 1907–08 Session, Vol. II, No. 7 'Report By The Military Board for the Year 1906' p. 93; *ibid.*, No. 169, 'Annual Report for the Year 1907 By The Inspector-General', p. 111
52 *CPP* 1906 Session, Vol. II, No. 43 'Annual Report For The Year 1905, By the Inspector-General, Major-General H. Finn' pp. 122–37
53 *CPP* 1906 Session, Vol. II., No. 45 'Military Board Report for the Year 1905' p. 99
54 *ibid.*, pp. 97–8
55 *ibid.*, 1907–08 Session, Vol. II, No. 169 'Annual Report For The Year 1907 By The Inspector-General' p. 125
56 *BPP* Vol. LIV, 1907, Cd. 3523 'Minutes of Proceedings of the Colonial Conference, 1907' pp. 94–99; same minutes in *CPP* 1907–08 Session, Vol. III, No. 11, p. 817
57 Colonial Conference, 1907, Subject No. 1 proposed for discussion by the Army Council 'The Strategical Conditions of the Empire from the Military Point of View' (Paper prepared by the General Staff), 14 March 1907, Cab 17/77, and, a copy of the same paper, Cab 11/118, PRO
58 *ibid.*
59 *ibid.*, Subject No. 2, 'Possibility of Assimilating War Organization Throughout the Empire', 14 March 1907, Cab 17/77, PRO
60 *ibid.*, Subject No. 3, 'Patterns and Provision of Equipment and Stores for Colonial Forces', 21 March 1907, Cab 17/77, PRO
61 *ibid.*, Subject No. 4, 'The Desirability that the Colonial Government should Give Their Orders for Ordnance Stores, Particularly Arms and Ammunition, Through the War Office', Cab 17/77, PRO
62 *BPP* Vol. LIV, 1907, Cd. 3523, p. 96
63 *ibid.*, pp. 96–7
64 *ibid.*, p. 103
65 *ibid.*, p. 117
66 G. A. Ellison to Clarke, 19 April 1907, with two enclosed draft resolutions, Cab 17/77, PRO
67 *BPP* Vol. LIV, 1907, Cd. 3523, pp. 95–6
68 Part I—General Principles Affecting National Defence, 7 December 1908, pp. 6–7, Cab 11/118; see also War Office to Under Secretary of State, Colonial Office, 15 December 1908, Cab 11/118, PRO
69 *BPP* Vol. LIV, 1907, Cd. 3523, pp. 111–16; Colonial Defence—Précis of Important Events connected with Question of the Employment of Colonial Military Forces on Imperial Service, 29 June 1909, paras. 14–16, pp. 5–6, Cab 11/125, PRO
70 Ewing to Prime Minister, 28 February 1907, MP 84/1, file no. 1856/1/10, AA
71 *BPP* Vol. LIV, 1907, Cd. 3337, Enclosure No. 1, Resolutions of Government of Commonwealth of Australia to be submitted to Colonial Conference, IV—Imperial Defence, p. 7

Notes

72 *ibid.*, Cd. 3523, pp. 83–84; and, Memorandum As To The Functions of The Committee of Imperial Defence, March 1907, Cab 17/77, PRO
73 *BPP* Vol. LIV, 1907, Cd. 3523, p. 107
74 *ibid.*, pp. 129–30, 474–5, 482
75 *CPD* Vol. XLII, 13 December 1907, Mr Deakin, p. 751
76 *BPP* Vol. LIV, 1907, Cd. 3523, pp. 102–04
77 *ibid.*, Cd. 3523, pp. 105–06
78 Deakin to Clarke, 8 January 1906 *Deakin Papers* Ms. 1540/15/3549–3551, ANL
79 *CPP* 1906 Session, Vol. II, No. 79 'Report on the Department of Defence For the Period from 1st March, 1901, to 30th June, 1906' para. 23, p. 40
80 *ibid.*, 1907–08 Session, Vol. II, No. 169 'Annual Report for the Year 1907 By the Inspector-General' p. 121
81 T. W. Tanner *Compulsory Citizen Soldiers* Alternative Publishing Co-operative Ltd, Waterloo, 1980, pp. 72–6
82 *ibid.*, pp. 123–4
83 A. Deakin quoted by A-M. Jordens in 'Against the tide: the growth and decline of a liberal anti-war movement in Australia, 1905–1918' *Historical Studies* Vol. 22, No. 88, April 1987, pp. 380–1. *Note*: I have emphasised '*self defence*'.
84 *CPD* Vol. XLII, Mr Deakin, 13 December 1907, pp. 7509–23
85 *ibid.*, pp. 7527–28
86 *CPP* 1907–08 Session, Vol. II, No. 149 'Land Defence of Australia: National Guard' pp. 67–73
87 *CPD* Vol. XLII, Mr Deakin, 13 December 1907, p. 7528
88 *ibid.*, p. 7529
89 *CPP* 1907–08 Session, Vol. II, No. 149, p. 69
90 *CPD* Vol. XLII, Mr Deakin, 13 December 1907, p. 7528–30
91 *ibid.*, pp. 7529–33; for Intelligence Corps, CG No. 62, 7 December 1907, p. 1430; for Australian Corps of Signallers, CG No. 63, 23 December 1905, p. 1000
92 *CPD* Vol. XLII, Mr Deakin, 13 December 1907, p. 7527
93 Hutton to Ommanney, 19 August 1903 *Hutton Papers* Vol. I, Add. Ms. 50078, ff. 304–5, BL
94 Hutton to Deakin, 24 January 1906 *Deakin Papers* Ms 1540/15/3553–3554, ANL; Hutton to Deakin, 19 January 1906 *Hutton Papers* Vol. VIII, Add. Ms. 50084, ff. 54–7, BL
95 Hutton to Forrest, 29 December 1908 *Hutton Papers* Vol. VII, Add. Ms. 50084, ff. 300–5
96 *CPP* 1907–08 Session, Vol. II, No. 129 'Report on The Swiss Military System Compiled in the Department of The Chief of Intelligence 1907' para. 1, p. 141
97 Bridges to Hutton, 17 December 1907 *Hutton Papers* Vol. XII, Add. Ms. 50089, ff. 58–9, BL

Chapter 10

1 G. P. Walsh 'Ewing, Sir Thomas Thomson' *ADB*, Vol. 8, MUP, Melbourne, 1981, p. 455
2 C. Coulthard-Clark *No Australian Need Apply* Allen & Unwin, Sydney, 1988, p. 46
3 Military Board Minute Book, 1907–08, Meeting of 29 September 1908, item (3), p. 356, CRS A2653, AA

An Army for a Nation

4 *CPD* Vol. XLVII, Mr Ewing, 8 October 1908, pp. 935–6
5 *ibid.*, Vol. XLVII, 14 October 1908, Sir John Forrest, p. 1129
6 Military Board Minute Book, 1907–08, Meeting of 27 July 1908, item (18), p. 296, CRS A2653, AA
7 *ibid.*, Meeting of 1 October 1908, item (6), p. 362
8 Chief of Intelligence to Minister of Defence, 22 February 1907, MP 84, file no. 1856/4/4, AA
9 Chief of Intelligence to Minister of Defence, 15 April 1907, MP 84, file no. 1856/4/4, AA
10 Private—Note on Central Administration, Etc., by G. S. Clarke, 1 May 1906 *Sydenham Papers* Vol. VI, Add. Ms. 50836, ff. 78–84, BL. *Note*: A note is enfaced on the document: 'Sent to Mr. Deakin. Given to Colonel Bridges'.
11 Memorandum by Minister for Defence, 19 June 1907, MP 84, file no. 1856/4/4, AA
12 *CPP* 1904 Session, Vol. II, No. 51 'Defence Forces—Memorandum By The Minister for Defence On the Administration and Control Of' para. 6(a), p. 358
13 General Orders, 1905, No. 3, 6 January 1905
14 Military Board Proceedings 1907–08, Meeting of 24 December 1907, item (3), p. 171, CRS A2653, AA
15 Bridges to Secretary Military Board, 24 June 1908, and enclosed Notes on Central Administration by G. S. Clarke *MBPHI* Vol. II, CRS A2657/ T1, AA
16 *ibid.*,; for Bridges' resolution that the Military Board should be organised like an operational headquarters, see Military Board Proceedings 1907–08, Meeting of 13 July 1908, item (30), p. 276, CRS A2653, AA
17 Bridges to Secretary Military Board, 24 June 1908, and enclosed Notes on Central Administration by G. S. Clarke *MBPHI* Vol. II, CRS A2657/ T1, AA
18 Minute by Tho. Ewing, 31 July 1908 *MBPHI* Vol. II, CRS A2657/ T1, AA
19 White to Hutton, 31 May 1908 *Hutton Papers* Vol. XII, Add. Ms. 50089, ff. 106–10, BL
20 Military Board Proceedings 1907–08, Meeting of 6 March 1908, item (16), p. 198, CRS A2653, AA
21 Bridges to Hutton, 8 June 1908 *Hutton Papers* Vol. XII, Add. Ms. 50089, ff. 60–3, BL
22 White to Hutton, 3 September 1908 *Hutton Papers* Vol. XII, Add. Ms. 50089, ff. 111–13, BL
23 White to Hutton 31 May 1908 *Hutton Papers* Vol. XII, Add. Ms. 50089, ff. 106–10, BL
24 White to Hutton, 3 September 1908 *Hutton Papers* Vol. XII, Add. Ms. 50089, ff. 111–13, BL
25 *CPD* Vol. XLVII, 29 September 1908, Mr Ewing, p. 438
26 Bills Introduced Together with Printed Amendments 1908, House of Representatives, A Bill for an Act Relating to Naval and Military Defence, Read 29 September 1908, Part III A—Obligations in Respect of Naval and Military Training, Sections 58A, 58B, 58F and 58L, pp. 330–2, PL
27 *CPD* Vol. XLVII, 29 September 1908, Mr Ewing, p. 439
28 *ibid.*, pp. 454–6
29 Bills Introduced Together with Printed Amendments 1908, House of Representatives, A Bill for an Act Relating to Naval and Military Defence, Read 29 September 1908, Section 54A, p. 330, PL
30 Bridges to Hutton, 29 September 1908 *Hutton Papers* Vol. XII, Add. Ms. 50089, ff. 64–5, BL
31 P. R. Heydon *Quiet Decision* MUP, Melbourne, 1965, p. 4

Notes

32 G. F. Pearce *Carpenter to Cabinet* Hutchinson & Co., London, 1951, p. 77
33 Military Board Minute Book 1908–11, Meeting of 23 December 1908, item (11), p. 18, CRS A2653, AA
34 R. Muirhead Collins, Representative of the Commonwealth in London, to Secretary, Colonial Office, 15 September 1908, Cab 17/48, PRO
35 Bridges to Hutton, 29 September 1908 *Hutton Papers* Vol. XII, Add. Ms. 50089, ff. 64–5, BL
36 Collins to Secretary, Colonial Office, 15 September 1908, Cab 17/48, PRO
37 Representation of the Commonwealth on the Imperial General Staff, under cover of Collins to Secretary, Colonial Office, 15 September 1908, Cab 17/48, PRO
38 *ibid.*; for draft of instructions drawn up in Department of Defence *MBPHI* Vol. II, CRS A2657/ T1, AA. *Note*: I have emphasised '*discuss the desirability*'.
39 J. A. La Nauze *Alfred Deakin* Angus & Robertson, Sydney, 1979, p. 519
40 White to Bridges, 19 February 1909 *Bridges Collection* Series I, Item 29, ADFAL
41 White to Bridges, 15 January 1909 *Bridges Collection* Series I, Item 26, ADFAL
42 J. Gooch *The Plans of War* RKP, London, 1974, pp. 137–8
43 *CPD* 1909 Session, Vol. II, No. 33 'Defence: Imperial General Staff—Correspondence Relating to Proposed Formation; including Major-General Hoad's Proposal with Regard to Australian Section, Etc.', 'The Imperial General Staff', W. G. Nicholson, December 1908, Part I—General Principles Affecting National Defence, pp. 429–30
44 *ibid.*, Part II—The Most Suitable and Efficient Organization for an Imperial General Staff, pp. 430–1
45 *ibid.*, Part I, p. 430
46 *ibid.*, Part III, p. 431
47 *ibid.*, Part I, p. 429
48 *ibid.*, Part IV—Present Means, And How to Utilize Them, For the Creation of an Imperial General Staff, p. 433
49 E. D. Ward, War Office, to Colonial Office, 15 December 1908, MP 84/1, file no. 1894/5/4, AA; *BPP* Vol. 51, 1909, Cd 4475 'Correspondence Relating to the Proposed Formation of an Imperial General Staff' Enclosure in No. 1, p. 3; *CPP* 1909 Session, Vol. II, No. 33, p. 425
50 The Imperial General Staff—Notes on the Proposal, J. G. Legge, Quarter-Master General, 24 February 1909 *MBPHI* Vol. II, CRS A2657/ T1, AA
51 *ibid.*
52 Comments By The Minister For Defence On The Proposals For An Imperial General Staff Forwarded by The War Office, February 13th 1909, G. F. P. [G. F. Pearce], 1 March 1909 *MBPHI* Vol. II, CRS A2657/ T1, AA
53 Application of *Army Act* to Colonial Troops when Employed on Active service with Imperial Troops, Colonial Defence Committee Minute No. 402M, 16 July 1908, Cab 8/4, PRO
54 Military Board Minute Book, 1908–11, Meeting of 18 and 19 January 1909, item (5), p. 29; Meeting of 25 January 1909, item 930, p. 33, CRS A2653, AA
55 White to Bridges, 25 March 1909 *Bridges Collection* Series 1, Item 31, ADFAL
56 Comments By the Minister for Defence on Memo of War Office, Dated 15th December 1908, On the Subject of Imperial General Staff, no date, *MBPHI* Vol. II, CRS A2657/ T1, AA. *Note*: The document is annotated: 'The previous

memorandum on the undermentioned subject submitted by the Minister is withdrawn'.
57 Andrew Fisher to Earl of Dudley, Governor-General, 26 March 1909 *MBPHI* Vol. II, CRS A2657/ T1, AA
58 Petherbridge, Acting Secretary, Department of Defence, to London, 12 February 1909; London to Melbourne, 13 February 1909, MP84/1, file no. 1894/6/46, AA
59 Memorandum by Governor-General's Office, 17 February 1909, re Telegram from Colonial Secretary to Prime Minister, 16 February 1909 *MBPHI* Vol. II, CRS A2657/ T1, AA
60 *CPP* 1909 Session, Vol. II, No. 33 'Major-General Hoad's Proposals with Regard to Australian Section, Etc.' February 1909, pp. 439–40
61 *ibid.*, Nicholson to Hoad, 12 February 1909, pp. 444–5
62 White to Bridges, 19 February 1909 *Bridges Collection* Series 1, Item 29, ADFAL
63 *CPP* 1909 Session, Vol. II, No. 33, Part IV, p. 433
64 White to Bridges, 4 March 1908 *Bridges Collection* Series 1, Item 25, ADFAL. *Note*: The date on this letter is clearly wrong. It should be 4 March 1909
65 White to Bridges, 22 January 1909 *Bridges Collection* Series 1, Item 27, ADFAL
66 *CPP* 1909 Session, Vol. II, No. 33 'Major-General Hoad's Proposals with Regard to Australian Section, Etc.' February 1909, paras. 11, 13, p. 440
67 *ibid.*, Nicholson to Hoad, 12 February 1909, pp. 444–5
68 Nicholson, quoted by J. Gooch, in *The Plans of War* p. 157
69 Hutton to Nicholson, 8 April 1904 *Hutton Papers* Vol. IX, Add. Ms. 50086, ff. 303–4, BL
70 Nicholson, quoted by J. Gooch, in *The Plans of War* p. 157
71 Bridges, CGS, to Minister of Defence, 23 April 1909 *MBPHI* Vol. II, CRS A2657/ T1, AA
72 Minute by G.F.P. [George Foster Pearce], 'Inspector Generals Report on I.G.S.', 29 April 1909 *MBPHI* Vol. II, CRS A2657/ T1, AA
73 E. T. Wallack, Adjutant General, to Secretary, 30 April 1909; J. M. Marwell, Chief of Ordnance, to Minister for Defence, 3 May 1909; J. G. Legge, Quarter Master General, to Minister for Defence, 3 May 1909 *MBPHI* Vol. II, CRS A2657/ T1, AA
74 S. A. Petherbridge to Minister, 5 May 1909 *MBPHI* Vol. II, CRS A2657/ T1, AA
75 A. Hunt to Official Secretary to the Governor-General, 25 May 1909 *MBPHI* Vol. II, CRS A2657/ T1, AA
76 C. Coulthard-Clark *A Heritage of Spirit* MUP, Melbourne, 1979, pp. 81–3
77 Pearce to Fisher, 14 May 1909 *Pearce Papers* file no. 419/80/2, Bundle 4, Item 2, AWM
78 Minute by Pearce 'The Following Alterations in the Military Board are Directed' 22 May 1909 *MBPHI* Vol. II, CRS A2657/ T1, AA
79 White to Bridges, 19 February 1909 *Bridges Collection* Series 1, Item 29, ADFAL
80 *CPD* Vol. LII, Mr W. M. Hughes, 13 October 1909, p. 4462
81 *BPP* Vol. 59, 1909, Cd. 4948 'Correspondence and Papers Relating to a Conference With Representatives of The Self-Governing Dominions on the Naval and Military Defence of The Empire' I-Correspondence Relating To The Summoning of The Conference, No. 7 New South Wales, p. 3
82 *ibid.*, No. 9, Australia, p. 3

Notes

83 N. Meaney *The Search for Security in the Pacific* Sydney University Press, Sydney, 1976, p. 178
84 Jose to Deakin, 2 April [1909] *Deakin Papers* Ms 1540/16/601, ANL
85 R. Lamont 'Jose, Arthur Wilberforce' *ADB* Vol. 9, Melbourne, 1983, pp. 523–4
86 Jose to Deakin, 2 April [1909] *Deakin Papers* Ms. 1540/16/601, ANL
87 Jose to Deakin, 28 April 1909 *Deakin Papers* Ms. 1540/16/556, ANL
88 Commonwealth Liberal Party Platform *Hume Cook Papers* Ms. 601/3/50, ANL; for draft platform, G. D. Meudell to Deakin, 22 April 1909 *Deakin Papers* Ms. 1540/16/1131, ANL; *Age* 26 May 1909, Melbourne, p. 7
89 Deakin to T. F. Farleigh, 18 May 1909 *Deakin Papers* Ms. 1540/16/575–6, ANL
90 The History of the Movement, 25 May 1909, pp. 17–18 *Hume Cook Papers* Ms. 601/3/63, ANL
91 *ibid.*, p. 20
92 *Age* 29 May 1909, Melbourne, p. 11
93 Governor-General to Secretary of State for Colonies, 1 June 1909, CP 78/9, Vol. I, p. 580, Copies of Secret and Confidential Despatches, Recorders and Acknowledgements from Governor-General to Secretary of State, AA

Chapter 11

1 J. A. La Nauze *Alfred Deakin* Angus & Robertson, Melbourne, 1979, p. 573
2 *Age* 10 June 1909, Melbourne, p. 5
3 *Age* 11 June 1909, Melbourne, p. 7
4 C. Carty Salmon to Deakin, 10 June 1909 *Deakin Papers* Ms. 1540/16/590, ANL
5 C. Carty Salmon to Deakin, 12 June 1909 *Deakin Papers* Ms. 1540/16/593, ANL
6 *Age* 11 June 1909, Melbourne, p. 6
7 *Age* 12 June 1909, Melbourne, p. 14
8 *ibid. Note*: I have emphasised *'as a whole'* and *'on this coast'*.
9 Sub-Committee To Consider The Proposals To be Laid Before the Imperial Conference on Defence, 30 June 1909—Points to which the attention of the Sub-Committee should be directed and Proposals for So Organizing the Military Forces of The Empire as To Ensure Their Effective Co-operation in the Event of War, Cab 17/78, PRO
10 C. Carty Salmon to Deakin, 12 June 1909 *Deakin Papers* Ms. 1540/16/593, ANL
11 *BPP* Vol. 59, 1909, Cd. 4948 'Imperial Conference—Naval and Military Defence of the Empire' B—Naval Defence, II—Admiralty Memorandum, 20 July 1909, pp. 21, 23, and IV—Australia, p. 25
12 *CPD* Vol. XLII, 13 December 1907, Mr Deakin, p. 751
13 Colonial Forces—Interchange of Military Units Between the Self-Governing Colonies and the Mother Country—Minute by the Chief of the General Staff, 10 May 1909, Cab 11/124, PRO
14 *BPP* Vol. 59, 1909, Cd. 4948 'Imperial Conference—Naval and Military Defence of the Empire', II—Proceedings of the Conference, pp. 18–19, and, C—Military Defence, pp. 28–52
15 *ibid.*, pp. 18, 30
16 *CPD* Vol. XLII, Mr Deakin, 13 December 1907, p. 7527

An Army for a Nation

17 *CPD* Vol. XLII, 13 December 1907, Mr Deakin, p. 751; Vol. LI, 21 September 1909, Mr Joseph Cook, pp. 3613–16
18 *ibid.*, p. 3622
19 *ibid.*, p. 3621–3
20 *Sydney Morning Herald* 22 September 1909, Sydney, pp. 9–10
21 *ibid.*, p. 3624. *Note*: I have emphasised '*up North*'.
22 A Bill for An Act Relating to Naval and Military Defence, House of Representatives, Brought in by the Minister for Defence, the Hon. Joseph Cook, Read 21 September 1909, LAGD
23 *CPD* Vol. LII, 13 October 1909, pp. 4472–3
24 *ibid.*
25 *Age* 27 September 1909, Melbourne, p. 7
26 *Age* 28 September 1909, Melbourne, p. 6, *Note*: I have emphasised '*to make our coasts secure*'.
27 *Sydney Morning Herald* 23 September 1909, Sydney, p. 6
28 *Sydney Morning Herald* 23, 24 September 1909, Sydney, p. 7; *Age* 27 September 1909, Melbourne, p. 7
29 *CA* Vol. 8, 1909, No. 15, pp. 201–33
30 *Note*: Deakin queried Kitchener's availability on 12 June 1909: Atlee Hunt to Governor-General, 12 June 1909, MP 84/1, file no. 1901/13/16, AA. Kitchener accepted Deakin's formal invitation of 9 July 1909: Kitchener to Prime Minister, 10 July 1909, MP 84/1, file no. 1901/13/16, AA
31 Kitchener to Clarke, 5 June 1909 *Sydenham Papers* Add. Ms. 50835, Vol. V, ff. 122–3, BL
32 *Daily Telegraph* 24 February 1910, Sydney, p. 7
33 *Age* 22 February 1910, Melbourne p. 6
34 Cablegram from the Prime Minister (Mr Alfred Deakin) to Viscount Kitchener (Commander-in-Chief in India), 9 July 1909, in G. Greenwood and C. Grimshaw (eds) *Documents on Australian International Affairs 1901–1918* Thomas Nelson (Aust), Melbourne, 1977, p. 246
35 R. B. Haldane, quoted by *Age* 25 September 1909, Melbourne, p. 10
36 *Sydney Morning Herald* 23 December 1909, Sydney, p. 6
37 Deakin to Kitchener, 10 August 1909, CP 10/1731, AA
38 Kitchener to Lady Salisbury, 12 February 1910, quoted by P. Magnus, in *Kitchener—Portrait of an Imperialist* John Murray, London, 1958, p. 244
39 *Sydney Morning Herald* 23 December 1909, Sydney, p. 6
40 British officer, quoted by G. Souter, in *Lion and Kangaroo* Collins, Sydney, 1976, p. 151
41 *Sydney Morning Herald* 6 January 1910, Sydney, p. 7
42 *Sydney Morning Herald* 5 January 1910, Sydney, p. 8
43 *ibid.*, 6 January 1910, p. 7
44 *Age* 10 January 1910, Melbourne, p. 10
45 *ibid.*, 12 January 1910, p. 7
46 *ibid.*, 11 February 1910, p. 5
47 *ibid.*, 12 February 1910, p. 11
48 *ibid.*, 19 February 1910, p. 12
49 *CPP* 1910 Session, Vol. II, No. 8 'Defence of Australia—Memorandum By Field Marshal Viscount Kitchener of Khartoum', Part I, para. 2, p. 87
50 *CPP* 1910 Session, Vol. II, No. 8, paras. 39, 42, 43, p. 93, para. 62, p. 95, para. 65, p. 96
51 *ibid.*, para. 68, p. 93
52 *ibid.*, pp. 83–104

Notes

53 *CA* Vol. IX, 1910, No. 37, Defence, pp. 98–102
54 *CPP* 1909 Session, Vol. II, No. 33, 'Defence: Imperial General Staff—Correspondence Relating to Proposed Formation; including Major-General Hoad's Proposal with Regard to Australian Section, Etc.' 'The Imperial General Staff' W. G. Nicholson, December 1908, Part I—General Principles Affecting National Defence, pp. 429–30
55 *ibid.*, paras. 40, 41, 55, 56, 111; Report of the Royal Military College for the Year 1910–1911, para. 32, p. 24, Archives Duntroon
56 C. D. Coulthard-Clark *A Heritage of Spirit* MUP, Melbourne, 1979, p. 91
57 Kirkpatrick to Bridges, 8 July 1909 *Bridges Collection* ADFAL
58 Kirkpatrick to Bridges, 2 September 1909 *Bridges Collection* ADFAL
59 Kiggell to Bridges, 6 October 1910 *Bridges Collection* ADFAL
60 J. L. Mordike 'Establishing The Royal Military College, Duntroon' Litt. B. Thesis, University of New England, 1981, pp. 85–94
61 Kiggell to Bridges, 6 October 1910 *Bridges Collection* ADFAL
62 Kirkpatrick to Bridges, 8 July 1909 *Bridges Collection* ADFAL
63 *CPP* 1910 Session, Vol. II, No. 8, para. 94, p. 100
64 *Age* 23 April 1910, Melbourne p. 11. *Note*: Pearce confirmed Kirkpatrick's appointment, *Age* 4 May 1910, p. 6
65 Minute by Attorney General 'Colonel Kirkpatrick—Appointment as Inspector-General, Military Forces' 2 May 1910; Memorandum by the Minister for Defence 'Appointment of Colonel Kirkpatrick as Inspector-General of Commonwealth Military Forces' no date, file no. 1902/5/28, MP 84, AA
66 *ibid.*
67 *Worker* 28 April 1910, Sydney
68 *Daily Telegraph* 23 April 1910, Sydney
69 Strickland to Pearce, 19 January 1910, AWM 3/2222, file no. 419/80/2, Bundle 3, Item 20 *Pearce Papers* AWM
70 G. F. Pearce *Carpenter to Cabinet* Hutchinson & Co., London, 1951, pp. 71–2
71 *CPD* Vol. LVI, 18 August 1910, Senator Pearce, pp. 1670–1
72 Minutes of the Military Board, 11 July 1910, Item 21 'Issue of Agenda Papers and Decisions of the Military Board' p. 392, AA
73 J. G. Legge, QMG and D. of O., 12 November 1910, CRS B197, file no. 1804/1/7, AA
74 G. F. Pearce, Minister for Defence, to Secretary Defence Department, 22 November 1910, CRS B197, file no. 1804/1/7, AA
75 C. M. Dobell, MOI(C), to DMO, 26 August 1910, WO 106/43, PRO
76 H. Wilson, DMO, to CIGS, 10 April 1911, WO 106/43, PRO
77 W. G. N. [Nicholson], CIGS, to S of S, 5 May 1911, WO 106/43, PRO
78 W. G. N. [Nicholson}, CIGS to DMO, 9 May 1911, WO 106/43, PRO
79 Secret Memorandum by the General Staff of 12 May 1911 No. 80C—Entitled: 'The Cooperation of the Military Forces of The Empire' Part IV, WO 106/43, PRO
80 Memorandum by the General Staff, No. 80-C Revised, 12 May 1911 'The Desirability of Such a General Uniformity of Organization Throughout the Military Forces of the Empire as may Facilitate Their Rendering Mutual Support and Assistance' WO 106/43, PRO
81 Report and Proceedings of a Sub-Committee of the Committee of Imperial Defence on the Military Needs of the Empire, 1909, I—The Assistance to be given by Great Britain to France if She is attacked by Germany, para. 17, p. ix, Cab 16/5, PRO

An Army for a Nation

82 B. Tuchman *August 1914: the First Month of the First World War* Papermac, London, 1980, p. 59
83 Memorandum by the General Staff, No. 80-C Revised, WO 106/43, PRO
84 Pearce *Carpenter to Cabinet* p. 79
85 G. F. Pearce to Secretary to the Prime Minister, 23 February 1911, reproduced in *Carpenter to Cabinet* pp. 83–5. *Note:* Cabinet approval acknowledged, *ibid.*, p.85.
86 *Times* 16 May 1911, London, p. 5
87 Pearce *Carpenter to Cabinet* p. 81
88 *ibid.*, p. 82
89 *CPD* Vol. LIX, Mr Deakin, 25 November 1910, pp. 6859–60
90 Questions of Defence (Military)—2nd Day, 17 June 1911, p. 20, WO 106/43, PRO
91 *ibid.*, pp. 20–1
92 *ibid.*, p. 21
93 *ibid.*, p. 22
94 *ibid.*
95 Bundle 4, Item 7, AWM 3/2222 *Pearce Papers* AWM
96 *Argus* 23 October 1911, p. 5; *The Times* 24 October 1911, p. 5; *Age* 14 October 1911, p. 12; *Age* 17 October 1911, p. 8; *Argus* 17 October 1911, p. 9
97 Memorandum by Senator The Hon. G. F. Pearce on Relinquishing Office as Minister of State For Defence, 23 June 1913, 10027, file 419/80/2, film 52, Bundle 5 *Pearce Papers* AWM; *Age* 1 April 1913, Melbourne, p. 9; Pearce, *Carpenter to Cabinet*, p. 98
98 *Argus* 23 October 1911, p. 7
99 J. Barrett *Falling In: Australians and 'Boy Conscription' 1911–1915* Hale and Iremonger, Sydney, 1979, pp. 69–70
100 R. Ward *A Nation For A Continent: The History of Australia 1901–1975* Heinemann Educational Australia, Richmond, 1977, pp. 85–6
101 Chapter I, 2. Strategic Considerations, p. 5, paras. VI, VII, IX, AWM 113, MH1-11 General Scheme of Defence 1913, AWM
102 *ibid.*, Chapter II, Organization, II—War, para (V), p. 21
103 G. M. Kirkpatrick, Inspector-General, to CGS, 19 September 1912; Investigation of Preparatory Plans of the General Staff, 17th January, 1913, Signed by G. M. K. [Kirkpatrick], 21 January 1913, MP 84, file no. 1855/1/4, AA; W. Perry, 'Hoad Sir John Charles' *ADB* Vol. 9, Melbourne, 1983, pp. 311–12
104 Denman, Governor-General, to Secretary of State for Colonies, 4 March 1913, CRS B197, file no. 1856/4/214, AA
105 J. M. Gordon, CGS, to Secretary for Defence, 4 October 1912, MP 84/1, file no. 1856/1/31, AA
106 Minute by G. F. P. [Pearce] to Secretary, 21 October 1912, *ibid.*
107 Andrew Fisher to Prime Minister, Dominion of New Zealand, 24 October 1912; Cablegram Massey to Fisher, 31 October 1912, *ibid.*
108 Proceedings of the Conference between Major-General A. J. Godley, CB, Commanding New Zealand Military Forces, and, Brigadier-General J. M. Gordon, CB, Chief of the General Staff, C. M. Forces, 18 November 1912, MP 84, file no. 1856/1/33, AA
109 B. J. V. Johnson 'Australia, New Zealand and Imperial Defence (Military) 1902–1914', MA thesis, Monash University, 1983, p. 167; C. E. W. Bean *Two Men I Knew* Angus & Robertson, Sydney, 1957, p. 90
110 Proceedings of the Conference between Major-General A. J. Godley, CB, Commanding New Zealand Military Forces, and, Brigadier-General J. M.

Notes

Gordon, CB, Chief of the General Staff, C. M. Forces, 18 November 1912, MP 84, file no. 1856/1/33, AA
111 *ibid*.
112 Andrew Fisher to Prime Minister of New Zealand, 23 January 1913, *ibid*.
113 C. E. W. Bean *The Official History of Australia in the War of 1914–1918*, UQP Edn, Vol. I 'The Story of ANZAC' UQP, St Lucia, 1981, p. 28
114 White to Hutton, 4 March 1913 *Hutton Papers* Vol. XII, Add. Ms. 50089, ff. 114–17, BL
115 *Age* 1 April 1913, Melbourne, p. 10. *Note*: I have emphasised '*in the Pacific*'.
116 *Age* 4 April 1913, Melbourne, p.7
117 Bean 'The Story of ANZAC', p. 24
118 *ibid*., pp. 33, 63, 87

Bibliography

Primary sources

1 Official

(a) Unpublished archives:

Australian Archives Office, Canberra
Department of External Affairs:
- CRS A6—Correspondence files 1901
- CRS A8—Correspondence files 1901

Governor-General's Office:
- CRS 78/9—Copies of secret and confidential despatches

Prime Minister's Office
- CP 103/12—Records of Imperial Conferences, 1897–1933

Army Office:
- CRS A2653—Military Board proceedings
- CRS A2657/ T1—Military Board Papers of Historical Interest, Vols I and II

Australian Archives Office, Melbourne
Department of Defence:
- B168—Correspondence files, 1901–1906
- B173—Secret correspondence files, 1905–1907
- MP 84—Correspondence files, 1906–1917
- B197—Secret and confidential correspondence files, 1906–1935

Bibliography

Australian War Memorial, Canberra
AWM 3—Department of Defence Central Registry files, 1902–1905
AWM 113—Military History Section Files and Historical Records

National Library of Australia, Canberra
Microfilm copy of Colonial Office records:

- CO 13—South Australia—Original Correspondence
- 13/152 Despatches, Offices and Individuals 1897
- 13/153 Despatches, Offices and Individuals 1898–1899
- CO 201—New South Wales—Original Correspondence
- 201/624 Despatches, Offices and Individuals 1898
- 201/625 Despatches, Offices and Individuals 1899
- CO 234—Queensland—Original Correspondence
- 234/67 Despatches, Offices and Individuals 1898
- CO 280—Tasmania—Original Correspondence
- 280/401 Despatches, Offices and Individuals 1899
- CO 309—Victoria—Original Correspondence
- 309/147 Despatches, Offices and Individuals 1898
- 309/148 Despatches, Offices and Individuals 1899
- CO 418—Australia (General), Original Correspondence
- 418/5 Despatches, Offices and Individuals 1898
- 418/6 Despatches, Offices and Individuals 1899

New South Wales Archives Office, Sydney
Colonial Secretary's Office:

- Copies of Letters to Naval and Military Officers, 21 December 1896–13 October 1899, Reel No. 2876

Public Records Office, London
Committee of Imperial Defence

- Cab 2   Minutes
- Cab 4   Miscellaneous memoranda (B series), 1903–1912
- Cab 5   Colonial defence memoranda, 1902–1939
- Cab 17   Correspondence and miscellaneous papers, 1902–1918
- Cab 18   Miscellaneous volumes, 1875–1919

Colonial Defence Committee:

- Cab 7   Minutes, 1878–1916
- Cab 8   Memoranda, 1885–1914
- Cab 9   Remarks, 1887–1914
- Cab 10   Secretary's minutes, 1912–1914
- Cab 11   Defence schemes, 1863–1914

Ad Hoc Committees:

- Cab 16/5 Inquiry into imperial defence—report and proceedings.

War Office:

- WO 32   Registered papers, general series, relating to all aspects of War Office business, 1855—1925
- WO 106   Papers of the Directorate of Military Operations and Intelligence, 1870–1925

(b) Published records

Commonwealth Parliamentary Debates 1901–1910
New South Wales Parliamentary Debates
Queensland Parliamentary Debates

Commonwealth of Australia Parliamentary Papers
1901–2 Session, Vol. II:

- No. A7, 'Further Report of the Federal Military Committee, 1901'
- No. A13, 'Defence Forces of the Commonwealth'
- No. A19, 'Report and Appendices Prepared by the Commonwealth Defence Pay Committee, Assembled at Sydney, New South Wales'
- No. A36, 'Minute Upon the Defence of Australia by Major-General Hutton, Commandant'
- No. 31, 'Defence Forces and Defence (Memorandum by Colonial Defence Committee)'
- No. 68, 'Military Forces of the Commonwealth (Reduction of Estimates—Report by Major-General Hutton)'

1903 Session, Vol. II:

- No. 37, 'Annual Report Upon the Military Forces of the Commonwealth for the Period January, 1902–30th April, 1903'
- No. 38, 'Military Forces of the Commonwealth: Scheme of Organization of, into a Field Force (for Interstate or Commonwealth Defence), and into Garrison Troops (for Local or State Defence)'

1904 Session, Vol. II:

- No. 25, 'Military Forces of the Commonwealth of Australia—Second Annual Report By Major-General Sir Edward Hutton'
- No. 51, 'Defence Forces—Memorandum By The Minister for Defence on the Administration and Control Of'
- No. 58, 'Defence Forces of the Commonwealth—Memorandum by a Committee in Regard to the Command and Administration of the Military and Naval Forces; Together with Memorandum Thereon by Senator Hon. A. Dawson, and, Major-General Sir E. T. H. Hutton'

Bibliography

1905 Session, Vol. II:

- No. 31, 'The Defence of Australia (Statement By The Honourable Alfred Deakin, M.P.)'

1906 Session, Vol. II:

- No. 43, 'Annual Report for the Year 1905 by the Inspector-General, Major-General H. Finn'
- No. 45, 'Military Board Report for the Year 1905'
- No. 62, 'Report of the Committee of Imperial Defence upon a General Scheme of Defence for Australia'
- No. 79, 'Report on the Department of Defence For the Period from 1st March, 1901, to 30th June, 1906'
- No. 87, 'Report of Committee of Officers Appointed By the Minister of State for Defence to Consider and Report upon The General Scheme of Defence of Australia as Submitted by The Committee of Imperial Defence'
- No. 109, 'Administration and Control of the Military Forces by a Board (Minute by Major-General H. Finn)'

1907–8 Session, Vol. II:

- No. 7, 'Report by the Military Board for the Year 1906'
- No. 129, 'Report on the Swiss Military System Compiled in the Department of the Chief of Intelligence 1907'
- No. 149, 'Land Defence of Australia: National Guard'
- No. 169, 'Annual Report for the Year 1907 By the Inspector-General'

1907–8 Session, Vol. III:

- No. 11, 'Colonial Conference, 1907—Minutes of Proceedings'

1909 Session, Vol. II:

- No. 33, 'Defence: Imperial General Staff—Correspondence Relating to Proposed Formation; Including Major-General Hoad's Proposal with Regard to Australian Section, Etc.'
- No. 75, 'Memorandum on Australian Military Defence and its Progress Since Federation'

1910 Session, Vol. II:

- No. 8, 'Defence of Australia—Memorandum By Field Marshal Viscount Kitchener of Khartoum'

1911 Session, Vol. II:

- No. 69, 'Royal Military College of Australia—Report for the Year 1910–11'

Royal Commissions—New South Wales
Report of the Royal Commission Appointed to Inquire into the Military Service of New South Wales—Appointed June 10, 1892, AWM

Commonwealth and Colonial Military Reports
Defence Scheme of New South Wales, by Major-General E. T. H. Hutton, 1 September 1894, ANL
Report and Summary of Proceedings Together with Appendices and Minutes of the Federal Military Conference Assembled at Sydney to Consider a General Scheme of Military Defence Applicable to the Australian Colonies and Tasmania, October 1894, AWM
Report of Military Conference, held at Sydney, 24 October 1894, 31 March 1895, ANL
Australian Federal Defence, Amended 12 February 1896, ANL
Report of the Military Committee of Inquiry, 1901, AWM

Commonwealth Bills
Draft Commonwealth Defence Bill—Drafted by the Federal Military Committee, 1901, BML
Commonwealth Defence Bill, 1901, PL
Draft Commonwealth Defence Bill—Drafted by E. T. H. Hutton, 25 February 1903, in *MBPHI*, Vol. I, CRS A2657/T1, AA
A Bill for an Act Relating to Naval and Military Defence, Read 29 September 1908, House of Representatives, PL
A Bill for an Act Relating to Naval and Military Defence, Read 21 September 1909, House of Representatives, LAGD

Commonwealth Acts
Constitution Act (63 and 64 Vict. Chapter 12, 9 July 1900), *Commonwealth Acts*, Vol. I
Defence Act, No. 20 of 1903, *Commonwealth Acts*, Vol. II, 1903
Defence Act, No. 12 of 1904, *Commonwealth Acts*, Vol. III, 1904
Defence Act, No. 15 of 1909, *Commonwealth Acts*, Vol. VIII, 1909
Defence Act 1903, As Amended by No. 12 of 1904 and No. 15 of 1909, *Commonwealth Acts*, Vol. VIII, 1909
Defence Act, No. 37 of 1910, *Commonwealth Acts*, Vol. IX, 1910
Defence Act, No. 15 of 1911, *Commonwealth Acts*, Vol. X, 1911

Commonwealth and Colonial Miscellaneous Records
Journals of the Senate, Vol. I, 1904 Session, 2 March–15 December 1904
Official Record of the Proceedings and Debates of the National Australasian Convention, March–April 1891, ANL
Official Record of the Debates of the Australasian Federal Convention, 3rd Edition, Vol. II, Melbourne, 1898, ANL
The *Year Book of Australia* for 1903, published under the auspices of the Government of the Commonwealth of Australia
Official Year Book of the Commonwealth of Australia, No. 2, 1909, published under the authority of the Minister of Home Affairs

Bibliography

Commonwealth of Australia Electoral Roll, State of New South Wales, Division of Eden–Monaro, 1906 and 1908

The Military Forces List of the Commonwealth of Australia, 30 June 1906

British Parliamentary Debates
Vol. XC, Fourth series, 1901

British Parliamentary Papers
Vol. 56, July 1887, C. 5091, 'Proceedings of the Colonial Conference 1887'
Vol. 49, August 1890, C. 6188, 'Correspondence Relating to the Inspection of the Military Forces of the Australasian Colonies by Major-General J. Bevan Edwards'
Vol. 40, 1904, Cd. 1789, 'Report of His Majesty's Commissioners Appointed to Inquire into the Military Preparations and Other Matters Connected with the War in South Africa'
Vol. 54, 1907, Cd. 3337, 'Despatch from the Secretary of State for the Colonies, with Enclosures Respecting the Agenda of the Colonial Conference, 1907'
Vol. 54, 1907, Cd. 3523, 'Minutes of Proceedings of the Colonial Conference, 1907'
Vol. 51, 1909, Cd. 4475, 'Correspondence Relating to the Proposed Formation of an Imperial General Staff'
Vol. 59, 1909, Cd. 4948, 'Correspondence and Papers Relating to a Conference with Representatives of the Self-Governing Dominions on the Naval and Military Defence of the Empire'

Imperial conferences
Proceedings of a Conference between the Secretary of State for the Colonies and the Premiers of the Self-Governing Colonies, At the Colonial Office, London, June and July 1897, ANL
Report of a Conference between the Right Hon. Joseph Chamberlain, MP, and the Premiers of the Self-Governing Colonies of the Empire, June and July 1897, ANL
Papers Relating to a Conference Between the Secretary of State for the Colonies and the Prime Ministers of Self-Governing Colonies, June to August, 1902

Royal Commissions—Great Britain
First Report of the Royal Commissioners Appointed to Inquire into the Defence of British Possessions and Commerce Abroad, 3 September 1881, PRO
Second Report of the Royal Commissioners Appointed to Inquire into the Defence of British Possessions and Commerce Abroad, 8 March 1882, PRO

Third and Final Report of the Royal Commission Appointed to Inquire into the Defence of British Possessions and Commerce Abroad, 22 July 1882, PRO

Report of His Majesty's Commissioners Appointed to Inquire into the Military Preparations and Other Matters Connected with the War in South Africa, 1904, PRO

2 Non-official

(a) Unpublished records

Collections of Private Papers—Australia
Barton Papers, Ms. 51, ANL
Bridges Collection, ADFAL
Chauvel Papers, Defence Regional Library, Canberra
Hume Cook Papers, Ms. 601, ANL
Deakin Papers, Ms. 1540, ANL
Finn Papers, 2nd Military District Museum, Sydney
Hopetoun House Manuscripts, mfm M936, ANL
Hutton Collection, Ms. 1215, ANL
General Hutton's Letters to His Wife, Ms. 1215, ANL
Pearce Papers, AWM
Vernon Papers, in possession of P. V. Vernon, Sydney

Collections of Private Papers—Great Britain
Chamberlain Papers, BU
Dilke Papers, BL
Hutton Papers, BL
Kitchener Papers, Ms. 30/57, PRO
Northcote Papers, Ms. 30/56, PRO
Sydenham Papers (Sir George Clarke), BL

(b) Published records

Newspapers and Periodicals
Age, Melbourne, 1901, 1902, 1903, 1904, 1909, 1910, 1911, 1913
Advertiser, Adelaide, 1902
Argus, Melbourne, 1901, 1902, 1903, 1904, 1905, 1911
Brisbane Courier, Brisbane, 1902
Bulletin, Sydney, 1893, 1901, 1902, 1904
Cooma Express—Monaro and Southern Districts Advertiser, Cooma, 1903
Daily Telegraph, Sydney, 1893, 1894, 1910
Herald, Melbourne, 1903, 1905
Kerang New Times, Kerang, 1903
Kerang Observer, Kerang, 1903

Bibliography

Montreal Daily Star, Montreal, 1902
Sydney Morning Herald, Sydney, 1893, 1894, 1895, 1896, 1901, 1902, 1903, 1904, 1905, 1909, 1910
The Times, London, 1911
Wellington Gazette, Wellington, 1903
Worker, Sydney, 1910

Books, Articles and Addresses
Coghlan, T. A., *Labour and Industry in Australia: From the First Settlement in 1788 to the Establishment of the Commonwealth in 1901*, Vol. 4, Oxford University Press, London, 1918
Colomb, P. H., 'The Functions of the Navy and Army in the Defence of the Empire', *Royal United Service Institution Journal*, vol. XL, July–December 1896, London
Deakin, A., *Federated Australia: Selections From Letters to the Morning Post 1900–1910*, edited and with an introduction by J. A. La Nauze, Melbourne University Press, Melbourne, 1968
Edwards, J. Bevan, 'Australasian Defence', *Proceedings of the Royal Colonial Institute*, vol. XXII, 1890–91, London
Egerton, H., *A Short History of British Colonial Policy*, Book IV, 'The Period of the Zenith & Decline of *Laissez Aller* Principles—1861–1885', 3rd edn, Methuen, London, 1910
Hutton, Major-General E. T. H., Introductory address to Lecture XX, 30 August 1893, *Journal and Proceedings of the United Service Institution of New South Wales*, vol. V, 1893, Sydney
——'A Co-operative System for the Defence of the Empire', *Proceedings of the Royal Colonial Institute*, vol. XXIX, 1897–1898, London, 1898
——'The Evolution of Mounted Infantry', *The Empire Review*, vol. I, no. 4, May 1901, London
Legge, J. G., 'Suggestions for an Australian Defence Force', *Journal and Proceedings of the United Service Institution of New South Wales*, vol. XI, 28 August 1899, Sydney
Miles (J. Maurice), 'Where to Get Men', *Contemporary Review*, vol. LXXXI, January 1902, London
Parkes, H., *Fifty Years in the Making of Australian History*, 2 vols., Longmans & Co., London, 1892
——*The Federal Government of Australasia—Speeches delivered on various occasions*, November 1889–May 1890, Turner & Henderson, Sydney, 1890
Pearce, G. F., *Carpenter to Cabinet: Thirty-seven Years of Parliament*, Hutchinson, London, 1951
Quick, J. and Garran, R. R., *The Annotated Constitution of the Australian Commonwealth*, Angus & Robertson, Sydney; Melville & Mullen, Melbourne, 1901

Todd, A. *Parliamentary Government in the British Colonies*, 2nd edn, Longmans Green, London, 1894
Tulloch, Major-General, 'Defence of Australia', Lecture delivered in Melbourne, 1891, ANL
Wilkinson, F., *Australian Cavalry: The New South Wales Lancer Regiment and First Australian Horse*, Angus & Robertson, Sydney and Melbourne, 1901
Weller, P. (ed.), *Caucus Minutes 1901–1949: Minutes of the Meeting of the Federal Parliamentary Labor Party*, vol. I, 1901–1914, Melbourne University Press, Melbourne, 1975

SECONDARY SOURCES

1 Books

Barrett, J., *Falling In: Australians and 'Boy Conscription' 1911–1915*, Hale and Iremonger, Sydney, 1979
Barton, L., *Australians in the Waikato War 1863–1864*, Library of Australian History, Sydney, 1979
Bean, C. E. W., *Two Men I Knew*, Angus & Robertson, Sydney, 1957
Bennett, S. (ed.), *Federation*, Cassell Australia, North Melbourne, 1975
Bond, B., *The Victorian Army and The Staff College*, Eyre Methuen, London, 1972
Booker, M., *The Great Professional: A Study of W. M. Hughes*, McGraw-Hill Book Company, Sydney, 1980
Calder, W., *Heroes and Gentlemen: Colonel Tom Price and the Victorian Mounted Rifles*, Jimaringle Publications, Melbourne, 1985
Coulthard-Clark, C. D., *A Heritage of Spirit: A Biography of Major-General Sir William Throsby Bridges, K.C.B., C.M.G.*, Melbourne University Press, Melbourne, 1979
—— *No Australian Need Apply: The Troubled Career of Lieutenant-General Gordon Legge*, Allen & Unwin, Sydney, 1988
Cunneen, C., *King's Men: Australia's Governors-General from Hopetoun to Isaacs*, George Allen & Unwin, Sydney, 1983
Dickey, B. (ed.), *Politics in New South Wales 1856–1900*, Cassell Australia, North Melbourne, 1969
Field, L. M., *The Forgotten War: Australian Involvement in the South African Conflict of 1899–1902*, Melbourne University Press, Melbourne, 1979
Gordon, D. C., *The Dominion Partnership in Imperial Defense 1870–1914*, John Hopkins Press, Baltimore, 1965
Gooch, J., *The Plans of War: The General Staff and British Military Strategy c.1900–1916*, Routledge and Kegan Paul, London, 1974
Greenwood, G. (ed.), *Australia: A Social and Political History*, Angus & Robertson, Sydney, 1955

Bibliography

Greenwood, G. and Grimshaw, C., *Documents on Australian International Affairs 1901–1918*, Thomas Nelson (Australia) in association with the Australian Institute of International Affairs and the Royal Institute of International Affairs, West Melbourne, 1977

Hamer, W. S., *The British Army: Civil–Military Relations 1885–1905*, The Clarendon Press, Oxford, 1970

Harries-Jenkins, G., *The Army in Victorian Society*, Routledge and Kegan Paul, London, 1977

Haycock, R. G., *Sam Hughes: The Public Career of a Controversial Canadian 1885–1916*, Wilfrid Laurier University Press, Canada, 1986

Heydon, P. R., *Quiet Decision: A Study of George Foster Pearce*, Melbourne University Press, Melbourne, 1965

Huntington, S. P., *The Soldier and the State: The Theory and Politics of Civil–Military Relations*, The Belknap Press of Harvard University Press, Cambridge, Massachusetts, 1967

Inglis, K. S., *The Rehearsal: Australians at War in the Sudan 1885*, Rigby, Sydney, 1985

James, R. R., *The British Revolution: British Politics 1880–1939*, Methuen and Co. Ltd, London, 1978

Johnson, D. H., *Volunteers at Heart: The Queensland Defence Force 1860–1901*, University of Queensland Press, St Lucia, 1975

Kennedy, A. L., *Salisbury 1830–1903: Portrait of a Statesman*, Murray, London, 1953

La Nauze, J. A., *Alfred Deakin: A Biography*, Angus & Robertson, Sydney, 1979

Lehmann, J. P., *The Image of Japan: From Feudal Isolation to World Power 1850–1905*, George Allen & Unwin, London, 1978

Luvaas, J., *The Education of an Army: British Military Thought 1815–1940*, Cassell, London, 1965

Magnus, P., *Kitchener: Portrait of an Imperialist*, John Murray, London, 1958

Mander-Jones, P. (ed.), *Manuscripts in the British Isles Relating to Australia, New Zealand and the Pacific*, Australian National University Press, Canberra, 1972

Martin, A. W. (ed.), *Essays in Australian Federation*, Melbourne University Press, Melbourne, 1969

Meaney, N. K., *The Search for Security in the Pacific, 1901–14*, Sydney University Press, Sydney, 1976

Mitchell, B. R. and Deane, P., *Abstract of British Historical Statistics*, Cambridge University Press, Cambridge, 1962

Morton, D., *Ministers and Generals: Politics and the Canadian Militia 1868–1904*, University of Toronto Press, Toronto, 1970

Norris, R., *The Emergent Commonwealth: Australian Federation: Expectations and Fulfilment 1889–1910*, Melbourne University Press, Melbourne, 1975

Pakenham, T., *The Boer War*, Weidenfeld and Nicolson, London, 1979

Pearce, G. F., *Carpenter to Cabinet—Thirty-Seven Years of Parliament*, Hutchinson and Co. Ltd, London, 1951

Preston, R. A., *Canada and 'Imperial Defense': A Study of the Origins of the British Commonwealth's Defense Organization 1867–1919*, University of Toronto Press, Toronto, 1967

Roberts, J. M., *A General History of Europe: Europe 1880–1945*, Longman, London, 1976

Reynolds, J., *Edmund Barton*, Angus & Robertson, Sydney, 1948

Sawer, G., *Australian Federal Politics and Law 1901–1929*, Melbourne University Press, Melbourne, 1956

Sinclair, K. (ed.), *A Soldier's View of Empire: The Reminiscences of James Bodell 1831–92*, The Bodley Head, London, 1982

Souter, G., *Lion and Kangaroo—Australia: 1901–1919—The Rise of a Nation*, Collins Australia, Sydney, 1976

Tanner, T. W., *Compulsory Citizen Soldiers*, Alternative Publishing Co-operative Ltd, Waterloo, 1980

Thompson, R. C., *Australian Imperialism in the Pacific: The Expansionist Era 1820–1920*, Melbourne University Press, Melbourne, 1980

Tuchman, B., *The Proud Tower: A Portrait of the World Before the War 1890–1914*, Hamish Hamilton Ltd, London, 1966

——*August 1914: the First Month of The First World War*, Papermac, London, 1980

Vernon, P. V. (ed.), *The Royal New South Wales Lancers 1885–1960*, Royal New South Wales Lancers, Sydney, 1961

Ward, R., *A Nation for a Continent: The History of Australia 1901–1975*, Heinemann Educational Australia, Richmond, 1977

Wieck, G. F., *The Volunteer Movement in Western Australia 1861–1903*, Paterson Brokensha Pty Ltd, Perth

Willard, M., *History of the White Australia Policy to 1920*, Melbourne University Press, Melbourne, 1923

Yarwood, A. T., *Asian Migration to Australia: The Background to Exclusion 1896–1923*, Melbourne University Press, Melbourne, 1964

2 Articles

Chandran Jeshurun, 'The Anglo-French Declaration of January 1896 and the Independence of Siam', *Journal of the Siam Society*, July 1970, vol. 58, Part 2

Cole, D., ' "The Crimson Thread of Kinship": Ethnic Ideas in Australia, 1870–1914', *Historical Studies*, vol. 14, no. 56, April 1971

Connolly, C. N., 'Manufacturing "Spontaneity": The Australian Offers of Troops for the Boer War', *Historical Studies*, vol. 18, no. 70, April 1978

——'Class, Birthplace, Loyalty: Australian Attitudes to the Boer War', *Historical Studies*, vol. 18, no. 71, October 1978

Bibliography

Encel, S., 'The Study of Militarism in Australia', *The Australian and New Zealand Journal of Sociology*, vol. 3, no. 1, April 1967

French, M., 'The Ambiguity of Empire Day in New South Wales, 1901–21: Imperial Consensus or National Division', *Australian Journal of Politics and History*, vol. 24, no. 1, April 1978

Grimshaw, C., 'Australian Nationalism and the Imperial Connection 1900–1914', *Australian Journal of Politics and History*, vol. 3, no. 2., May 1958

Jones, R. 'Tryon in Australia: 1887 Naval Agreement', *Journal of the Australian War Memorial*, no. 10, April 1987

Jordens, A.-M., 'Against the Tide: The Growth and Decline of a Liberal Anti-War Movement in Australia, 1905–1918', *Historical Studies*, vol. 22, no. 88, April 1987

Penny, B., 'Australia's Reactions to the Boer War—A Study in Colonial Imperialism', *Journal of British Studies*, vol. 7, November 1967

Perry, W., 'Military Reforms of General Sir Edward Hutton in New South Wales 1893–96', *The Australian Quarterly*, December 1956

——'Lieutenant-General James Gordon Legge—Australia's First Wartime Chief of the General Staff', *The Victorian Historical Journal*, vol. 48, no. 3, August 1977

Trainor, L., 'British Imperial Defence Policy', *Historical Studies*, vol. 14, no. 54, April 1970

Thompson, S. G., 'An Officer and a Gentleman', *Law Society Journal*, May 1985

Ward, R., 'Two Kinds of Australian Patriotism', *Victorian Historical Magazine*, vol. 41, no. 1, February 1970

3 Theses

Atkinson, L. D., Australian Defence Policy: A Study of Empire and Nation, 1897–1910, PhD thesis, Australian National University, 1964

Cuneen, C., The Role of Governor-General In Australia, 1901–27, PhD thesis, Australian National University, 1973

Glenister, R., Desertion without Execution, BA Hons thesis, La Trobe University, 1984

Johnson, B. J. V., Australia, New Zealand and Imperial Defence (Military) 1902–1914, MA thesis, Monash University, 1983

Millar, T. B., History of the Defence Force of The Port Phillip District and Colony of Victoria 1836–1900, MA thesis, University of Melbourne, 1957

Mordike, J. L., Establishing the Royal Military College, Duntroon: A Study in British and Australian Attitudes, LittB thesis, University of New England, 1981

Zwillenberg, H. J., Citizens and Soldiers: The Defence of South Australia 1836–1901, MA thesis, University of Adelaide, 1970

Index

Afridi campaign, 60
Alien Immigration Act, 94, 96; Japanese reaction, 129
Alien 'Restriction' Act, see Alien Immigration Act
Altham, Edward, 110
Anderson, Sir John, 59, 91; Australian section of Colonial Office, 50
Ardagh, Sir John, 57; Director of Military Intelligence, 55–6
Army Council, Universal Military Training, 204–05
Army Headquarters, 83, 131, 132, 140, 146
Army Service Corps, formation, 28
Arnold-Forster, Mr, 57–8
artillery, 27–8; garrison artillery 102; field artillery 102; training program, 133
Asquith, Prime Minister, 210
Australian Army, 66, 72, 87; chain of command, 72, 73; Hutton and, 101–02
Australian Commonwealth Horse, 1st, 2nd, 3rd, 4th Battalions, 138
Australian Constitution, 72; British control over Australian forces, 49–51; capital punishment, 100; conscription, 82; draft, 50; Liberal defence policy, 212; military chain of command, 73; Section 87, 145; Section 89, 145
Australian Federation for Defence, 37–8; Federal Defence scheme and Royal Navy, 38
Australian Military Forces, object of, 206

Australian National Defence League, 185, 210
Australian Natives Association, 206

'Blue Water' theory, 57
Balfour, Lord, 86,170
Barrett, Senator John, 152
Barton, Edmund, 66, 81, 83, 84, 89–90, 93, 96–8, 105, 108, 149; Morant affair, 98–9; with Hutton, 92
Batchelor, Egerton, attends Imperial Conference of 1911, 238
Beatson, General, 98
Beauchamp, Governor of New South Wales, 61
Bell, Francis Dillon, 2
Berry, Graham, 6
Bigge, Sir Arthur, 96–7
Bodell, James, 2
Boer War, 62–6, 77–80, 83, 85–7, 97, 168; Morant affair, 98; Esher Committee, 152; volunteers, 201
Borden, Sir Fredrick, 181, 206, 239
Braddon, Sir Edward, 79, 107
Braithwaite, William, 149
Bramston, John, 50
Brassey, Lord, 53–4
Bridges, William Throsby, 170, 173, 192–3, 195–6, 200–01, 208–09, 231–2; *Defence Act*, 205
British *Army Act*, 39, 46, 58, 72, 74; Australian soldiers on active service, 52, 54, 127, 205

306

Index

British General Staff, 204–05; creation, 180; papers, 180
British Military Society, 138
Brodrick, Mr St John, 87–93, 99–101, 104, 109, 118, 130, 148
Burns, James, 60–1, 135, 155

cadet corps, 71, 75, 184, 187
Camberley Staff College, 22–3
Cambridge, Duke of, 27; Hutton and, 37, 39, 43, 109
Canada, 86–8, 90, 91; unit exchange, 58
Carnarvon Commision, 7–8; British aims since, 202; conclusions, 8, 22
Carnarvon, Lord, 7
Carrington, Lord, 62
Chamberlain, Joseph, 47–50, 52, 55, 58, 63, 78, 85–6, 90–1, 113, 164; Boer War, 60, 62; Hutton and, 86, 148; Morant affair, 99–100
Chaplain's Department, 133
Chapman, Austin, 141, 153, 160
Chauvel, Charles, 4
Chauvel, Sir Harry, 4–5
China, 48
Chippindall, George, 70
citizen soldiers, Easter camps, 133; in garrison force, 145; Overseas service liability, 205
Civil Branch, 131
Clarke, Sir George, 100–02, 132, 193–6, 164, 170, 180
Clauson, John, 89
Collins, Robert, 107, 117, 131–2, 159–60
Colomb, Sir John, 56–8
Colomb, Philip, 44, 56
Colonial Ammunition Company, 179
Colonial Conference,108, 166; 1887, 9; 1897, 48, 54, 58; 1902, 113,105, 107; 1907, 202
Colonial Defence Committee, 8, 40–5, 48, 60, 63, 64, 83, 84, 89, 97, 120, 167–8; Australian involvement in Imperial operations, 15, 49, 51, 53, 55, 134; military federation, 14–15, 36, 38; Morant affair, 100
colonial forces, 4, 7–8, 12–14, 17, 24; Australian forces, 20, 42, 46; federation, 10, 21; Sudan, 6, 15
Colonial Office, 47, 50, 58–61, 90–1; Australian commitment to overseas service, 51, 54, 64, 204

Committee of Imperial Defence, 142, 170, 182
Committee on Supply, 105–06
Commonwealth Forces, 69
compulsory military service, 77, 79, 81–2, 187, 191, 207
Connaught, Duke of, 109
Constitutional Convention (1897), 107
Cook, James Hume, 79, 153
Cook, Joseph, 80, 233; Defence Bill, 218
Cooke, William, 82
Cooma, 140–1
Corps of Signallers, 187
Council of Defence, Australian, 161, 163, 173
Cowper, Earl, 44
Cox, Charles, 62
Creswell, Captain, 167
Crimea, 86
Crimean War, 1
Crouch, Richard, 127, 153
Cruickshank, George, 82
Currie, Sir Philip, 25

Dalley, William Bede, 5
Dawson, Senator Andrew, 160, 161
Deakin, Alfred, 52–3, 73, 165, 187, 191, 212; as Prime Minister, 199–201, 210, 214; on Defence issues, 166, 181, 185–6, 189, 216
Defence Act, 40, 74, 130, 132, 198, 205; Australian service overseas, 168, 188; of 1903, 127–8, 152; *see also* Federal *Defence Act*
defence of Australia, 69, 101, 107; active, 38, 69, 102
Defence Bill, 80–4, 1st, 71–5; 2nd, 76, 78–84, 92, 93; Ewing's, 198–9; Joseph Cook's, 218–20; of 1903, 123–7, 151
defence spending, Britain, 44–5, 48, 85
Department of Defence, 67, 83, 107, 131, 134, 201
Department of External Affairs, 166
Dibbs, Sir George, 26–7, 34–7
Dickson, Sir James, 67
Dilke, Sir Charles15, 56–8, 60, 109
Disraeli, Benjamin, 6
doctrine, no longer along British lines, 188
Downes, Francis, 70
Drake, James, 40

307

dreadnoughts, 210–11, 214
Drury, Colonel, 40
Duff, Sir Robert, 25, 30, 36

Easter military training camp 1903, 148
economic depression, 27
Edward VII, King, 109, 148, 155, 157, 191
Edwards, George, 81
Edwards, Sir James Bevan, 11–15, 38, 57, 228
Edwards, Richard, 79
Elgin Commission, 83
Engineers, Corps of, 27–8, 133; Corps of Australian Engineers, 133
Esher Committee, 152, 161, 170
Ewing, Thomas, 191–2, 196–8, 182, 189, 201, 209

Fashoda incident, 55
Federal *Defence Act*, 70–1, 75, 87
Federal Defence Council, 39
Federal Defence Scheme, 87
Federal Liberal Party, 211–13
Federal Military Committee, 68–70
Federation, 19, 21, 43, 63–4; of Australian Colonial Forces, 35–7, 43, 56, 107, 132
Ferguson, Mr, 192
Fiji, 77
Finn, Harry, 70, 172, 176, 178
Fisher, Andrew, 199, 206, 238
Forrest, Sir John, 67–8, 73–6, 81–4, 115, 191; Barton and, 149; defence, 67, 123–7, 134; Garrison forces, 146; Hutton and, 92, 103, 123, 128, 151, 188
Foxton, Justin, 214, 221
France, 24, 55
French Indochina, 64
French–Russian Alliance, 55
French, Major-General, 62–3, 70, 87

Garran, Robert, 73
Gillies, Duncan, 37
Glynn, Patrick, 107
Godley, Major-General Alexander, 244
Gordon, General Charles, 5
Gordon, Joseph, 70, 178, 244
Greenoaks, 26
Grey, Sir Edward, 239
Griffith, Arthur, 40

Griffith, Sir Samuel, 10

Hackett, John Winthrop, 78
Haig, Sir Douglas, 202–3, 231
Haldane, Richard Burdon, 180–82, 237
Hamilton, Sir Ian, 90, 129
Handcock, Peter, 99, 100; wife learns of execution, 100
Higgins, Henry Bournes, 77–83, 107–8, 127
Higgs, Senator William, 152
Hilliard, Maurice, 142
Hoad, John, 179, 196, 200–02, 206, 209, 243; and Haig's paper, 206–7; and Hutton, 157–8, 176
Holland, Sir Henry, 9–10
Hopetoun, Lord, 90, 94, 104–5; Morant affair, 100
Hughes, William Morris, 78, 210
Hunter Valley, 136–7
Hutton, Edward, 22–43, 55, 58, 69, 85–118, 131–32, 154–68, 188; Forrest and, 122, 126, 128, 146–48, 188

Imperial Army, 54–6
Imperial Conference, 1909, 214
Imperial Defence, Colonial involvement, 7–8, 53, 56, 58; Boer War, 62–3
Imperial Defence Committee, 38
Imperial General Staff, 195, 203
Imperial Military Reserve, 97, 111–13, 116
India, 22, 53, 64, 77, 203
infantry, 27, 38, 54, 133; 3rd Infantry Brigade, 104; conversion to mounted, 104, 139–40; establishment of regiments, 137
Innes, Glen, 142
Inspector-General, 177; Hoad's appointment as, 178–9; and Hoad's scheming, 207–8; Kirkpatrick's appointment as, 232–3; excessive power of, 235
Intelligence Corps, 187
Intercolonial Convention, 1883, 3
Intercolonial Military Conference, 75
Isaacs, Isaac, 59; Morant affair, 100

Jameson raid, 55
Japan, 48, 88, 189; alliance with Britain, 94, 128–9, 165; defeat Russian navy, 165

Index

Jervois, Sir William, 3, 7, 15
Jeune, Sir Francis, 52
Jose, Arthur, 211

Key, Sir William, 9
Kingston, Charles, 49, 59, 128, 96
Kirkpatrick, George, 231–2, 172, 243
Kirwin, John, 79, 144
Kitchener, Lord, 85, 98–100, 223–4, 233–4; Morant affair, 99–100
Knutsford, Lord, 10

Labor Party, 81–2, 96, 137, 210
Lambley, Reverend, 81
Lansdowne, Lord, 54–5, 63, 70, 87
Laurier, Sir Wilfrid, 90
Lee, George, 148; Easter camp 1903, 148–50
Legge, James, 189, 191, 206, 235
Legge, William, 70
Le Mesurier, Havilland, 175
Lenehan, Robert, 99
Light Horse, 133, 135, 137–8; 4th Light Horse, 104; 6th Light Horse, 104; Australian Light Horse (NSW Lancers), 136; No. 2 Squadron 3rd Australian Light Horse Regiment, 141; No. 6 Squadron 10th Regiment, 135; Squadrons, 102; Upper Clarence Light Horse, 4
local manufacture, stores and equipment, 179, 184, 187
Lyne, Joseph, 70
Lyne, Sir William, 62, 116, 212
Lyster, John, 144
Lyttelton, Sir Neville, 180

Markwell, William, 139
Matheson, Senator Alexander, 152
Mauger, Samuel, 80, 151
Maurice, Sir John, 45
Mawson, Herbert, 140
McCay, James, 107, 127, 163, 193
McDonald, Charles, 80, 127
McKenna, Reginald, 210
McLean, Allen, 142–3
McMillan, Sir William, 79, 82
Meade, Robert, 22–3, 25, 42–3
medical services, 133, 187; Australian Army Medical Corps, 133
Mekong, 24–5
Melbourne Cavalry Corps, 135

Melbourne Volunteer Rifle Regiment, 1
Military Board, 161, 163, 191–3, 208–9, 235
military displays, 28–30
militia, 71, 86, 107
Minto, Lord, 90
Morant, Harry 'Breaker', execution, 99
Morning Post, 174
mounted brigade, active defence, 38
mounted infantry, 54, 86–93, 97, 104–05, 133–9

Nathan, Captain, 41–2, 63
National Australasian Convention, 19, 50
National Australian Convention, 49, 53
Naval Agreement of 1887, 8, 9, 105, 113
Navy, Australian, 214–16
Neild, John, 154–6
New Caledonia, 64,
New Guinea, 6, 64
New South Wales Artillery Regiment, 28
New South Wales Government, 61, 100
New South Wales Lancers, 4, 27, 29, 60, 64, 135, 139, 155; Boer War, 62
New South Wales Regiment of Cavalry, 28, 30
New Zealand, 97, 111, 204, 244
Nicholson, Sir William, 102–03, 109, 180, 202, 208, 236
Norman, Sir Henry, 38, 52, 57, 58
Northcote, Lord, 156, 176–7

O'Keefe, Senator David, 153–4
Ommanney, Sir Montagu, 91–3, 101, 109, 117–18, 121, 128, 164
Ordnance Department, Ordnance Store Corps, 134

Papua, 3, 6
Parkes, Sir Henry, 6, 16–17, 19, 36–7; Tenterfield address, 17
Parnell, John, 196
Parramatta, RMS, 25–6
part-time volunteers, 1–2
Peace, Humanity and Arbitration Society, 81
Peace Society of New South Wales, 185
Peacocke, Captain, 25, 39, 40
Pearce, Senator George Foster, 200, 205, 209–10, 233–4, 238–42
Peninsular War, 86, 135, 155
Petherbridge, Samuel, 208

Playford, Senator Thomas, 175

Queensland Government, 62, 100, 144
Quick, John, 73

Reay, William, 149
1st Regiment of New South Wales Rifles, 1
Reid, George, Premier, 37, 41–2, 50, 52, 57, 60–1, 62, 79, 80; Reid–McLean Government collapses, 166
Rentoul, Reverend Professor John, 81
rifle clubs, 71–2, 134–5
Roberts, Lord, 89, 91, 109, 148
Rose, Staff Sergeant, 142
Rosebery, Lord, 24–5, 30
Royal Australian Artillery band, 64
Royal Australian Artillery Regiment, 133
Royal Colonial Institute, 55, 58, 86, 102
Royal Military College, Sandhurst, 105
Royal Navy, 8–9, 14, 17, 38, 39, 44, 56, 63–4, 101, 105, 108, 210, 216
Royal United Service Institution, 44
Rushall, Alexander, 135
Russia, 7, 31–2, 55
Ryrie, Granville de Laune, 141
Ryrie, Harold, 141

Salisbury, Lord, 55
Salmon, Charles Carty, 215
Sawers, William, 79
Scott, Rose, 185
Scratchley, Peter, 3
Seddon, Richard, 107, 112
See, John, 136
Service Corps, 69, 102, 133
Signallers, Corps of, 187
Smith, Senator Miles Staniforth
Smith, Sydney, 107
Soldiers' Wives League, 26
South Africa, 78, 86, 88, 204; war, 61, 81,
South Australian Government, 62
Spence, William, 81
Stanhope, Edward, 10–11
submarine mining units, 133
Sudan campaign, 5–6, 19, 40–1, 52, 62–4
Swiss military scheme, 157, 170, 178

Tasmanian Government, 62, 100
telegraph, 3

Tennyson, Lord, 119, 128–9, 150–1, 159, 167
Thring, Henry, 8
Todd, Alpheus, 51
training, 133, 203, 207; citizen soldiers, 132–3, 138
Transvaal, 59–61
Tryon, George, 8, 9
Tulloch, Major–General Alexander, 21–2, 31–2, 36, 40–1
Turner, Sir George, 96, 145

uniform, 133; Melbourne Cavalry Corps, 135
unit exchange proposal, 58–9
United Service Institution of New South Wales, 33–4
United States, 55, 64
universal military training, 186, 211–12, 215, 243
Upper Clarence Light Horse, 4

Verite letter, 30
Veterinary Department, 133
Victorian Government, 61, 62
Victorian Mounted Rifles, 4, 27, 149
Victorian Rangers, 142
Victorian Yeomanry Corps, 1
Volunteer Rifle Corps, 1
volunteers, 71, 78–9, 82, 102–03, 141, 144, 201

Waikato campaign, 2
Walker, Mr Critchett, 36
Wallack, Ernest, 145, 196
War Office, 38, 44, 53–62, 87, 190, 201, 203, 206–07
Watson, John, 77, 81, 107
Western Australian Government, 62, 145
White Australia policy, 96, 129
White, Brudnell, 196–9, 207, 244–5
Whitehall committees, 7
Wilkinson, James, 79, 142
Wilkinson, Spencer, 56
Williams, Surgeon-General, 161
Willis, Henry, 142
Wilson, Henry, 236
Witton, George, 99
Wolseley, Lord, 43–5, 54, 56, 63
Wolseley Ring, 23–4, 56
Wood, Evelyn, 54
Wyndham, Colonel, 64

Extracts From the Meeting at the War Office on 17 June 1911

Pearce: 'The reason animating the Commonwealth Government in bringing this question forward was . . . that whilst we hold strongly the view that our forces are raised for local defence—and indeed our Defence Act does not authorise us to send any soldiers oversea . . . nevertheless we know that the spirit animating the forces is such that in the event of any serious war, even without any compulsion or pressure on the part of the Government, there would be a considerable number of those forces who would volunteer for oversea service if considered necessary or advisable. As that is so it seemed to us that our local General Staff ought to know what is in the minds of the Imperial General Staff as regards what use such forces should be put to so that they could be employed in their various Dominions in arranging schemes for mobilisation or transportation of the troops, and so that they could be guided in the preparation of such a scheme by the general idea that the Imperial Staff had as to the use to which such troops could be put . . .'

Borden: 'The idea which is in the mind of Senator Pearce is really, as I understand the object, or one of the principal objects, of the establishment of the Imperial General Staff. That being the case and the matter having been dealt with in 1907, and again especially in 1909, it would seem to me a work of supererogation to discuss the matter or to pass any resolution with reference to this matter at this time. . . Now it seems to me that that is enough, and I should very much prefer, as far as I am concerned, that we should not do anything more. I think that is sufficient.'

Pearce: 'I should like to say that I quite agree with Sir Frederick Borden that nothing further than that as a general agreement is necessary in the way of a resolution, but the object of the Australian Government in bringing it forward, is to bring this question again before the various Dominions, in order to ascertain whether they are taking any action, or propose to take any action, in connection with their local sections of the Imperial General Staff to give effect to that idea. During the time that has elapsed since then we in the Commonwealth have taken action as a result of that agreement towards standardising our units on mobilisation and our equipment but there is something more than that to be done, that is to say, the preparation of schemes of mobilisation by the local sections of the Imperial General Staff in order to enable that uniformity to be availed of. My only object is that we have the various Dominions here represented, there should be a general understanding—there does not need to be any resolution—that the local section of the Imperial General Staff are to work aolong those lines.'

Nicholson: 'Your idea is that just as in this country we have our scheme of local defence and we also have a scheme